A MIRROR FOR HISTORY

A MIRROR FOR HISTORY

How Novels and Art Reflect the Evolution of Middle-Class America

MARC EGNAL

THE UNIVERSITY OF TENNESSEE PRESS
Knoxville

Copyright © 2024 by The University of Tennessee Press / Knoxville.
All Rights Reserved. Manufactured in the United States of America.
FIRST EDITION.

Library of Congress Cataloging-in-Publication Data
Names: Egnal, Marc, author.
Title: A mirror for history : how novels and art reflect the evolution
   of middle-class America / Marc Egnal.
Description: Knoxville : The University of Tennesee Press, 2024. | Includes biblio-
   graphical references and index. | Summary: "In this book, Marc Egnal argues that
   the arc of middle-class culture reflects the evolution of the economy from the
   near-subsistence agriculture of the 1750s to the extraordinarily unequal society
   of the twenty-first century. By using literature and art to explain the shifts in
   values over this lengthy span and highlighting class conflict within the American
   economy over time, Egnal offers particularly unique insights into the development of middle-class America. By delving into a myriad of fictional characters
   and their complex worlds, Egnal sheds light on an array of issues including the
   shifting roles of women in society, the resulting changes in masculinity, waning
   religious beliefs through the centuries, and a broad exploration of African American characters"—Provided by publisher.
Identifiers: LCCN 2024000431 (print) | LCCN 2024000432 (ebook) |
   ISBN 9781621908678 (hardcover) | ISBN 9781621909040 (paperback) |
   ISBN 9781621908685 (pdf) | ISBN 9781621908869 (kindle)
Subjects: LCSH: United States—Civilization. | Middle class—United States. |
   Literature and society—United States—History. | Arts and society—
   United States—History. | American fiction—History and criticism. |
   Social values—United States—History.
Classification: LCC E169.1 .E394 2024 (print) | LCC E169.1 (ebook) |
   DDC 305.5/50973—dc23/eng/20240206
LC record available at https://lccn.loc.gov/2024000431
LC ebook record available at https://lccn.loc.gov/2024000432

To my grandchildren:
KYE, FRASER, TAYLOR, AND MINA.

CONTENTS

Introduction: Of Novels, Paintings, Ngrams,
and the Middle Class ... 1

1 Prelude: From Austerity to Sentimentality, 1750–1788 ... 15

Part One: The Sentimental Era ... 27

2 Years of Uncertainty, 1789–1819 ... 31
3 Soaring Spirits, 1820–1851 ... 45
4 Retreat from the Heights, 1852–1869 ... 61

Part Two: The Genteel Era ... 81

5 Cheerful Towns, Troubled Cities, 1870–1890 ... 87
6 The Edifice Crumbles, 1891–1919 ... 109

Part Three: The Modern Era ... 131

7 Businessmen, Romantics, and Rebels, 1920–1940 ... 137
8 Anxious Conformists, 1941–1960 ... 161

Part Four: The Postmodern Era		179
9	New Realities, 1961–1990	185
10	Beset on All Sides, 1991–2020	211
	Conclusion	237
	Acknowledgments	241
	Sources for artwork	243
	Notes	245
	Index	303

ILLUSTRATIONS

Ngrams

IN.1. *middle class*, 1800–2019	13
P1.1. *weep*, 1800–2019	28
2.1. *betray* and *deceit*, 1800–2019	36
2.2. *seduce*, 1800–1980	38
3.1. *father* and *mother*, 1800–2019	50
3.2. *strong women*, 1840–1900	54
3.3. Two periods when the frequency of *romantic* rose sharply, 1800–1980	58
4.1. Four periods of mounting racism: *nigger*, 1800–1980	68
4.2. *woman's rights* and *woman's suffrage*, 1820–1915	71
4.3. Two child-centered periods: *childhood*, 1800–2019	75
5.1. Three crusades against drink: *temperance*, 1800–2019	91
5.2. *trustworthy* and *virile*, 1825–1985	102
6.1. Two periods of maternalism: *loving mother*, 1820–2019	119
P3.1. *damn*, 1860–1970	132
P3.2. *conformity, diversity,* and *multiculturalism*, 1900–2019	132
P3.3. *Kiwanis* and *Rotarians*, 1900–1980	133
P3.4. Hierarchy in the modern era: *executive* and *manager*, 1860–2019	134
P3.5. *character* and *personality*, 1800–1990	135
7.1. *strong women*, 1900–2019	149
P4.1. *shit, fuck,* and *asshole*, 1940–2019	181
9.1 *black middle class*, 1920–2019	188
9.2 *violence, robbery,* and *apocalypse*, 1920–2019	191

9.3. *corporate power* and *corporate greed*, 1850–2019	193
9.4. *grandparents, nurturing, toddler,* and *babysitter,* 1860–2019	204
10.1. *tramps* and *homeless,* 1820–2019	216
10.2. *women's liberation* and *feminism,* 1950–2019	225
10.3. *brotherhood* and *sisterhood,* 1900–2019	226

Paintings

1.1. Robert Feke, *Isaac Royall and Family*	20
1.2 Charles Willson Peale, *The Peale Family*	22
2.1. Washington Allston, *Elijah in the Desert*	42
3.1. Thomas Cole, *The Oxbow (The Connecticut River near Northampton)*	59
4.1. Thomas Cole, *Niagara Falls*	77
4.2. Frederic Church, *Niagara*	78
4.3. Albert Bierstadt, *The Rocky Mountains, Landers Peak*	79
5.1. Winslow Homer, *Snap the Whip*	103
5.2. Winslow Homer, *The Life Line*	104
5.3. Thomas Eakins, *The Courtship*	106
5.4. Thomas Eakins, *Portrait of Walt Whitman*	107
6.1. George Bellows, *Cliff Dwellers*	127
6.2. Max Weber, *The Liberty Tower from the Singer Building*	128
7.1. Charles Sheeler, *American Landscape*	157
7.2. Edward Hopper, *Room in New York*	159
8.1 Jackson Pollock, *One: Number 31, 1950*	176
9.1 Betye Saar, *The Liberation of Aunt Jemima*	208
10.1 Kara Walker, *Alabama Loyalists Greeting the Federal Gunboats*	235

INTRODUCTION
Of Novels, Paintings, Ngrams, and the Middle Class

Art and literature have always been deeply entangled with Americans' view of themselves. In his Nobel Prize acceptance speech in 1930, Sinclair Lewis explained, with his tongue firmly in his cheek, how authors can succeed in the United States. "To be not only a best seller in America but to be really beloved," Lewis states, "a novelist must assert that all American men are tall, handsome, rich, honest, and powerful at golf; that all country towns are filled with neighbors who do nothing from day to day save go about being kind to one another; [and] that although American girls may be wild, they change always into perfect wives and mothers." Lewis, whose acerbic view of small towns led to works like *Main Street* (1920) and *Babbitt* (1922), rejected such cant and declared: "We are coming out, I believe, of the stuffiness of safe, sane, and incredibly dull provincialism."

A Mirror for History uses novels, like Lewis's, as well as paintings, and quantitative data (particularly "Ngrams") to understand the outlook of the American middle class between 1750 and 2020. Despite the significance of literature for this book, it is a historical study, not a work of literary criticism, a field that has its own methodology and goals, and typically focuses on fewer novels and examines them in greater detail.[1] *A Mirror for History* also looks at the development of the economy, an area with singular importance for the contention that ties the story together. The book argues that the arc of middle-class culture reflects the evolution of the economy from the 1750s, when the "middling folk" emerged as a recognizable group, to the fractious present, when extremes of wealth threaten the very existence of that cohort.

The analysis of middle-class values as reflected in literature, art, and Ngrams is a journey, and as for any voyage of exploration, there is a need to carefully pack our bags and bring the right tools. The balance of the introduction looks at the equipment necessary for the trip. It scrutinizes the methodology that links literature and painting to the development of the economy. It examines the Ngram database in more detail. And it discusses the middle class, a group that is central to this analysis.

I

An intrepid traveler who wants to use literature (along with art and Ngrams) as a key to understanding society must pack not only stacks of novels but also guidebooks on methodology. Despite nineteenth-century German historian Leopold von Ranke's dictum to write history "as it actually happened" (*wie es eigentlich gewesen*), modern writers recognize that theoretical constructs underpin every interpretative work.

Still, the first question that looms as we push open the gates to begin our journey is this: why use novels as one of the principal sources for this analysis? Other materials, the ensuing chapters make clear, remain important. Chapter 1, covering 1750–1788, looks at evolving worldviews before the first American work of fiction appeared (although this chapter considers the impact of European literature). But novels hold great importance for this study. Books have an extraordinary reach. Although polls of American reading habits are recent and show a declining interest in literature, even in 2014, 43 percent of adults read at least one work of fiction during that year.[2] Novels boast a richness and complexity that no other source offers. They present deeply layered characters and intricate social orders. They are like the pieces of amber that trap the atmosphere of ancient times and allow scientists to study the earth in earlier millennia. They are time machines that offer a privileged view of the past.

Finding meaning in novels, however, is a perilous undertaking. During the twentieth- and twenty-first centuries, scholars elaborated a variety of hypotheses to suggest how informed readers might best proceed. Often these methodologies are frameworks that shine in the hands of brilliant practitioners but fail to offer clear guidelines for less-skilled acolytes. These models come with labels such as New Criticism, Deconstructionism, New Historicism, Structuralism, Post-Structuralism, Marxism, Feminism, and Post-Colonialism. Some of these approaches highlight particular bodies of material that earlier critics overlooked. Some methodologies disdain looking outside the novel, while others (like this book) assert that the social context offers great value. Almost all writers argue for the close reading of texts.[3]

Except for a few didactic novels, such as Edward Bellamy's *Looking Backward* (1888) or Upton Sinclair's *The Jungle* (1906), the meaning of a book cannot be inferred from the words of any single character but only from the totality of the work. In a 2014 interview, Philip Roth cautions: "The thought of the novelist lies not in the remarks of his characters or even in their introspection but in the plight he has invented for his characters, in the juxtaposition of those characters and in the lifelike ramifications of the ensemble they make—their density, their substantiality, their lived existence actualized in all its nuanced particulars, is in fact his thought metabolized."[4] In short, there is no handy Baedeker or (to change the metaphor) simple algorithm to provide readers step-by-step instructions for extracting the significance of a work.[5]

Hence, the first step in using novels to understand their times involves humility and recognition of the challenges involved in exploring texts. Explanations that begin with an author's intent are rarely satisfactory. For example, in James Fenimore Cooper's *The Pioneers* (1823), Judge Marmaduke Templeton might seem to be the spokesperson for Cooper's views. The judge, modeled after Cooper's wealthy landowning father, expounds many of the opinions Cooper sets forth in other essays. But the oddly named, illiterate Nathaniel Bumppo, who is disdainful of civilization and often in trouble with the law, turns out to be a far more engaging character. Encouraged by the enthusiasm of readers (who liked Natty better than the judge), Cooper traced the career of the sharpshooting backwoodsman in four subsequent novels. Who then is the author's standard-bearer in *The Pioneers*? Clearly, both men and neither of them—for the novel depicts many individuals. Only an analysis of the entire work, rather than a focus on any particular character, can do justice to a book.

A Mirror for History engages in an extensive dialogue with scholarly studies. Indeed, it is hard to imagine an analysis without these colloquies. Many writers explore contested terrains, delving into crucial questions. Does Louisa May Alcott's *Little Women* (1868–69) promote the cause of women's rights? Is Ernest Hemingway's *For Whom the Bell Tolls* (1940) about social justice? Does Ralph Ellison's *Invisible Man* (1952) provide an incisive critique of racism? Thoughtful answers emerge only after encounters with many points of view.

Equally challenging is the task of using literature to understand changes in society. A few scholars vociferously reject the contention that historical context has relevance in the analysis of novels. Fortunately, most researchers today take a different viewpoint. In his introduction to the seven-volume *Cambridge History of American Literature* (1994), Sacvan Bercovitch remarks: "At no time in literary studies has awareness of history—or more accurately, theorizing about history—been more acute and pervasive. It is hardly too much to say that what joins all the special interests in the field, all factions in our current critical dissensus, is an overriding interest in history: as the ground and texture of ideas, metaphors, and myths; as the substance of the texts we read and the spirit in which we interpret them."[6]

In analyzing novels, *A Mirror for History* follows certain guidelines. It recognizes the danger of generalizing from a single text or even a handful of texts. Hence, this study looks at many novels for every decade and highlights the shared outlooks that illuminate those years. Similarly, in examining change over time, the analysis explores multiple works and focuses on the *longue durée*. Individual novels might chronicle a military campaign, an outbreak of disease, or a political upheaval. But particular events, even ones seemingly as earth-shattering as the two World Wars or 9/11, have only an incidental impact on literature when viewed across a broad spectrum of novels. The Civil War ended slavery, but its reverberations are less evident in books by White authors. Far more important are long-term changes in society, such as the sharp rise in the standard of living beginning around 1820, the impact of industrialization in the late nineteenth century, the growing influence of a business civilization in the 1920s, or soaring inequality in the twenty-first century. Authors respond in different ways to these developments, but few books are untouched by such transformations.

Any examination of the ties between history and literature also must look closely at the assumptions underpinning the book's central argument: that "the arc of middle-class culture reflects the evolution of the economy." Every part of that statement needs unpacking. To begin, reference to "middle-class culture" could suggest that each era boasted a single uniform worldview, which the ensuing chapters make clear was never the case: wide-ranging, often antagonistic, beliefs characterize every period. Moreover, the contention that the outlook of the middle class "reflects the evolution of the economy" might, for some readers, hint at economic determinism. The title of the book, which suggests that novels (along with art) were a "mirror for history," could raise similar concerns.

This study, however, eschews determinism. The chapters that follow make explicit that there are no iron-clad links between the economy and the outlook of the middle class, or between that worldview and literature and painting. Perhaps the most thoughtful guide to these issues lies in the work of Raymond Williams, who spent much of his life pondering the connection between society and culture. He concludes, "We have to revalue 'determination' toward the setting of limits and the exertion of pressure, and away from a predicted, prefigured and controlled content."[7] In any given year, as this book emphasizes, American society gave rise to a broad range of artifacts. For example, in the early 1880s, readers would have encountered three strikingly dissimilar, newly published novels: Lew Wallace's

Christian adventure story, *Ben-Hur;* Henry James's study of an innocent abroad, *The Portrait of a Lady;* and Mark Twain's moral fable, *The Prince and the Pauper.* If society can be thought of as a mirror, it is a fragmented, shattered pane that projects a multitude of disparate images. Moreover, the Black experience often provides (to change the metaphor) a counterpoint to the dominant themes sounded by White authors. Nor does influence go only in a single direction. Books, particularly, popular ones, help shape perceptions and influence how people live their lives.

Still, the emphasis on the ways novels *mirror* social change captures an important aspect of the work's argument. Instead of using that term, I might have stated: "In each era, American society gave rise to a particular range of cultural expressions linked to the social and economic conditions." That lengthier statement broadens the import of "mirror" and suggests a spectrum of colors, not one specific line in that band. The set of possibilities alters with the growth of American society, and the nature of that evolution provides the narrative of this work.[8] For example, the previously mentioned novels of the early 1880s responded to the advent of industrialization. A corollary of this approach must be emphasized: novels are analyzed as part of the period in which they were created, regardless of the time frame of the narrative. So, E. L. Doctorow's *Ragtime* (1975) is viewed as a work of the 1970s, although it discusses America in the early twentieth century. Toni Morrison's *Beloved* (1987), which explores the horrors of slavery, is examined along with other postmodern works of the 1980s.[9]

Another key question must be addressed: how were novels chosen for this study?[10] No one person or team of readers (until machines take over our work) could possibly keep pace with the exponential growth of American novels. In the 1820s, about fifteen novels were published each year. With new methods of bookmaking and the demands of a broader reading audience, output soared. Between 1837 and 1857, American-authored works of fiction averaged over one hundred annually. By the 1880s, over one thousand novels appeared every twelve months, and the pace has only quickened. Early in the twenty-first century, American writers turned out more than fifty thousand novels each year. That amounts to more than a new title every ten minutes.[11]

So, choices must be made. To begin with, *A Mirror for History* examines works from the literary "canon"—the set of books valued by critics and often taught in courses. To be sure, academic studies have moved beyond the days when a small group of celebrated White males defined reading lists. In recent years, novels by women and members of various minorities have entered the literary pantheon. These highly praised works are often richly textured and have much to say about society and its values.[12]

A Mirror for History also looks at bestsellers—a category that only at times overlaps with the canon. For middle-class readers, the division between popular works and "good literature" was evident as early as the 1850s. Susan Warner's *The Wide, Wide World* and Maria Cummins's *The Lamplighter* sold in the hundreds of thousands, while Melville's *Moby-Dick* and Hawthorne's novels languished. After 1870, with genteel values now characterizing bourgeois society, the division between the two streams widened. The most popular authors affirmed Victorian pieties, while dissenting writers, like William Dean Howells, Henry James, Kate Chopin, Theodore Dreiser, and Frank Norris, challenged those beliefs—and sold far fewer books. Only a handful of novels, like Twain's *Adventures of Huckleberry Finn* and Edith Wharton's *House of Mirth*, claimed success in both camps. Works such as *Moby-Dick*, Stephen Crane's *Maggie*, Kate Chopin's *The Awakening*, or Charles Chesnutt's *Marrow of Tradition*, which met with indifference when first published, can provide powerful insights into their times. But the fact that readers shunned them suggests they were out of step with popular taste in important ways. By the same measure, bestsellers that modern critics might consider of less intrinsic value can shed a bright light on the outlook of the reading public.[13]

The selection is also topical. In a work that covers a broad span of American history, few themes are more important than race. *A Mirror for History* looks at how White writers viewed Blacks, and more particularly how African American novelists regarded themselves and their community. Black writers, from Frank J. Webb and Martin Delany in the 1850s, to Frances Harper and Paul Laurence Dunbar at the turn of the nineteenth century, to the titans of the Harlem Renaissance, to Toni Morrison and Alice Walker, and more recently, Jesmyn Ward, Colson Whitehead, and Edward Jones, all illuminate America's troubled soul. Most chapters also examine the changing role of women and the evolution of masculinity, and these themes too helped choose novels.

A Mirror for History focuses on the "mainstream" literature that the middle class enjoyed, not on the dime novels, "story papers," pulp fiction, and romance novels directed at a working-class audience. Some scholars refer to the works read by the more affluent as "middlebrow" or "highbrow" in contrast to "lowbrow" or mass market fiction. To be sure, there was overlap in readership among these categories. But the language, story lines, and values expressed in the dime novels differed from those in middle-class works. Mass market fiction, which emerged as a genre in the 1840s, appears in this study only as a counterpoint.[14]

II

Each chapter also explores art and suggests how this visual medium illuminates middle-class values. Discussing novels and paintings, Henry James remarks:

"Their inspiration is the same, their process (allowing for the different quality of the vehicle) is the same, their success is the same. They may learn from each other, they may explain and sustain each other."[15] Novels do the heavy lifting in this book; their rich texture allows the exploration of topics such as the role of religion and the status of women. Art refines that analysis. For example, paintings of the 1830s and 1840s (such as those by Thomas Cole) illustrate the close connection many White Americans felt to the divine. Similarly, the evolution of the art of Winslow Homer and Thomas Eakins, like the changing perspectives in the novels of Twain and Howells, reveals the impact of industrialization in the late nineteenth century.

Several concerns guide the use of painting in this work. Like the discussions of novels, investigations of art explore form as well as content. In the early twentieth century, the cubist-inspired art of Alfred Stieglitz's circle signaled their rebellion against genteel values. In the 1950s, the large canvases of abstract expressionists such as Jackson Pollock and Mark Rothko involved those artists in a complex dialogue with a society that emphasized conformity. Race remains important in painting as well as in literature; recent art by African Americans documents a range of responses to social injustice. Finally, the ready availability of images shapes the study of this medium. Art books make reviewing the complete oeuvre of a painter far easier than efforts to command the collected works of a prolific novelist. The eighteen illustrations included in this book stand in for a much larger universe of pictures.[16]

Still another question can be posed: why not include music, architecture, and poetry? Like novels and painting, these forms of expression mirrored changes in the world of the middle class. The answer is more practical than theoretical. Each of those art forms brings in its train, like a lengthy Silk Road caravan, a weighty literature and extensive methodological discussions. In a work that uses novels as an important source, painting was judged the most readily accessible complement to fiction.

III

The Ngram database, the basis for the twenty-seven graphs in the book, comprises another key source for this study. It sheds light on social change and expands upon the insights drawn from literature. Including these quantitative data comports with Franco Moretti's insistence on the value of "distant reading." Moretti asserts that "the trouble with close reading ... is that it necessarily depends on an extremely small canon. ... At bottom it's a very theological exercise—very solemn reading of very few texts." He continues: "Distant reading ... allows you to focus on units that are much smaller or much larger than the text: devices, themes, tropes—or genres and systems."[17]

The origins and dimensions of the Ngram database suggest its strengths and limitations. In 2004, engineers at Google began making digital copies of books. They undertook a task of herculean proportions. Since the invention of the printing press, more than 129 million books have been published; by 2017, Google had digitized over twenty-five million of them. The project encompasses works in seven languages, although two-thirds of the books scanned are in English. Most of the volumes have appeared since 1800; English-language authors, for example, published only five hundred thousand works between 1500 and 1800. Google initially selected 5.2 million books from those scanned to establish the Ngram database. The researchers chose this group based on the quality of the page scans and the completeness of "metadata," including date, place, and language of publication.[18]

Anyone visiting the Ngram Web page to run English-language word searches finds a short, and not entirely satisfactory, list of possible filters.[19] The one used in this book is "American English (2019)," which limits the search to English-language books published in the United States in 2019 or earlier. These works, however, can be of many sorts, including legal or technical documents, reprints of foreign books, sermons, political tracts, and American fiction. Bestsellers (such as the works of Mark Twain) appear in multiple editions, adding weight to their lexicons. However, because Google worked with the repositories of major libraries, dime novels and pulp fiction are underrepresented. Relatively few publications were issued in America before 1800, so graphs before that date are often marked by wild gyrations. Most charts in this work begin in 1800 or later.

Another challenge for this analysis of words is changes in meaning. Some terms, like "rake," "swell," and "creep," carry multiple denotations—and are typically not graphed. Nor are words whose meanings have evolved over time, such as "sissy" (from "little sister" to "weakling"). Dictionaries and linguistic studies, like the University of Pittsburgh's "Keywords Project," help track those transformations.[20]

Often denotations stay the same, but the baggage that words lug around changes. A powerful database, the Corpus of Historical American English (COHA), provides insights into those associations. COHA, based on more than one hundred thousand texts, allows searches by decade for "collocates"— words appearing near the target word. So, while the key meaning of *sin* ("an offense against religious or moral law") may remain constant, during the first half of the nineteenth century it was most often linked to *shame, evil, misery,* and *sorrow*. By the late twentieth century, the term was used far less often, and its companions were *mortal* and *original*. Similar change occurred with *romantic* ("marked by imaginative or emotional appeal"), whose use soared in the 1820s and again in the 1920s (see figure 3.3). In the 1820s, it was associated with *wild, scenery,* and *picturesque,* and in the

1920s—think Jay Gatsby—with *temperament*. Especially when analysis stretches over lengthy periods, these pages explore such changes in usage.[21]

Ngram word searches generate graphs, like the twenty-seven presented in this book; but what exactly is being measured? The numbers on the left axis are percentages indicating for each year the proportion of all words (or phrases) in the scanned books that match the term selected. If you search for "the," a very common word, the results show that in most years about 5 percent of all words (Google calls them "unigrams") are a match. More typical results are much lower. For example, the use of "weep," displayed in figure PI.1, peaks in 1850 at about 0.002 percent. Of every one hundred thousand words in books published at midcentury, two of them are "weep."[22]

Two technical concerns also must be noted. Graphs use a "running average" of three years to lessen the "noise" that might come from focusing on annual data. In some instances—all clearly labeled—charts present lines with different scales. While the frequency of a word might be multiplied by, say, ten, the shape of each curve remains true. This approach allows the comparisons of trends where one word or phrase is used far less often than the other.

Google allows users of the database to conduct a still finer-grained analysis—but that sorting must be undertaken manually. For any word queried, Google provides a list of the books that include the term. For "weep" in the Ngram American English database (2019), 1843–52, 410 books are listed. All are published in the United States, but many are reprints of works first issued elsewhere, for example, the plays of William Shakespeare and the poetry of John Milton. The listed volumes include novels, collections of sermons, and issues of the *Southern Literary Messenger*. In sum, the Ngram American English database is a useful handbook for what Americans wrote, but it is a still better guide for what middle-class Americans were reading.

Finally, while the aura of "scientific history" might hover over these graphs, they are simply one body of evidence that must be used with care. As the numbers on the left axes suggest, these plottings tabulate words or phrases that in some cases appear infrequently. The Ngram and COHA databases are too important to ignore. They provide important clues and open up avenues of enquiry. But novels and art, not these quantitative sources, comprise the most important material for exploring the changing outlook of Americans.[23]

IV

Few concepts are more crucial to this work than that of the middle class. *A Mirror for History* chronicles the evolution of this group's values.[24] But what is the "middle class" and when did it emerge? An examination of this cohort provides a foundation for the chapters that follow.

If there is any agreement among social scientists about the American middle class, it rests with the elusive nature of this stratum. "Studying the middle class," Debby Applegate remarks, "offers all the frustrations of an optical illusion—what seems plain as day out of the corner of the eye can become hopelessly muddled when examined directly."[25] G. D. H. Cole underscores the problem of defining this group: "Clearly membership in the middle class or classes [is] not simply a matter of income... Nor is it exclusively a matter of... profession or calling. Nor again is it exclusively a matter of education, or of manners." Thus, no single metric defines the middle class. The bounds of this group resemble not hard lines but blurred, uncertain demarcations. Moreover, the composition of this cohort has changed over time. Where the stratum centered on shopkeepers, artisans, and well-off farmers in the eighteenth century, its mainstay in the twentieth century was businesspeople, managers, and professionals. Still, imprecision or a changing composition hardly negates the group's existence. Contemporaries recognized the importance of this class, while the scholars who emphasize its elusiveness eagerly parse its behavior. As Applegate wryly notes, "For most historians, the middle class is something they know when they see it."[26]

Researchers clash over when the American middle class emerged. Some, like Stuart Blumin and Mary Ryan, argue that a coherent group appeared only in the decades before the Civil War.[27] Others, like Jackson Main in *The Social Structure of Revolutionary America*, place the origins of this group in the eighteenth century. Main notes that, in the 1770s, "the middle class in America consisted of small property holders who were usually self-employed."[28] In a recent study, Emma Hart notes, "Increasingly, historians of eighteenth-century America are becoming equally confident about the importance of 'middling' people to the story of late colonial society."[29] If the criterion for a social class is widespread self-identification, then the emergence of the "middle class" cannot be dated before the twentieth century. But if, more properly, shared values and the remarks of many contemporary observers document the existence of a social group, then (as this book affirms) the American middle class appeared in the mid-eighteenth century. Not until the first decade of the nineteenth century, however, was the nomenclature resolved, with "middle class" becoming the accepted term for the group. Before that the stratum had various labels, combining "middle" or "middling" with "class," "orders," "folk," and "people." (This study occasionally uses "middling" folk, people, order, or class as a synonym for "middle class.")

A brief narrative of the rise, further rise, and decline of the American middle class puts flesh on these theoretical bones. Although the constituent elements of this group had long existed, around 1750 commentators began referring to the "middling folk" and their role in society. In a verse praising his adopted colony, Pennsylvania, Benjamin Franklin made clear his admiration for these individuals. He wrote:

> But who her Sons, that to her Int'rest true,
> Still plan with Wisdom and Zeal pursue?
> These found most frequently in Life's *Middle State*,
> Rich without Gold, and without Titles great.[30]

In 1747, Franklin called on the "middling People" to form militia companies, as the wealthy lawmakers who headed the colony's two parties seemed indifferent to the dangers posed by King George's War. With his newspaper, almanacs, and public persona, Franklin, more than any other individual, became the spokesman and guide for the "middling" people.[31]

As the conflict with Britain deepened, commentators regarded the middle class as the bulwark against British tyranny—and the individuals who could relieve the burden of debt oppressing the colonies. In 1767, "A TRADESMAN" remarked in the *New-York Journal*, "Are we more Frugal? Is Grain cheaper? Are our Importations less?—not to mention the Play-House and Equipages, which it is hoped none but People of Fortune frequent, or use.... Surely it is high Time for the middling People to abstain from *every Superfluity*, in *Dress, Furniture,* and *Living.*"[32] Patriot writers favorably compared the middle class to the elite, whose virtue had been weakened by luxury. "Trust not in the Rich, they trust in their Wealth, and will sneak in an Hour of Distress," one editorialist remarked. "If the middle Class sleep, Perdition is just before us." Another writer opined that if "rights are preserved, it must be through the virtue and integrity of the middling sort of people, as farmers, tradesmen, etc. who despise venality, and best know the sweets of liberty."[33]

By the end of the eighteenth century, many individuals recognized the middle class as a powerful, coherent group whose views mattered. When the first American novels appeared in 1789, middle-class readers formed the audience for these works—and provided most of the authors. Charles Brockden Brown, a prominent member of the first generation of American novelists, acknowledged the importance of this collectivity. "Poverty is far from being a spur to genius," he observed. "Wealth is far less unfriendly, though its influence is certainly not propitious to it. It is the middle class that produces every kind of worth in the greatest abundance. We must not look for fertility on the hill top, nor at the bottom of the glen. It is only found in the plains and intermediate slopes."[34]

In the decades before the Civil War, both the composition and views of the middle class continued to evolve. By the 1850s, between 25 and 40 percent of the adult male population in Northern towns and cities was engaged in nonmanual labor—and these individuals comprised an important component of the growing middle class.³⁵ A contributor to the *New York Tribune* in 1855 emphasized the range of occupations gathered under this heading: "Our population [in New York City] is mostly made up of the middle class, (if there be any classes in democratic America). We have a large sprinkling of builders, master-masons, carpenters &c.; we have merchants and brokers . . . printers, bookbinders, book keepers, clerks, [and] journeymen of every trade."³⁶ A new ethos shaped the outlook of this group. Members of this cohort, lauding domesticity and piety, accorded women an exalted place within the family and church. Historians who assert that this era marked the emergence of the middle class conflate a particular phase in the existence of this group with its first appearance.³⁷

Nineteenth-century commentators also suggested the bounds of wealth defining the group. "The most valuable class in any community," Walt Whitman remarked in 1858, "is the middle class, the men of moderate means, living at the rate of a thousand dollars a year or thereabouts."³⁸ Two decades later, writer Lydia Maria Child presented comparable numbers. "By the middle class," she noted in 1877, "I mean farmers and mechanics, who work with their *hands*, own a house, with or without acres of land, with incomes from their own labor, varying from $300 a year to $1,500."³⁹

When Theodore Dreiser wrote his novels at the beginning of the twentieth century, marking someone as "middle class" had become commonplace. In *Sister Carrie* (1900), the author notes that Carrie "was a fair example of the middle American class—two generations removed from the emigrant." George Hurstwood, the other protagonist, muses that, "When some one of the many middle-class individuals whom he knew, who had money, would get into trouble, he would shake his head."⁴⁰

The prosperity of the 1920s and the success of the industrial economy after World War II broadened the membership of this class and changed its composition. Professionals and businesspeople in the 1920s and then white-collar workers in the 1950s became the mainstay of the group. Americans increasingly called themselves *middle class*—a change reflected in the Ngram data. The use of this phrase rose sharply between 1926 and 1937 and climbed still further between 1943 and 1970 (fig. IN.1).⁴¹ This cohort remained overwhelmingly White. Although a small Black bourgeoisie emerged in the nineteenth century, a numerically significant African American middle class dates from the 1960s (fig. 9.1).⁴²

Since the 1970s, the middle class, both White and Black, has been under siege, and the terrain it commands has contracted like those low-lying islands whose shores are eroded by rising seas. Deindustrialization, the decline of unions, and the growing extremes in wealth all threaten the group in the middle. Ngram data

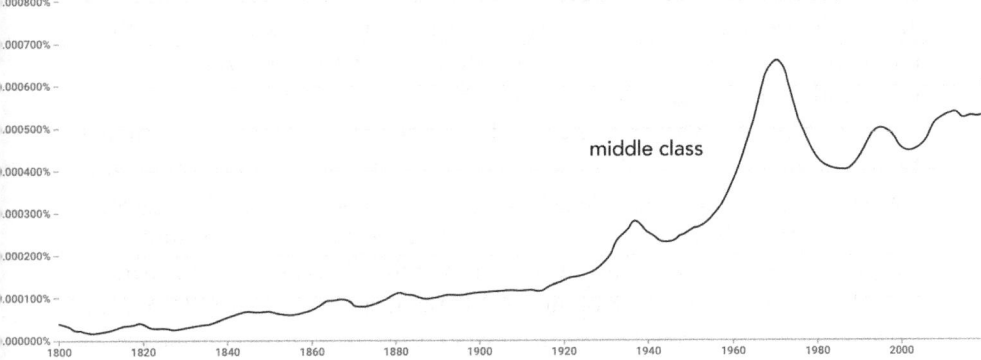

IN.1. FREQUENCY OF *MIDDLE CLASS* IN AMERICAN ENGLISH (2019), NGRAM DATABASE, 1800-2019.

indicate that the use of the term has fallen off.[43] Even weakened, this group remains central to American society. Gallup regularly asks adult Americans in which social class they place themselves. The most common response remains "upper middle" or "middle class," although the proportion identifying with those cohorts declined from 63 percent in 2000 to 51 percent in 2015, while those declaring themselves "working and lower" class rose over the same span, from 33 percent to 48 percent.[44] Despite the emergence of an anxious "Precariat," as some now term this stratum, the middle class remains a key to American culture today as it has since the mid-eighteenth century.

V

Finally, for anyone entering a capacious building, like this investigation of American values, a discussion of the architecture is essential. Chronology orders the sections and chapters. Chapter 1 covers the years from the mid-eighteenth century, when the middle class emerged, to 1788, just before the first American novel appeared. That analysis forms a prelude to the ensuing four periods. These epochs are the sentimental era (1789–1869), genteel society (1870–1919), modern America (1920–60), and postmodern America (1961–present). But why these periods?[45]

These units reflect fundamental shifts in the economy and in the outlook of the middle class. Although the termini might vary, the four epochs also underlie many studies of art and fiction. They shape multiauthor volumes such as, *Cambridge*

History of American Literature, *The Columbia History of American Literature*, and *The Cambridge History of the Novel*. More than social historians may realize, these four periods, familiar to students of literature and painting, provide a valuable framework for understanding the evolving beliefs of Americans.[46]

Each era highlights a distinct period of economic development and a response to the question—how should middle-class Americans behave? The sentimental era manifested the outlook of a largely rural society. "Middling folk" distinguished themselves from the strata above and below them by their ability to emote—to shed tears when authors or painters plucked at their heart strings. The genteel period celebrated the triumph of small-town America, with its demand that good citizens (invariably, White, Protestant, Anglo-Saxon) adhere to well-defined codes of behavior. Big cities shaped the modern period. Members of the middle class balanced the freedoms of postgenteel society with the pressures for conformity from a pervasive business culture. In postmodern America, with the locus of the middle class shifting to the suburbs, a different tension animated society. These years were marked by the clash between the chaos that came from rejecting time-honored institutions and the determination to establish a new order based on compassion and progressive values. The introductions to each of the four sections explore these overviews more fully.

Generalizations about these eras, clearly, are broad brushstrokes. There is a need to look not just at the forest, but also at the trees, branches, and leaves. If social science explanations are sometimes polarized between *splitters* and *lumpers*, both approaches are required to explain change over time.[47] The book emphasizes not only the themes that mark the periods, but also the crosscurrents and the changes within those epochs—patterns of development that are almost as important as the larger units.

The story begins before the first American novel was written. It starts with Benjamin Franklin, Poor Richard, and the outlook of the newly emergent American middle class in the mid-eighteenth century.

1
Prelude
From Austerity to Sentimentality, 1750–1788

Like most autobiographies, Benjamin Franklin's account of his life is not a full and frank retelling of his worldly progress. He downplays his assiduous cultivation of those in power and quest for the patronage that helped propel him from one position to the next, posts that included clerk of the assembly, postmaster, and colonial agent. There is no mention of his prolonged, unsuccessful campaign to become royal governor of Pennsylvania or his hope of being honored as a British undersecretary of state. Those plans required him to play the courtier and mute his criticism of British policy. Instead, Franklin ascribes his rise in the world to two qualities: industry and frugality. ("I mention this industry the more particularly and the more freely," he remarks, "tho' it seems to be talking in my own praise, that those of my posterity, who shall read it, may know the use of that virtue, when they see its effects in my favour throughout this relation."[1]) The explanation he chose, and emphasized in his other writings, fits well with his times, making his *Autobiography* and almanacs indispensable guidebooks for the middle class, which had emerged around 1750.[2]

The appearance of this new group preceded by about four decades the first American-authored novels and the full-blown expression of middle-class views. During those forty years, the outlook of this cohort, or at least many members within it, evolved from the austere values Franklin preached to a sentimentality that was in keeping with the European novels Americans had begun to read. Painters, who flourished in the New World before novelists did, help document this transition. These developments, which reflected changes in the economy, suggest the strong foundations for the emotion-filled era that emerged in the late 1780s.

I

Between 1750 and 1788, the polities that would form the Thirteen Colonies and (after independence) the United States experienced a lengthy expansion and then a gradual slowdown—fluctuations that shaped not only economic activities but also the outlook of the new middle class. The buoyant beginnings to this era—the expansion actually dates from 1745—lifted up individuals who had once struggled to get by. For the first time, many took note of a "middling" group of prosperous farmers and tradesmen. As growth continued in the 1750s, 1760s, and 1770s, more women and men enjoyed not just the bare necessities but "amenities" such as West Indian sugar and British-manufactured cloth and ironware. With the rise in the standard of living, the austere doctrines of the midcentury years no longer seemed appropriate, and those beliefs gradually gave way to an acceptance of some luxuries and a celebration of emotion. Growth stagnated during the Revolutionary War and the hard times that followed. Nonetheless, the sentimental turn, first apparent in the 1760s, was there to stay, and would characterize the mindset of many middle-class Americans, as well as the novels and art that appeared after 1788.

The mechanics of this expansion demand closer scrutiny. The era of growth between 1745 and 1775 reflected an upsurge in Europe. Business activity in the colonies, like the planets in Isaac Newton's clockmaker universe, was one component in an intricate system with many moving parts. The mainspring of development was the European economy and particularly British growth. When English demand for West Indian products surged, colonial exports, such as flour, wheat, lumber, and livestock, directed to the Caribbean increased in value. Continental purchases of the tobacco Britain re-exported also played a pivotal role. Expansion in Britain enlarged the flow of capital to the New World. At the same time, advances in England's industries boosted output, while quotations for those textiles and ironware remained relatively flat.

The colonists benefited from the confluence of those trends.[3] The most striking indication of the new prosperity was the increased consumption of imported goods. Judged against the free population, per capita purchases of manufactured goods increased about 30 percent between 1730-45 and 1760-75.[4] Observers testified to the changes. "Within these 25 years," a Virginia trader remarked in 1766, "1000 due to a merchant was looked upon as a sum immense and never to be got over. Ten times that sum is now spoke of with indifference.... Luxury and expensive living have gone hand in hand with the increase of wealth. In 1740 I don't remember to have seen such a thing as a Turkey carpet in the country except a small thing in a bedchamber, now nothing are so common as Turkey or Wilton carpetts, the whole

Furniture of the Roomes Elegant & every appearance of Opulence. All this is in a great measure owing to the Credit which the Planters have had from England."[5] In 1764, a New Yorker put the case more simply: "The manner of living among all ranks of people is now at a much higher rate than formerly."[6]

Still, the shortcomings of this expansion must be underscored. Slaves, who comprised 20 percent of the population, did not share in the bounty. Even for the free citizenry, the pace of growth remained far slower than the blistering ascent that began after 1820. Many "middling folk" recognized that uncertainty defined their world. Wars repeatedly disrupted Atlantic trade and roiled markets within the colonies. Bad luck or poor planning could turn the daily wagers that merchants made into losses, with dire consequences for many townspeople. In 1757 Franklin interjected a dark note of caution into "Father Abraham's Speech," a widely reprinted discourse that prefaced that year's *Poor Richard's Almanac*. This collection of a hundred adages drawn from earlier editions of the almanac warned, "Do not depend too much upon your own *Industry*, and *Frugality*, and *Prudence*, though excellent Things; for they may all be blasted, without the Blessing of Heaven."[7]

After independence, even this modest advance faltered, and the economy would not resume its ascent until the 1790s. The War for Independence, which stretched from 1775 to 1783, crippled commerce. At different times, British forces occupied Boston, Philadelphia, and Charleston, and they remained in New York throughout the war. The Royal Navy blockaded the coast, making shipping difficult. The contending armies—with their forced marches and demands for men and provisions—disrupted farming, while rampant inflation of the continental and state currencies rendered transactions more difficult. Infusions of French specie as well as gains from privateering and military purchases only slightly softened these blows. Problems continued after the Peace of Paris in 1783. The weak central government, unable to pay its debts, hindered recovery, as did restrictions on American trade with the British West Indies. Indigo production, deprived of a British bounty, disappeared, while rice and tobacco shipments remained well below prewar levels.

Still, hopeful signs pointed to improving conditions after 1788. The western lands gained by the fledgling republic promised future wealth. Freed from the British yoke, Americans established banks and entered into direct trade with the Far East. The grain-growing middle states profited from shortages in Europe. The writing and ratification of the Constitution in 1787–88 laid the foundation for a strong national government. If the standard of living rose little after the mid-1770s, it still remained well above the level recorded at midcentury. There was no reversion to the austerity Franklin preached; the "middling folk" clung to their newfound comforts.[8]

II

The colonial middle class, which emerged at midcentury, embraced an outlook that lauded hard work and self-denial. These tenets were well suited for strivers whose foothold on the ladder of success remained precarious but were determined to climb higher. No one voiced this philosophy more fully than Franklin, who began as a poor apprentice, established himself as a respected printer, and eventually became a prosperous political leader. With various tracts, and with his almanac and newspaper, the *Pennsylvania Gazette,* Franklin guided this middle stratum. In a 1748 pamphlet, "Advice to a Young Tradesman," he explains: "In short, the Way to Wealth, if you desire it, is as plain as the Way to Market. It depends chiefly on two Words, Industry and Frugality."[9] Franklin expanded on this advice with the adages compiled in "Father Abraham's Speech." The oration advises: "Keep thy Shop, and thy Shop will keep thee," "The sleeping Fox catches no Poultry," "Plough deep, while Sluggards sleep, and you shall have Corn to sell and to keep," and "He that hath a Calling hath an Office of Profit and Honour."[10]

Others reinforced this outlook. Benjamin Rush, who gained acclaim as a doctor and humanitarian, provides a similar account of his early days as a physician. With no family connections, and many of the older practitioners critical of his emphasis on diet and exercise rather than medicine, Rush had a hard time establishing his practice. His eventual success, he explains, came from Franklinesque virtues. "From the time of my settlement in Philadelphia in 1769 'till 1775," he recalls in his memoirs, "I led a life of constant labor and self-denial. My shop was crowded with the poor in the morning and at meal times, and nearly every street and alley in the city was visited by me every day."[11]

The insistence on *industry* and *frugality* distinguished the new middle class from the elite. Before the 1740s, virtually all the "conduct" books that instructed individuals how to behave were directed to the upper class. Conspicuous by their absence were admonitions to work hard or limit expenditures. The wealthy relied on servants and slaves to perform arduous tasks, and everywhere the consumption of houses, clothes, horses, and expensive schooling comprised the measure of success.

Still, even in these midcentury years, the picture of a frugal, industrious class of farmers and craftspeople must be carefully qualified. As trade statistics make clear, the lure of low-priced British goods was too strong for many well-intentioned individuals. Significantly, Franklin concludes "Father Abraham's Speech" with a note of despair. "Thus the old Gentleman ended his Harangue," Franklin notes. "The People heard it, and approved the Doctrine, and immediately practised the contrary, just as if it had been a common Sermon; for the Vendue opened, and they began to buy extravagantly, notwithstanding all his Cautions, and their own Fear of Taxes." The contradiction between lofty goals and self-interested behavior does not negate the importance of the advice promoted by Franklin, Rush, and others. Rather, it shows that their statements embodied aspirations, which many applauded and some—but not all—of the "middling sort" adhered to. The emphasis on industry and frugality remained sound, relevant advice for a class of strivers living in difficult times.[12]

III

Members of the new middle class also agreed on the importance of restraining personal emotions. This behavior fit well with the times: personal sentiments were a luxury in which a struggling class could not afford to indulge. But how do we know how the colonists felt? A growing body of scholarship sheds light on the feelings of colonial Americans. This research draws upon diverse materials, including private letters, "conduct" books, tracts, newspaper articles, portraiture, guides to childrearing, and records of the European novels imported and read. These studies, which look at the colonists from many vantage points, sketch in the same broad picture. They note the emotional restraint of the 1750s and the gradual turn toward sentiment after 1760.

The works dealing with emotional restraint at midcentury explore concerns of class, gender, and race as well as the division between public and private sentiments. Anger served as a marker of class. Members of the middle class (and gentry) demonstrated restraint; the less wealthy did not. Advertisements for runaways noted their unbridled emotions. A 1747 announcement sought information about "a Irish servant man, named Francis Grachams; he is a short lad, about 21 or 22 years of age ... short red hair, and talks English short and quick, and passionately, as if angry."[13] Racial lines traced a similar fissure. In *Plain Truth*, the 1747 pamphlet Franklin used to stir the "middling folk" into forming a militia, the printer asserts that the enemy might bring wild, dark-skinned soldiers to Pennsylvania. Franklin remarks: "Who can, without the utmost Horror, conceive the Miseries ... when your Persons, Fortunes, Wives and Daughters, shall be subject to the wanton and unbridled Rage, Rapine and Lust, of *Negroes*, *Molattoes*, and others, the vilest and most abandoned of Mankind?"[14]

However important lines of class and race were for questions of emotion, the divisions did not extend to gender. Both male and female members of the middle and gentry classes were directed to rein in their emotions. Neither men nor women wrote love letters to their intended mate before marriage, whatever sentiments they might share with a friend of the same sex. When a child died, husbands and wives admonished each other to repress displays of grief.[15]

Colonial portraiture also documents this era of emotional restraint. Before 1770, paintings reveal little familial affection. *Isaac Royall and Family*, 1741 (ptg. 1.1), by the prolific Boston painter Robert Feke, typifies these early efforts. In a discussion of this portrait and other similar ones, art historian Margaretta Lovell remarks: "The children . . . pose stiffly in their mothers' arms; they are still, composed, obedient, attentive, and easily overlooked minor actors in the complex tableaux. The women sit in quiet horizontal groups and direct their attention to the spectator."[16] Karin Calvert's study of colonial art similarly underscores the absence of demonstrably warm family ties—or even childhood—during this era. Before midcentury, Calvert notes, none of the portraits with children included items such as toys, schoolbooks, or cribs. Girls were dressed as small adults, as were boys

1.1. ROBERT FEKE, *ISAAC ROYALL AND FAMILY*, 1741.

after ages six or seven (before that they typically wore petticoats like girls). Even between 1750 and 1770, less than 10 percent of the portraits of children included the artifacts associated with the young. Few of the paintings made before 1770 illustrate parental affection, even when infants are portrayed.[17]

IV

By the 1760s, with the rise in the standard of living, members of the middle and upper class gradually abandoned austerity and embraced sentiment. Scholars underscore this change. In *Passion Is the Gale*, Nicole Eustace notes that her study "centers on the heart of the century, from the 1740s through the 1770s, when colonial ideas about emotion would be tested and ultimately transformed."[18] Similarly, in *Sensibility and the American Revolution*, Sarah Knott remarks that "Before the [post-1763] imperial crisis ... colonial North America was embedded in sensibility's early-eighteenth-century genealogy. Only in the second half of the century, around and with that crisis, however, did sensibility take on a central place in American history."[19]

Portraits reflected this change, with the prominent artist Charles Willson Peale exemplifying the new approach. Peale was not only a gifted painter, he also advocated a new, more gentle approach to childrearing. He was enamored of the work of Jean-Jacques Rousseau, whose novel *Emile* (1762) called on parents to foster their children's intellectual and emotional development. Peale placed over his fireplace an allegorical print celebrating Rousseau as the "liberator of childhood."[20] Peale's portraits are filled with couples and friends who look at each other with affection and show love for their offspring. *The Peale Family* (ptg. 1.2) is a good example. He painted this group portrait in 1772–73, making only a few minor changes in 1808; Peale placed himself on the left, holding a palette and bending over his brother. Near him, his wife holds their infant child. John Adams saw the picture in 1776 and commented that the faces showed "a pleasant happy cheerfulness" and "a familiarity in their air towards each other."[21] More broadly, art historian Karen Calvert found that while from 1730 to 1770 only 1 percent of family groupings depicted a nuclear family, fully 27 percent did so between 1770 and 1810.[22]

The revolutionary movement furthered the growth of sentiment by breaking down distinctions between the tight-lipped upper orders and the passionate lower class. A united, heartfelt opposition to British tyranny became the order of the day. A 1765 account of a funeral for "Liberty" in Rhode Island declared that "The Concourse of Mourners and Spectators was prodigious, consisting of Persons of all Ranks, from the highest, even down to the Blacks, who seemed, from a sense of their Masters Sufferings to join the Mourning Course."[23] Thomas Paine's widely

1.2. CHARLES WILLSON PEALE, *THE PEALE FAMILY*, 1772–1773, 1808.

reprinted pamphlet, *Common Sense*, declared in 1776 that "The Cause of America ... is the Concern of every Man to Whom Nature has given the Power of feeling."[24]

V

The turn toward sentiment after 1760 was also reflected in the English and continental novels that Americans imported and read in ever greater numbers. These works would have a far-reaching impact on the fiction that New World writers produced after 1788—an influence evident both in themes pursued and in specific references. The first American novel, William Hill Brown's *The Power of Sympathy* (1789), tells the story of Thomas Harrington, who, thwarted in a love affair, kills himself with a copy of Johann Wolfgang von Goethe's *The Sorrows of Young Werther* at his side. In Hannah Foster's *The Coquette* (1797), Mrs. Richman presciently warns the heroine, Eliza Wharton. "I do not think you seducible," Richman remarks, "nor was [Samuel Richardson's] Clarissa till she made herself the victim by her own indiscretion."[25]

Sentimental novels appeared in Europe well before they did in America— reflecting societies in which vibrant middle classes coalesced decades before such groups formed in North America. By the early eighteenth century, the "middling sort" of people were a clearly recognized stratum within English society. As in the New World, the middle class practiced austerity before parading its emotions. The first English novel, Daniel Defoe's *Robinson Crusoe*, published in 1719, embodied that restraint. Critics like Ian Watt justly label Crusoe a *homo economicus*, or "economic man." Shipwrecked and stranded on an island for twenty-eight years, Crusoe succeeded by embodying the middle-class virtues of self-denial and hard work.[26]

The leap into sentimental literature came with Samuel Richardson's best-selling epistolary novels, *Pamela; or, Virtue Rewarded* (1740) and *Clarissa; or The History of a Young Lady* (1748). Both tell stories of aristocrats who sexually assault women of lower rank. In *Pamela*, Mr. B (his full name is never provided) repeatedly tries to seduce Pamela, but then reforms—and the two eventually marry. Clarissa Harlowe, however, fares less well. In *Clarissa*, the lustful aristocrat, Robert Lovelace, drugs and rapes the heroine, who falls ill and dies. Both books, written from the vantage of the middle class, criticize the self-serving morals of the aristocracy.[27]

Richardson's success opened the floodgates for sentimental literature. Several English authors contributed to the mania. Henry Fielding's *Shamela* (1741) and *Joseph Andrews* (1742) directly respond to *Pamela*, while his *Tom Jones* (1749) reflects the new license to explore sex and romance. Horace Walpole's *The Castle of Otranto* (1764) was one of the first "gothic" novels, bringing together romance and medieval settings. Laurence Sterne in *A Sentimental Journey through France and Italy* (1768) introduces emotion into travel writing.[28]

The extraordinary acclaim that greeted Richardson was not lost on continental authors. Two wildly successful books depicted tragic love triangles. In *Julie; or, The New Heloise* (the original French title, *Julie, ou la nouvelle Héloïse* [1761]), by the Swiss-born Jean-Jacques Rousseau, the lovely Julie d'Étange, at her parents' insistence, marries M. de Wolmar, but never stops loving Saint-Preux and reaffirms those feelings as she lies dying at the end of the novel.[29] Goethe's *The Sorrows of Young Werther* (or in its original German, *Die Leiden des jungen Werthers* [1774]) was equally heart-rending—and popular. In this tale, Charlotte spurns the love-stricken Werther and weds Albert. Overcome by grief, Werther commits suicide. Both were soon translated into English and widely reprinted.[30]

VI

The growing interest in these European novels both reflected and encouraged Americans' turn toward emotions. Beginning in 1760, three British-born booksellers helped bring sentimental works to New World readers. In America the passion for "sensibility" was hardly universal and was for the most part limited to middle- and upper-class individuals in the largest towns. The colonists' enthusiasm for the new literature remained a faint echo of the mania that touched England and the continent. Some individuals grumbled about these works; for example, Philadelphia lawyer Alexander Graydon dismissed Rousseau's *Confessions*, arguing that the writer was "tiresome when he dwells upon his sensibilities, which he does too much."[31] Still, change was evident, and these book importers fostered an outlook that would grow ever more important in the new nation.

James Rivington was better known to Americans for his politics than for his role in introducing the new European literature. Except for George Washington, the revolutionaries reviled him. That anger was understandable: Rivington's newspaper, *New-York Gazetteer*, attacked the patriots and continued to do so during the British occupation of New York. Few Americans, however, knew about his divided loyalties: secretly in Washington's pay, he passed along information about British troop movements.[32]

Rivington also played a noteworthy role in the literary history of early America. Coming from a well-established London family of booksellers, he arrived in New York in 1760 with a "very heavy" stock of books. Several novels celebrating personal emotion had been imported earlier or reprinted in the colonies, but Rivington was the first bookseller to actively promote sentimental literature. In 1762, he advertised Thomas Leland's recently published *Longsword, Earl of Salisbury*, noting it could "not fail of affecting every Reader of Sensibility." That same year, Rivington announced the new English translation of Jean-Jacques Rousseau's *La Nouvelle Héloïse*, comparing the work to Samuel Richardson's heart-rending novel *Clarissa*. He noted that it was "equally well received [as] the celebrated Clarissa Harlowe, to which it bears some Resemblance."[33]

Like Rivington, John Mein became better known in the colonies for his politics than for his bookselling. Born in Scotland, and always passionately loyal to Britain, Mein arrived in Boston in 1764 and opened a printing house and bookstore. In 1769–70, Mein's newspaper, the *Boston Chronicle*, vehemently denounced the boycott of British goods, angering the common folk and more affluent patriots. In 1770, the threat of mob violence and arrest forced Mein to leave Boston, and he returned home the following year.[34]

Before clashing with the patriots, Mein contributed to Boston culture and promoted sentimental literature. In 1765, he established Boston's first "circulating library." This institution lent books for just a few pence a week—an approach that for most readers proved far more attractive than the outright purchase of volumes or membership in a "social library" (like Franklin's Library Company) with its large initial fees. In announcing his plan, Mein welcomed both men and women. "Something of this kind has been long wanted," he remarked, "to amuse the *Man of Leisure* [and] . . . *Men of business*" and to "insinuate knowledge and instruction, under the veil of entertainment to the FAIR SEX." In a society where women were subordinate, Mein and other booksellers affirmed the value of female consumers. Mein enumerated the different sorts of people who would benefit from his collection. He noted that he had works for the *"Divine* and the *Christian,"* for the *"Student of Physic,"* and the *"Physician."* Some books would please the *"Man* who delights in speculation and solitude." Finally, the circulating library would allow the *"Man of Taste* and *Sentiment"* to "enjoy all the pleasure—the painful pleasures attending an exquisite sensibility."[35]

The catalogue Mein issued made clear that in the mid-1760s the market for sentimental fiction in colonial America remained small. Only a fourth of the seven hundred titles he enumerated were fiction, and only some of those works came from the new emotional literature. More than a third of the collection focused on religion and philosophy.[36]

The third bookseller, Robert Bell, was the most ardent of the three in promoting sentimental literature. His career suggests the growing importance of the new fiction in the 1770s and 1780s. Bell arrived in Philadelphia in 1768 after a stint as a bookseller in Dublin and, unlike Rivington and Mein, remained on good terms with the patriots (in 1776, he published Tom Paine's *Common Sense*). Initially, Bell had little interest in promoting emotional literature. His first auction catalogue, issued in 1768, was directed simply to "the Lovers of Literary Entertainment, Amusement and Instruction." In announcing the sale, he declared, "Reading helps polish the Mind, and renders me fitter for polite conversation."[37]

But Bell's approach to fiction changed after the strong sales of Laurence Sterne's *Sentimental Journey*, which he published in 1770. He also printed Goethe's *The Sorrows of Young Werther*, adding on the title page that the book had "received the approbation of every reader of taste and sentiment." In 1774, he established a circulating library in Philadelphia and made his new passion clear to all. Bookplates in the two thousand volumes stated that Bell's library was "where sentimentalists, whether ladies or gentlemen, may become readers." An observer remarked that in Bell's shop near Saint Paul's Church *"sentimental-mongers"* could be seen along with "young blushing writers" and "smart politicians."[38]

During the war years Bell expanded his efforts to promote the new literature. When John Witherspoon, president of the College of New Jersey, labeled him the Sentimentalists' "Provedore" (or purveyor), Bell seized upon the term and soon advertised himself as the "humble Provedore to the Sentimentalists." He traveled to Massachusetts and Rhode Island to sell these novels, declaring to the inhabitants of Providence that he offered "FOOD for SENTIMENTALISTS." His evening auctions, one rival remarked, were "as good as [a] play to attend." In 1778, he published a collection of European works under the title *Miscellanies for Sentimentalists*. His announcements emphasized that the volumes offered would appeal to "persons in the middle walk of life" as well as to "Gentlemen of affluent fortunes."[39]

Tabulations of the novels listed in various catalogues, along with analysis of the works Americans reprinted in full or in abridged versions, highlight the importance of emotional literature. Historian Robert Winans lists the two dozen works of fiction found most often in 140 catalogues issued by American booksellers and circulating libraries between 1750 and 1800. About half of the twenty-four are sentimental novels. These bestsellers include such familiar titles as Richardson's *Pamela* and *Clarissa*; Sterne's *Sentimental Journey*; Fielding's *Joseph Andrews* and *Tom Jones*; Goethe's *The Sorrows of Young Werther*; Oliver Goldsmith's *The Vicar of Wakefield* (1766); and Rousseau's *Emilius and Sophia* (1762), although not his *Emile* or *La Nouvelle Héloïse*. Several sentimental novels, less well-known today, make the list. Among them are Frances Burney's *Evelina* (1778) and Henry Brooke's *The Fool of Quality* (1765)—a work in which, as a critic remarked, "every emotion is a rapture or an agony."[40]

Sentimental fiction also dominated the books reprinted in America in full or in abridged editions. Of the five complete novels printed in America before 1775, three were sentimental works: *Pamela, Sentimental Journey*, and *The Vicar of Wakefield*. (The other two were Samuel Johnson's *Rasselas* and *Tristram Shandy*, an experimental novel that is difficult to categorize; it appeared as part of the complete works of Laurence Sterne printed in 1774.) Four of the five novels issued repeatedly in abridged versions were sentimental ones. They included three works of Richardson, *Pamela, Clarissa,* and *Sir Charles Grandison* (1754), and Fielding's *Tom Jones*. The other work frequently shortened was Defoe's *Robinson Crusoe*.[41]

More broadly, libraries became more numerous and their holdings larger—all of which contributed to the spread of sentimental fiction. David Kaser's study of library catalogues shows that between 1765-89 and 1790-99, the average number of titles doubled from 718 to 1,413. At the same time, the proportion of books devoted to fiction rose from 27 percent to 37 percent. In fact, readers favored novels by even greater percentages, as studies reveal that works of fiction were borrowed more frequently than other books. Readership expanded throughout the new nation. One observer remarked in 1789: "It is scarce possible to conceive the number of readers with which even every little town abounds. The common people are on a footing, in point of literature, with the middle ranks in Europe. They all read and write, and . . . almost every little town now furnishes a circulating library."[42]

The changes of these years set the stage for the Sentimental Era, which would commence, boldly and unmistakably, with the first American-written novel in 1789.

PART ONE
The Sentimental Era

The first American-authored novel, William Hill Brown's *The Power of Sympathy* (1789), opens the era with a bold manifesto: "Hail *Sensibility!* Sweetner of the joys of life! Heaven has implanted thee in the breasts of children to sooth the sorrows of the afflicted, to mitigate the wounds of the stranger who falleth in our way."[1] From 1789 to 1869, the middle class celebrated sentiment, an outlook that distinguished this group from the elite, whose lives were seemingly given to dissipation, and from the poor who lacked the leisure to indulge their feelings. As Shirley Samuels declares (while stretching the temporal reach of this epoch), "Sentimentality is literally at the heart of nineteenth-century American culture."[2]

The outlook had its roots in a rural society and the middle class's increasing wealth, gains that dated from the late colonial period. This measure of prosperity allowed the group to move beyond its earlier commitment to frugality and industry. The turn toward emotion brought together the "imagined communities" of like-minded individuals who populated a nation of farms and scattered urban places. Even in 1850 only 15 percent of Americans called towns and cities home. During these decades, the middle class consisted, in the countryside, of the more affluent farmers and, in the towns, professionals and artisans.[3] These families, and particularly the wives and daughters, relished the widening flood of novels. Much of this fiction, such as the works of James Fenimore Cooper and Harriet Beecher Stowe, had a rural setting. In the towns, the "middling folk" who visited galleries and exhibits enjoyed the work of landscape painters, including Thomas Cole, Frederic Church, and Albert Bierstadt.

Any exploration of the period must look more closely into two questions: What exactly was sentimentality? And what dates demarcate the era? Observers agree that sentimental literature involves heightened emotions, often including a flood of tears.

28 SENTIMENTAL ERA

"Characters in sentimental novels," notes Cindy Weinstein, "cry for all sorts of reasons: they have lost a child or a parent, seen a loved one fall from spiritual grace, endured cruel treatment. . . . There is indeed a contagion of weeping, but the targeted weeper is, of course, the reader."[4] One indication of the high-water mark and gradual ebb of sentimentalism rests with the frequency of *weep*, which crested in the mid-1840s and declined in the following decades (fig. P1.1). Still, a full understanding of the era and of sentimental literature and art, must move beyond tears, and focus on "heightened emotions." That broader definition encompasses the anguished protagonists of the early national period; the seekers and lofty heroes in novels by James Fenimore Cooper, Nathaniel Hawthorne, and Herman Melville; and the sentimentality that marked many of the books published after midcentury.

Scholars underscore other aspects of this literature. Some critics pronounce this outlook (as David Reynolds notes) "socially conservative." Jane Tompkins remarks, "the fiction we label as 'sentimental' . . . . blots out the uglier details of life," while Laura Wexler observes, "The energies [sentimentalism] developed were intended as a tool for the control of others." In this reading, tears dissolved cries for change and turned anger inward.[5] Others vigorously dissent. Samuels comments, "Perhaps the most powerful instance of sentimental work thus appears in the mid-nineteenth century conjunction of feminist and abolitionist discourse." Weinstein concurs, remarking that many sentimental works "fiercely challenge the patriarchal regime."[6] Like the sea god Proteus, sentimental literature has many shapes and can seem hard to capture. The next three chapters illustrate how authors used this style to depict a wide variety of female roles.

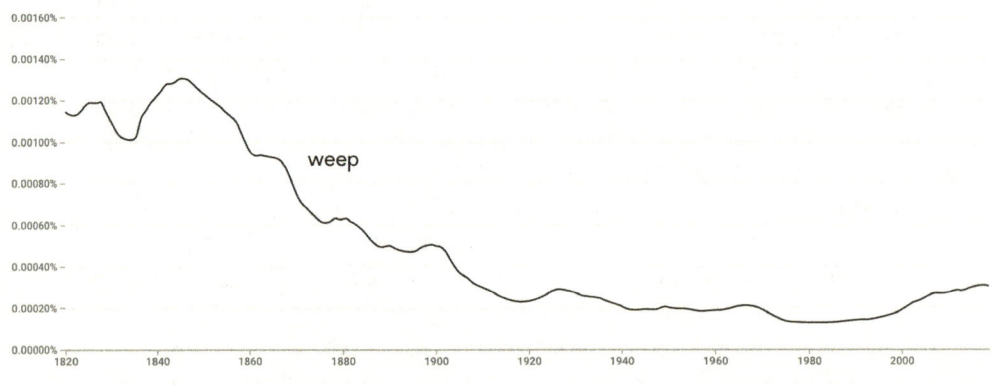

P1.1. FREQUENCY OF *WEEP* IN AMERICAN ENGLISH (2019) NGRAM DATABASE, 1800–2019.

Painting similarly targeted viewers' emotions. During the first decades of the era, artists like Washington Allston and John Vanderlyn presented dramatic, often heartwrenching scenes.[7] From the 1820s through the 1860s, the focus was on landscape and the sublime beauty of the natural world. (In sketching these expanses, artists, like most European Americans, ignored the dispossession of the original inhabitants—or saw it as the inevitable consequence of advancing "civilization.")

Scholars propose various dates for the reign of sentimentality. Ann Douglas contends that this worldview "dominated the literary market in America from the 1840s through the 1880s," while David Reynolds notes that the "standard view is that between 1800 and 1860 America was flooded with [sentimental] novels and poetry volumes."[8] But as the quotation opening this overview suggests, geysers of emotion also erupted in the early national period. In *Revolution and the Word*, which deals with the literature of those early decades, Cathy Davidson remarks that her focus is on "the sentimental origins of the American novel."[9]

A Mirror for History suggests that the most plausible dates for the era are 1789 to 1869, although for some middle-class Americans—including many painters and those who devoured the new European novels—the turn toward sensibility began earlier. Sentimentality waned by the late 1860s, with Louisa May Alcott's *Little Women* (1868–69) marking a suitable close to the era. Douglas observes that "After the Civil War, no longer backed by any significant segment of the male (or female) cultural elite, feminine literary sentimentalism became by definition lowbrow."[10] The woman's rights crusaders, who were increasingly vocal after midcentury, disdained teary-eyed views of the world. Many post–Civil War novelists, sometimes called "Realists," also distanced themselves from excessive emotion. In 1865, Henry James declared himself "utterly weary of stories about precocious little girls."[11] Two decades later, in *The Rise of Silas Lapham*, William Dean Howells cruelly satirized an imagined novel, *Tears, Idle Tears*, which is described as "a famous book with ladies. They break their hearts over it."[12] The market for landscape painting declined precipitously in the 1870s.

Important changes also occurred within the epoch—an evolution the next three chapters explore. The era of slow growth before 1820, the buoyant entrepreneurial economy of the next three decades, and then the gradual encroachment of bureaucracies and finance capital shaped society, fiction, and painting. By the late 1860s, the center of gravity for the middle class had shifted from rural America to small towns (or, in some instances, to city neighborhoods that felt like small towns). The emphasis on sentiment yielded to an insistence on manners and proper behavior.

2
Years of Uncertainty, 1789–1819

Charles Brockden Brown's life, like the orreries, the small models of the solar system that eighteenth-century scientists built, seemed to contain within it all the components of this period of slow growth. The economic gains of these years were evident in the support his "middling" family offered the young author. With wealth drawn from mercantile and real estate enterprises, his parents provided him a classical education and paid his expenses as he began his writing career. But the challenges that burdened so many in this era of wild economic swings also afflicted Brown. His critically acclaimed novels sold poorly, and he gave up writing fiction. He joined his brothers in an importing firm, but that business soon collapsed. Moreover, the sentimentality that marked the age filled his letters. His failures and the onset of "consumption" fueled his melancholy. "When have I ever known," he asked, "that lightness and vivacity of mind which the divine flow of health, even in calamity, produces in some men? . . . never; scarcely ever; not longer than a half an hour at a time, since I have called myself man." In 1810, at age thirty-nine, he died.[1]

The stumbling, slowly growing economy shaped not only Brown's life but also the outlook of many middle-class Americans. The novels of this era mirror those turbulent times, presenting fictional worlds marked by uncertainty, deceit, irreligion, and fears. Paintings by individuals such as Washington Allston capture the same dark emotions. In many respects, these years belong more to the "long" eighteenth century than to the bumptious, optimistic decades that would characterize the United States after 1820.

I

Any understanding of middle-class views during this era must begin with scrutiny of the economy and its fitful growth. Life improved for "middling folk" between 1789 and 1820, but not dramatically, and many observers focused on the gyrations in the economy and the impact of disruptive events rather than on the slight material gains.

Growth resumed after the difficult years of the Revolutionary War and its aftermath. While foreign commerce stood at a lower ebb in 1790 than in 1775, it rebounded during the Napoleonic Wars, which continued with only brief respites from 1793 to 1815. Claiming to be a neutral country exempt from seizures on the high seas, the United States brought Far Eastern goods to Europe and marketed the produce of the West Indian islands. New wealth reshaped the great trading centers. New York expanded steadily, surpassing Philadelphia in population, while the buildings Charles Bulfinch designed in Boston testify to the increasing affluence of that city.[2]

But harnessing national growth to foreign trade made for a bumpy ride. Re-exports fell off during periods of peace, for example, in 1797 and 1802–1803, and plummeted when the United States became more deeply entangled in the European conflict. Britain and France did not share America's liberal interpretation of trade laws and captured nearly fifteen hundred vessels between 1802 and 1812. Trade was still more gravely affected when the United States responded to these affronts with an embargo in 1807–1809 and war in 1812. The embargo produced the worst of times. Exports declined by almost 80 percent and imports by nearly 60 percent; jails were filled with debtors—in New York City alone thirteen hundred men were imprisoned. Empty stores blighted the waterfronts in the port cities.[3]

Even during boom times trade did not provide the engine of growth that domestic commerce and manufacturing would in later years. Most White Americans, like their forebears in the colonial period, accepted that their lives would be only marginally better than those of their parents. The ways they farmed, traveled, and clothed themselves changed little. Transportation remained dependent on the power of horses and wind. Local weavers, bent over their hand looms, provided most cloth.

Because the angle of ascent was so slight, each challenge to the well-being of Americans seemed far more jarring than comparable problems would be after 1820. During these years, citizens faced wild swings in the economy; a yellow fever epidemic in Philadelphia; domestic rebellions in western Pennsylvania and Louisiana; the dangerous contagion of revolutions in France and Haiti; partisan strife; a vice president who conspired with the enemy; a second war with Britain; and secessionist plots in New England. For many, these were perilous times.

Observers underscored the weakness of an economy based on foreign trade rather than domestic exchanges and manufacturing. "There is no word in the English language that more deceives a people than the word *commerce*," political economist Hezekiah Niles remarked in 1814. Most people "associate with it an idea of great ships, passing to all countries—whereas the rich commerce of every community is its *internal*; a communication of one part with other parts of the same ... In the United States, (were we at peace) our *foreign* trade would hardly exceed a *fortieth* or *fiftieth* part of the whole *commerce* of the people."[4] Kentucky politician Henry Clay made the same point in the early 1820s. He extolled the "American System" of manufacturing and internal commerce, while criticizing the "European System" that prevailed before 1820. That "system is anomalous," Clay observed. "It can succeed only in the rare occurrence of a general state of war throughout Europe."[5]

Perhaps the most significant developments of these years were the steps Americans took to lay the foundations for the soaring growth that emerged after 1820. The "transportation revolution," which would so dramatically change society, began in these decades. In 1811, construction commenced on the National Road, a highway that took several decades to complete and would accelerate the settlement of Ohio, Indiana, and Illinois. Key initiatives transforming water travel also date from this period. In 1817, New Yorkers started digging the Erie Canal, that all-important 363-mile-long ditch, which would be completed in 1825. (In 1816, the United States had only one hundred miles of canals.) Robert Fulton launched his steamboat, the *Clermont*, on the Hudson in 1807, and rejoiced in 1811 when the *New Orleans* completed the first powered trip on the Mississippi River. Paddle wheelers, however, came to dominate trade on the western waters only in the 1820s.[6]

Advances in manufacturing, finance, and cotton cultivation also proved auspicious. Beginning in the 1790s, small yarn mills (which served local weavers) proliferated in the Northeast. But the turning point for American textile production came in 1813 when Francis Cabot Lowell established in Waltham, Massachusetts, an integrated mill for making cotton cloth. Production climbed, particularly in the 1820s, with new factories in Lowell (1822) and Chicopee (1823). Government action set the banking system on a sounder footing. The business community had complained loudly after the demise of the first Bank of the United States in 1811. During the war, the government was unable to honor its obligations, while most banks outside New England abandoned specie payment. The chartering of the Second Bank of the United States in 1816 provided a welcome note of stability. Finally, the spread of cotton culture promised the White citizenry robust growth in the Deep South. The entry of new states—Louisiana (1812), Mississippi (1817) and Alabama (1819)—and the acquisition of valuable territories—Louisiana (1803) and Florida (1819)—seemed to assure long-term prospects for plantation owners, as well as the spread of slavery.[7] These developments, however, pointed to future expansion, not to immediate prosperity. Slow long-term growth defined the milieu in which novelists and artists labored.

II

The stumbling economy helped shape an era with unsettled narratives and duplicitous characters. But just how did weak economic development lead to troubled story lines? To begin with, fiction during these years repeatedly portrayed the fragile nature of worldly success. After 1820, reflecting more buoyant long-term growth, the master narrative of American literature would change. The new assumption, for middle-class individuals, would be personal progress, and such optimism would characterize fiction well into the twentieth century, excepting only a few decades. But so often in the novels of the early national period, a looming Wheel of Fortune threw down the many while elevating the few.

The catalogue of characters whose economic circumstances suddenly worsened includes Lucy Eldridge's father, Mrs. Crayton, and Charlotte Temple in Susanna Rowson's *Charlotte Temple* (1791); Reuben, Rachel, and the LaVarones in Rowson's *Reuben and Rachel* (1798); Major Peter Sanford in Hannah Foster's *The Coquette* (1797); Updike Underhill in Royall Tyler's *The Algerine Captive* (1797); Sophia Courtland, Martinette de Beauvais, and the Dudleys in Charles Brockden Brown's *Ormond* (1799); Sarsefield and Weymouth in Brown's *Edgar Huntly* (1799); Jane Talbot, her brother, and father in Brown's *Jane Talbot* (1801); and Alonzo and his father in Isaac Mitchell's *Alonzo and Melissa* (1804). The list easily could be lengthened.[8]

Many noted how common such vicissitudes were. Hearing about Weymouth's decline from riches to rags, Edgar Huntly remarks, "What a mournful tale! . . . Our countrymen are prone to enterprise, and are scattered over every sea and every land in pursuit of that wealth which will not screen them from disease and infirmity, [and] which is missed much oftener than found."[9] Discussing the fate of a particular family, the LaVarones, the narrator in *Reuben and Rachel* observes: "Human happiness is futile! A fire broke out in the neighborhood, and their house was consumed amongst a number of others, and as their property was not insured, a few hours reduced them from a state of competence to absolute beggary."[10] One of the few figures who prospers in *Alonzo and Melissa* battens on those disasters: "He had loaned money, and taken mortgages on lands and houses for securities; and as payment frequently failed, he often had opportunities of purchasing the involved premises at his own price."[11]

Remarkably, literary critics who often differ with one another, agree that uncertainty marks the fiction of the early national period. In *The Columbia History of the American Novel,* Jeffrey Rubin-Dorsky roundly declares: "The hallmark of the early American novel is its instability, an uncertainty and confusion in almost every area related to fiction making."[12] Analyses of Charles Brockden Brown's works underscore this ethos. Michael Gilmore observes: "His novels teem with misplaced and discovered manuscripts, characters compulsively pouring out their life stories while other characters listen avidly, intercepted letters and overheard conversations, plagiarisms, forgeries, and verbal mimicries."[13] Critics make the same point about other novels, such as Hugh Henry Brackenridge's *Modern Chivalry* (1792–1815) and Royall Tyler's *The Algerine Captive* (1797).[14]

Brown's principal novels amply illustrate this argument: all four hinge on deception. *Wieland; or, The Transformation* (1798) exemplifies the danger wreaked by these subterfuges. The story, set in a spacious home near Philadelphia, focuses on the fate of a brother and sister, Theodore and Clara Wieland. Theodore is happily married with four children. Everything changes, however, when a disheveled Irish immigrant, Carwin, arrives at the Wieland mansion and is invited to stay. About the time that Carwin appears, Theodore begins hearing a voice that purports to issue divine commands. At the urging of that voice, Theodore murders his wife, children, and a servant girl. He is about to kill Clara when Carwin reveals that he is a ventriloquist. Distraught, Theodore commits suicide.[15]

Edgar Huntly is another tale of confused identities and a world destabilized. Edgar encounters a sleepwalker, Clithero, who claims that only by accident was he near the tree where one of Edgar's friends was recently murdered. Edgar believes Clithero, and the two men draw close, but then Clithero disappears. Edgar is unsettled when he learns that Clithero is in fact a homicidal maniac. What Edgar finds even more disturbing is the discovery that he too is a sleepwalker. He wakes up far from home, is forced to fight rampaging Natives and a fierce panther, and then realizes that while asleep he has hidden a set of letters crucial to understanding his circle of friends.[16]

Dangerous deceptions also mark Brown's *Arthur Mervyn; or, Memoirs of the Year 1793* (1799) and *Ormond* (1799). *Arthur Mervyn* is set against the background of the yellow fever epidemic that devastated Philadelphia. The story focuses on young Arthur Mervyn and his friendship with Thomas Welbeck, who appears to be a prosperous businessman. Mervyn innocently assists Welbeck with a series of projects, until he discovers that the man is a heartless embezzler, a villainous seducer, and a murderer. Mervyn then struggles to right the wrongs that Welbeck (and he) have committed. On occasion, Mervyn appears to spin his own webs of deception.[17] (Reading those ambiguous passages, Jane Tompkins comments, "There is nothing to do at such times except plunge ahead, hoping that the uncertainty will be cleared up soon."[18]) *Ormond* follows the adventures of Constantia

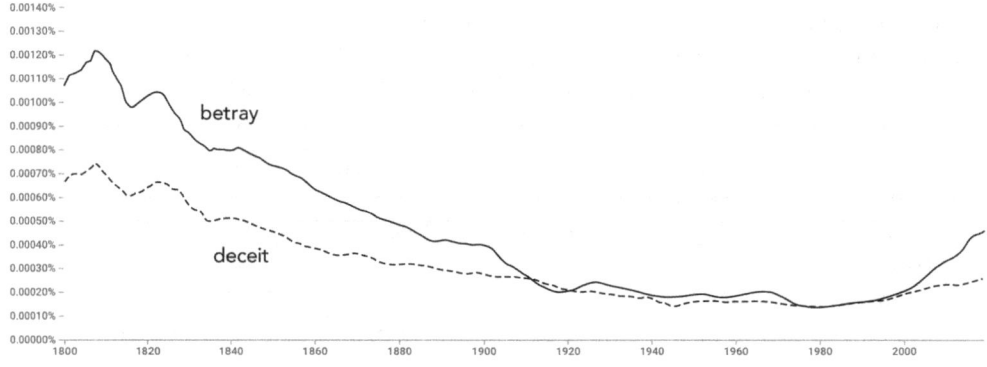

2.1. FREQUENCY OF *BETRAY* AND *DECEIT* IN AMERICAN ENGLISH (2019), NGRAM DATABASE, 1800–2019.

Dudley and her father, who is forced into bankruptcy when he takes a likeable young man, Thomas Craig, as a partner and Craig proves to be a thief. Meanwhile, the duplicitous Ormond pursues Constantia. Ormond is educated, affluent, and seemingly well-mannered. But as the narrator notes, his "appearances were merely calculated to mislead and not to enlighten." Ormond turns out to be a schemer and a rapist.[19]

Nor was deception limited to Brown's works. The many novels that focused on seduction had deceit at their core, as did the books that included women cross-dressing as men. The rampant mercantile dishonesty that touched so many in these stories further expands the category. Ngram analysis supports these readings. The use of *betray* and *deceit* (and the related word *disguise*) peaked in the first years of the century (fig. 2.1).

III

Women recorded gains during these years, although viewed in a broader perspective these advances were limited and reflected the halting pace of economic development. Looking ahead to the decades from 1820 to 1850, several developments expanded women's roles. The sharp ascent of the standard of living was a rising tide that lifted many boats. Growing wealth supported the reality of "two spheres," allowing many middle-class women to stay home and cultivate domestic virtues. Rapid growth also fostered an unbounded individualism and reform movements—including woman's rights. Finally, the spread of a raucous, disputatious political democracy brought more people—including women—into the public square. These trends appeared, however, only as vague hints in the early national period.

Literature documents the progress women made during these years. Novels written *by* and *for* women gave individuals who had long been overlooked a voice and recognition they lacked in the colonial era. Cathy Davidson summarizes her contribution to this debate: "*Revolution and the Word* was among the first books to attribute agency both to female protagonists (they are not simply passive in the face of men) and to the female reader (who could take away from the plot an inspiration to personal strength and power)."[20] Similarly, Carroll Smith-Rosenberg sees Eliza Wharton, the seduced and abandoned heroine of Foster's *The Coquette*, as the standard-bearer for a new group of women who "anxiously embraced individualism, risk, and the new capitalism."[21]

Several sentimental novels that focused on the challenges women faced became bestsellers. Rowson's *Charlotte Temple* sold almost forty thousand copies before 1810, while Foster's *The Coquette* went through thirty editions by 1840. In *The Coquette*, Eliza Wharton's disastrous attempt to defy norms engaged readers. Eliza rejects her friend's sensible advice to stay with Reverend Boyer, a trustworthy but dull clergyman, and turns instead to the unscrupulous if lively Major Peter Sanford. Eliza explains to her friend: "My reason and judgment entirely coincide with your opinion, but my fancy claims some share in the decision, and I cannot yet tell which will preponderate.... From a scene of constraint and confinement, ill-suited to my years and inclination, I have just launched into society. My heart beats high in expectation of its fancied joys." Her fling with Sanford comes to no good. Abandoned, she dies after giving birth to a baby who expires as well.[22]

Novels called for more female education. During the colonial era, girls received less schooling than boys and were less literate. Gradually, during the first half of the nineteenth century, literacy rates for White women rose to the levels achieved by men—a development eagerly promoted by male and female writers. Between 1790 and 1830, educators opened 196 academies and seminaries exclusively for female students.[23] The first American-authored novel, William Hill Brown's *The Power of Sympathy*, argues for educating women. "*The female mind*," one character observes in this didactic work, "*is competent to any task*, and the accomplishments of an elegant woman depend on a proper cultivation of her intelligent powers."[24] Even Enos Hitchcock's *Memoirs of the Bloomsgrove Family* (1790), which affirms that women should remain homemakers, tells parents: "Every work, which has in view the improvement of their children, and especially their daughters, whose education has been, hitherto, too much neglected, must be received with avidity by them."[25]

The literature of these years includes a series of "outliers"—bold women who defy the norm. In Brown's *Ormond*, Martinette de Beauvais is a cross-dresser and fearless soldier. "If thou wert with me at Paris," she tells the protagonist, Constantia, "I could show thee a fusil of two barrels, which is precious beyond any other relic, merely because it enabled me to kill thirteen officers at Jemappe."[26] Constantia also pushes the limits for acceptable female roles. She gains an education, finds work to support her ailing father, rebuffs wealthy suitors for whom she has no love, and finally stabs and kills the would-be rapist, Ormond.[27] Herman Mann's *The Female Review* (1797) recounts the story of Deborah Sampson, who dressed as a man to fight in the Revolutionary War. In *The History of Constantius and Pulchera* (1794), by an unknown author, Pulchera disguises herself as Lieutenant Valorus.[28] Leonora Sansay's *Secret History; or, The Horrors of St. Domingo* (1808) presents the adventures of remarkable women who escape from or exact revenge upon abusive husbands.[29]

Still, the gains were limited, and observers justly emphasize the restrictions that narrowed women's roles. Kristin Comment notes: "Late eighteenth-century American novels in general, such as *The Power of Sympathy* (1789), *The Coquette* (1797), and *Charlotte Temple* (1791, 1794) demonstrate a clear interest in the control of women's bodies as a means of preserving the 'virtue' of the republic."[30] In her biography of novelist Susanna Rowson, Marion Rust similarly underscores the constraints confronting women in this period.[31]

The pervasiveness of seduction along with the presence of many conventional female characters underscores the lack of progress. Accounts of lustful men and fallen women echo earlier narratives such as Samuel Richardson's *Pamela* and *Clarissa*. The message of the cautionary tales written on both sides of the Atlantic is clear: punishment awaits those women (but not men) who transgress. *The Coquette* teaches readers that, while Elizabeth Wharton's flirtations may seem attractive, the

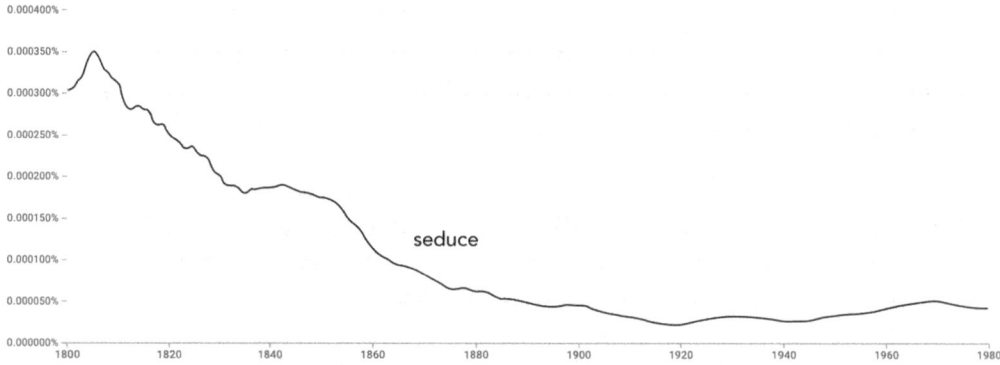

2.2. FREQUENCY OF *SEDUCE* IN AMERICAN ENGLISH (2019) CORPUS, NGRAM DATABASE, 1800–1980.

wiser course is subordination to a dull, traditional husband. The Ngram database for *seduce* illustrates the prevalence of this theme during the early national period and its diminished importance in later years (fig. 2.2).

Narratives of seduction are inextricably tied to social hierarchy. Repeatedly, novels of the early national period bring together a mercenary elite male—an army officer, an aristocrat, an affluent landowner—with a less wealthy middle-class woman. Such a relationship marks *The Power of Sympathy*, in which wealthy Thomas Harrington pursues Harriot Fawcett. Harrington confesses to a friend, "Now, Mr. Worthy, I must take the liberty to acquaint you that I am not so much of a republican as formally to wed any person of this class."[32] In *The Coquette*, Major Peter Sanford, who describes himself as a "rake," seduces Eliza Wharton but spurns a permanent relationship with a woman of such modest means.[33] In *Charlotte Temple*, the heroine's head is turned by a soldier, Montreville, who wants only a fling, not a wife. In *Ormond*, the aristocratic title character first takes advantage of Helena Cleves (who commits suicide) and then tries to do the same with Constantia Dudley (who kills him in self-defense). The first half of Rowson's *Reuben and Rachel* details a series of aristocratic seductions and betrayals of less wealthy women. Sansay's *Secret History* recounts various attempts by elite Frenchmen to take advantage of lower-status women.[34]

After 1820, a booming economy fostered democratic ways, a wealthier middle class—and new roles for women. Disparities in wealth persisted, but increasingly "middling folk" rejected the elitist attitudes that had underpinned the tales of seduction. The passion for equality was too fierce a sun to allow such malevolent shadows. There still were illicit romances (as in Nathaniel Hawthorne's *The Scarlet Letter*), but scenes in which a powerful man took advantage of a poorer woman became less common in literature and society.[35]

IV

Religion also reflected these years of uncertain economic growth. The great expansion of faith among the middle classes came after 1820, as piety and evangelical beliefs spread along with increasing affluence. Such religiosity lay in the future; for the middle (and upper classes), the early national period was marked by a notable lack of fervor. The religious ties of the wealthier colonists had broken down in the aftermath of independence. Southern states disestablished Anglicanism, while Congregationalism weakened in New England. Overall, the proportion of Americans who were church members declined from about 17 percent in 1775 to 14 percent in 1800. This declension was hardly countered by the Deism, favored by some affluent individuals like Franklin and Jefferson, or the emergence of

Unitarianism, promoted by a few New England divines who questioned harsh Calvinistic doctrines. During these years, the campaigns of dissenters, particularly Baptists and Methodists, targeted less wealthy persons.[36]

The novels of Brown, himself a freethinker, reveal the lack of fervor characterizing many "middling folk." As a young man, Brown entertained dangerous notions, contending Jesus was a moral philosopher rather than a divinity and was the worthy peer of Mahomet, Confucius, and Pythagoras. The controversial books that engaged Brown, such as the works of Mary Wollstonecraft and William Godwin, suggest an upbringing similar to the one that Clara Wieland (in the novel *Wieland*) says shaped her life and her brother's. "Our education had been modelled by no religious standard," she confesses. "We were left to the guidance of our own understanding, and the casual impressions which society might make upon us."[37]

Significantly, several individuals depicted by Brown as virtuous have little interest in Christianity. In *Ormond*, Constantia Dudley, a heroine who is praiseworthy in every other way, is a nonbeliever. The narrator, Sophia Courtland, announces: "It becomes me to confess, however reluctantly, thus much concerning my friend [Constantia]. However abundantly endowed in other respects, she was a stranger to the felicity and excellence flowing from religion."[38] Similarly, in *Jane Talbot*, Henry Colden, an admirable man and the love of Jane's life, is another freethinker. Jane remarks: "I have found a man without religion. . . . I do not cease to regard unbelief as the blackest stain, as the most deplorable calamity that can befall a human creature; but I still *love* the man."[39] Although these books affirm the worth of Christian doctrines, the skepticism voiced by leading characters is striking.[40]

Other works quietly laud non-Christian faiths. Updike Underhill, the hero of Royall Tyler's *The Algerine Captive*, spends seven years as a slave in a Muslim land, engaging during that time in a spirited debate with a local mullah. The religious leader offers him a lesson in cultural relativism: "Born in New England, my friend, you are a Christian purified by Calvin. Born in the Campania of Rome, you would have been a papist. Nursed by the Hindoos, you would have entered the pagoda with reverence, and worshipped the soul of your ancestor in a duck."[41] Tyler nowhere counters this reasoning. A reviewer in a Boston journal noted that, because "the author has so decidedly given the Mollah the best of the argument, that the adherence of Updike to Christianity seems the effect rather of obstinacy than of conviction."[42] In *Modern Chivalry*, Brackenridge mocks backwoods preachers and explores the value of the Koran and Vedas.[43] Even in *Memoirs of the Bloomsgrove Family*, the author, Enos Hitchcock, a conservative minister, includes an anecdote that depicts a principled Muslim and a corrupt Christian.[44]

V

Finally, the uncertain pace of recovery after 1789 also influenced how novelists, painters, and, more broadly, members of the middle class viewed the natural world. Scholars have long emphasized the links between how people live and what they see. In an essay on "wilderness," William Cronon observes, "As we gaze into the mirror it holds up for us, we too easily imagine that what we behold is Nature when in fact we see the reflection of our own unexamined longings and desires."[45] Art historian E. H. Gombrich concurs, noting our vision of the world "is to a remarkable degree determined by the habits and expectations generated by a particular culture."[46] In Puritan America, where the survival of frontier communities remained precarious, settlers regarded the wild backcountry with fear. In 1662, Michael Wigglesworth called the West, "A waste and howling wilderness."[47] Fast forward 170 years to the 1830s, when a frothy, rapidly growing society fostered an exalted view of humanity. Ralph Waldo Emerson, James Fenimore Cooper, and others imagined that in the forest depths humans could commune with the divine.

In their view of the wilderness, the artists and authors of the early national period stood somewhere between the fears of the Puritans and the exuberance of the Transcendentalists. Observers shunned uncharted expanses, but celebrated woods and mountains when those features formed the backdrop to cozy homes and cultivated fields. English critics like William Gilpin, who noted the pleasures of those grand vistas, shaped the outlook of writers and artists on both sides of the Atlantic. Gilpin, one of the first to elaborate the concept of the "picturesque," praised a particular scene because "it is what the painter properly calls a *whole*. There is a fore-ground, a middle-ground, and distance—all harmoniously united."[48] Edward Huntly, the eponymous hero of Brown's novel, stands on a high hilltop and gazes on just such a "harmonious" landscape: "A large part of this chaos of rocks and precipices was subjected, at one view, to the eye. The fertile lawns and vales which lay beyond this, the winding course of the river, and the slopes which rose on its farther side, were parts of this extensive scene. These objects were at any time fitted to inspire rapture."[49] Similarly, in Mitchell's *Alonzo and Melissa* the two lovers describe the place where they hope to settle after marriage: "It was a pleasantly situated village, surrounded by rugged elevations, which gave an air of serenity and seclusion to the valley they encircled.... On the west, forests unevenly lifted their rude heads, with here and there a solitary field, newly cleared, and thinly scattered with cottages." Diverse but unified elements mark these "picturesque" spots.[50]

At the same time, writers of the early national period regarded the forests themselves and the trackless western lands as forbidding locales. Nowhere is this better exemplified than in *Edgar Huntly*. Brown prefaces his work by telling the reader that "puerile superstition and exploded manners, Gothic castles and chimeras, are the materials" usually drawn upon when "calling forth the passions." He then emphasizes that "the incidents of Indian hostility, and the perils of the Western wilderness, are far more suitable; and for a native of America to overlook these would admit of no apology." Brown illustrates those perils when Edgar, while sleepwalking, wanders outside the pale of civilization. Awakened, he encounters bands of hostile Natives, dangerous animals, and settlers who shoot at him, thinking he is one of the Indians on the warpath. Even the very ground conveys danger: "No fancy can conceive a scene more wild and desolate than that which now presented itself. The soil was nearly covered with sharp fragments of stone. Between these, sprung brambles and creeping vines, whose twigs, crossing and intertwining with each other, added to the roughness below, made the passage infinitely toilsome."[51]

Artists embraced similar views of the natural world. Not until the 1820s and 1830s would painters depict luxuriant forest scenes where a divine presence seemed to infuse the landscape. Painters in the early national period, much like novelists,

2.1. WASHINGTON ALLSTON, *ELIJAH IN THE DESERT*, 1817–1818.

took a grimmer view of the unsettled expanses. Washington Allston, perhaps the most important American painter during these decades, shared an outlook not far removed from Brown's. As Allston later recollected, he "developed a strong love for the wild and marvelous," often depicting individuals in extreme emotional states, such as the mad, half-naked man in *Tragic Figure in Chains* (1800).[52] He also admired the craggy landscapes of the seventeenth-century Italian artist, Salvator Rosa. Allston remarked that "the Soul of this master was in unison with his own; he felt a strange pleasure in brooding over his dark rocks and gloomy wildness and shuddered at, yet could not but admire the noble ferocity of the banditti."

In *Elijah in the Desert* (1817–18), Allston captures some of the "gloomy wildness" he saw in Rosa's work. In this painting, the prophet crawls through a bleak landscape, seemingly near death, with only ravens to feed him (ptg. 2.1). John Vanderlyn's *The Murder of Jane McCrea* (1804) similarly depicts the dangers of America's wild expanses (as well as racist views of Indigenous people). The painting, set in a forest, shows two half-clothed natives with knife and tomahawk killing an innocent White woman.[53] Sentimentality would remain the language of expression, but across a broad range of areas change came after 1820 as growth quickened.

3
Soaring Spirits, 1820–1851

"I once met an American sailor," French traveler Alexis de Tocqueville recalled, "and asked him why his country's ships are made so that they will not last long. He answered offhand that the art of navigation was making such quick progress that even the best of boats would be almost useless if it lasted more than a few years." Tocqueville, who visited the US in 1831–32, used this encounter to underscore the links between the rapid economic progress that (White) Americans experienced and their belief in human perfectibility. "Every man sees changes continually taking place," he continued. "His setbacks teach him that no one has discovered absolute good; his successes inspire him to seek it without slackening. . . . [H]e is ever striving toward that immense grandeur glimpsed indistinctly at the end of the long track humanity must follow. It is hard to realize how much follows naturally from this philosophic theory of the indefinite perfectibility of man and what a prodigious influence it has."[1]

The quickening pace of development after 1820 had a far-reaching, and sometimes contradictory impact on the outlook of the middle class. It encouraged, as Tocqueville noted, many to believe in human perfectibility, and its corollary, a heightened sense of individualism. But the rising standard of living also fostered "domesticity" and new distinct spheres for men and women. These trends, and more broadly, a celebration of prosperity, shaped literature and art—and reinforced the turn toward emotions, which was the hallmark of the age.

I

Around 1820, the US economy experienced a momentous turning point: centuries of slow growth gave way to a long epoch of sustained, rapid development. Despite the peaks and troughs of the business cycle, "middling folk" now saw dramatic improvements in their lives.

A person born in 1820 came into a world in which communication between towns went no faster than a fleet horse. Nearby farms raised the variety of foodstuffs that households required. Except in the port cities, local spinners and weavers provided most clothing. A few steamboats plied river routes, but they remained an oddity. The high price of books kept these works beyond the reach of those who worked with their hands. By 1850, that world was unrecognizable. Telegraphs and railroads tied together far-flung places. Ready-made clothing became the norm for many. Steamships and canal boats brought the blessings of commerce to millions of once isolated people. ("He [i.e., 'man']," wrote Ralph Waldo Emerson, "no longer waits for favoring gales, but by means of steam, he realizes the fable of Aeolus's bag, and carries the two and thirty winds in the boiler of his boat."[2]) Novels were no longer luxury goods—thanks to advances in papermaking and printing. More ominously, the bustling economy rested in part on slavery, which also expanded during these decades.[3]

What changed the pace of development from the lumbering rhythms of a horse-drawn cart to the breakneck speed of a railroad engine careening down the track belching thick black smoke? Most economic historians agree with George Rogers Taylor's *The Transportation Revolution, 1815–1860*, which observes: "Transportation developments were so revolutionary and were so fundamental to the economic growth of the country that . . . they seemed to require the central position they have been given."[4] A plethora of improvements broadened local markets and created the beginnings of a national one. Among these advances were well-constructed highways, including the National Road, which went from Maryland to Illinois; a constellation of canals, with the Erie as its crown jewel; larger, faster, and more numerous steamboats; and a railroad network that began in the late 1820s and gradually knit together the eastern United States.

Improved transportation pulled in its wake a host of related changes. The accelerated movement of goods fostered manufacturing on an ever-larger scale. Shoes made in Lynn, Massachusetts, could be sold in the South, while cloth from nearby Lowell, found an outlet in the West. Water and rail routes inspired Cyrus McCormick to select in 1847 the small, muddy town of Chicago as the site of his reaper works. Farmers shifted from a diversity of crops to fewer, more lucrative ones. The Jeffersonian idyll of a nation of self-sufficient yeomen quietly faded. Tocqueville captured the spirit of the countryside. "It is unusual," he observed, "for an American farmer to settle forever on the land he occupies . . . A farm is built in the anticipation that, since the state of the country will soon be changing with the increase in population, one will be able to sell it for a good price."[5] More broadly, the transportation revolution changed the force propelling American growth from the faltering pull of foreign commerce to the powerful tug of domestic trade.[6]

Finally, and significantly for the ethos of these years, small enterprises characterized the economy (particularly outside the slave South). Most employees were not factory workers or corporate managers. Even in the textile center of Lowell, Massachusetts, the large mills employed only one third of the workers. Most businesses, including shoemaking, iron foundries, and flour mills, hired fewer than ten individuals. And who could be more entrepreneurial than the millions of farmers who worked their own land with the assistance of family members and perhaps a hired hand or two? They bought and sold their homesteads as well as foodstuffs. This bustling, rapidly growing society with its small units of production had a far-reaching impact on the culture as well as the comforts of Americans.[7]

II

One result of the surging economy was a new optimism that buoyed the middle class—and recast fiction. Writers celebrated the rising standard of living, a striking change from the cautionary tales of earlier years. Starting around 1820, authors noted the acceleration in American growth. In "The Legend of Sleepy Hollow" (published as part of *The Sketch Book* [1819–20]), Washington Irving contrasts the "peaceful spot" where the story takes place with "the great torrent of migration and improvement, which is making such incessant changes in other parts of this restless country."[8] James Fenimore Cooper paints a similar picture in *The Pioneers* (1823). The novel opens with a paean to the prosperous settlements of western New York: "Beautiful and thriving villages are found interspersed along the margins of the small lakes . . . and neat and comfortable farms, with every indication of wealth about them, are scattered profusely through the vales." The energy of the settlers drove these improvements: "In short, the whole district is hourly exhibiting how much can be done, in even a rugged country . . . where every man feels a direct interest in the prosperity of a commonwealth."[9]

A new master narrative marked American literature: instead of emphasizing the fragility of worldly fortunes, authors toasted the ascent of the middle class. At the end of *The Prairie* (1827), Cooper summarizes the bright future that lay ahead for Paul Hover and his family. "By that progressive change in fortune," the narrator remarks, "which in the republic is often seen to be so singularly accompanied by a corresponding improvement in knowledge and self-respect, he went on, from step to step, until his wife enjoyed the maternal delight of seeing her children placed far beyond the danger of returning to that state from which both their parents had issued."[10] Most novels eschewed the tragic lurches of the wheel of fortune so common in earlier periods.

A paradox, however, lurked beneath this celebration: Americans gloried in the rising standard of living but criticized acquisitive individuals. In *The Jacksonian Persuasion*, Marvin Meyers observes, "The Jacksonians wanted to preserve the virtues of a simple agrarian republic without sacrificing the rewards and conveniences of modern capitalism."[11] Although men with an eye on the main chance populated the North and much of the South, authors created and readers preferred tales about individuals who disdained money-making. Cooper's bestselling Leatherstocking series traces the adventures of Natty Bumppo, who had few possessions apart from his rifle. The protagonists in novels by Catharine Maria Sedgwick, John Pendleton Kennedy, William Gilmore Simms, or Hester Prynne in Hawthorne's *The Scarlet Letter* (1850) had many qualities—including courage and compassion—but pursuing riches was not among them.

Underscoring that dislike for business, at least in the world of fiction, was the caricature of the sharp-dealing Yankee, a depiction that regularly marked novels, particularly those authored by New Yorkers and Southerners. Such individuals recur in Cooper's books. In *The Pioneers*, New Englander Jotham Riddel engages in a series of questionable schemes and is denounced by Judge Marmaduke Temple, as "that dissatisfied, shiftless, lazy, speculating fellow!"[12] In the first two books of the Littlepage trilogy, *Satanstoe* and *The Chainbearer* (both 1845) Yankee Jason Newcome schemes to acquire land without paying rent, and then conspires with squatters to market their ill-gotten lumber. In *The Redskins* (1846), the final book in the trilogy, Jason's grandchildren lead the Anti-Rent War. The works of South Carolinian William Gilmore Simms offer similar negative portrayals. In *Guy Rivers* (1834), the sharp dealings of peddler Jared Bunce provoke the ire of the local community. One settler remarks, "Why, he kin walk through a man's pockets, jest as the devil goes through a crack or a keyhole, and the money will naturally stick to him, jest as ef he was made of gum turpentine." [13] Americans applauded prosperity, but not the wheeler-dealers who made these good times possible.

III

The rising standard of living fostered sharply contrasting roles for women. Recognizing how economic expansion could give rise to these different outlooks is a key to understanding the era. On the one hand, increasing wealth made possible more comfortable lives; for the first time, many women could stay home and stand apart from income-producing activities. That new arrangement underpinned the doctrine of the "two spheres"—the separation of men's and women's worlds—and the growing emphasis on piety.

On the other hand, the dynamic entrepreneurial economy, with its small units of production, encouraged individualism, self-reliance, and an extraordinary faith in human potential. This second set of ideas boosted democracy (at least for adult White males); inspired Transcendentalism, the philosophy that Emerson expounded; and spurred a host of reform movements, including woman's rights. These two outlooks may be thought of as a tidal current and an equally powerful undertow, often in opposition but at other times blending indistinguishably into each other. This account begins with the ascent of domesticity and the piety that marked many in the middle class.

Fully understanding the growing importance of the "two spheres" and its significance for women—as well as for literature and art—requires a journey through a vast body of critical literature.[14] Since the publication in 1966 of Barbara Welter's essay "The Cult of True Womanhood, 1820–1860," scholars have debated the nature or even the existence of "domesticity." Observers agree about the key role the economy played in creating these new relationships and concur that domesticity reordered the lives only of certain women. Cathy Davidson and Jessamyn Hatcher underscore that the concept applies, at most, to "white, middle-class, Northeastern, and putatively heterosexual women."[15]

On other questions involving domesticity, scholars differ—and the dialogue is instructive. One long-standing debate turns on whether the "two spheres" oppressed or benefited women. Some, like Welter in her seminal article, assert that the new doctrines punished women, turning them into "the hostage in the home."[16] An opposing school suggests domesticity empowered females. Jane Tompkins, for example, states: "I will argue that the popular domestic novel of the nineteenth century represents a monumental effort to reorganize culture from the woman's point of view."[17] This valuable debate, in which both sides put forth cogent points, sheds light on the restrictions and opportunities women found in the new ordering of society.[18]

Even more significant is the question—again vigorously debated—whether domesticity in fact characterized middle-class families and the novels they read during these years. Amy Kaplan declares, "Domesticity dominated middle-class women's writing and culture from the 1830s through the 1850s."[19] Using a single literary example ("The Wife," a story from Irving's *Sketch Book*), Jeanne Boydston concludes that domesticity, or what she calls the "pastoralization of housework," "shaped much of the fiction of the period." She contends it was an "essential . . . part of the worldview of antebellum northeasterners."[20] But other literary critics so qualify the idea of domesticity as to nearly banish the concept. More than three decades after Welter's essay, Mary Kelley observed: "Where Welter's womanhood was a seamless ideology with transparent directives, the fiction I read was shot through with ambivalence, tension, and contradiction. And where she had found docile compliance with the ideology's prescriptions, I detected acts of subversion."[21] This debate is an invitation to look more closely at the evidence.

There can be no question that much *prescriptive* writing during these three decades preached the doctrine of the two spheres. A good starting point is Catharine Beecher's *A Treatise on Domestic Economy* (1842), a work that literary critic Lora Romero calls "probably the single most influential statement of domesticity."[22] Beecher begins with *subordination*: "It is decided . . . she ["woman"] take a subordinate station, and that, in civil and political concerns, her interests be intrusted to the other sex, without her taking any part in voting, or in making or administering laws." Despite the whiff of oppression in those comments, Beecher and others viewed domesticity as a striking advance over patriarchy. Women were now cherished for their nurturing and moral role. "In matters pertaining to the education of their children," Beecher explains, "in the selection and support of a clergyman, in all benevolent enterprises, and in all questions relating to morals or manners, they have a superior influence." Indeed, the fate of the republic depended on women: "The mother forms the character of the future man. . . . Let the women of a country be made virtuous and intelligent, and the men will certainly be the same."[23] Sermons, editorials, and treatises with remarkable consistency and enthusiasm expounded similar messages.[24]

Reflecting the new doctrines of domesticity, *mother,* which had long been less commonly used than *father,* began a sharp ascent in 1820 and continued its rise

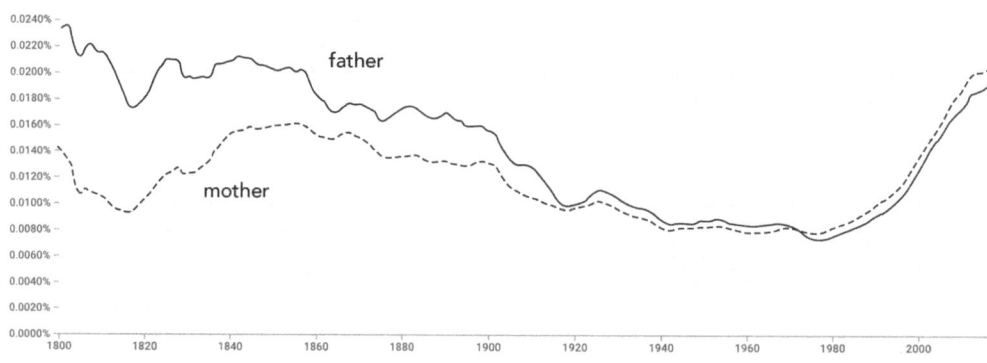

3.1. FREQUENCY OF *FATHER* AND *MOTHER* IN AMERICAN ENGLISH (2019), NGRAM DATABASE, 1800–2019.

until the end of the Sentimental Era. (Another surge in the use of *mother*—as well as *father*—would come in the 1980s, and is discussed in chapter 9.)

But what was true for tracts, treatises, and didactic works did not apply as fully to novels in the period from 1820 to 1851. To be sure, in the literature of these years some unmarried women displayed the submissiveness and piousness the guidebooks praised. But this fiction included few married couples who exemplify the doctrine of the two spheres. Typically, storylines culminated in marriages, not in years of wedded bliss, and adhered to Ira Gershwin's dictum: "The climax of a plot / Should be the marriage knot."[25] Similarly, few stories illustrate the mother-child bonding that was so central to domesticity. Hester Prynne, the heroine of Hawthorne's *Scarlet Letter*, clearly cares for her daughter, Pearl. But as an adulterous, single mother, Hester hardly embodies the virtues Beecher extolled. Even Susan Warner's *The Wide, Wide World* (1850), the first of the sentimental bestsellers, begins with Ellen Montgomery's mother, who is ill, leaving her child so that she and her husband can seek medical treatment in Europe. Indeed, fictional women were more often independent and assertive than domestic and submissive.

Although maternalism was rarely found in novels before 1852, another aspect of the new domestic morality *was* evident: the increasing strength of evangelical Christianity among "middling folk." Beginning in the 1820s, rapidly growing sects, whose rise dated from the eighteenth century, turned their attention to the middle class. For the Methodists and Baptists, who traditionally had reached out to the less wealthy, the new orientation led to far-reaching institutional changes. Churches that had relied on camp meetings, unlettered itinerants, and hellfire and brimstone, now moved toward a settled, educated ministry and tamer sermons. The Presbyterians, who long had been more staid, also evolved—meeting their competitors halfway. They too now directed their efforts toward the more affluent. Charles Grandison Finney, who was well-educated and well-spoken (and originally a lawyer), led the revitalized church. Beginning in 1825, he stormed across upstate New York, presiding over a series of wildly successful revivals. Nathan Hatch notes that Finney "conveyed the indigenous methods of popular culture to the middle class."[26] Many of these ministers (though not always Finney) became upholders of conventional beliefs, including the doctrines of domesticity.

Across a range of sects, theology moved away from the harsh tenets of Calvinism and toward an affirmation of human self-worth that fit with the prosperous times and the optimistic outlook of the middle classes. The Ngram database makes clear that the frequency of words signaling Calvinist beliefs, including *sin, devil, Satan,* and *damnation,* all declined after the first decades of the century.

Indicative of the new piety that attracted literate, middle-class audiences was the growing interest in Bible reading. By the 1830s, the American Bible Society and other groups were distributing annually more than one million Holy Testaments along with millions of tracts and other religious books. In *The Wide, Wide World,* an extraordinarily religious book (Warner claimed she wrote the novel "on her knees"), the Bible figures prominently. Early in the narrative, Ellen goes shopping with her ailing mother and is nearly delirious at the prospect of owning her own copy. Entering the bookstore, her "wits were ready to forsake her. Such beautiful Bibles she had never seen, she pored in ecstasy over their varieties of type and binding, and was very evidently in love with them all."[27]

By the 1840s, the impact of evangelicalism was unmistakable, and became an important facet of sentimental literature during the middle decades of the century. James Fenimore Cooper's novels trace the arc of ascending piety. His works in the 1820s bear the stamp of skepticism, reminiscent of Charles Brockden Brown's books. For example, in *The Pioneers,* Judge Temple, who is in most respects an admirable individual, stands apart from any faith. One observer notes that the Judge has "an over carelessness about his sowl. It's nather a Methodie, nor a Papish, nor Prasbetyrian, that he is, but jist nothing at all." Similarly, Natty Bumppo rebuffs the efforts of the local preacher to bring him into the church. Natty remarks, "I never know'd preaching come into a settlement, but it made game scearce, and raised the price of gun-powder."[28]

Cooper's novels of the 1840s reflected the piety that reshaped the author's own life. Mabel Dunham, who stands at the spiritual center of *The Pathfinder* (1840), is the model of a pious woman. Even Natty has become far more of a Christian. The reader learns that "Pathfinder prayed often, daily if not hourly—but it was mentally, in his own simple modes of thinking, and without the aid of words at all."[29] In *The Deerslayer* (1841), Natty frequently talks about God and Christianity, even telling his Native companion, Chingachgook: "You'll be Christianized one day, I make no doubt, and then 'twill all come plain enough."[30] Three late works, *The Wing-and-Wing* (1842), *The Oak Openings* (1848), and *The Sea Lions* (1849), have strong Christian themes. For example, the conclusion of *The Wing-and-Wing,* a naval story set in Napoleonic times, focuses on Ghita Caraccioli's efforts to win the protagonist, Raoul Yvard, for Christ. She tells him that the "Holy Spirit delights in the penitent and sorrowful. Oh! dearest, dearest Raoul, if thou *would'st* but pray!"[31]

IV

Alongside domesticity and piety, a contrasting ideology gathered strength, providing middle-class women with the basis for a more outspoken, independent role in society. This set of beliefs exalted the individual—and would profoundly influence the literature and art of these decades. Individualism, like the celebration of true womanhood, emerged from a soaring economy dominated by small enterprises. The emphasis on self-reliance and human "perfectibility" fostered the demand for woman's rights as well as a wide array of reform movements, including abolition, temperance, and utopian communities.

Although strong women appeared occasionally in novels of the early national period, after 1820 they became commonplace. Catharine Sedgwick's *Hope Leslie* (1827) reveals the new outlook. Guided by her compassion and deep sense of justice, Hope faces down pirates, escapes from Indians, and twice frees prisoners who have been unjustly confined. Were such heroines unusual and at odds with a world defined by domesticity, as some critics suggest? Judith Fetterley asserts that *Hope Leslie* provides a "radical" argument against a worldview that "reifie[d] the separation of public and private by gender."[32] Lucy Maddox labels Sedgwick's novel a "self-consciously feminist revision of male-transmitted history."[33] But James Machor, drawing upon a close reading of contemporary reviews, disagrees and sees such boldness as the norm. He notes that there was "little if any evidence that antebellum readers experienced *Hope Leslie* as a pyrotechnic challenge to the culture's dominant assumptions about gender and racial norms."[34]

In fact, assertiveness defined the behavior of many unmarried women in these decades. Tocqueville observes: "Long before the young American woman has reached marriageable age, the process of freeing her from her mother's care has started stage by stage. Before she has completely left childhood behind she already thinks for herself, speaks freely, and acts on her own. All the doings of the world are ever plain for her to see.... [S]he is full of confidence in her own powers, and it seems that this feeling is shared by all around her."[35]

Hope Leslie is only one of many fictional women in this era who embodied such qualities and fought Native Americans, defied British soldiers, held jobs (like surveyor) normally performed by men, or demonstrated physical and mental courage. These women not only populate Sedgwick's fiction, but also appear in Cooper's novels, including Cora Munro in *The Last of the Mohicans* (1826), Ursula "Dus" Malone in *The Chainbearer*, and Judith Hutter in *The Deerslayer*. They are prominent in John Pendleton Kennedy's work, notably Mildred Lindsay and Mary Musgrove in *Horse-Shoe Robinson* (1835); and are found in William Gilmore Simms's novels, for example, Moll Granger in *The Yemassee* (1835). Of course, not every woman in these works was daring; some were more timid and "ladylike." But novel after novel celebrates self-reliant females.

An exception underscores these observations. Washington Irving depicts a paragon of "true womanhood" in "The Wife," a tale highlighted by critic Jeanne Boydston. In that story, the wife lovingly supports her husband, who has been "smitten with sudden calamity"—a bankruptcy. Significantly, the events unfold in

England, where Irving lived from 1815 to 1832, and the relationship between husband and wife reflects more a British than American ethos. The stories in *The Sketch Book* set in America depict very different sorts of marriages; for example, in "Rip Van Winkle," shrewish Dame Van Winkle shows few signs of wifely subordination.

Beginning in the late 1830s, the woman's movement encouraged middle-class women to present still bolder views—an outlook reflected in literature. Outspoken individuals began to challenge long-accepted frameworks. In 1837, Sarah Grimké published her *Letters on the Equality of the Sexes,* and in 1845 Margaret Fuller issued *Woman in the Nineteenth Century.* Both writers demanded equality. "We would have every arbitrary barrier thrown down," Fuller wrote. "We would have every path laid open to woman as freely as to man."[36] Woman's rights leader Susan B. Anthony affirmed that no single publication had a greater influence on the subsequent protests than Fuller's tract. A turning point in the campaign for equality came with the woman's rights convention held at Seneca Falls, New York, in 1848, which launched a movement that would soon spread across much of the North.[37] The Ngram graph for *strong women* suggests the spread of this movement, showing a strong upward surge beginning in the 1840s and continuing through the Civil War (fig. 3.4).

By midcentury the impact of the woman's rights movement on literature was unmistakable, even if most works occupied a middle ground where new demands were acknowledged but not fully endorsed. Hester Prynne, the protagonist of Nathaniel Hawthorne's *The Scarlet Letter,* voices far-ranging views. The narrator explains: "She assumed a freedom of speculation then common enough on the

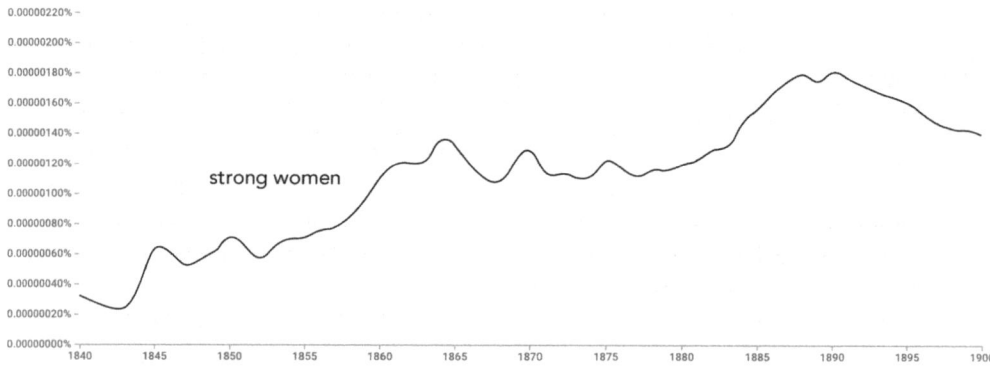

3.2. FREQUENCY OF *STRONG WOMEN* IN AMERICAN ENGLISH (2019) NGRAM DATABASE, 1840–1900. FIGURE 7.1 CONTINUES THIS GRAPH AFTER 1900.

other side of the Atlantic, but which our forefathers, had they known of it, would have held to be a deadlier crime than that stigmatized by the scarlet letter." Hester imagines a new world: "As a first step, the whole system of society is to be torn down, and built up anew. Then, the very nature of the opposite sex, or its long hereditary habit, which has become like nature, is to be essentially modified, before woman can be allowed to assume what seems a fair and suitable position."[38] Still, any depiction of *The Scarlet Letter* as a feminist novel can be challenged. David Leverenz notes that Hester "avoids any struggle for public power except to preserve her conventional role as mother." Indeed, Hester's speculations about the future of women come as somewhat of a surprise. Chillingworth, her husband, not Hester, confesses to being "the book-worm of great libraries."[39]

Cooper's final novel, *The Ways of the Hour* (1850), also engages the woman's movement. Some critics view the book as an attack on the Married Woman's Property Act, adopted by New York in 1848. "Cooper's principal target," Barbara Bardes and Suzanne Gossett remark, was "the disaster he foresaw in economic freedom for women."[40] The plot turns on the trial of the feminist Mary Monson, who is accused of killing and robbing an older couple. The Manhattan lawyer Dunscomb expounds (it might seem) Cooper's opinions. He condemns the anti-rent agitation, which disturbed landowners like Cooper, and attacks the new marriage property laws. Another character, Anna Updyke, lauds domesticity. But when those comments are considered within the broad context of the narrative, the author's views of the woman's movement become more complex. Mary's speeches are forthright. "Men have not dealt fairly by women," she notes. "Possessing the power, they have made all the laws, fashioned all the opinions of the world, in their favour.... If a woman think differently from those around her, she is expected to conceal her opinions, in order to receive those of her masters." When her lawyers falter in court, she conducts her own defense and wins the case. The reader also learns that her estranged husband had married her for her inheritance, and that the Married Woman's Property Act had foiled his intentions. Considered in its entirety, the book offers a mixed verdict on the woman's movement.[41]

V

The exaltation of the individual also led many in the middle class to adopt a new view of men's role. The rapidly growing, entrepreneurial society fostered a beau ideal: the self-made man. Henry Clay coined the term in 1832, praising "the enterprising and self-made men, who have whatever wealth they possess by patient and diligent labor."[42] Readers embraced strong-minded, self-reliant protagonists such as Natty Bumppo in Cooper's Leatherstocking series; Horse-shoe Robinson,

Kennedy's eponymous hero; and the daring figures in Simms's works, such as Ralph Colleton in *Guy Rivers* and Gabriel Harrison in *The Yemassee*. These men have few counterparts in the literature of the early national period.

Still, observers had conflicted views about exalting the self-reliant male. Emerson presents one side of this heated debate. With his unblinking celebration of great men, Emerson took the ethos of these years to its logical extreme. "Every true man," he wrote, "is a cause, a country, and an age; requires infinite spaces and numbers and time fully to accomplish his design; —and posterity seem to follow his steps as a train of clients."[43] Emerson praised these individuals for their *character*, a term whose use peaked in the antebellum decades and that connects self-reliant men to the creation of a just society (fig. P3.5). Emerson observes aphoristically, "Character is this moral order seen through the medium of an individual nature." According to the COHA database, *moral* was the word most closely associated with *character* in this period.[44] Emerson lifted these self-reliant individuals above any carping criticisms, observing, "Society everywhere is in conspiracy against the manhood of every one of its members. . . . Whoso would be a man, must be a nonconformist."[45] Unlike some of his contemporaries, Emerson saw no danger in the unbridled liberty he granted such persons.[46]

Hawthorne and Melville were also fascinated by titanic figures, but unlike the "Sage of Concord," they recognized the dangers of excessive self-reliance.[47] While both novelists laud men who seek higher truths, they sharply criticize self-centered individuals who ignore the feelings of others. Thus, in *The Scarlet Letter*, the Reverend Arthur Dimmesdale accuses Roger Chillingworth, who pursues the minister with unslakable malice, of violating "the sanctity of a human heart."[48] Similarly flawed protagonists are evident in Hawthorne's stories. In "The Birthmark," a scientist seeks to perfect his wife by removing a blemish on her face; when he does so, she dies. In "Rappaccini's Daughter," another researcher believes he has immunized his daughter to the toxic flowers in his garden, but the antidote he compounds kills her. In "Ethan Brand," the protagonist's quest for the "Unpardonable Sin" culminates when he finds that failing in his own heart. He ends his life by walking into a lime furnace.[49]

Melville's critique of such lofty figures is similar. In *Moby-Dick*, he suggests the proper balance for conducting life. The novel censures Ahab's megalomania (the captain declares, "I'd strike the sun if it insulted me") and shows how this pathology leads to the destruction of the *Pequod* and its crew.[50] Ishmael embodies a more admirable mix of traits. Like Ahab (and unlike the first mate, Starbuck), Ishmael is a seeker, exploring larger philosophical issues. But cosmic currents never sweep him away. "[B]y many prolonged, repeated experiences, I have perceived," he states, "that in all cases man must eventually lower, or at least shift, his conceit of attainable felicity; not placing it anywhere in the intellect or the fancy; but in the wife, the heart, the bed, the table, the saddle, the fire-side, the country."[51] In short, the resolution to the challenges posed by the era of self-made men lies in an amalgam of individualism and domesticity.

VI

The exaltation of the individual also led to a new view of nature. Writers and painters illustrate how the once frightening forests now became places where men and women could commune with the divine. This outlook brought together several strands that marked the decades from 1820 to 1850. Only during an era in which many held an unbounded belief in human perfectibility could writers imagine this discourse with God. The reverence for the wilderness also dovetailed with the widespread disdain, in literature at least, for money-making and city life. "In the wilderness," observes Emerson, "I find something more dear and connate than in streets or villages. In the tranquil landscape, and especially in the distant line of the horizon, man beholds somewhat as beautiful as his own nature."[52]

Cooper's five Leatherstocking novels, which trace the career of Natty Bumppo, apostrophize a God who dwells in the uncharted forests. In *The Pioneers*, the scout tells Oliver Effingham about a majestic waterfall. "To my judgment, lad," he remarks, "it's the best piece of work that I've met within the woods; and none know how often the hand of God is seen in a wilderness, but them that rove it for a man's life."[53] The ensuing novels elaborate that theme. In *The Pathfinder*, Natty repeatedly testifies to the holiness of the woods. "That towns and settlements lead to sin, I will allow," he remarks, "but our lakes are bordered by the forests, and one is every day called upon to worship God, in such a temple." Natty tells another friend: "I have endivoured to worship garrison-fashion, but never could raise within me, the solemn feelings and true affection, that I feel when alone with God, in the forest. There I seem to stand face to face, with my master."[54] In *The Deerslayer*, Natty declares, "the whole 'arth is a temple of the Lord to such as have the right mind."[55] Thus, by the 1840s, Cooper's views of religion drew upon both traditions: he shared the piety of the newly evangelized middle class, and he celebrated the pantheism expounded by Emerson and other Transcendentalists.

Other writers echoed Cooper's view of the natural world as God's holy place. In William Gilmore Simms's *Guy Rivers*, an otherwise unremarkable tale of derring-do in frontier Georgia, the hero Ralph Colleton pauses in a particularly lovely grove. The reader learns, "He could not help acknowledge, as, indeed, must all who have ever been under the influence of such a scene, that in this, more properly and perfectly than in any other temple, may the spirit of man recognise and hold familiar and free converse with the spirit of his Creator."⁵⁶ In Lydia Maria Child's *Hobomok* (1824), the title character, a Native American, perceives (the Christian) God when in the woods. "Though the intellect be darkened," the narrator remarks, "there are rays from God's own throne, which enter into the peacefulness and purity of the affections, shedding their mild lustre on the ignorance of man. . . . He had never read of God, but he had heard his chariot wheels in the distant thunder, and seen his drapery in the clouds."⁵⁷

The soaring use of *sublime* was another marker of the elevated view of nature during these years. The frequency of the term peaked during this period, then declined precipitously after midcentury. The word often describes God's presence in the wilderness. In *The Deerslayer,* for example, Cooper notes that Natty "loved the woods for their freshness, their sublime solitudes, their vastness, and the impress that they everywhere bore of the divine hand of their Creator."⁵⁸

References to *romantic* also climbed during the 1820s and 1830s, similarly testifying to the deep, spiritual appreciation of nature (fig. 3.3). The word often described a wild, barely tamed landscape. In Cooper's *The Pioneers,* a rock-strewn mountainside gives "that romantic character to the country, which it so eminently possesses."⁵⁹ In the *Last of the Mohicans,* the two sisters, Alice and Cora, pause in a secluded spot and gaze "upon its romantic though not unappalling beauties."⁶⁰ The resurgence of *romantic* a century later was tied to personality and is discussed in chapter 7.⁶¹ As noted in the introduction, the COHA database links *romantic* to "wild," "scenery," and "picturesque" in the antebellum era, and to "temperament" in the 1920s.

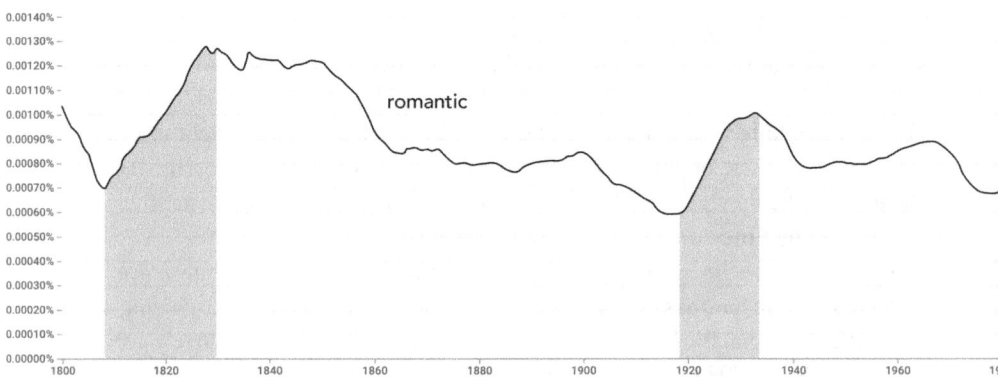

3.3. TWO PERIODS WHEN FREQUENCY OF *ROMANTIC* ROSE SHARPLY IN AMERICAN ENGLISH (2019) NGRAM DATABASE, 1800–1980

3.1. THOMAS COLE, *THE OXBOW (THE CONNECTICUT RIVER NEAR NORTHAMPTON)*, 1836.

The same view of nature characterized painting, and particularly the canvases of Thomas Cole, leader of the Hudson River School. Viewing the White Mountains of New Hampshire, Cole remarked, "It is here, in such sublime scenes that man sees his own nothingness; and the soul feels unutterably . . . How kind the Creator has been to us—Nature opens her treasures; and a rich banquet is ever spread for our enjoyment."[62] Cole conveyed God's magnificence with canvases on which (as Donald Ringe notes) "the small figures in the middle distance . . . are all but engulfed by the surrounding space."[63] *The Oxbow (The Connecticut River near Northampton)* (ptg. 3.1) illustrates the artist's approach to composition. A self-portrait of Cole with his easel in the center foreground is dwarfed on the left by a forest and storm, and on the right by the magnificent Connecticut River and cultivated fields.[64] After midcentury, artists would continue to focus on landscapes, but their view of nature evolved as society became more stratified.

4
Retreat from the Heights, 1852–1869

After midcentury, the economy gradually grew more bureaucratic, and the bold individualism that had marked literature and art no longer appealed to middle-class readers and viewers. Few writers looked more acerbically at these developments than Herman Melville and Nathaniel Hawthorne, who briefly lived as neighbors in western Massachusetts. Both men lamented the meager sales of their books—and the extraordinary success of the domestic fiction written by women. "Dollars damn me . . . ," Melville exclaimed, "What I feel most moved to write, that is banned—it will not pay. Yet, altogether, write the *other* way I cannot." Still, he would try. He informed Nathaniel's wife, Sophia, that his new novel, *Pierre* (1852), would be "a rural bowl of milk," and assured his English publisher the work would be "very much more calculated for popularity than anything you have yet published of mine." But *Pierre* was a disaster commercially—and artistically.[1] Hawthorne too tried to respond to popular tastes. Critics praised *The House of the Seven Gables* (1851) as a novel full of "tenderness and delicacy" of sentiment. Hawthorne, however, vowed never to repeat that experiment. "I doubt whether the public will stand for two quiet books in succession," he sighed. Exasperated, he told his publisher, William Ticknor, in 1855: "America is now wholly given over to a d—d mob of scribbling women, and I should have no chance of success while the public taste is occupied with their trash—and should be ashamed of myself if I did succeed."[2]

During two decades after midcentury years, the views of many in the middle class traced a retreat from their admiration of men who thundered at God or plunged into the forests to commune with the divine. As bureaucracies redefined the economy and domesticity appeared to triumph, the age of heroic males gradually faded. Along with novels, painting changed, as artists no longer viewed the landscape as God's sublime handiwork. Emotion still suffused depictions of nature, but more attention was paid to detail and less to the presence of a higher power.

Yet, any examination of the outlook of the middle class in these years must move beyond the narrative of declension and the fall from the Emersonian heights of the 1830s and 1840s. For the first time in the young republic, a group of African American novelists vigorously expounded their own perspectives. And while domesticity seemed triumphant in the early 1850s (much to the chagrin of Melville and Hawthorne), that triumph was short-lived. The woman's rights crusade fostered a cohort of outspoken women, both in society and literature. Making their case involved sentiment, that was the mark of the times, as well as a demand for new roles. Finally, domesticity and the middle class's growing affluence meant a heightened interest in children.

I

The standard of living for middle-class Americans continued to rise during the 1850s and 1860s (even with the disruptions of the Civil War) but equally significant was the gradual transformation of the economy, as large businesses gradually emerged and the world of daring men-on-the-make slowly faded. These developments would have a far-reaching impact on fiction and art.

Farmers grew more dependent on financiers and industrialists. In 1850, George Boutwell (who later became governor of Massachusetts) told a group of Concord farmers that agriculture had become "a very different pursuit from what it was twenty years ago." "All of you," he stated, are now "equally dependent upon the great laws of production, exchange, and consumption." One Concord resident, Henry David Thoreau, wholeheartedly agreed. In *Walden; or Life in the Woods* (1854), he notes, "On applying to the assessors, I am surprised to learn that they cannot at once name a dozen in the town who own their farms free and clear. If you would know the history of these homesteads, inquire at the bank where they are mortgaged."[3]

Western farmers also found themselves increasingly entangled with distant financiers and manufacturers. In 1851, Austin Corbin, a New Hampshire native, moved to Davenport, Iowa, and soon began to market western mortgages to eastern investors. In the 1860s, he expanded his business as the Corbin Banking Company, joining other financial companies in channeling eastern money to the booming West. Soaring purchases of agricultural equipment intensified the demand for funds. Between 1850 and 1858, farmers bought over seventy thousand harvesters and mowers, machines that might cost $115 and last five years, no small investment for a struggling homesteader.[4]

The business world changed as well, with corporations increasingly elbowing aside individual proprietorships. Beginning in the 1840s, most states outside the South adopted general incorporation laws, eliminating the need for lawmakers to review each application. Limited liability and the ability to raise funds from many sources proved powerful inducements to entrepreneurs. During the 1850s, four east-west railroads—the Baltimore & Ohio, the Pennsylvania, the Erie, and the New York Central—took the lead in developing elaborate managerial structures and new accounting procedures, and in soliciting public financing. By 1859, foreign and domestic investment in US railroad securities had surpassed the billion-dollar mark, with many of these funds channeled through New York brokers.[5]

An army of managers and clerks served the needs of the new businesses. The New York City census of 1855 found clerking to be the third most important male occupation, trailing only laborers and servants. These individuals, pivotal figures in the emerging economy, tabulated not only profit and loss, but also a host of new metrics, such as depreciation and return on equity. It seems apt that while Melville's Ahab, with his heaven-defying ambitions, characterized the preceding period, Bartleby, the self-effacing scrivener (or copyist) from Melville's 1853 story of that name became the standard-bearer for these years.[6]

The flood of immigrants that washed across both urban and rural America, leaving only parts of the South untouched, also helped reshape the economy. The newly arrived laborers assisted middle-class families and expansion-minded corporations. Almost all the Irish who fled the potato famine of the mid-1840s were poor, as were some of the Germans who arrived after the 1848 revolutions. Many of these individuals became household servants, while others helped lay the thousands of miles of railroad track added in the 1850s. The Irish also entered the New England textile mills, replacing native-born farm women, driving down wages, and ending the paternalistic boardinghouse system.[7]

The Civil War accelerated the shift from a nation of self-made men to one of large corporations. The triumphant Republicans pushed through a series of landmark measures that strengthened the national economy. They abolished slavery; created a system of national banks; established a uniform currency, the greenback; planned a transcontinental railroad; founded land grant colleges; and offered free land to homesteaders. Organizing for victory encouraged business leaders, like Tom Scott of the Pennsylvania Railroad, and future magnates, like Andrew Carnegie, to think in continental terms.[8]

Still, the changes of the 1850s and 1860s marked only the first steps to full-blown industrialization. Railroads moved goods long distances, but the process involved multiple bills of lading and arrangements with separate roads. A unified national market emerged only in the 1880s, when trunk lines consolidated transportation networks. And only then did large corporations, manufacturing uniform goods for consumers across the country or producing materials for the burgeoning cities, come to dominate the economy. Only in the last decades of the century would a large, impoverished working class characterize the American scene.[9]

II

The transformed economy of the 1850s and 1860s, with its larger firms and expanding bureaucracies, reshaped views of masculinity. The age of the independent, assertive man was passing. Writers turned from portraying heroic individuals like Natty Bumppo, or titanic figures like Ahab, to depicting more settled men who wrestled with problems but rarely conversed with God or engaged in battles with good and evil.

The change was evident in the works of male novelists who wrote both before and after midcentury. Melville, for example, moves from the daring adventurers of *Typee* (1846) and *Omoo* (1847) and the seekers in *Moby-Dick* (1851) to the confused and rigidly moralistic hero of *Pierre*; Bartleby the scrivener in the 1853 story; Amasa Delano, the limited, self-satisfied New England captain in *Benito Cereno* (1855); and the bewildering, shape-shifting protagonist of *The Confidence-Man* (1857). Similarly, after *The Scarlet Letter,* Hawthorne's male characters no longer engage in quests for ultimate truths or sign pacts with the devil. Instead, Hawthorne populates his books with such men as the gentle reformer Holgrave in *House of the Seven Gables* (1851); the passive, ineffective Coverdale and arrogant Hollingsworth in *The Blithedale Romance* (1852); the well-meaning Kenyon and the seemingly half-human Donatello in *The Marble Faun* (1860). Even William Gilmore Simms shifted with the times. Instead of the dashing figures of his earlier novels, the protagonist of *Woodcraft* (1854) is the Falstaffian Captain Porgy.[10]

Similarly, few heroic men stand out in the books written by women. In Harriet Beecher Stowe's *Uncle Tom's Cabin* (1852), the "good" men, such as Mr. Shelby, Senator Bird, and Augustine St. Clare, do the right thing (and not always that) only when prodded by a female.[11] In E.D.E.N. (Emma Dorothy Eliza Nevitte) Southworth's novels, positive male figures are typically less prominent—and usually less interesting—than the villains. For example, in *The Hidden Hand* (1859), scoundrels such as Gabriel Le Noir, Black Donald, and Ira Warfield, command the reader's attention far more than upright Herbert Greyson, who marries the heroine, Capitola. In other cases, key male figures are nearly absent, like Mr. March in Louisa May Alcott's *Little Women* (1868–69).

The middle class no longer exalted adventuresome, independent men, but now praised qualities more suited to the world of corporations—and the rhythms of home life. Ministers and other opinion makers instructed men to be trustworthy, caring, and dependable. Figure 5.2 shows the increasing importance of *trustworthy* during these decades. For many men, however, the turn to those quieter virtues remained unsettling. Tim Prehal remarks the "general call for the recovery of 'the masculine character' sounded among middle-class men who felt their lives to be suffused with 'feminine' refinements and sentiments."[12] During the 1850s and 1860s, the growth of sports, particularly baseball, and the expansion of men's clubs, suggested another side to male identity. A fuller response to such longings came only at the end of the century with the emergence of "virile manhood."[13]

III

Balanced against that story of declension was the emergence of two movements, one led by outspoken African Americans and the other by White women demanding their rights. Both left a deep imprint on literature. A survey of the views of White writers provides a crucial context for understanding the accomplishments of Black authors. Racist depictions of Blacks had been a staple of American literature at least since James Fenimore Cooper portrayed the house servant Caesar in *The Spy* (1821). During the 1830s and 1840s, Southern writers, such as William Gilmore Simms, John Pendleton Kennedy, and Nathaniel Beverly Tucker presented a variety of Black characters who conformed to long-standing stereotypes. These authors (and their northern counterparts like Cooper) portrayed African Americans as happy, intensely loyal individuals, with even freed slaves remaining close to their former owners. While occasionally brave (servants rescue masters in Simms's *The Yemassee* [1835] and Cooper's *Satanstoe* [1845]), they lack intelligence, foresight, and the ability to formulate larger plans.[14]

Those negative depictions continued after midcentury. No book was more important in presenting the Black character to Whites than Stowe's bestseller, *Uncle Tom's Cabin*. Stowe added important new elements to the familiar condescending portrait. Her goal, as she states in the preface, was "to awaken sympathy and feeling for the African race, as they exist among us." Stowe praises Blacks for their receptivity to Christianity. "It is the statement of missionaries," she observes, "that, of all races of the earth, none have received the Gospel with such eager docility as the African."[15] Uncle Tom, Christlike in his teachings and martyrdom, epitomizes those sentiments. Stowe also appeals to her readers by underscoring Blacks' attachment to their families.[16]

Stowe groups African Americans according to their skin color, with the "whiter" individuals more self-assertive and intelligent. Both George Harris and Cassy (who briefly is Simon Legree's concubine) can "pass," and both are clever and defiant.

By comparison, black slaves are slow-witted. They might be buffoons like Black Sam, or faithful, saintly individuals like Tom—but they clearly are members of an inferior race. Such stereotypical portraits comported with the prejudices of Stowe's readers, including the many who denounced slavery. Richard Hildreth was one of the few authors before Stowe to suggest the impact of "white blood." In *The Slave: or Memoir of Archy Moore* (1836, reissued in an enlarged edition, 1852), Hildreth depicts a near-white bondsman who inherited a "proud spirit, sensitive feelings and ardent temperament" from his White father.[17]

A few White novelists sympathetic to the cause of antislavery provide a more balanced picture of Blacks. Most of the African Americans in Southworth's novels are childish, but the nurse Nancy Grewell in *The Hidden Hand* challenges that rule. She helps raise and defend the heroine Capitola. As Jordan Landry notes, Southworth, in a striking reversal of standard practices, "disguises the African American woman as white by leaving her race uncoded until near the end of Nancy's story."[18]

Even more significant are the proud, dark-skinned individuals who inhabit the novels of Herman Melville, a vehement opponent of slavery. The romantic descriptions of the South Sea islanders in *Typee* and *Omoo* can possibly, as Eleanor Simpson suggests, "be accounted for largely in terms of the literary convention of the 'noble savage.'"[19] But Melville's early seafaring novels, *Redburn* (1849) and *White Jacket* (1850), include African American seamen, portrayed with no condescension. In *Moby-Dick* several of the nonwhite individuals are still more admirable. The South Sea harpooner, Queequeg, is an impressive figure, searching in his own way for the secrets of the universe, and more than once saving lives. "Queequeg," Ishmael observes, "was George Washington cannibalistically developed." The African Dagoo fearlessly holds his own when taunted by White sailors. Pip, the cabin boy, after abandonment for hours in the ocean, changes from a happy-go-lucky entertainer to a seer, gifted in his insanity. "Hands off from that holiness!" Ahab tells a sailor.[20] Babo, the rebellious slave in "Benito Cereno," is another imposing if malevolent figure. The reader does not see Babo directly; rather, as Jean Yellin notes, "as a configuration of features which we later learn are carefully painted masks."[21] Clearly, Melville has created another powerful, dark-skinned individual who defies the stereotype of the infantilized Black.[22]

In the context of the widespread racism that characterized novels (with those few exceptions), the enforced illiteracy of slavery, and the limited schooling offered free Blacks, the emergence of talented, outspoken African American writers in the 1850s is noteworthy. Some of the authors—William Wells Brown, Frederick Douglass, and Hannah Crafts (the pen name for Hannah Bond)—were escaped slaves. Others—Frank J. Webb, Martin R. Delany, and Harriet E. Wilson—were free born. Works by Black authors provide a window into a group too often defined by others. Few of their novels, however, had a wide readership. Delany's unfinished *Blake; or the Huts of America* (1859–61) was serially published in the *Weekly Anglo-African* and not issued as a book until 1970. Crafts's *The Bondwoman's Narrative* (c. 1855–59) remained in manuscript until its publication in 2002.[23]

In portraying men, Black novelists rejected Stowe's linkage between whiteness and intelligence. Douglass states that Madison Washington, the defiant protagonist of *The Heroic Slave* (1853), is "black, but comely."[24] Similarly, Webb describes Walters, a highly successful businessman in *The Garies and Their Friends* (1857), as "above six feet in height, and exceedingly well-proportioned; of jet-black complexion, and smooth glossy skin."[25] Delany remarks that the protagonist of *Blake* is "a pure Negro—handsome manly and intelligent."[26] And when Brown re-wrote *Clotel* (1853) for distribution to soldiers during the Civil War, he emphasized that Jerome, one the principal characters, was "of pure African origin."[27]

These writers were less consistent, however, in depicting African American women: many of the most attractive women in these novels are mulattas. In these instances, the standards found in novels by White authors prevail. *Clotel* follows the lives of five mixed-race women, including Clotel and her sister Althesa, both of whom are Thomas Jefferson's daughters. All are desired by men, Black and White, and four meet a tragic end. In *Blake*, Delany portrays the hero's wife, Maggie, as "a dark mulatto of a rich, yellow, autumnlike complexion, with a matchless, cushionlike head of hair, neither straight nor curly, but handsomer than either."[28] In Wilson's *Our Nig* (1859), the heroine Frado is described as "real handsome and bright, and not very black, either."[29] Several modern commentators decry those portraits. "The mulatta figure," Ann duCille notes, "stands in some of this criticism as a kind of man-made antifeminist outlaw, whose ubiquity represents an insult to authentic black womanhood."[30]

Broadly viewed, a dialogue between assimilation and rebellion characterizes African American novels. Rising prosperity nurtured a small Black middle class, providing opportunities that several authors elaborate.[31] In *Clotel,* Brown describes Blacks who advanced through education and industry, adding in the preface to the London edition an account of his own entrepreneurial successes—and setbacks.[32] Webb's novel portrays a middle-class African American family, the Ellises. Mr. Ellis owns his own home; his daughters attend lectures at the library company; and his son, Charlie, after a brief spell as a "bad boy," gains employment as a printer. Walters, another prominent African American figure in the novel, is a real estate magnate and said to be "worth half a million."[33] Not all modern commentators applaud this tack, with some scholars (as Anna Mae Duane notes) criticizing Webb's outlook and the idea that Blacks "need, above all, in America to get rich."[34]

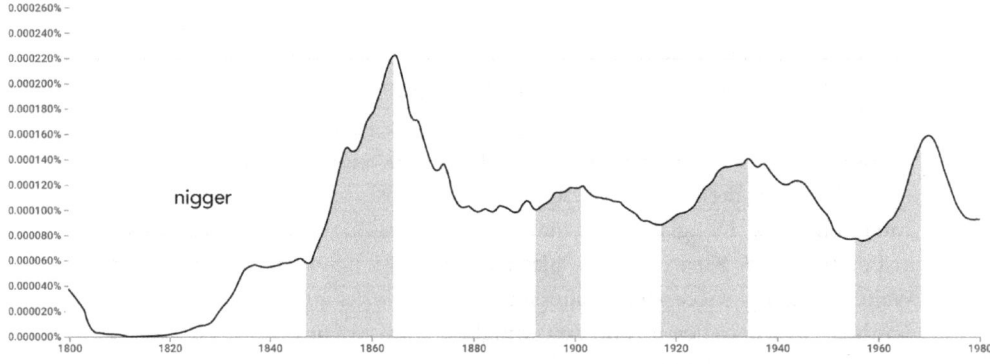

4.1: PERIODS OF MOUNTING RACISM: PLOTTING SHARP INCREASES IN THE FREQUENCY OF *NIGGER* IN AMERICAN ENGLISH (2019) NGRAM DATABASE, 1800–1980.

Still, all these novels detail the oppressive environment that Blacks faced in the South and North. *Blake, The Heroic Slave,* and *The Bondwoman's Narrative* underscore the cruelty of slaveowners, while *The Garies* and *Our Nig* focus on discrimination in the North. *Clotel* illustrates the harsh conditions in both sections. In chapter after chapter of *The Garies,* Webb documents the discrimination that confronted Northern Blacks in public conveyances, housing, schools, and burial grounds. An Irish-led riot besieges Walters's home and nearly kills Mr. Ellis. As one sympathetic White character notes, "I never knew prejudice more rampant than it is at this hour." Figure 4.1, which tracks the term *nigger,* underscores that observation. It highlights four periods (1847–64; 1892–1901; 1916–34; 1957–69) in which use of that odious term rose sharply.[35]

Several novels celebrate slave revolts. Madison Washington, the protagonist of Douglass's *The Heroic Slave,* leads the uprising on the brig *Creole.* Douglass retells the story of the 1841 episode when slaves took over the vessel, sailed it into the British port of Nassau, and were declared free. In *Blake,* Henry (as Blake is known in the first part of the book) passes from state to state throughout the South with seeming impunity, preaching rebellion. He carries the same message to Cuba, joining a diverse group of rebels. Once anointed leader of that coterie, he announces: "You know my errand among you; you know my sentiments. I am for war—war upon the whites."[36] The novel breaks off before the actual revolt occurs. Even the wealthy businessman Walters in the *Garies* has a defiant side. He hangs a picture of the Haitian leader Toussaint Louverture in his parlor, telling a White friend, "All white men look at it with interest. A black man in the uniform of a general officer is something so unusual that they cannot pass it with a glance." Walters organizes a stout, armed defense when rioters attack his house.[37]

This outpouring of literature by Black novelists did not continue after the Civil War. Although racism persisted and even deepened, the end of slavery removed the deep injustice that had spurred many writers. Not until the turn of the century, when lynching and campaigns for disenfranchisement intensified, would another important, engaged set of African American writers emerge.[38]

IV

Along with African Americans, a second group—White women—challenged the narrative of declension that marked these years of expanding bureaucracies. Any full description of women's literature after midcentury, as in the decades before 1850, must examine opposing outlooks. The growing wealth of middle-class families provided the backdrop for what seemed to be the triumph of "true womanhood." At the same time, the continuing and extraordinary growth of the woman's rights movement fostered a literature of defiance.

Many observers, like Melville and Hawthorne, felt that literary domesticity reigned supreme at midcentury. The prime exhibit for this case is Stowe's *Uncle Tom's Cabin*, a work Jane Tompkins calls, "the most important book of the century."[39] It sold a record three hundred thousand copies in the United States the first year, and a half million by 1857; large sales were also recorded abroad. Stowe's novel exalts the idea of two spheres, with women the keepers of the home and bearers of morality, while men deal with the rough-and-tumble of politics and commerce. The novel epitomizes the precepts that Harriet's older sister, Catharine, set forth in her 1842 *A Treatise on Domestic Economy*. Stowe exalts maternalism, with loving mothers the most admired women in the novel. The apotheosis of the mother reflected the gradual evolution of middle-class values. The ascent of the term *loving mother*, illustrated in figure 6.1, was part of a cultural change that dated from the 1820s.

While Stowe's women serve as moral guides, they remain subordinate to men in most dealings with the larger world.[40] Critics underscore the grave restrictions on women's power. Elizabeth Ammons notes that the opening scenes on the Shelby farm illustrate how "white men buy and sell black people while the white woman stands by powerless to intervene."[41] Amy Lang remarks how little impact the Ohio housewife Mrs. Bird has on society, even while persuading her senator husband to help the runaway Eliza. When Mrs. Bird confesses, "I don't know anything about politics," Lang comments: "It articulates her powerlessness."[42]

How typical—for the fiction of this era—was Stowe's portrayal of women? Some aspects of Stowe's world reappeared regularly. During the first half of the 1850s, several bestselling works limned a society in which woman's subordination was unquestioned, and marriage was the presumed goal for all girls. For example, in Mary Jane Holmes's popular *Tempest and Sunshine* (1854), men typically are wise and self-assured and a woman's fondest hope is to marry such an exalted creature. Similarly, in Caroline Lee Hentz's *The Planter's Northern Bride* (1854), Eulalia, the New Englander of the title, adores her future husband, the Georgia planter Moreland. The book by Hentz, who was born in Massachusetts but lived many years in the South, was perhaps the best-known Southern response to *Uncle Tom's Cabin*. Nina Baym ties the themes of the novel together: "Hentz recognizes that patriarchy is an institution affecting women as well as slaves; but since she is defending it for the slave, she must defend it for women as well."[43]

Two other popular novels of the early 1850s also affirm the natural dominance of men and the desirability of marriage. Susan Warner's *The Wide, Wide World* (1850) and Maria Cummins's *The Lamplighter* (1854) trailed only *Uncle Tom's Cabin* in their sales during these midcentury years. Both books underscore the value of womanly submissiveness. "I will always do whatever you tell me—just as I used to—no matter what anybody else says," Ellen Montgomery, heroine of *The Wide, Wide World* tells John, who will be her future husband.[44] In *The Lamplighter*, Gertrude Flint gives up her post as a teacher to better serve her future husband, William. Gertrude's good friend Emily Graham captures the flavor of these relationships when she briefly protests a marriage proposal, "O, no, Philip! Do not speak of it! Think of my frail health and my helplessness!" But she quickly relents, and her marriage and Gertrude's conclude the book.[45]

These novels also share an intense, evangelical Christianity. Although piety was the mark of the age, appeals to the Savior were less common in the literature that questioned the subordination of women. Few novels have more direct references to Christ the martyr and comforter than *Uncle Tom's Cabin*, *The Wide, Wide World*, and *The Lamplighter*. Such prayers are also evident, particularly in deathbed scenes, in *The Planter's Northern Bride* and *Tempest and Sunshine*.[46]

In their piety and their refusal to challenge domesticity—or even suggest other possibilities for women—these novels can be grouped with *Uncle Tom's Cabin*. None, however, fully replicates Stowe's elaborate universe. They do not, for example, depict moral women guiding erring men. Few nurturing maternal figures mark the narratives of *Tempest and Sunshine*, *The Wide, Wide World*, or *The Lamplighter*.

Narratives celebrating "true womanhood" would continue during the sentimental era and, indeed, well after 1870. The growing affluence of the middle class allowed more and more women to focus on the domestic sphere. But increasingly another, more militant point of view challenged the tenets of domesticity.

V

Unlike so many crusades that faltered as the economy turned from the bumptious individualism of the 1830s and 1840s, the woman's movement only gathered strength after midcentury. Millennialism, utopian communities, dietary reform, and even abolition (subsumed into the political process) waned, while the demand for woman's rights waxed.

Drawing on a growing cadre of educated, middle-class women, protests strengthened following the Seneca Falls Convention of 1848. Women now regularly gathered in county and state meetings and, beginning in 1850, in National Woman's Rights Conventions. A national conclave met almost every year from 1850 to the Civil War. Speakers fanned out across the North, spreading the word. During the 1860s, several organizations bolstered the movement. In 1863, Elizabeth Stanton and Susan B. Anthony formed the Woman's Loyal National League to promote rights for Blacks and women. Three years later, the Eleventh National Woman's Rights Convention created the American Equal Rights Association with Lucretia Mott as president. Divisions over whether the demand for Black rights should take precedence led in 1869 to a split in the movement and the formation of rival alliances: the National Women's Suffrage Association and the American Women's Suffrage Association. Campaigns led by both groups (they would unite in 1890) further broadened the movement. As figure 4.2 indicates, the term *woman's rights* rarely appeared before the mid-1840s, but then became more common, peaking in the early 1870s. The frequency of *woman's suffrage* soared after the turn of the century as the campaign for voting redirected the energy of politicized individuals.[47]

The resurgent woman's movement made certain that domesticity was not the only ideology guiding middle-class women. During the 1850s and 1860s, more and more novels questioned the idealized version of the two spheres. Increasingly, writers highlighted women's unrealized aspirations and remarked how men's bad

4.2. FREQUENCY OF *WOMAN'S RIGHTS* AND *WOMAN'S SUFFRAGE* IN AMERICAN ENGLISH (2019) CORPUS, NGRAM DATABASE, 1820–1915.

behavior undermined traditional relationships. Few authors dismissed marriage as a desirable goal or wholeheartedly supported radical critiques; but in raising concerns about domesticity, they opened a spirited dialogue and made works of fiction into fields of contestation.

By the mid-1850s, many novels written by American authors questioned the idyllic picture of two spheres that Stowe, Hentz, and Holmes had depicted. (Indeed, after 1855, those three novelists would register their own dissents.) Some of these works directly referenced the woman's movement, although most did not. The novels of E.D.E.N. Southworth are a good starting point for understanding this literature. No American novelist had more readers in the second half of the nineteenth century. During the 1850s and 1860s, twenty-five American-authored books sold more than several hundred thousand copies; Southworth wrote five of them. Even in subsequent decades, when Stowe's sales slackened, Southworth's star remained in the ascendant. An 1874 survey of libraries in New England, New York, and Michigan found Southworth's books the most frequently borrowed. (Following her, in order, were Mary Jane Holmes, Augusta Evans, and two English authors, Charles Reade and Charles Dickens.)[48]

In Southworth's novels, marriages are far from happy; fathers and husbands are often cruel; submissive women are regularly punished, while bold women are rewarded. For example, in *The Discarded Daughter* (1852), Alice Chester, accepting her father's guidance, marries General Aaron Garnet, a calculating, self-centered individual. After years of coldness, Garnet suddenly showers Alice with kisses when he wants her to sign away her rights to a vast estate. An old friend and family adviser urges her not to give up her claim to the plantation: "Don't you be kissed out of it, Alice, for you can leave it to your beloved daughter, who will need it." But Alice, eager for the marriage to work and trusting her husband, signs the deed only to find the next day that Garnet disinherits her and her daughter.[49] In *The Hidden Hand*, the protagonist, a daring young woman, Capitola Black, defeats a series of villains who seek to molest, rob, or control her. At the same time, three more passive, traditional women, whose actions provide a counterpoint to Capitola's boldness, are subject to imprisonment, abandonment, and commitment to an asylum.[50]

Southworth's books horrified the defenders of domesticity—a response particularly evident during the first half of the 1850s. A reviewer of *The Discarded Daughter* complained that Southworth "makes her men too uniformly bad or silly, savage or stupid, malignant and mean or mulish." Sarah Josepha Hale, editor of the very proper *Godey's Lady's Book*, commented about Southworth's first four novels that the author "seems carried by a fervid imagination ... beyond the limits prescribed by correct taste or good judgment."[51] Still, Southworth was no wild-eyed rebel.

She too labored in the contested middle ground that marked the literature of these years. She did not campaign for woman's rights and continued to believe in happy marriages as an ideal; at the end of *The Hidden Hand*, for example, Capitola finds a loving husband.[52]

A survey of other fiction shows Southworth had much company in questioning domesticity. Hawthorne's *The Blithedale Romance* focuses on the actions of Zenobia, a feminist. "It is my belief...," she states, "that, when my sex shall achieve its rights, there will be ten eloquent women where there is now one eloquent man." But Zenobia too is conflicted; she falls hopelessly in love with a chauvinistic male, Hollingsworth, and when spurned commits suicide.[53]

Fanny Fern's bestselling novel *Ruth Hall* (1855) offers another sharp critique of traditional marriage. Although Fern rarely invokes the language of woman's rights orators, it is hard imagining this book written without those protests. The author, who was born Sara Payson Willis, describes a struggle that closely parallels her own life and makes clear that the challenges facing her protagonist are ones that females confront daily. When dealing with her unhappiness as a wife, "Ruth kept her wise little mouth shut." The author comments, "Ah! Could we lay bare the secret history of many a wife's heart, what martyrs would be found, over whose uncomplaining lips the grave sets its unbroken seal of silence."[54] Still, Ruth Hall's assertiveness also has strong maternalist roots; many of the bold steps she took in pursuing her career came from her desire to provide for her children.[55]

Other established authors also distanced themselves from the "cult of true womanhood." Just before her death in 1856, Caroline Lee Hentz, who earlier had written *The Planter's Northern Bride*, penned an essay, "The Sex of the Soul," questioning male dominance. A man, Hentz notes, views himself as "lord of creation." However, the "relative intellectual powers of men and women" will not be known until "*both* sexes are subject to the same mental discipline."[56] Earl Yarington's overview of Mary Jane Holmes's work points out that the author of *Tempest and Sunshine* dealt in her later novels with issues such as woman's suffrage, race relations, and class conflict.[57] Stowe's outlook also shifted; the next chapter examines the changes signaled in *My Wife and I* (1871). Even William Gilmore Simms evolved with the times. The South Carolinian had brave women in his earlier novels, but never one as defiantly independent as the widow Mrs. Eveleigh in *Woodcraft*. She rejects the hero's proposal of marriage, telling him: "I have been too long my own mistress to submit to authority. I have a certain spice of independence in my temper, which would argue no security for the rule which seeks to restrain me."[58]

Two popular novels of the 1860s similarly challenge traditional norms, but stop short of fully advocating woman's rights. Augusta J. Evans's *St. Elmo* (1866) chronicles the life of an orphan, Edna Earl, who is adopted by a wealthy family, and goes on to write a highly acclaimed book that weaves together art history and cultural studies. Having climbed to that intellectual peak, she marries the misanthropic St. Elmo Murray, who disapproves of working women. On their wedding day, he declares, "To-day I snap the fetters of your literary bondage. There shall be no more books written." Clearly, this is a work of profound contradictions. Susan Harris remarks, "The ending of *St. Elmo* does not come as a logical sequence to the events preceding it; Edna's apparent acquiescence in St. Elmo's interdict alone flatly contradicts every explicit or implicit statement she has made prior to the last chapter."[59] But Harris's analysis misses the deep crosscurrents in the book. While researching various cultures, Edna discovers that the proper role for women is subordination. The narrator explains: "Jealously she contended for every woman's right which God and nature had decreed the sex. The right to be learned, wise, noble, useful, in woman's divinely limited sphere [and] the right to modify and direct her husband's opinions, if he considered her worthy and competent to guide him. . . . But not the right to vote; to harangue from the hustings; [or] to trail her heaven-born purity through the dust and mire of political strife." For Evans, women can be writers and moral guides, but never politicians or voters.[60]

While Louisa May Alcott's *Little Women* (1868–69) also is balanced in its approach to women's roles, Alcott clearly favors assertive women. Some critics read the novel as a casebook in repression. Richard Brodhead asserts: "The March sisters learn the standard lessons of women's domestic education: mandatory other-directedness, the cure of 'temper,' the curtailment of selfish will, and so on."[61] Such readings, however, miss the full impact of the story. Barbara Sicherman, who studied the response of readers, remarks, "There is no evidence that Alcott's contemporaries read the book in this way. . . . [M]ost early critics admired *Little Women*'s spirit; some even found the author transgressive."[62] To be sure, Alcott shows her affection for the traditional roles chosen by three of the March sisters: Beth, Amy, and Meg. But as readers and critics alike agree, the central figure in the novel is Jo March, whose independence and determination to become an author reflects Alcott's own path. Jo persists in her resolve to write books, despite obstacles that include criticism from those she loves.[63]

In sum, the growing wealth of these decades, along with the increasing leisure and literacy that marked women's lives, encouraged domesticity—but also animated the woman's movement and critiques of "true womanhood." The dialogue between these differing views shaped the literature of these years.

V

Still another group—children—became more important in both fiction and society. The celebration of mothers and the newfound reverence for boys and girls were inextricably connected. Affluence, smaller families, and more years of schooling turned the attention of society to the young. Before 1850, few novels present children as fully developed characters. Often adulthood started at a remarkably early age. In *Charlotte Temple* (1791), Charlotte is thirteen when she meets the man who will seduce her, and fifteen when she runs off with him. Similarly, in *Hope Leslie* (1827), the heroine seems to skip her childhood, quickly becoming a young adult who faces difficult moral decisions. Since the colonial period, various guidebooks had been instructing parents on childrearing, with an emphasis on developing the child's moral sense. But almost never did these manuals introduce young individuals with their own, distinct worldviews.

The increased attention paid to children before midcentury, even if the focus came in didactic texts rather than novels, laid the foundation for their presence in literature after 1850. Ngram data show that references to *childhood* became increasingly common between 1815 and 1850 (fig. 4.3). A second rise in the use of this term came after 1980 and is discussed in chapter 9. The differences between the two periods—as illustrated by the collocates in the Corpus of Historical American English—is revealing. *Childhood* in the antebellum period was linked to *innocence, sunny,* and *sports,* while in the postmodern era the comparable words are *unhappy, trauma,* and *abuse.*[64]

Around midcentury, authors began to include children in their narratives, with depictions that fit well with the broader currents of these years. Their pathetic deaths plucked readers' heartstrings, confirming the 1850s as the high-water mark of sentimentality. Few scenes were more moving (for contemporaries), or stretched

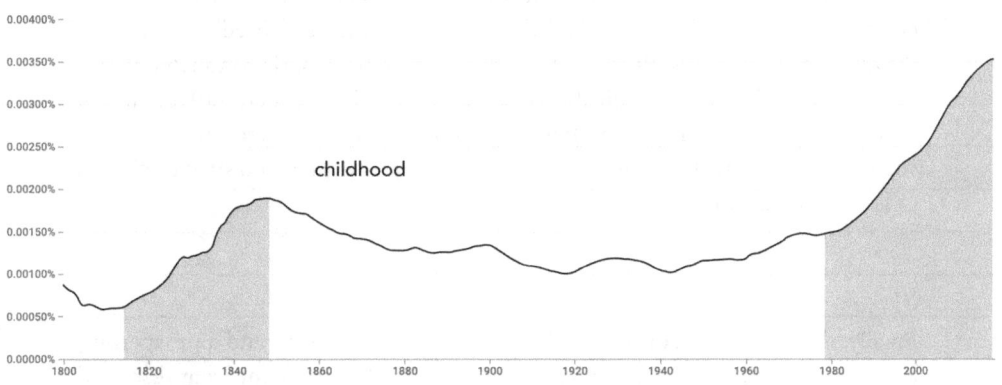

4.3: TWO ERAS OF NURTURING: PLOTTING INCREASES IN THE FREQUENCY OF *CHILDHOOD* IN AMERICAN ENGLISH (2019) CORPUS, NGRAM DATABASE, 1800–2019.

over more chapters, than the slow departure of Eva in *Uncle Tom's Cabin* or the demise of Beth in *Little Women*. Children also exhibited a spontaneity that echoed the teachings of Transcendentalists like Emerson, Amos Bronson Alcott, and Lydia Maria Child. Alcott, the father of Louisa May, noted that a child was "a Type of Divinity," adding, "Herein is our nature yet despoiled of none of its glory."[65] Among these spirited, and sometimes wild, children were Pearl in *The Scarlet Letter*, Garnet "Nettie" Seabright in *The Discarded Daughter*, Effie in *The Planter's Northern Bride*, and (before she became a young woman) Capitola Black in *The Hidden Hand*.

Depictions of youth also highlight middle-class society's evolving view of the proper balance between obedience and freedom. Two bestsellers of the early 1850s—Warner's *The Wide, Wide World* and Cummins's *The Lamplighter*—confront the reader like stern schoolmarms, delivering sermons that instruct girls on the importance of submissiveness.[66] But the popularity of these lessons in humility, like the seeming triumph of domesticity, was deceptive. None of Warner's or Cummins's subsequent books sold as well as their first novels, and, more broadly, the trend in childrearing was toward liberality.[67] Loving guidance not coercion became the new watchword. The sharp decline in the usage of *obedience* during these years underscores that change.

Around midcentury, scholars conclude, gendered values came to shape childrearing. Anger, for example, was regarded as destructive for girls but useful for boys, at least in particular circumstances. Girls increasingly played with dolls, with sales rising strongly after the Civil War.[68] Another sign of gendered differences was the appearance of "bad boy" novels during these decades. Thomas Bailey Aldrich's *The Story of a Bad Boy* (1869) is sometimes considered the beginning of a series that would include Mark Twain's *Tom Sawyer*. However, Webb's earlier work, *The Garies and Their Friends*, which profiles young, spirited Charlie Ellis, fits well under this rubric. The "bad boys," as the narratives by Webb, Aldrich, and Twain make clear, were more scamps than miscreants and (the reader is assured) will become respectable men. In this literature, boys misbehaved while girls conducted themselves more sedately.[69] Qualifications, however, must hedge such stark contrasts. Often the most free-spirited children, like Pearl and Capitola, were female; writers such as Louisa May Alcott and Henry James repeatedly depicted strong-minded girls and young women.

VI

Finally, the changing economy with its incipient bureaucracy and a prosperous, largely rural middle class was also reflected in the developments that reshaped painting. Just as novelists moved beyond depictions of men communing with the divine, so painters no longer saw their mission as exalting God's handiwork. To fully understand the links between the evolving economy and painting, it is necessary to see how art between 1850 and 1870 both resembled and differed from the works completed from 1820 to midcentury.

Continuities were important. Landscape painting characterized both periods; these canvases appealed to the emotions of a middle class whose locus remained in the countryside. Contemporary art critics underscored the importance of the genre. In 1865, James Jackson Jarves observed that "The thoroughly American branch of painting, based upon the facts and tastes of the country and people, is the landscape."[70] Prominent among those depicting nature were six artists: Frederic Edwin Church, Albert Bierstadt, John Frederick Kensett, Sanford Robinson Gifford, Fitz Hugh Lane, and Martin Johnson Heade. Late-nineteenth-century critics labeled them "The Hudson River School," noting their themes and the influence of Thomas Cole, who had begun to paint the Catskills in the 1820s. But since the

4.1. THOMAS COLE, *NIAGARA FALLS*, 1830.

appearance of an influential 1954 article by art historian John Baur, modern writers refer to the group as "luminists," emphasizing their rich, atmospheric handling of light. Their inspiring canvases, with magnificent sunsets and breathtaking vistas, fit well with the worldview of a middle class that, since the 1820s, was proud of its prosperity, dominant position, and heartfelt sentiments.[71]

Luminist paintings, however, differ in substantial ways from the pre-1850 landscapes. Some scholars, it must be noted, challenge that assertion. They argue that Emerson and the Transcendentalists influenced Thomas Cole's successors as much as the master himself. Art historian Barbara Novak asserts that "the luminist looked at nature, as Emerson did 'with a supernatural eye,' and with a clarity that was for Thoreau 'as if I touched the wires of a battery.'"[72] But unlike Cole, none of these six painters spoke about God dwelling in Nature. Those who noted literary influences pointed not to Emerson but to a variety of authors; for example, the writings of Alexander von Humboldt, the Prussian naturalist and explorer, shaped Church's views.[73] The contrast between landscapes before and after midcentury is evident in two views of Niagara Falls, one by Thomas Cole completed in 1830 (ptg. 4.1) and the other by Church in 1857 (ptg. 4.2). Cole portrays the falls as part of God's grandeur. Two Native Americans, small figures in an expansive landscape, contemplate the scene, which includes not only the cataract, but also stately mountains, rich fall colors, and sunset-tinged clouds. By contrast, Church, working on an enormous

4.2. FREDERIC CHURCH, *NIAGARA*, 1857.

4.3. ALBERT BIERSTADT, *THE ROCKY MOUNTAINS, LANDERS PEAK*, 1863.

canvas (seven feet by three feet) confronts the viewer with the power of the falls. His painting combines the two qualities that, paradoxically, defined the landscapes of the 1850s and 1860s: a direct appeal to the emotions and an obsessive concern with detail.[74]

For a generation that wept over the death of Eva in *Uncle Tom's Cabin* and Beth in *Little Women*, luminist painting similarly targeted the heart—and often touched a vein of patriotic fervor. The *New York Times* reviewer remarked about Church's *Niagara*, "Having no visible standing place, the viewer is propelled giddily out over the rushing upper rapids at the Canadian brink of the falls to come full face with the terrifying spectacle of the great river hurtling into the gulf."[75] Many also regarded such paintings through the lens of American triumphalism. Viewing Church's *Niagara*, an editorialist observed, "It is inspired not only by the irresistible cataract, but... by the broad continent we call our own, by the onward march of civilization, by the conquering of savage areas."[76] A writer commented in similar, glowing jingoistic terms about Bierstadt's *The Rocky Mountains, Lander's Peak* (1863) (ptg. 4.3), "He who lays his ear to the wild grass may perhaps hear the distant tramp, not of buffaloes, but of civilization, coming like an army with banners."[77] Church and Bierstadt marketed their "Great Pictures" with single-picture exhibitions, tours, reproductions, and brochures. The popularity of these two artists and the prices they commanded far outpaced the other luminists. Henry Tuckerman's encyclopedic *Book of the Artists* (1867) devotes a chapter each to Church and Bierstadt, discusses Kensett and Gifford as part of a survey of landscape painters, and ignores Lane and Heade.[78]

Perhaps surprisingly, the luminists also paid fastidious attention to detail in constructing their emotion-laden pictures. These artists grounded their grand vision on careful observation rather than reverence for an in-dwelling God. Tuckerman remarks that Church "goes to nature, not so much with the tenderness of a lover or the awe of a worshipper, as with the determination, the intelligence, the patient intrepidity of a student; he is keenly on the watch for facts, and resolute in their transfer to art."[79] In an age of scriveners and train schedules, observers cherished those details. In 1860, twenty-four-year-old Samuel Clemens gazed reverently upon Church's *The Heart of the Andes* when it was exhibited in St. Louis. He told his brother Orion, "I have just returned from a visit to the most wonderfully beautiful painting which this city has ever seen.... I have seen it several times, but it is always a new picture.... We took the opera glass, and examined its beauties minutely, for the naked eye cannot discern the little wayside flowers, and the soft shadows and patches of sunshine, and half-hidden bunches of grass and jets of water which form some of its most enchanting features."[80] Tuckerman similarly praises Bierstadt, Kensett, and Gifford for the accuracy of their observations. Still, for all these artists such careful transcription was only a means to an end. Gifford pointedly noted that "attention should not be diverted to details, if the feelings are to be appealed to."[81]

The reign of landscape painting ended with seeming abruptness after 1870 as the locus of middle-class America shifted from rural expanses to small towns. Those artists, such as Bierstadt, who continued to paint as they had in the 1860s, found that interest in their work and the prices they commanded fell off sharply.[82]

PART TWO
The Genteel Era

As the nation shifted from a largely rural economy to one dominated by towns, sentimentality gave way to gentility. The new worldview emerged from tight-knit communities of like-minded White Protestants who now could readily observe each other's behavior.

Several questions organize this overview. To begin, why call the period from 1870 to 1919 "the genteel era"? After all, these were years of rapacious robber barons, violent attacks on African Americans in the South, massive immigration, labor strife, angry farmers, pestilent tenement houses, campaigns for women's suffrage, relentless warfare against Native Americans, and eventually, extensive reforms. But for White, middle-class Americans, and for the novelists and painters whose works provide key documents for this study, the genteel outlook initially towered above all other concerns. These virtues shaped the views of the bourgeoisie.

Second, what were those virtues? The list was lengthy and evolved during these fifty years. Core values included the importance of caring communities and loving families, Protestantism, chastity, temperance, honesty, separate spheres for men and women, optimism, a belief in progress, the elevation of Anglo-Saxons, and good manners. While some of these traits dated back to the sentimental period and earlier, and many would survive into the modern era, only between 1870 and 1919 was this cluster of beliefs dominant in middle-class America.[1]

The genteel era and genteel values, however, have a bad name—an opprobrium only partly deserved. Too often, these years are seen through the eyes of those who early in the twentieth century fought against what they considered a rigid, judgmental worldview. In 1911, the Spanish-born, American-raised philosopher George Santayana described the "genteel tradition" as outmoded and oppressive. Speaking in Berkeley, California, Santayana discussed the two sides of the American character. "The truth is," he noted, "that one-half of the American mind, that not occupied intensely in practical affairs, has . . . floated gently in the back-water, while, alongside, in invention and industry and social organization, the other half of the mind was leaping down a sort of Niagara Rapids." "The one is all aggressive enterprise," he declared, "the other is all genteel tradition."[2]

Many observers in the 1910s and 1920s echoed Santayana's condemnation. For example, in 1922, Harold E. Stearns edited a volume of thirty essays by younger authors—all of whom railed against the older values. Stearns himself commented, "The genteel tradition . . . has stolen from the intellectual life its own proper obsessions, gaiety and laughter." Van Wyck Brooks dismissed the novels of the preceding era: "But what immediately strikes one, as one surveys the history of our literature during the last half century, is the singular impotence of its creative spirit."[3] (Middle class themselves, these critics rarely put forth a more trenchant argument: that genteel values subordinated women and excluded those outside the charmed circle of affluent Anglo-Saxon Protestant society. Throughout that half-century, writers typically condescended to African Americans, immigrants, Native peoples, and in general, the less wealthy.)

The critique put forth by Santayana and his followers was only half right, even discounting its ethnocentricity. It captured this ideology in its final, rigid, and defensive years. But it ignored the "better angels" of this tradition, most in evidence when these beliefs first coalesced. Those more positive traits included a concern for others, an emphasis on loving families, and optimism.

Third, how fully did these small-town values reflect the composition of society? Unquestionably, America became more urban during these years. By 1880, the percentage of the population living in places with 2,500 people or more had climbed to almost 28 percent (from 15 percent in 1850). New England and the Middle Atlantic states, where many writers and readers lived, boasted an urban majority in the 1870s. Before 1870, a preponderance of stories, like Catharine Maria Sedgwick's *Hope Leslie,* James Fenimore Cooper's Leatherstocking series, and Harriet Beecher Stowe's *Uncle Tom's Cabin,* had rural settings. Now tales unfolded in towns and cities.

Still, small towns loom larger in genteel-era literature than their relative weight in the population might suggest. The prominence of those communities was particularly marked in the literature of the 1870s, with many novels set in peaceful villages, such as Spindlewood in Stowe's *Pink and White Tyranny* (1871), St. Petersburg in Twain's *The Adventures of Tom Sawyer* (1876), Deephaven in Sarah Orne Jewett's 1877 novel of the same name, and South Bradfield, the home of the heroine of Howells's *Lady of the Aroostook* (1879). The grip of those irenic towns on popular culture remained strong even after 1900. Works such as Kate Wiggin's *Rebecca of Sunnybrook Farm* (1903) and

Eleanor Porter's *Pollyanna* (1913), both set in small, caring communities, topped the bestseller lists in the early twentieth century.

These villages, however, never held more than a sliver of the population. In 1870, merely 6 percent of Americans lived in communities with between twenty-five hundred and ten thousand people, and by 1890 that figure had inched up to only 8 percent. Far more individuals inhabited cities of fifty thousand or more and their numbers grew more rapidly (13 percent in 1870, 19 percent in 1890).[4] Still, books about harmonious towns, like the dime novels about the Wild West, attracted a large audience in the industrializing nation. Middle-class city dwellers enjoyed reading about simpler times, just as working-class readers relished the tales of Western derring-do. Mark Twain, who set most of his novels in small towns, observed in 1882: "Human nature cannot be studied in the cities except at a disadvantage—a village is the place. There you can know your man inside and out—in a city you know but the crust; and his crust is usually a lie."[5] Twain himself had moved with his wife, Olivia Langdon, to a city—Hartford, Connecticut.

Although relatively few Americans lived in villages, a "small town" feeling shaped the lives of many in the middle and upper classes during the early genteel era. A national market and standardized goods did not prevail until the 1880s, and even then many enclaves were left untouched. Well-off city dwellers often lived within tight-knit circles. Booth Tarkington's popular books, *Penrod* (1914) and *The Magnificent Ambersons* (1918), detail the existence and then gradual decline of such neighborhoods within a fictional Midwestern city. Edith Wharton, who was born in New York City in 1862, remembered the society of her childhood as a friendly, caring community, giving no hint that she lived in a teeming metropolis of more than a million. "The small society into which I was born," she remarked, "was 'good' in the most prosaic sense of the term." She fondly recalled its "moral treasures."[6]

The same, relentless social forces that laid the foundation for the genteel era would hasten its demise. Urbanization continued apace, with most of the gains recorded in the larger centers. By 1920, cities of fifty thousand or more accounted for 31 percent of the American population, while villages, like Twain's fictional St. Petersburg, held only 9 percent. Industrialization conjured into being an army of poorly paid workers. Many of these laborers were immigrants who arrived speaking strange languages and practicing faiths alien to Protestants. The dramatic changes in society encouraged ever more vocal dissent among novelists and painters.[7]

Fourth, what was the relationship between novelists and painters and gentility, particularly as the nation moved further away from the heyday of small towns? Throughout the era, bestselling authors and acclaimed artists enthusiastically broadcast traditional values. These novelists populate their novels with kindly, pious men and women who contentedly inhabit separate spheres. Good-hearted children leap from these pages— girls and boys who are loveable even when they get into scrapes and are admirable when they overcome adversity. Such works include John Habberton's *Helen's Babies* (1876), Margaret Sidney's *Five Little Peppers and How They Grew* (1880), Frances Burnett's *Little Lord Fauntleroy* (1886), Wiggin's *Rebecca of Sunnybrook Farm*, Porter's *Pollyanna*, and Tarkington's *Penrod*. Religious themes also shape novels, including Lew Wallace's *Ben-Hur* (1880) and Harold Bell Wright's *The Shepherd of the Hills* (1907). Only a few popular books, such as Mark Twain's *Adventures of Huckleberry Finn* (1884) and Edith Wharton's The *House of Mirth* (1905), defy these norms.[8]

Beginning in the 1880s, however, reflecting a society that was being transformed by industrialization and immigration, dissenting novelists increased in number and significance. These authors, although only occasionally making the bestseller lists, are the individuals most studied today. Among White authors, their ranks include William Dean Howells, Henry James, Sarah Orne Jewett, Kate Chopin, Frank Norris, Theodore Dreiser, Twain, and Wharton. They challenged genteel assumptions about women, piety, and human nature. Around the turn of the century, they were joined by a group of African American novelists whose work represents the most significant outpouring of Black writing since the 1850s. These individuals, including Charles Chesnutt, James Weldon Johnson, and Paul Laurence Dunbar, criticized the racism, always endemic in genteel society, that now worsened with the campaigns for disenfranchisement.

Still, few individuals attacked all aspects of gentility, and every rebel in some way remained entangled in traditional values. Stephen Crane's *Maggie: A Girl of the Streets* (1893) presents a very ungenteel heroine: a Bowery girl who falls into prostitution. But the story concludes with a genteel quandary: can such an individual, whose life was buffeted by larger forces, gain admission into heaven? It was the sort of question that the author, who was the son of a Methodist minister, might well ask. Similarly, Frank Norris, often seen as a fierce critic of his times, affirms male dominance and sexual modesty.[9] The two principal dissenting literary movements of these years—Realism, which flourished in the 1880s, and Naturalism, whose heyday came during the ensuing two decades—are best viewed within this framework of rebellion and accommodation. These writers were like schools of brightly colored fish swimming in a genteel sea. To understand them fully, we must look both at the individuals and their environs.

The mavericks were themselves caught up in a relentless pace of change with the revolutionaries of one decade becoming the stodgy conservatives of the next. In her autobiography, *A Backward Glance* (1933), Edith Wharton remarks that "Howells was the first to feel the tragic potentialities of life in the drab American small town; but the incurable moral timidity which [he displayed] again and again checked him on the verge of a masterpiece."[10] She was equally critical of James, whom many praised for venturing into new areas. Wharton notes that "James was essentially a novelist of manners, and the manners he was qualified by nature and situation to observe were those of the little vanishing group of people among whom he had grown up."[11] But Wharton herself, who shocked many defenders of the genteel with books such as *The House of Mirth* and *Ethan Frome* (1911), was hardly immune to these shifting viewpoints. A new generation of authors, including F. Scott Fitzgerald, criticized her as hopelessly old-fashioned. She protests: "The amusing thing about this turn of the wheel is that we who fought the good fight are now jeered at as the prigs and prudes who barred the way to complete expression—as perhaps we should have tried to do, had we known it was to cause creative art to be abandoned for pathology!"[12]

During this half century, painting, responding to the same social currents, boasted its own traditionalists and dissenters. Here too the rebel painters of one decade seemed tame ten years later. And here too the bolder spirits faced an indifferent or resentful public. Thomas Eakins, who beginning in the 1880s pushed portraiture into new dimensions, sold few paintings. Similarly, after the turn of the century, hostility greeted those artists, like Alfred H. Mauer, Frank Stella, and Arthur Dove, who brought abstract painting to America.

Finally, how should the period be dated? A few writers place the commencement of this era well before the Civil War. Curiously, Frederic Carpenter calls Hawthorne, "one of the greatest writers of the genteel tradition," while Henry Nash Smith sees him as a leading opponent of gentility.[13] William Dillingham, more typically, dates the start of this epoch after the sectional conflict, though he brings it to a close in 1900. The "genteel tradition," he notes, "refers to that literature in America from about 1870 to the turn of the century which was molded by the 'polite' manners and the rigorous taboos of refined society."[14]

Clearly, there's no normative answer, but dating the genteel tradition from the 1870s makes the most sense. Some facets of this ideology, like piety or the emphasis on two spheres, appeared earlier. But with its concern for manners and (at least initially) for caring neighbors, the advent of the genteel tradition must be set in the 1870s with the triumph of small-town life. This ideology provided a new response to the question, "What defines the middle class?" From the 1780s to 1870, the answer was *emotion*, the ability to empathize with the joys and trials of others. After 1870, as the middle class settled down into towns and close, caring communities in larger cities, the answer became *good manners* and an adherence to a well-defined code of behavior. Writers like Henry James, William Dean Howells, and Mark Twain now lambasted sentimentality, signaling the passing of an era. Appeals to the reader's emotions became less common, even in bestselling novels.

Most scholars (Dillingham, noted above, is an exception) agree that the genteel tradition broke down in the 1910s, which is when Santayana put forth his critique. Katrina Bachinger singles out that decade in her study of those "who took part in the 'Gunpowder Plot' that blew up the old parliament of critical values."[15] In *The End of American Innocence: The First Years of Our Own Time, 1912–1917,* Henry May agrees, offering an equally violent metaphor: "We can still see the massive walls of nineteenth century America apparently intact, and then turn our spotlight on many different kinds of people cheerfully laying dynamite in the hidden cracks."[16] With those detonations, the emerging hegemony of big cities, and the advent of a world in which business dominated middle-class life, the genteel era finally gave way to the modern period.

5
Cheerful Towns, Troubled Cities, 1870–1890

William Dean Howells was distressed by the transformation of the country he so cherished. Howells, born in 1837, grew up in a small southern Ohio community, and remembered his early years as blissful. "I can recur to the time only as a dream of love and loving," he remarked, adding, "I must still recur to the ten or eleven years passed in Hamilton as the gladdest of all my years."[1] Howells's worldly ascent was rapid: he learned the printer's trade, read widely, wrote furiously and well, and by his early twenties, landed a job for a Republican newspaper in Columbus. A campaign biography of Lincoln helped him secure the post of US consul in Venice, and after the war the *Atlantic* recruited him as an editor. Novels and essays followed, as did a new, well-paid position at *Harper's Monthly*. Despite his success, Howells was saddened by the feeling that the loving world of his childhood was disappearing, overwhelmed by industry and inequality. In 1888, he informed his friend Henry James: "After fifty years of optimistic content with 'civilization' and its ability to come out all right in the end, I now abhor it, and feel that it is coming out all wrong in the end, unless it bases itself anew on a real equality."[2]

Others shared Howells's rueful perceptions. During the eventful twenty years from 1870 to 1890, America changed from a country of small towns and caring communities to an industrial nation shaped by a flood of immigrants and an expanding proletariat. Many writers and painters, including those whose works were most popular, celebrated the virtues that gave small-town life its optimistic cast. But others, like Howells, dissented and increasingly, in their books and paintings, criticized the norms shaping genteel society.

I

The striking shift in the outlook of middle-class observers reflected the evolution of the economy during this twenty-year span. Although the 1870s and 1880s resembled each other in the rapid expansion of rail lines and industry, in fact the two decades embodied different stages in the process of growth. Understanding those differences illuminates the changing world that novelists, painters, and others perceived and described.

Historian Robert Wiebe calls the United States in the 1870s a "society of island communities." He states: "Small-town life was America's norm in the mid-seventies," and observes, "however much they [townsfolk] actually relied upon an outside world, they still managed to retain the sense of living largely to themselves." Subsequent decades, Wiebe notes, brought "the breakdown of this society."[3]

Wiebe's contentions remain apt: much of the United States in the 1870s was characterized by communities only loosely connected to the national economy. Although small towns accounted for only a sliver of the population, compassionate, isolated settlements, even within larger cities, characterized the decade. Shopkeepers and craftspeople were usually familiar faces. The neighborhood butcher dressed meat; a nearby brewer supplied beer; a long-established baker provided bread. General stores provided a jumble of unbranded goods without fixed prices. Even local time was a patchwork; clocks in adjoining towns might be an hour ahead or behind. Freight shipments required a welter of arrangements, as goods were shifted from one short line to another or (in the South and West) from trains running on one gauge to another.[4]

All that changed in the 1880s as links of iron and steel tied together disparate communities, creating a national market. By the beginning of the decade, four great trunk lines had emerged, moving freight smoothly from the East Coast to the Midwest. In 1883, far-sighted (and self-interested) railroad executives established a set of uniform time zones, and in 1886 shifted track widths throughout the nation to the eastern standard of 4' 8 1/2". The various lines added over seventy thousand miles of track—more than ever before. All was in place for companies to create standardized brands for a national market.[5]

Entrepreneurs seized those opportunities. A wave of consolidation and innovation transformed the goods Americans purchased. Continuous flow production allowed the Campbell Soup company of Camden, New Jersey, and H. J. Heinz and Company of Pittsburgh to sell foodstuffs across the country. Cincinnati soap maker Procter & Gamble turned out two hundred thousand cakes of Ivory soap each day. The advent of the modern refrigerated car helped Chicago meatpackers like Gustavus F. Swift sell their products across the North. The Pillsbury brothers marketed their milled grain widely; James Duke cornered the market on machine-made cigarettes; brewers Pabst and Schlitz of Milwaukee, and Anheuser and Busch of St. Louis developed national brands of beer. John D. Rockefeller had begun his campaign to control the refining and marketing of kerosene with his domination of the Cleveland market in the 1870s. Now his firm, Standard Oil, moved aggressively to establish a national monopoly. References to *corporate power* marked their high point in the 1880s (fig. 9.3).[6]

New approaches to marketing accompanied increases in production. Merchant capitalists erected department stores, luxurious "palaces of consumption," in the major cities. These stores had pre–Civil War antecedents, but only in the 1880s did they assume their modern form, with a focus on retail customers, fixed prices, and lavish displays. Mail-order sales reached the smallest towns. Aaron Montgomery Ward had founded his business in 1872, and in the 1880s marketed wares nationwide. In 1887, Ward's catalogue featured 540 pages with over twenty-four thousand items. Advertising became important as never before, boosting department store sales and national brands.[7]

The rise of big business also transformed the workforce, conjuring a disgruntled proletariat and an army of clerks. The number of workers increased by 1.4 million in the 1880s, more than double the rise in the preceding decade. About 40 percent of industrial operatives lived below the poverty line, laboring in abhorrent conditions—squalor that fueled the soaring number of strikes. The Knights of Labor, a loose organization that attracted workers from a variety of industries, ballooned from fifty thousand members in 1884 to over seven hundred thousand in 1886, before collapsing with the repression that followed the bloody clash in Chicago's Haymarket Square. Industrialization also attracted immigrants: over five million individuals arrived in the 1880s, easily the highest level for any decade in the nineteenth century. The number of clerical workers, a group that included bookkeepers, typists, and secretaries, doubled in the 1880s.[8] The industrial nation of 1890 stood worlds apart from the "island" communities that characterized society in 1870.

II

The dramatic changes in the economy profoundly influenced fiction and art. In the 1870s, an array of novelists and painters exalted small-town values, elaborating an outlook that for many would continue to have strong appeal. Beginning in the 1880s, however, dissenters presented the harsher realities of a changing nation and explored new roles for women and men.

The blessings that seemed to shower on the "island communities" in the 1870s infused mainstream fiction with optimism, creating a template that would guide popular writers for the next half century. This was an idyll untroubled by the repression of Blacks in the South and Native Americans in the West. Ignoring such conflicts, the works of this decade highlighted caring villages and loving families. Mark Twain's *The Adventures of Tom Sawyer* (1876) epitomizes that outlook. When Tom, Joe Harper, and Huckleberry Finn were feared lost, "the villagers conducted their concerns with an absent air, and talked little; but they sighed often." And when the boys reappeared in the middle of a church service, the townsfolk mightily rejoiced. The hymn, the "Old Hundred swelled up with a triumphant burst" until "it shook the rafters." Huck, the local outcast, benefitted from that warmth. "Aunt Polly, it ain't fair," Tom remarks, "Somebody's got to be glad to see Huck." His aunt replies: "And so they shall. I'm glad to see him, poor motherless thing."[9]

That caring world marks other novels of the 1870s. Sarah Orne Jewett's *Deephaven* (1877) relates the adventures of two Boston women, Kate and Helen, who summer in the small Maine town where Kate's great-aunt Miss Brandon had lived. The two visitors receive a characteristically warm welcome. Helen notes: "When it was known that we had arrived in Deephaven, the people who had known Miss Brandon so well . . . seemed to consider themselves Kate's friends by inheritance, and were exceedingly polite to us, either in calling upon us or sending pleasant messages. Before the first week had ended we had no lack of society."[10] The inhabitants of Spindlewood, the village that provides the setting for Harriet Beecher Stowe's *Pink and White Tyranny* (1871), are cut from the same cloth. Not only John Seymour, the well-off protagonist, but also most residents care deeply about community programs. The narrator remarks: "The people had, of their own accord, raised a subscription for a library, which was to be presented to John that day, with a request that he would select the books."[11]

In the 1870s, evil typically came from outside the virtuous community of Anglo-Saxon Protestants. In *Tom Sawyer*, the "half-breed," Injun Joe, is the villain. In Henry James's *The American* (1877), a Parisian family, the Bellegardes, radiates malevolence. Similarly, in James's *Daisy Miller* (1879), an Italian, Giovanelli, tries to seduce the innocent American heroine, a pursuit that leads to her death.[12] In *Pink and White Tyranny*, Stowe blames the French for the bad habits American women display. The narrator intones, "France, unfortunately, is becoming the great society-teacher of the world."[13]

In these gardens of gentility, drunkenness was a noxious weed. Few individuals are more loudly condemned in Howells's *The Lady of the Aroostook* (1879) than the drunkard Hicks. His behavior shocks Lydia Blood, a small-town girl and the "lady" of the title. The narrator comments: "She could hardly have seen in South Bradfield a man who had been drinking. Even in haying, or other sharpest stress of farmwork, our farmer and his men stay themselves with nothing stronger than

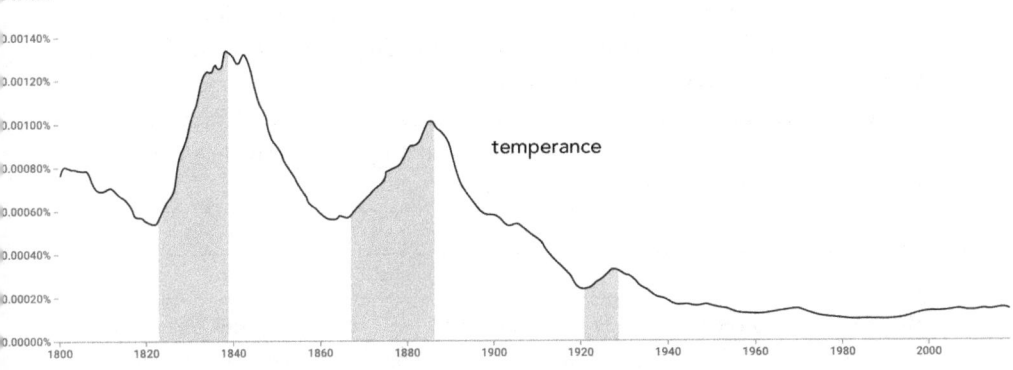

5.1: THREE PERIODS WHERE THE FREQUENCY OF *TEMPERANCE* ROSE SHARPLY IN AMERICAN ENGLISH (2019) NGRAM DATABASE, 1800–2019.

molasses-water, or, in extreme cases, cider with a little corn soaked in it; and the Mill Village, where she had taught school, was under the iron rule of a local vote for prohibition."[14] In *Tom Sawyer*, the schoolboys mock the schoolmaster who had become "pretty well fuddled."[15] And in Spindlewood, where Stowe's *Pink and White Tyranny* is set, John Seymour leads a successful temperance campaign. He rejoices: "It was a complete victory; and, since then, there hasn't been a more temperate, thrifty set of people in these United States."[16]

Figure 5.1, which shows periods in which the use of *temperance* rose sharply, maps the three prolonged battles against drink: the antebellum reform movement, the crusade in Victorian America, and Prohibition in the 1920s. The Woman's Christian Temperance Union, founded in 1873, led the charge in the late nineteenth century.

The harmonious world of the 1870s even welcomed industrialists: the antagonisms evident in later decades had not yet emerged. James's *The American* sets wealthy Christopher Newman in a favorable light. To be sure, Newman lacks a deep appreciation of culture, a deficiency he is determined to correct. But he has risen in the world, as James makes clear, thanks to an admirable constellation of strengths: "[M]any of the qualities that make a great deed were there: the decision, the resolution, the courage, the celerity, the clear eye, and the strong hand." He is a moral individual who "never [had] a stomach for dirty work. He was blessed with a natural impulse to disfigure with a direct, unreasoning blow the comely visage of temptation."[17] Similarly, Stowe in *Pink and White Tyranny* praises industrialists

John and Grace Seymour: "The brother and sister had been left joint heirs of a large manufacturing property, employing hundreds of hands, in their vicinity; and the care and cultivation of these work-people, the education of their children, had been most conscientiously upon their minds."[18]

In sum, the novels of the 1870s portray communities that were loving, temperate, respectful of business leaders, and troubled only by malevolence that came from a few evil-minded outsiders.

III

By contrast with the sunny villages of the 1870s, the towns and cities of the 1880s were darkened by the pallor of industrialization, conflict between the classes, and the widening gap between rich and poor. The impact of those changes emerged only gradually, however, and did not affect all novels. Three well-known writers—Twain, Howells, and James—highlight the powerful currents reshaping the nation. Although their styles and subject matter differed, all three authors chronicle the declension of a once harmonious society.

The changing perspective that marked Twain's work is visible in three novels: *The Prince and the Pauper* (1881), *Adventures of Huckleberry Finn* (1884), and *A Connecticut Yankee in King Arthur's Court* (1889). *The Prince and the Pauper* takes only a small step away from the world of the 1870s, although at first blush it seems a far less genteel novel than *Tom Sawyer*. In this tale of exchanged identities in sixteenth-century England, individuals are burned alive, women and children are beaten, and gangs of thieves roam the land. However, the violence is muted by being set in the distant past, and the novel concludes with identities restored, evil punished, and good rewarded. The "prince," Edward Tudor, who learns first-hand about cruelty from his adventures as a poor boy, becomes a wise monarch. "The reign of Edward VI," the narrator intones, "was a singularly merciful one for those harsh times."[19] Contemporary observers and literary scholars agree that *The Prince and the Pauper* never strays far from genteel norms. *Harper's* pronounced the book "charged with a generous and ennobling moral," while the *Atlantic Monthly* said the story was "pure and humane in purpose."[20]

Twain's next book, *Huckleberry Finn*, while set in the same village of St. Petersburg as *Tom Sawyer*, takes still another stride away from the cheerful world of the 1870s. No longer is evil the exclusive province of outsiders. Miss Watson, who owns Jim, is a slave trader; Judge Thatcher takes Huck's $6,000 for a "consideration" of $1, with no assurance the funds will be returned; Huck's father, "Pap," who was never depicted in *Tom Sawyer*, suffers delirium tremors, imprisons and beats Huck, and dies in a brothel that is washed down the river in a flood. Poverty is evident:

rats infest the home of Judith Loftus, a sometime slave catcher. Farther down the river, the Shepherdsons and Grangerfords, handsome, church-going gentry, are engaged in a homicidal feud.

Even Huck's decision to free Jim challenges the genteel world. "All right, then, I'll *go* to hell," Huck declares, when he resolves to help the runaway slave gain his freedom. Readers in the 1880s, as today, agreed Huck's actions were right. But Twain is also asserting that at times moral individuals must defy social norms. (Huck's dealings with Jim involve, of course, issues of race. The next chapter looks more closely at race relations in the genteel era.) While *Huckleberry Finn* sold well, some guardians of culture expressed their ire. "If Mr. Clemens cannot think of something better to tell our pure-minded lads and lasses," sniffed Louisa May Alcott, "he had best stop writing for them."[21]

Still, *Huckleberry Finn* does not present as decisive a departure from gentility, as Twain's later novels would. The ending, with Tom's return to the story, mutes the book's critique. The reader learns that Miss Watson has freed Jim, the Judge has kept Huck's money safe, and Pap has died. Huck's moral fervor fades, as Tom propounds his elaborate plans to liberate Jim (cruelly withholding the information that Jim is already free). Modern critics, with few exceptions, are troubled by the ending, but Twain's contemporaries, deeply immersed in genteel values, were not. Richard Hill remarks: "Of the dozens of 1885–1900 essays I have examined, only one critic, T. S. Perry, disliked the ending in particular." Most agreed that Tom was portrayed in a "delightfully humorous fashion."[22] But it is hard not to see Tom's romantic schemes as silly, and even mean-minded. The light-hearted pranks of the 1870s fit poorly with the harsher world of the 1880s.[23]

Connecticut Yankee still more incisively critiques the industrializing nation and makes clear Twain's mounting pessimism. Hurled back into the sixth century, Hank Morgan strives to bring the benefits of nineteenth-century civilization to Arthurian England. He introduces newspapers, the telegraph, railroads, bicycles, and soap, and speaks nobly about democracy and human dignity. But the destructive, imperious nature of the modern world overwhelms all such benefits. Morgan chooses "The Boss" as his title, and readily and sometimes capriciously kills those who displease him. The final orgy of slaying begins when Launcelot corners the newly established stock market, angering other knights. The nobility and church condemn Hank and attack his fortified enclave. Morgan responds by using electrified fences and Gatling guns to kill twenty-five thousand knights.

Three novels by Howells—*A Modern Instance* (1882), *The Rise of Silas Lapham* (1885), and *A Hazard of New Fortunes* (1889)—present a similar progression, mirroring the deepening social conflicts of the 1880s. *A Modern Instance* tells the story of newspaper reporter Bartley Hubbard and his wife who move from the small

Maine town of Equity to Boston. Eventually their marriage collapses, and Bartley flees to Indiana. Amy Kaplan notes that, while critics have often focused on the couple's bitter divorce, an "equally modern" aspect of the work is the "rise of the mass media and its formation of a new kind of public."[24] With the soaring importance of advertising revenue, money has begun to corrode traditional values. While still in Equity, Hubbard transforms the local paper "upon the modern conception," turning it into a money-making gossip sheet.[25] In Boston, Hubbard agrees wholeheartedly with the editor Witherby, who declares, "I'm not going to contend that a newspaper should be run solely in the interest of the counting room. Not at all! But I do contend that, when the counting-room protests against a certain course the editorial room is taking, it ought to be respectfully listened to."[26] Howells contrasts Hubbard's aggressive capitalist values with the views of two old-fashioned moralists: Hubbard's father-in-law and the Boston lawyer Atherton.

The Rise of Silas Lapham marks still another step into the turbulent world of industrializing America. Silas's "rise" is a moral one; the book charts his financial decline from his eminence as a wealthy paint manufacturer hoping to enter Boston society, to his bankruptcy and return to Vermont. The novel explores the era's sometimes questionable business ethics. Silas had ousted his first partner but comes to regret his actions and offers restitution. Later, when Silas's business is failing, two prospective buyers knock on his door—but in each case he would have to deceive the purchaser. Although others urge him to grab the money, Silas refuses, leading to his downfall.[27] The novel also suggests the elite's fears of the restless lower classes. Wealthy Bromfield Corey frets about the large homes standing idle during the summer, remarking: "If I were a poor man, with a sick child pining in some garret or cellar at North End, I should break into one of them, and camp out on the grand piano."[28] An earlier draft was even stronger: Howells wrote about "applying dynamite" to those houses. And *Silas Lapham* documents the emergence of new immigrant groups. Jewish leaders persuaded Howells to delete antisemitic references before the work, which originally appeared in serial form, became a book.[29]

Even more than *Silas Lapham*, *A Hazard of New Fortunes* transports the reader into a world of labor strife and class conflict. The novel follows the activities of Basil March, who moves from Boston to New York to edit a magazine. An uneducated Pennsylvania millionaire, Jacob Dryfoos, bankrolls the publication; a fiery German socialist, Berthold Lindau, works for it as a translator; an unreconstructed Southerner, Colonel Woodburn, joins March's circle—all making for lively exchanges on the issues of the day. Dryfoos boasts of breaking a union, angering Lindau, who asks, "How much money can a man honestly earn without wronging or oppressing some other man?" and continues, "It is the landlords and the merchant princes, the railroad kings and the coal barons (the oppressors to whom you instinctively give the titles of tyrants)—it is these that *make* the millions, but no man *earns* them."³⁰ Woodburn too rails against Northern capitalists. The climax of the book is a streetcar strike. Lindau is beaten by the police and dies, while Dryfoos's son, who tries to calm the situation, is fatally shot.

Still, *A Hazard of New Fortunes*, while critical of industrial society, is no socialist tract. Howells passionately cared about the treatment of workers and the poor; despite the scorn of many, he demanded clemency for the anarchists convicted in the 1886 Haymarket Riot. But he placed his faith in discourse, not in revolution, and that spirit underpins the novel. In 1887, he wrote in *Harper's*: "Men are more like than unlike one another; let us make them know one another better, that they may all be humbled and strengthened with a sense of their fraternity."³¹

The same reflection of a changing society is evident in two works by Henry James: *The Portrait of a Lady* (1881) and *The Princess Casamassima* (1886). In several ways, *Portrait* steps beyond the optimistic world of the 1870s. The novel tells the story of Isabel Archer, who leaves Albany, New York, for Europe, spurns several suitors, receives a sizable inheritance, and weds Gilbert Osmond in a marriage that soon proves to be an unhappy one. James debunks the cheerful, romantic outlook that Isabel brings with her from America. Soon after she arrives in England, Isabel is introduced to Lord Warburton. "Oh, I hoped there would be a lord; it's just like a novel," she exclaims.³² The narrator summarizes Isabel's romantic mindset: "She spent half her time in thinking of beauty and bravery and magnanimity; she had a fixed determination to regard the world as a place of brightness, of free expansion, of irresistible action; she thought it would be detestable to be afraid or ashamed."³³ Her naivete proves dangerous. As one critic notes, "genuine knowledge of evil is fatally lacking in the girl's equipment for the quest on which she is about to embark."³⁴ In another departure from the optimism of the 1870s, the malevolent figures—Osmond and Madame Merle—are not foreigners, as they were in *The American* and *Daisy Miller*, but Americans residing in Europe.

Isabel's sustained commitment to Osmond and their marriage in the face of his cruelty and deceit also implicitly criticizes genteel values. Osmond cares little for Isabel or her views and is imperious in his commands. To Isabel's chagrin, he overrides his daughter Pansy's wishes and tries to marry Pansy off to Lord Warburton. Osmond weaves a circle of deceit about his daughter's birth, claiming that her mother died in childbirth, when in fact (as Isabel discovers) Pansy is the product of his affair with Madame Merle. Isabel also learns that Merle has manipulated her, persuading her to marry Osmond so they can gain her fortune. Given her painful awareness of these betrayals, Isabel's decision at the end of the book to return to Italy and Osmond after visiting a dying friend in England, discomfits most modern readers. "He was not one of the best husbands," Isabel reflects, "but that didn't alter the case. Certain obligations were involved in the very fact of marriage, and were quite independent of the quantity of enjoyment extracted from it."[35] Contemporary reviews suggest genteel critics approved Isabel's decision. Still, in setting traditional values against the background of a toxic marriage, James provides a discourse far removed from the loving families of the 1870s.[36]

Like other novels of the second half of the 1880s, James's *The Princess Casamassima* highlights the harm that industrialization has wreaked on society. In 1869, James moved to London, where the book is set, with the title character, Christina Light, like James, a transplanted American. The story follows Hyacinth Robinson from his earliest days to his career as a bookbinder, his friendship with Christina (who married an Italian noble and became the Princess Casamassima), and finally into his involvement in a shadowy revolutionary movement and suicide. The novel details the squalid conditions of the poor, observing that "the deep perpetual groan of London misery seemed to swell and swell and form the whole undertone of life."[37] And like Howells in *A Hazard of New Fortunes*, James gives socialists a voice; Eustache Poupin, one of Hyacinth's mentors, took part in the Paris Commune of 1871. However, neither James nor his hero ultimately favors violent change. During a trip to Paris, Hyacinth came to feel that preserving the glories of civilization was more important than railing against oppressors. "What was supreme in his mind to-day was not the idea of how the society that surrounded him should be destroyed," the narrator remarks, "it was, much more the sense of the wonderful, precious things it had produced, of the brilliant, impressive fabric it had raised." James's letters make clear that he shares these views.[38]

Other novelists joined Twain, Howells, and James in depicting the 1880s as a more troubled decade than the 1870s. Constance Fenimore Woolson's *For the Major* (1883) seems at first to present another happy genteel community, Far Edgerley. But as the novel unfolds, the reader discovers that the title character, the Major, suffers from dementia, while his wife and daughter engage in an elaborate charade to hide the truth from both their neighbors and the Major. The narrative also highlights his wife's tragic backstory in which her first husband absconded with their son. Mary Murfree's *The Prophet of the Great Smoky Mountains* (1885) depicts the hardscrabble life of moonshiners and others in the Tennessee mountains. George Washington Cable's *The Grandissimes: A Story of Creole Life* (1880) portrays the violent landscape of Louisiana in the early nineteenth century. Racial tensions, long-lived family feuds, and clashes between Creoles and Americans shape a tale of love and revenge. Helen Hunt Jackson's *Ramona* (1884) shows the harsh treatment of Native peoples after the Americans conquered California. And even Louisa May Alcott's *Jo's Boys* (1886), which concludes the saga of Jo Bhaer (née March), is less cheerful than its predecessor, *Little Men* (1871). In this final novel, one of Jo's charges, Dan, kills a man, is jailed, experiences redemption, and then is shot dead in the West.[39]

Many books of the 1880s depict a seismic change in the treatment of children, as the loving villages of the 1870s gave way to communities that no longer nurtured young people. The new realities are evident in the lives of Huck Finn and Buck Grangerford in *Huckleberry Finn*; Pansy in *Portrait of a Lady*; young Hyacinth in *The Princess Casamassima*; several children in *For the Major*; and others in *Jo's Boys*.

Finally, it must be noted that the emphasis on mounting social conflict reflects only one portion of the books the middle class read in these two decades. Looked at through the lens of bestsellers—novels that sold at least 375,000 copies in the 1870s and five hundred thousand in the 1880s—the landscape has a more cheerful and pious cast. Popular works applaud churchgoers. John Habberton's *Helen's Babies* (1876), which amply illustrates that religiosity, follows a bachelor who for some weeks must take care of his young nephews. The two boys are insatiable in their desire for stories—but only tales from the Bible. And, having lost their brother, they engage in charming discourses about heaven. In Alcott's *Little Men*, the boys go to church and learn how Christ cares for the poorest among us. Even *Tom Sawyer* testifies to conventional piety; respectable St. Petersburg is a church-going, Bible-reading community. Lew Wallace's bestseller, *Ben-Hur* (1880), interweaves the adventures of the hero and the life of Christ. Only *Huckleberry Finn* among the bestsellers defies this generalization, with an irreverence that displeased many guardians of the genteel.

The popular books that acknowledge the gap between rich and poor mute this conflict. Margaret Sidney's *The Five Little Peppers and How They Grew* (1881) shows how disparate classes can come together. Thanks to a friendship that develops among the children, wealthy Mr. King and his son adopt the impoverished Peppers, and the two families then live blissfully together in the Kings' large mansion. The many sequels underscore the popularity of this harmonious fantasy. Similarly, Frances Hodgson Burnett's *Little Lord Fauntleroy* (1886) unites the affluent and indigent. Cedric Errol, a poor boy growing up in New York, turns out to be the only heir of an English earl. While the earl hopes to make his grandson (who becomes Lord Fauntleroy) a proper aristocrat, Fauntleroy defies stuffy norms and teaches his grandfather the importance of compassion for all classes.[40]

Thus, the outlook of the middle class was divided, and particularly so in the 1880s. Many novels, and particularly ones that have entered the modern canon, limned the darker currents of an industrializing nation. But such volumes shared the stage with popular works steeped in genteel optimism.

IV

The activism of White women during the 1870s and 1880s is reflected in literature.[41] Some novels acknowledge the woman's movement, even when they regard it with ambivalence—or scorn. Wallace's *Ben-Hur* notes the existence of assertive women—but also shows the author's disdain for them. The book contrasts two women who might be drawn from the 1880s rather than the time of Christ. Iras is assertive and confident, while Esther is gentle, loving, and childlike; both vie for the hero's love. The narrator comments that Iras and Esther "were acquainted; this one was shrewd and worldly; the other was simple and affectionate, and therefore easily won." In the end, Iras proves deceitful, taking part in a treacherous scheme, while Ben-Hur falls in love with and marries Esther, who matures as a lovely woman.[42]

Stowe's *My Wife and I; or Harry Henderson's History* (1871) is similarly ambivalent, but Stowe's recognition of feminism in this work is significant, as she and her sister Catherine Beecher had long been among the leading traditionalists. The novel follows the adventures of Harry Henderson as he first dreams about then actively seeks a wife. Not surprisingly, the book praises gentle homemakers, like Harry's mother and Eva Van Arsdel, the woman Harry falls in love with and marries. But the work also presents an outspoken feminist, Audacia Dangyereyes, whom Barbara Bardes and Suzanne Gossett suggest is modeled after the reformer Victoria Woodhull.[43] Although Audacia is broadly satirized, the novel introduces two women who are favorably portrayed and, while hardly radicals, are determined to move beyond traditional roles. Both Harry's cousin Caroline and Eva's sister Ida resolve to become doctors. "In that profession," Caroline declares, "I don't doubt I might do a great good, be very happy, have a cheerful home of my own, and a pleasant life work."[44]

Henry James also demonstrates an awareness of the woman's movement, even as he shies away from backing those protests. Before arriving in Europe, Christopher Newman, hero of *The American*, "had thought very little about the 'position' of women, and he was not familiar either sympathetically or otherwise, with the image of a President in petticoats."[45] In *Portrait of a Lady*, James gently mocks Isabel's friend Henrietta Stackpole, a reporter who is "in the van of progress." She had come to Europe to "write a series of letters . . . from the radical point of view—an enterprise the less difficult as she knew perfectly in advance what her opinions would be and to how many objections most European institutions lay open."[46] Only at the end, when Harriet falls in love, marries an Englishman, and decides to stay in England, does James soften her portrait.

With *The Bostonians* (1886), James devotes a full novel to the woman's rights movement and on balance is critical of the campaign. The work is shaped by a love triangle in which Olive Chancellor, an austere Boston woman's rights crusader, and her distant cousin, Basil Ransom, a handsome Mississippi lawyer, compete for the affections of Verena Tarrant, a young, attractive individual who delivers electrifying speeches on women's issues. In general, outspoken women come across poorly. Olive, for example, "hated men, as a class," while Verena is malleable, with her views shaped by others, first by her father then by Olive.[47] Basil scoffs at these reformers, observing about women in general, "My plan is to keep you at home and have a better time with you there than ever."[48] Neither the Southerner Basil, who at one point is compared to John Wilkes Booth, nor the humorless New Englander Olive, can be considered spokespersons for James. Still, as Bardes and Gossett suggest, "the plot tends to confirm Basil's judgements."[49] In the climactic scene, Basil, who is determined to take Verena away from Boston and her life as public speaker, arrives at the Boston Music Hall just before she delivers a major address. He demands she leave with him, and Verena, though flustered by the request, acquiesces.

More broadly, James's fascination with, but ultimately negative view of assertive women is evident in his heroines: they are headstrong and attractive, but deeply flawed in self-destructive ways. The independence of these women can be endearing. Daisy Miller spurns the counsel of the Americans in Rome. She tells one older man: "I have never allowed a gentleman to dictate to me, or to interfere with anything I do."[50] In *Portrait*, Isabel Archer defies the conventional, rejecting marriage proposals from two wealthy, eligible men. Equally independent-minded, Princess Casamassima leaves her husband and uses her wealth to support a group of conspirators. But daring as these women may be, they all have a grave failing: they make foolish choices in the men they pursue. Daisy's involvement with Giovanelli leads to her death. Isabel Archer's marriage to Gilbert Osmond condemns her to lifelong misery. The princess falls in love with the self-centered revolutionary Paul Muniment. Cruelly, he tells her: "I *do* consider that in giving your money—or rather, your husband's—to our business you gave the most valuable thing you had to contribute."[51] By repeating the same tale over and over again (and Verena Tarrant fully fits this pattern), James is telling the reader: admire these lovely independent souls all you want, but they lack the wisdom to manage their lives.

Other writers are far more sympathetic to the woman's movement. Louisa May Alcott's *Little Men: Life at Plumfield* (1871) continues the story of Jo's marriage and career. In this sequel, Alcott contrasts two ten-year-old girls: Meg's daughter, Daisy, and Annie "Nan" Harding, who comes to Plumfield for an education. Daisy is feminine; she "knew nothing about women's rights; she quietly took all she wanted." Nan, on the other hand, wants to be a healer, and Jo encourages her in that pursuit.[52] Alcott's next novel, *Work: A Story of Experience* (1873) explores

Christie Devon's life. Christie asserts her right to work early in the novel, telling her aunt, "there's going to be a new Declaration of Independence... I mean that being of age, I'm going to take care of myself." But Alcott does not yet endorse suffrage. Christie attends a meeting where women "demand the ballot before one-half of them were quite clear what it meant, and the other half were as unfit for it as any ignorant Patrick bribed with a dollar and a sup of whiskey."[53]

Jo's Boys (1886) concludes the Plumfield saga and confirms Alcott's development as a woman's rights advocate. Daisy and Nan are now twenty. Alcott remarks: "Daisy, as sweet and domestic as ever, was her mother's comfort and companion. ... Nan began to study medicine at sixteen, and at twenty was getting on bravely; for now, thanks to other intelligent women, colleges and hospitals were open to her." The two girls also differ in their views of suffrage, with Nan making the better case. Nan tells her friends, and the reader, "Daisy is a dear, but inclined to be an old fogy; so I stir her up; and next fall she will go and vote with me." While visiting Plumfield, Jo's father announces approvingly, "The woman's hour has struck."[54]

Other novels criticize the restrictions on women. Cable's *The Grandissimes* is set in New Orleans around 1805, seemingly uninviting terrain for a discussion of women's rights. But listen to the cutting insights of Clotilde, who faces genteel poverty after her father gambles away the family estate and is killed in a duel. "We are compelled not to make a living," she laments. "Look at me: I can cook, but I must not cook; I am skillful with the needle, but I must not take in sewing; I could keep accounts; I could nurse the sick; but I must not." She pointedly asks her mother: "Do you not see why it is that this practical world does not permit ladies to make a living? Because if they could, none of them would ever consent to be married. Ha! Women talk about marrying for love; but society is too sharp to trust them, yet!"[55] Sarah Orne Jewett's *A Country Doctor* (1884) also notes the limits on women's choices. The novel tells the story of Anna Prince, an orphan who is raised by the local doctor in her small country town and decides to pursue her mentor's profession. Anna must surmount the censure of townsfolk and relatives and, even more gravely, inform the young man she loves that they cannot marry—as the roles of wife and doctor are incompatible. She tells him that if they wed, "I know that the days would come when I should see, in a way that would make me long to die, that I had lost the true direction of my life and had misled others beside myself. You don't believe me, but I cannot break faith with my duty."[56] The graph for *strong women* reaches its nineteenth-century peak in 1890 before falling off in the 1890s (fig. 3.2).

Still, even during the height of the "first wave" of feminism, many works ignored the rights movement. Most bestsellers, such as Habberton's *Helen's Babies* and Sidney's *The Five Little Peppers and How They Grew*, were set firmly in the realm of the two spheres. Alice Mayton, whom the protagonist in *Helen's Babies* pursues and wins, "unhesitatingly leaves her destiny to be shaped by his love." Mrs.

Pepper has her hands full tending her large brood and shows little interest in broader demands.[57]

Mark Twain's novels of the 1870s and 1880s similarly feature traditional women. Some are warm-hearted and lovely, like Mary in *Tom Sawyer* or Sophia Grangerford and Mary Jane in *Huckleberry Finn*. Others chatter away, like Sandy in *Connecticut Yankee*. A few personify evil, for example, Tom Canty's grandmother and the prince's sister, the future "bloody Mary," in *Prince and the Pauper*, and Morgan Le Fay in *Connecticut Yankee*. Still, none has the depths of the leading male characters. Some critics argue that Judith Loftus in *Huckleberry Finn* and Roxy in *The Tragedy of Pudd'nhead Wilson* (1894) defy that rule.[58] The next chapter discusses Roxy and disputes the case for her exceptionalism. Judith Loftus also seems a weak peg for any Twain defense. Her appearance in the narrative is brief, her home is slovenly, and while she sees through Huck's disguise as a girl, she is taken in by the story he spins about being a runaway servant. Ruth Bolton, in *The Gilded Age: A Tale of Today* (1873), which Twain coauthored with Charles Dudley Warner, also might appear to be an exception to the generalization about Twain's women. Ruth, a young Quaker woman, resolves to become a doctor and defends her decision in spirited exchanges. What's most significant, however, is that Warner, not Twain, wrote the chapters depicting Ruth. The parts that Twain created feature weak, one-dimensional women such as Colonel Beriah Sellers's all-too accommodating wife.[59]

Although the women in William Dean Howells's novels seem to be more flesh-and-blood creatures than those in Twain's books, they too adhere to traditional roles. When young, they look for a husband; when married, they are helpmates. The *obiter dicta* that Howells scatters through his work document his belief in the separate spheres. For example, in *Silas Lapham*, the narrator explains: "Up to a certain point in their prosperity, Mrs. Lapham had kept strict account of all her husband's affairs; but as they expanded, and ceased to be of the retail nature with which women successfully grapple, the intimate knowledge of them made her nervous."[60]

Thus, the woman's rights movement remained a powerful force into the 1880s—even if it was often ignored in popular literature. The intensification of the suffrage campaign after 1900 was accompanied by racism and xenophobia, and a decline in these broader demands for women's rights. A vocal woman's rights movement, one that had a far-reaching impact on literature, would not reemerge until the 1970s.[61]

V

The genteel society of the 1870s and 1880s exalted the stable, dependable ideal of manhood, which had emerged at midcentury. A set of domestic and business-friendly virtues had elbowed aside the credo of the self-made man. Playing and watching sports became an approved outlet for individuals in small towns and

GENTEEL ERA

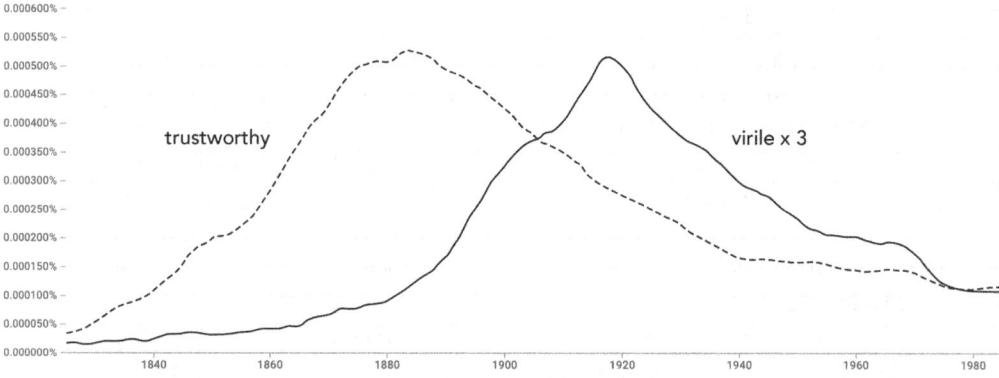

5.2: FREQUENCY OF *TRUSTWORTHY* AND *VIRILE* IN AMERICAN ENGLISH (2019) NGRAM DATABASE, 1825–1985.

cities. Parents, ministers, and peers encouraged behaviors that helped men flourish at home and at work. As historian Michael Kimmel notes, "In place of the scramble for wealth, men were advised to return to more stately and Protestant virtues, such as industry, usefulness, and thrift: to substitute virtues of personality for success; and do a good job."[62] Another student of masculinity, E. Anthony Rotundo, emphasizes the importance of trustworthiness: "Faith in a man's word loomed large in this world because so much significant business was done privately, man-to-man."[63]

During the 1870s and early 1880s, the best men were kind, good-hearted, caring, thoughtful, steady, and dependable, but not given to daring deeds, strikingly courageous, or physically strong. The use of *trustworthy*, which serves as a proxy for a variety of genteel virtues, soared during these years, reaching a peak in 1883 (fig. 5.2).[64] Novels presented sterling exemplars, including John Seymour in Harriet Beecher Stowe's *Pink and White Tyranny*; Harry Henderson in Stowe's *My Wife and I*; Harry Burton in John Habberton's *Helen's Babies*; Mr. King in Margaret Sidney's *The Five Little Peppers and How They Grew*; Tom Corey in William Dean Howells's *The Rise of Silas Lapham*; and Basil March in Howells's *A Hazard of New Fortunes*. By the late 1880s, as conditions worsened and the underpinnings of gentility weakened, a new more aggressive ideal would emerge. As figure 5.2 suggests, praise for those who were *trustworthy*, declined, while a contrary value, *virile*, rose—a development discussed in the next chapter.

VI

The changes in American society between 1870 and 1890 shaped not only fiction, but also the art of Winslow Homer and Thomas Eakins, the two best-known American painters of this era. While the two men differed in style and subject matter, both depicted the optimistic world of the 1870s and the more troubled times of the 1880s.

Born in Boston in 1836, Homer came into his own as an artist in the 1870s when he portrayed a loving, rural setting similar in spirit to the St. Petersburg of Twain's *Tom Sawyer*. Largely self-taught with no formal art lessons before age twenty-three, Homer apprenticed with a lithographer, and then during the Civil War served as a freelance illustrator for *Harper's Weekly*. His oil painting *Prisoners from the Front* (1866) garnered him early acclaim. In the 1870s, Homer's art took a new turn with his depictions of the joyous society of small-town and rural America. He painted happy children, usually boys, playing together as in *Snap the Whip* (1872) (ptg. 5.1). Other canvases portray a country school with well-behaved youngsters; a boy protecting his small brother from a threatening bull as they cross a field; children

5.1. WINSLOW HOMER, *SNAP THE WHIP*, 1872.

5.2. WINSLOW HOMER, *THE LIFE LINE*, 1884.

cuddling a kitten; boys sailing; and young people coming together for a clambake. Reviewing an exhibition of Homer's art, a contemporary critic aptly remarked: "The impressions of those children ... convey the idea of wholesome, hearty and artless youngsters ... [who are] yet full of that sense of dawning responsibility and amenableness to reason that makes the seriousness of childhood so wholly inscrutable."[65]

Another aspect of the harmonious, optimistic world of the 1870s was the confident women Homer painted. We see them teaching school, chatting with young men, undertaking farm chores, and reading novels. Nothing quite like these lovely, poised figures exists in earlier American art, in which women rarely were portrayed individually—except in commissioned portraits. An art critic writing in the *New York Evening Post* observed, "Here are the American shepherdesses which only Mr. Homer paints—self-possessed, serious, independent ... free-born American women on free-soil farms, who had had a free-school education, who read newspapers, who have the sense of ownership, and whose bodies are symmetrically and generously proportioned."[66] They are the counterparts of the quietly assertive women depicted in the 1870s by Alcott, Stowe, and Jewett. (Still another facet of this optimistic world are Homer's dignified portrayals of African Americans.[67])

In the early 1880s, Homer's art, along with American society, grew unmistakably grimmer. Virtually every biographer sees the first years of the decade, and particularly his sojourn, 1881–82, in the small English fishing port of Cullercoats, as a turning point in his career. Children, sunny farmsteads, and attractive, leisured women—all disappear from his work. In their stead, Homer painted the stolid working women he observed on the beaches of Cullercoats and the grey sea behind them. In 1883, after his return to the United States, he closed his New York studio and moved to a house on the rocky peninsula at Prout's Point, Maine, where he would live until his death in 1910. During the 1880s, his Prout's Neck paintings typically showed men and women confronting an angry ocean. In *The Life Line* (1884), Homer depicts a dramatic rescue from a foundering ship (ptg. 5.2).[68]

The exceptions to the tempestuous seascapes that comprised the mainstay of Homer's work in the 1880s are intriguing. One set of more cheerful works came from the visits he made to Florida and the Caribbean; the other from the hunting and fishing trips, taken with his brother, in the Adirondack Mountains of upstate New York. These sunnier paintings, largely watercolors in contrast to his oil paintings of stormy seas, did not signal a return to the loving world of the 1870s. They feature no children, no fair maidens, no peaceful farmyards. Indeed, a few Caribbean scenes are as storm-tossed as anything viewed from Prout's Neck. Still, hunters paddle along tranquil waters and dappled trout leap from streams in Homer's North Woods pictures, while in his Bahama sketches dark-skinned West Indians hunt turtles on sun-filled beaches. Such scenes, I would contend, confirm rather than undercut the gloominess of Homer's vision after 1880. They resemble Washington Irving's "Sleepy Hollow," which presents a tranquil spot in a time of frantic change. There is joy, Homer's watercolors suggest, but only if you travel far from the somber locales that mark much of the eastern United States.[69]

Thomas Eakins's paintings also reflect the change from the optimistic, domestic society of the 1870s to the sullen, troubled world of the 1880s. Before scrutinizing those canvases, one must address the psychological explanation some art historians use to explain his work. These scholars argue that personal tragedies led Eakins to paint gloomy canvases. John Wilmerding remarks that Eakins's "critical fortunes or misfortunes found vivid expression in the faces who sat or stood before him, mirroring his own emotional and spiritual state."[70] Evidentiary problems, however, weaken this explanation. Henry Adams, who offers a book-length Freudian analysis of the artist, asserts that Eakins had an unhappy childhood—a conclusion other researchers dispute. Indeed, while somber notes mark Eakins's art only after the mid-1880s, several of the blows he received came much earlier. Those shocks include the death of his mother in 1872 and the widespread condemnation of his 1875 masterpiece, *The Gross Clinic*. A psychological explanation has at best limited applicability. Homer's art changed in parallel and dramatic ways from the 1870s

5.3. THOMAS EAKINS, *THE COURTSHIP*, 1876.

to the 1880s—and no biographer suggests that his reinvention mirrored personal trauma.[71]

The evolution of Eakins's art is striking. Between 1870 when Eakins returned from Europe and about 1885, the vast majority of his canvases were filled with happy domestic scenes or sunlit outdoor portrayals of men rowing, sailing, fishing, and hunting. While studying in Paris, he had set forth his agenda: "I love sunlight and children and beautiful women and men, their heads and hands, and most everything I see, and some day I expect to paint them as I see them."[72] Works from this period include *Baby at Play, Baseball Players Practicing, Max Schmitt in a Single Scull, Home Scene,* and *In Grandmother's Time. The Courtship* (1876) (ptg. 5.3), a consciously nostalgic picture, depicts a woman spinning—an unusual activity in the 1870s.[73]

After 1885, the domestic and sunny outdoor scenes virtually disappear, and Eakins turned almost exclusively to portraiture, with an emphasis on dark, psychological studies. Elizabeth Johns declares, "Thomas Eakins was a painter of portraits."[74] But only after 1885, as table 5.1 shows, is that assertion true. The portraits

5.4. THOMAS EAKINS, *PORTRAIT OF WALT WHITMAN*, 1887–1888.

Eakins completed in the 1880s and later years rarely depict happy individuals; some of his subjects appear on the verge of tears, others are caught in moments of deep contemplation, or are weakened by the ravages of age. More than one sitter rejected the final product. Eakins's portraits depict stormy inner tides just as Homer's seascapes portray the rough outer ones. The portrait of *Walt Whitman* (1887–88) is a good example of the gravitas marking these canvases (ptg. 5.4). (Whitman valued the likeness and the two men became good friends.) Eakins remarked that, in portraying Whitman, "I began in the usual way, but soon found out that the ordinary methods wouldn't do—that technique, rules and traditions would have to be thrown aside; that, before all else, he was to be treated as a *man*."[75]

TABLE 5.1. PORTRAITS AS PERCENTAGE OF EAKINS'S PAINTINGS[76]

1870–74	32.0
1875–79	38.9
1880–84	36.4
1885–89	73.7
1890–94	100.0
1895–99	85.4
1900–04	100
1905–09	94.3

6

The Edifice Crumbles, 1891–1919

Edith Wharton, like other writers in the first decades of the new century, was determined to present the sordid truth about lives once considered idyllic. She recollected in her autobiography: "For years I had wanted to draw life as it really was in the derelict mountain villages of New England. . . . In those days the snow-bound villages of Western Massachusetts were still grim places, morally and physically: insanity, incest and slow mental and moral starvation were hidden away behind the paintless wooden house-fronts of the long village street, or in the isolated farm-houses on the neighbouring hills." Unsurprisingly, proper folk denounced both *Ethan Frome* (1911) and *Summer* (1917), the two novels that emerged from Wharton's resolve. "When 'Summer' appeared," she noted, it "was received with indignant denial by many reviewers and readers; and not the least vociferous were the New Englanders who had for years sought the reflection of local life in the rose-and-lavender pages of their favourite authoresses." "'Ethan Frome,'" she added, "shocked my readers less than 'Summer': but it was frequently criticized as 'painful', and at first had much less success than my previous books."[1]

Between 1890 and 1919, the United States experienced wrenching changes brought on by industrialization, immigration, and wild swings in the economy, further undercutting the foundations of genteel society. Dissenting writers and artists ever more fiercely challenged prevailing beliefs. The rebels included Wharton, an important school of novelists, the naturalists, and several pathbreaking painters. African American authors pushed back against the upsurge in racial violence. The guardians of tradition did not go quietly: they spurned the books that depicted harsh realities and mocked "modern" art. The most popular authors affirmed the tenets of gentility and presented demeaning portraits of Blacks. Still, during these three decades, the dissidents steadily gathered strength, providing a broad critique that by the 1910s sounded the death knell for the genteel era.

I

Changes in the economy provide a crucial backdrop for the evolving outlook of the middle class. Business activity traced a broad arc: conditions worsened until about 1900, and then very gradually improved. For common folk, few periods in US history were more difficult than the last decade of the nineteenth century. Laborers, factory operatives, and skilled craftspeople were hit hard by a depression that began in 1893 and did not fully end until 1899. Some modern estimates place unemployment in these years as high as 18 percent. Armies of ragged men descended on cities and state capitals, demanding food and work. References to *tramps* hit an all-time high in 1896 before trailing off (fig. 10.1). Farmers also faced grave hardships. Agricultural prices, falling since the end of the Civil War, reached their nadir in the late 1890s. African Americans across the South, terrorized by violence and campaigns for disenfranchisement, confronted particular difficulties.[2]

The indifference or hostility of governments compounded those problems. Jane Addams, who in 1889 established a settlement house in a poverty-stricken Chicago neighborhood, reported: "The policy of the public authorities of never taking an initiative ... is obviously fatal in a neighborhood where there is little initiative among the citizens ... The streets are inexpressibly dirty, the number of schools inadequate, sanitary legislation unenforced, the street lighting bad ... and the stables foul beyond description."[3] A few governors were sympathetic to the poor, but most were not, nor was the federal government. In 1892, Pennsylvania state militia broke the strike at the Homestead Steel Works near Pittsburgh; two years later, federal troops and a court injunction ended the stoppage at the Pullman Works in Chicago. Supreme Court decisions restricted union activities, struck down railroad regulation, and declared oligopolistic corporate practices outside the purview of the Sherman Antitrust Act of 1890.[4]

While the first, unmistakable signs of improvement appeared around the turn of the century, many observers would not notice the change for another decade. Agricultural prices began a slow, steady climb, providing the basis for two decades of rural prosperity. Industrial output grew strongly. Just as significantly, consolidation transformed the corporate world, bringing benefits to workers as well as capitalists. Between 1897 and 1901, financiers combined thousands of smaller companies into larger ones. The new enterprises, like US Steel and International Harvester, sought stability in dealing with their competitors and workers. The National Civic Federation, formed in 1900, reflected these goals. Its membership included an impressive array of corporate titans and union leaders. The organization promoted labor agreements, limitations on child labor, and new safety standards.[5]

City, state, and national governments now took the first steps to check the ravages of industrialization. Municipal reformers instituted "Gas and Water Socialism," regulating an array of utilities. Thirty states outlawed child labor, and many adopted labor and fire-safety laws to lessen the danger posed by dangerous work conditions. Federal policies had a still broader impact. Theodore Roosevelt, who became president in 1901, finally secured meaningful railroad regulation, a step that farmers had long demanded. Thanks in part to the furor provoked by Upton Sinclair's *The Jungle* (1906), Roosevelt gained Congressional approval in 1906 for the Meat Inspection Act and the Pure Food and Drug Act. Working conditions remained abominable in many factories and mines, fueling the growth of radical labor unions and the Socialist Party. Still, during the first decades of the new century the country gradually became more prosperous, and the world of unregulated capitalism, where few voices defended employees and consumers, had come to an end.[6] The rise and fall of references to *corporate greed*, which peaked in 1908 (fig. 9.3), suggests both the unchecked behavior of corporate magnates in these years and the impact of the reforms directed at those TR called "malefactors of great wealth."[7]

Along with the broad swings in the economy, a second development—the continuing growth of cities—reshaped Americans' outlook. In 1890, the United States had four centers with over five hundred thousand people; by 1920, twelve places had surpassed that mark, and one in four Americans lived in metropolises of more than one hundred thousand. In 1920, slightly over half of Americans inhabited urban places—compared to just over a third in 1890. In New England and the Middle Atlantic states, three-fourths of the inhabitants were urbanites.[8] The growth of cities, with their polyglot populations, mix of religions, and lack of a larger sense of community, dissolved the homogeneity that had underpinned genteel values. Booth Tarkington's *The Magnificent Ambersons* (1918) profiles Midland (a fictionalized Indianapolis) over the course of many decades. Early in the new century, the automobile and streetcar changed Midland's geography, immigrants its makeup, while impersonal relations replaced the old close-knit ties. The narrator observes, "People no longer knew their neighbours as a matter of course: one lived for years next door to strangers—that sharpest of all changes since the old days—and a friend would lose sight of a friend for a year, and not know it."[9] A new world had emerged.

II

These tumultuous, difficult years led many to question the cheerful affirmations of gentility. The dissent that had begun in the 1880s now intensified. Any understanding of this new wave of protests must begin by examining an important group of writers: the naturalists, whose heyday lasted from 1893 to 1913. That analysis, in turn, requires an exploration of the critical literature. Most scholars today highlight four White men—Theodore Dreiser, Frank Norris, Stephen Crane, and Jack London—as leaders of the school. But that grouping is a construct. Observers at the beginning of the twentieth century did not single out the foursome, and only Norris called himself a naturalist. Only he spoke about the influence of Émile Zola, now considered the patron saint of this school. Even the term *naturalism* had a different meaning. It referred to the belief that scientific observation rather than divine revelation should underlie enquiries.[10]

The critic Vernon Parrington in 1930 was the first to label Dreiser, Norris, and Crane naturalists (London would be added later) and provide a modern definition of the term. Reflecting the biases of that time, Parrington included no male or female African American authors, or White female novelists, explicitly rejecting the claims of Edith Wharton and Willa Cather. Drawing from the work of the men he termed naturalists, Parrington limned the traits of this genre. In these novels, he notes, individuals are driven by "the deeper instincts, the endless impulses. The three strongest instincts are fear, hunger, sex." Moreover, "From much emphasis on animal impulses the naturalist may turn man into an animal." He also observed that the school was marked by a "bias toward pessimism" and "a philosophy of determinism."[11]

Later writers built upon Parrington's work, perpetuating his emphasis on Dreiser, Norris, and Crane, and adding London to that trinity in the 1950s. The works of these four men, steeped in pessimism and focusing on the less wealthy, became the touchstones for defining the genre. Critics welcomed into the naturalist fold a bevy of later writers, including many from the "proletarian" 1930s (such as John Steinbeck, James Farrell, and Erskine Caldwell) as well as more recent authors such as Cormac McCarthy.[12]

An edifice, even a long-standing one, erected upon a shaky foundation of bias and questionable assumptions cannot go unchallenged. The current view of naturalism does more to obscure than illuminate writing at the turn of the twentieth century. Two problems stand out. First, this approach privileges the work of four White male writers and diminishes the role of African Americans as well as female authors of any race. To be sure, most surveys of naturalism now mention Wharton, Cather, and Kate Chopin, as well as the African American Paul Laurence Dunbar. But adding names to the bottom of the list does not address the dominance of Dreiser et al. There is a need to set naturalism firmly in its historical context and *de-center* the four writers who now define the field. Imagine if instead of Crane, Norris, London, and Dreiser, the leading naturalists were Wharton, Chopin, and

Cather. The key traits of the genre would no longer be poverty, violence, pessimism, and a focus on the lower classes. Instead, social customs, the role of women, and the activities of the well-to-do would be foregrounded. The definition offered in the following paragraphs does not argue for that reversal, but it does urge that the foursome no longer be privileged.

Second, the temporal extension of naturalism conflates books from different periods and ignores the specific worldview of the "classic" naturalists. Individuals writing around 1900, but not in later eras, believed that scientific "laws" of heredity and environment governed human action. The belief in those immutable rules had deep roots in the difficult conditions present at the turn of the century. These writers and many of their peers doubted the ability of humans to guide their lives in the face of larger, sinister forces. After 1913, the return of prosperity and the impact of progressive legislation were like the spring sun melting the ice on a frozen river. Old ideas gave way; the gloomy fixities of Darwin and Marx yielded to the uncertainties of Einstein.[13]

If the traditional analysis is flawed, what interpretation better explains this genre? How can this literature be more fully grounded in its era? This chapter suggests redefining naturalist novels as *the works in which the "laws" of heredity or the impact of environment, or both, strongly influence characters' behavior.* This approach sets aside the critical baggage that has long shaped understandings of naturalism, and makes no assumptions about authors male or female, Black or White. It begins with no conclusions about whether naturalism is biased toward optimism or pessimism, lower-class or upper-class characters, bestsellers or more obscure works. As will be seen, this definition *broadens* the naturalist canon during the "classical" period, 1893–1913, and *excludes* most later works.[14]

This re-visioning also sets naturalism firmly within the intellectual framework that flourished at the turn of the twentieth century. Few "laws" were more persuasive for these writers than those they deduced from Darwinism, and particularly the idea of the "survival of the fittest"—a phrase coined by Herbert Spencer from his reading of Darwin.[15] While this approach no longer privileges Dreiser, Norris, Crane, and London, it certainly includes them. Their fiction provides important insights for any understanding of naturalism.

To begin, the works of these four men show the force of heredity and particularly the power of innate characteristics, sometimes transmitted through generations. For example, in Dreiser's *Jennie Gerhardt* (1911), we learn how bloodlines lead Jennie, the low-born heroine, to value the gifts that her wealthy lover provides. Dreiser explains, "From some far source, perhaps some old German ancestors, she had inherited an understanding and appreciation of all this."[16] Jack London's *The Call of the Wild* (1903), which tells the story of a powerful dog, Buck, kidnapped from California and taken to the Yukon, similarly illustrates the power of such ancestral traits. When Buck encounters the rough conditions of the north, "the domesticated generations fell from him. In vague ways he remembered back to the youth of the breed, to the time the wild dogs ranged in packs through the primeval forest and killed their meat as they ran it down."[17]

While the nature of these innate traits varied greatly, their force was unmistakable. In Norris's *McTeague* (1899), the title character repeatedly succumbs to his bestial nature. The narrator observes, "The brute that in McTeague lay so close to the surface leaped instantly to life, monstrous, not to be resisted."[18] Frank Cowperwood, whose career is traced in Dreiser's *The Financier* (1912), enters the world endowed with business skills: "He was a financier by instinct, and all the knowledge that pertained to that great art was as natural to him as the emotions and subtleties of life are to a poet."[19]

These novels also underscore the power of the environment, which sometimes appears to take on a life of its own. In Norris's *The Octopus* (1901), the growing and marketing of wheat shapes human lives. In the conclusion, Norris remarks: "*But the* WHEAT REMAINED. Untouched, unassailable, undefiled, that mighty world-force, that nourisher of nations . . . indifferent to the human swarm, gigantic, resistless, moved onward in its appointed grooves."[20] Dreiser and Crane single out the city as an oppressive or, for some, an energizing force. In *Sister Carrie* (1900), Dreiser depicts Carrie as the "victim of the city's hypnotic influence."[21] In *Maggie: A Girl of the Streets* (1893), Crane demonstrates how an unforgiving city, as well as a broken family and predatory men, constrict the heroine's world, leading to her suicide. As Crane explained to a friend, *Maggie* "tries to show that environment is a tremendous thing in the world and frequently shapes lives regardless."[22]

References to Darwinian ideas—the belief in a world where only the fittest survive—further highlight the role of environment. In Dreiser's *The Financier*, such rules benefit ambitious, talented Frank Cowperwood. When young Frank learns that a lobster has killed a squid in a local aquarium, he takes the lesson to heart. The incident "made a great impression on him," the narrator remarks. "It answered in a rough way that riddle which had been annoying him so much in the past: 'How is life organized?' Things lived on each other—that was it. Lobsters lived on squids and other things. What lived on lobsters? Men, of course! Sure, that was it! And what lived on men? he asked himself. Was it other men?"[23]

This emphasis on heredity and environment suggests a framework for analysis—one that reveals the breadth of naturalist writing in the twenty years after 1893. The three best-known novels Wharton wrote during these years bear the mark of this school. Darwinism shapes *The House of Mirth* (1905) and *The Custom of the Country* (1913). In *The House of Mirth*, when spiteful upper-class New Yorkers expel the heroine Lily Bart from their ranks, she finds herself ill-suited for any employment and eventually commits suicide. Wharton describes her plight in good Darwinian language: "Inherited tendencies had combined with early training to make her the highly specialized product she was: an organism as helpless out of its narrow range as the sea-anemone torn from the rock."[24] In *Custom of the Country,* Undine Spragg, who is all too willing to cast away conventions and husbands, flourishes, while Ralph Marvell, her first husband, sinks into despair and kills himself. Like Lily Bart, Ralph sees that heredity has kept him from responding to new conditions: "Gradually, he saw that the weakness was innate in him. He had been eloquent enough, in his free youth, against the conventions of his class; yet when the moment came to show his contempt for them they had mysteriously mastered him, deflecting his course like some hidden hereditary failing."[25] In *Ethan Frome* (1911), rural poverty keeps Ethan from his dreams, much as the Bowery defeats Maggie. Ethan reflects on his doomed life: "The inexorable facts closed in on him like prison-warders handcuffing a convict. There was no way out—none. He was a prisoner for life, and now his one ray of light was to be extinguished."[26]

Environment plays a powerful role in both Chopin's and Cather's novels. In Chopin's *The Awakening* (1899), a host of influences transform Edna Pontellier during her residence at Grand Isle on the Louisiana Gulf Coast and in New Orleans. They include the seemingly loose morals of the creole families, the music played by her friend, Mademoiselle Reisz, and the sea ("the voice of the sea is seductive.").[27] In Willa Cather's *O Pioneers!* (1913), the land itself shapes human lives, much as it does in Norris's *The Octopus.* Alexandra Bergson's involvement with the farmland of the Divide, a fertile region in central Nebraska, proves the key to her success: "For the first time, perhaps, since that land emerged from the waters of geological ages, a human face was set toward it with love and yearning . . . Her eyes drank in the breadth of it, until her tears blinded her. Then the Genius of the Divide, the great, free spirit which breathes across it, must have bent lower than it ever bent to a human will before."[28]

Among African American writers, Paul Laurence Dunbar stands out for the influence of naturalism in his novels, and particularly in *The Sport of the Gods* (1902). Much as in *Sister Carrie,* the city is a powerful influence. "To the provincial coming to New York for the first time, ignorant and unknown," the narrator explains, "the city presents a notable mingling of the qualities of cheeriness and gloom. . . . [S]omething will take possession of him that will grip him again every time he returns to the scene. . . . The subtle, insidious wine of New York will begin to intoxicate him." That "insidious wine" helps explain the downfall of the members of the Hamilton family, who come to New York after the father, Berry, is falsely accused of theft and jailed.[29]

Bestsellers demonstrate a similar ethos. In Winston Churchill's *The Crisis*, a tale of the Civil War and the bestselling book of 1901, the principal characters are linked to their ancestral pasts, much as Jennie Gerhardt channels earlier generations. The hero, Stephen Brice, observes Carl Richter, a German friend: "A trick of the mind opened for Stephen one of the histories in his father's library in Beacon Street, across the pages of which had flitted the ancestors of this blue-eyed and great-chested Saxon. He saw them in cathedral forests, with the red hair long upon their bodies. . . . And it seemed to him that in the end the new Republic must profit by this rugged stock."[30] Edgar Rice Burroughs's *Tarzan of the Apes* (1912) underscores the power of inherited traits. Tarzan, raised by apes, is the son of an English noble couple who were marooned on the coast of Africa and die while he is still an infant. Thanks to his bloodlines, young Tarzan is not cowed when he faces an angry gorilla: "In his veins . . . flowed the blood of the best of a race of mighty fighters."[31] Similar assumptions shaped Zane Grey's *Riders of the Purple Sage* (1912). The story, set in the West of the 1870s, turns on the battle between the Mormons and rancher Jane Withersteen, who is aided by two gunslingers, Bern Venters and Lassiter. The narrator explains Jane's explosive rage: "Her forefathers had been Vikings, savage chieftains who bore no cross and brooked no hindrance to their will. Her father had inherited that temper. . . . Jane Withersteen realized that spirit of wrath and war had lain dormant in her."[32]

Significantly, after 1913, few works highlight the influence of environment or heredity on fictional characters. Naturalism, as redefined in this chapter, had come to an end as American society gradually grew more prosperous and stable. Almost all the pre-1913 naturalists' later works—for example, Cather's *My Ántonia* (1918) or Wharton's *Summer* (1917) and *Age of Innocence* (1920)—lack the hallmarks of the genre. The same observation marks the "proletarian" novels of the 1930s often mentioned as naturalist works. For example, John Steinbeck's *Grapes of Wrath* (1939) is replete with lyrical passages about the social transformations that led the Okies to move west. But "larger forces" do not shape character. Ma Joad focuses on preserving the family, while Tom Joad and Jim Casy are "seekers," who ultimately find their purpose in helping others who are less fortunate. Links between modern writers such as Cormac McCarthy and the naturalists are even more tenuous.

This redefinition of naturalism highlights the strong connection between society and literature during the twenty-year span, 1893–1913. At no other time did individuals feel less in control of their lives and more in the grip of outside forces. These were years of raw, unregulated industrial capitalism; floods of seemingly unassimilable immigrants; and rapid, uncontrolled urbanization. The curve tracing Americans' belief in human potential, which had reached its apogee in the 1840s, sounded its nadir in 1900. More broadly, the naturalists, with their conviction that social laws shaped human behavior, struck a resounding blow against the foundations of genteel society. Their works undermined the assumption that free will and a beneficent deity governed the world.

III

Changes in society after 1890 also reshaped masculinity—challenging genteel-era norms. As conditions worsened in the 1890s, old definitions of manhood no longer served: a world defined by Darwinian struggle cried out for stronger men. Crude strength alone, however, could never satisfy genteel-era readers. The best men had to be also sensitive and caring. As Gail Bederman observes, "middle-class white men" constructed "powerful manhood in terms of both 'civilized manliness' and 'primitive masculinity.'"[33] Figure 5.2 shows that while *virile* rose sharply during these years, reaching a peak in 1917, *trustworthy*, even if on the decline, remained important.

Heroes combining the seemingly contradictory qualities of civilized and primitive masculinity delighted readers, and figure prominently in the bestsellers of the era. Other novels might have better reflected the travails of American men, but book purchasers spurned those tales. Few tracked Hurstwood's tragic demise in *Sister Carrie*; sales amounted to only 456 copies in the first year.[34] Nor could many wholeheartedly applaud Frank Cowperwood, the protagonist in Dreiser's *The Financier*. Cowperwood succeeds financially, but he cares little for the feelings of those around him, even abandoning his wife and children.

Four popular works help define the sensitive, "primitive man." The hero in Owen Wister's *The Virginian* is a steely-eyed cowboy. He hangs a friend caught rustling cattle, and guns down Trampas, a bully. But the Virginian (whose name is not given) can as easily comfort a crying child: the grateful mother "saw the baby grow quiet in the arms of the Virginian." The Virginian takes his new bride camping and prepares dinner: "He had brought much with him; but for ten minutes he fished, catching trout enough. When at length she came riding over the stream at his call, there was nothing for her to do but sit and eat at the table he had laid." He even cleans up after the meal![35]

Bern Venters and Lassiter in Grey's *Riders of the Purple Sage* are similarly strong and caring. While both kill bad guys in their effort to protect Jane Withersteen, both are remarkably domestic. After Venters falls in love with Bess Erne, whom he accidentally wounds, he nurses her back to health in a secluded canyon. Bringing several pieces of crockery to their campfire, he remarks, "Don't you think we needed something? That tin cup of mine has served to make tea, broth, soup—everything." Lassiter is equally thoughtful. He develops a warm friendship with Fay, an orphan Jane has adopted. Jane wonders, "How could Lassiter smile so at a child when he had made so many children fatherless?" He also helps Jane look after an elderly woman: "His great brown hands were skilled in a multiplicity of ways which a woman might have envied." Cathryn Halverson comments: "That the men in Grey's novel are drawn to the home demonstrates their civilized instincts, whereas the violence that accompanies this transition maintains their masculinity."[36]

Burroughs's Tarzan demonstrates the same balance. He is the proud killer of animals and (Black) men. Despite herself, Jane Porter is attracted to this richly muscled primitive man, and particularly so after he kills a menacing great ape: "When the long knife drank deep a dozen times of Terkoz' heart blood, and the great carcass rolled lifeless upon the ground, it was a primeval woman who sprang forward with outstretched arms toward the primeval man who had fought for her and won her." Tarzan, thanks to the noble lineage that shapes his actions, is more than a brute. After he carries Jane away, he places her "upon the soft grasses" of his bower, while he "stretched himself upon the ground across the entrance." When she awakes, he has brought her breakfast, "and with his knife opened and prepared the various fruits for her meal."[37]

Finally, John Thornton in London's *The Call of the Wild* is cut from the same cloth. He is beast-like himself when he rescues Buck from a cruel family: "Suddenly, without warning, uttering a cry that was inarticulate and more like the cry of an animal, John Thornton sprang upon the man who wielded the club." Moreover, Thornton "was unafraid of the wild. With a handful of salt and a rifle he could plunge into the wilderness and fare wherever he pleased as long as he pleased. Being in no haste, Indian fashion, he hunted his dinner in the course of the day's travel." But Thornton is also, as Buck quickly realizes, a loving man: "Other men saw to the welfare of their dogs from a sense of duty and business expediency; he saw to the welfare of his as if they were his own children, because he could not help it."[38]

Like naturalism, the cult of the primitive man faded as society grew wealthier. When Cole Porter wrote "Find Me a Primitive Man" in 1929 ("I could be the personal slave / of someone just out of a cave") new conceptions of masculinity predominated.

IV

Women became more independent in the three decades after 1890 and moved away from the stern restrictions of gentility. References to *strong women* were higher during the first two decades of the new century than they would be before the 1970s (fig. 7.1). Still, there is a need to strike a careful balance. Unlike the decades before

6.1. TWO PERIODS OF MATERNALISM: FREQUENCY OF *LOVING MOTHER* IN AMERICAN ENGLISH (2019) NGRAM DATABASE, 1820-2019.

1890, novels rarely mention women's rights; there is an odd disconnect between the suffrage campaign, which achieved success in 1920, and the literature of the period. But the advances women made were unmistakable. While the increase in shopping can be viewed with ambivalence, the gradual lifting of the stigma on adultery and even the critique of traditional motherhood reveals progress. A few authors also criticized patriarchy and portrayed feisty, independent women.

Some women now rejected their time-honored role of mother and helpmeet. The precipitous decline of *loving mother*, beginning in the late 1890s, illustrates this change (fig. 6.1). To be sure, there were kindly parents in the fiction of these years, particularly in the works of Willa Cather. But what is noteworthy is how many women abjured traditional roles. In Crane's *Maggie*, the mother is dissolute and vindictive. Ida Farange in Henry James's *What Maisie Knew* (1897) dislikes her child ("Mamma doesn't care for me," Maisie observes). In Chopin's *The Awakening*, Edna Pontellier labels her children her "antagonists," and does not let concern for them prevent her suicide. The novel also gently disparages Adèle Ratignolle, a beatific "mother-woman." Undine Spragg in Wharton's *The Custom of the Country* has no time for her son until she launches a custody battle to extort funds from her husband.[39]

With increased wealth, women in the late genteel era shopped more—a development that critics have variously assessed. Miriam Hansen declares that "for middle-class women" shopping "meant a liberation from the narrow confines of domestic space"; William Leach concurs, underscoring the "emancipating impact of consumer culture."[40] Novelist Robert Herrick is more cynical. In *Together* (1908), a fictional study of several couples, the narrator comments: "So Woman, no longer the pioneer, ... blossoms, as what? The Spender! She is the fine flower of the modern game ... The Man has the money, and the Woman has—herself, her body and her charm. She traffics with man for what he will give, and she pays with her soul." Lori Merish suggests a balance, underscoring the "limits of consumerism as a site of female power," and remarking that women were "both subjects and objects of exchange."[41]

What is clear is that consumerism runs through period novels like gold embroidery on a dark satin gown. Authors now celebrate the passion for finery—a far cry from *Pink and White Tyranny* (1871), in which Harriet Beecher Stowe portrays Lillie Seymour's love of "fine French dresses" as a moral failing. Fashion seduces Dreiser's women. In *Sister Carrie*, the heroine is entranced by the outfits she sees: "Fine clothes were to her a vast persuasion; they spoke tenderly ... 'My dear,' said the lace collar she secured from Partridge's, 'I fit you beautifully; don't give me up.'"[42] In *The Financier*, clothes glamorize Aileen Butler, who becomes Cowperwood's paramour, and in *Jennie Gerhardt* the humble protagonist is delighted when her wealthy lover outfits her: "Could this be really Jennie Gerhardt, the washerwoman's daughter, she asked herself, as she gazed in her mirror at the figure of a girl clad in blue velvet, with yellow French lace at her throat and upon her arms?"[43]

Rich fabrics drape Wharton's heroines while colorful tulles adorn their hats. In *The House of Mirth*, Lily Bart observes, "If I were shabby no one would have me: a woman is asked out as much for her clothes as for herself." The novel opens with Lily in debt to her dressmaker. Early in *Custom of the Country*, Undine Spragg and her mother visit stores hunting for elegant gowns. The reader learns they "had succumbed to the abstract pleasure of buying two or three more, simply because they were too exquisite, and Undine looked too lovely in them." Merish aptly observes, "As with Undine Spragg (*The Custom of the Country*), Lily Bart's passion for men is much less convincingly rendered than her passion for things."[44]

Women also benefited from the gradual lifting of the stigma on adultery. Society had long judged men less harshly for such transgressions. Few developments were more important in shattering the hegemony of genteel values than the changing approach to woman's misdeeds. Reading this literature, however, demands a note of caution. Many of the breakthroughs came in novels that sold poorly; bestsellers rarely criticized established views.

The process of change was gradual, with two works of the 1890s more affirming than challenging traditional views of adultery. The sad fate of the heroine in *Maggie* (1893) shows the cost of these infractions. When Maggie's adulterous affair is discovered, neighbors roundly condemn her and her family drives her out of her home—and ultimately, to her death. Chopin's *The Awakening* (1899) is another cautionary tale. The work was daring in showing Edna's Pontellier's sexual awakening. But Edna's liaison with Alcée Arobin, pursued despite friends' warning, brings despair, not pleasure. She walks to the beach to end her life, saying "over and over to herself: 'Today it is Arobin; tomorrow it will be someone else. It makes no difference to me.'"[45]

With the new century came fresh perspectives in the discussion of extramarital relations. Dreiser's *Sister Carrie* (1900) opens with what seems to be a genteel admonition: "When a girl leaves home at eighteen, she does one of two things. Either she falls into saving hands and becomes better, or she rapidly assumes the cosmopolitan standard of virtue and becomes worse." But as Jennifer Fleissner points out, "Despite Dreiser's rehearsal of these two familiar options for the novelistic heroine, they prove remarkably inadequate to the narrative arc of his own ingénue, Carrie Meeber." Enticed by material comforts, Carrie moves in with Charles Drouet. Her "average little conscience" troubles her, but not to the point of renouncing Drouet. The authorial voice questions accepted values: "For all the liberal analysis of Spencer and our modern naturalistic philosophers, we have but an infantile perception of morals." Carrie's approach to Hurstwood, who has also been wooing her, is more traditional. She is angered when she discovers he is married and agrees to live with him only if he divorces his wife and weds her, which he does in an arrangement that proves a sham.[46]

Dreiser's next two novels similarly challenge conventional beliefs. In *Jennie Gerhardt*, the heroine has adulterous relations with two wealthy men, and a child with one of them. But Jennie, whom Dreiser portrays as the spirit of purity, remains unsoiled by these ties: "She could not be readily corrupted by the world's selfish lessons on how to preserve oneself from the evil to come." As in *Sister Carrie*, the narrator attacks older views: "'Conceived in iniquity and born in sin,' is the unnatural interpretation put upon the process by the extreme religionist, and the world, by its silence gives assent to a judgement so marvelously warped. Surely there is something radically wrong in this attitude." *The Financier* (1912) also flouts tradition. Its Darwinian framework implicitly justifies Cowperwood's amorality. The financier delights in his affair with Aileen Butler, who shares his outlook: "Cowperwood's laissez-faire attitude had permeated and colored her mind completely. She saw things through his cold, direct 'I satisfy myself' attitude. . . . As for him, he saw nothing wrong with the sex relationship. Between those who were mutually compatible it was innocent and delicious." Not all readers agreed; a New York reviewer of Dreiser's novel remarked, "His hero has no more conscience or decency than a pig."[47]

Wharton also attacks genteel views of adultery. In *The House of Mirth*, false charges of illicit relations bring down Lily Bart. Discussing the novel in her autobiography, Wharton remarks: "A frivolous society can acquire dramatic significance only through what its frivolity destroys. Its tragic implication lies in its power of debasing people and ideals."[48] In *The Custom of the Country* (1913), Undine Spragg lands on her feet and has some claim to the reader's sympathy despite four marriages and a torrid affair. The critic Ariel Balter notes that in the novel "marriage is portrayed as nothing more than a calculated profitable investment." In the end, "society," despite its professed morals, accepts her back into its fold. The narrator observes, "It was only necessary to give people the time to pretend they had forgotten; and already they were all pretending beautifully."[49]

In *Summer* (1917), Wharton takes aim at the narrow morality of small towns. Charity Royall, pregnant with her lover Lucius Harney's child, rejects the judgements others offer. Harney, who will marry another woman, tells Charity, "I'm so sorry dear ... that this should have happened." Her response? "She threw her head back proudly, 'I ain't ever been sorry—not a minute.'" She rejects the censure of local moralists: "There was no sense of guilt in her now, but only a desperate desire to defend her secret from irreverent eyes, and begin life again among people to whom the harsh code of the village was unknown." She does make that new beginning and marries her former guardian.[50]

In Cather's *My Ántonia*, the proud, attractive heroine, Ántonia Shimerda, flourishes despite having a child out of wedlock. Although seduced and abandoned, she soon finds and marries a good man, who loves her daughter, Martha, "like she was his own." Together, they prosper and have ten more children. Martha grows up to marry well and have her own thriving family. By the end of the genteel era, the stigma of adultery, if not wholly effaced had lessened.[51]

Some authors also note the oppressive nature of patriarchy. Charlotte Perkins Gilman's short story "The Yellow Wallpaper" (1892) details a woman's descent into madness after her physician husband decides to treat her anxiety by locking her in a room and prohibiting her from working or seeing other people. The woman, who narrates her descent, comments, "If a physician of high standing, and one's own husband, assures friends and relatives that there is really nothing the matter with one but temporary nervous depression—a slight hysterical tendency—what is one to do?" *The Awakening* paints Léonce Pontellier as a similarly dominant male. Although Edna rebels by having an affair, she remains bound to Léonce. She tries to crush her wedding ring, "But her small boot heel did not make an indenture, not a mark upon the little glittering circlet."[52]

A handful of novels portray strong, independent women. The title character in *Iola Leroy* (1892) by the African American writer Frances Harper is a resolute, light-skinned woman who is rescued from slavery by Union soldiers, becomes a nurse, a salesperson in the North, and then returns to the South to help her people. Determined to improve herself, she remarks, "I have a theory that every woman ought to know how to earn her own living. I believe that a great amount of sin and misery springs from the weakness and inefficiency of women."[53] In *The Country of the Pointed Firs* (1896), Sarah Orne Jewett transports the reader to Dunnet Landing, a town populated by self-reliant, caring women, and ineffectual men.[54] Caroline Meeber in *Sister Carrie* must be added to the list of independent women, even though she makes no ringing pronouncements about female development and seeks work only when no longer supported by a man. Still, her success as an actor testifies to her remarkable grit and ability. The women in Willa Cather's novels are far more determined and successful than the men. In *O Pioneers!*, Alexandra Bergson is a better farmer, and simply a better person than her brothers. *My Ántonia* provides an array of female success stories. Lena Lingard becomes a sought-after dressmaker; Tiny Soderball makes a fortune speculating in land claims and running a lodging house in the Yukon; Mrs. Gardner owns and manages the best hotel in Black Hawk; Frances Harling stands out as a grain dealer; and Ántonia Shimerda teaches her husband ("a city man") how to farm.[55]

Such outspoken novels hardly characterize the period. None had sales that matched the bestsellers, in which women were typically more subordinate. But along with the new activities open to middle-class women, and the changing views of sexual relations, these works struck resounding blows against gentility. The edifice was crumbling.

V

African American novelists also critiqued genteel values and the assumption that non-Whites were inferior. But these protests came amid worsening race relations, particularly after 1890, and the drumbeat of stereotypical views in the works of White authors.

During the last decades of the nineteenth century, fiction by White novelists, with few exceptions, regarded people of color negatively. Southern writers like Joel Chandler Harris and Thomas Nelson Page populate their works with African Americans who are happy, loyal, ignorant, and often foolish.[56] Helen Hunt Jackson takes a similar, highly critical view of Native Americans. Jackson wrote *Ramona* (1884) to protest genocidal policies toward Indians in California. But as John Gonzalez suggests, the book views "human culture through the sequential stages of savagery, barbarism, and civilization," with Natives on that first rung.[57]

Mark Twain shares the condescension that White writers show to Blacks—a topic vigorously and voluminously debated by critics, with much of the scholarly discussion focusing on Jim in *Huckleberry Finn*.[58] The novel certainly makes the reader care about Jim as a person. It shows his love of family and kindness toward

Huck, and in those qualities, Jim resembles Uncle Tom in Stowe's novel. But Jim, like Uncle Tom, lacks the intelligence and the cognitive skills that these authors grant White people. Jim believes he was bewitched when he awakens and sees his hat on a tree where Tom and Huck placed it. After Huck's purported death, Jim is completely unnerved when he meets him (compare Tom Sawyer's calmer reaction to the same situation). Jim is fooled by Huck's story when they are briefly separated by a small island in their journey down the Mississippi, and he cannot perceive, as Huck does, the fraudulence of the "Duke" and the "Dauphin."[59]

Roxy in Twain's *Pudd'nhead Wilson* presents a similar picture, although she too has her advocates and detractors among scholars.[60] Roxy, like Jim, cares passionately about her child (until her son proves a total miscreant). But like other Blacks in Twain's work, her cognition is limited. For example, in advising her son, she stumbles over the concept of "percentage." She states, "tell 'em you'll pay 'em intrust, en big intrust, too—ten per—what you call it?" "Ten per cent a month?" "Dat's it. Den you take en sell yo' truck aroun', a little at a time, en pay de intrust."[61] No Whites and none of the protagonists in novels written by African Americans would ever sound so foolish.

George Washington Cable's *The Grandissimes* (1880) stands out during the genteel era as one of the few White-authored books to present Blacks in a favorable light. Although he was born into a slaveholding family and fought in the Confederate army, Cable became an advocate of racial equality and eventually fled to Massachusetts. *The Grandissimes*, set in New Orleans in 1803, not only details the depth of Southern prejudice but also presents several strong-minded Black characters. They include African Americans who openly mock their masters, and most memorably the unyielding slave Bras-Coupé, born "in Africa and under another name, a prince among his people." Bras-Coupé refuses to do field work, kills the "driver," and escapes into the swamps before he is finally captured and sentenced to death.[62]

During the 1890s and early 1900s, as campaigns for disenfranchisement swept across the South, violence against Blacks rose and racism intensified. As figure 4.1 illustrates, the use of *nigger* increased during these years, as did lynching. Almost every year between 1891 and 1901 over a hundred Blacks became the "strange fruit" hanging from Southern trees.[63]

Several writers voiced that new virulent outlook, with few authors more outspoken than Thomas Dixon, Jr. His novel *The Clansman* (1905), set during Reconstruction, became the basis for D. W. Griffith's 1915 movie, *The Birth of a Nation*. Gone are the happy, sometimes silly Blacks of earlier fiction. Instead, *The Clansman* depicts corrupt, self-serving African American lawmakers ("barbarism strangling civilization by brute force"), vengeful Northern politicians urging the freedpeople to take up arms, and in the climactic scene of the novel, the brutal rape of a White mother and daughter by savage Blacks ("a single tiger spring, and the black claws of the beast sank into the soft white throat and she was still"). The Ku Klux Klan emerges to right those wrongs.[64]

Bestsellers, frequently laced with reference to "primitive" African origins, perpetuate this mean spirit. Burroughs's *Tarzan* depicts Africans as cannibals and Tarzan as the proud slayer of these savages—often by hanging. He proclaims himself, "KILLER OF BEASTS AND MANY BLACK MEN." (Critic Gail Bederman calls Tarzan "a one-man lynch mob."[65]) The young protagonist of Tarkington's *Penrod* puts on a "show" with African American boys as the chief attraction. The sign reads: "SHERMAN THE WILD ANIMAL CAPTURED IN AFRICA, HERMAN THE ONE FINGERED TATOOD, WILD MAN VERMAN." Upton Sinclair's *The Jungle* portrays African Americans in Chicago in equally harsh tones: "One might see brawny Negroes stripped to the waist and pounding each other for money, while a howling throng of three or four thousand surged about, men and women, young white girls from the country rubbing elbows with big buck Negroes with daggers in their boots.... The ancestors of these black people had been savages in Africa."[66]

African American writers responded to these difficult times with the first significant outpouring of Black fiction since the 1850s.[67] Frances Harper's *Iola Leroy* (1892), written before the worst years of strife, is a surprisingly optimistic novel. In the conclusion, Iola announces, "My heart . . . is full of hope for the future. Pain and suffering are the crucibles out of which come gold more fine than the pavements of heaven."[68] Subsequent books by Black writers forcefully condemn White oppression. Charles Chesnutt's *The Marrow of Tradition* (1901) presents a fictionalized account of the 1898 riots in Wilmington, North Carolina—clashes that culminated in the slaughter of African Americans and the establishment of a White supremacist government. Chesnutt describes the White mob's unchecked rage: "'Kill the niggers!' rang out now and then through the dusk, and far down the street and along the intersecting thoroughfares distant voices took up the ominous refrain,— 'Kill the niggers! Kill the damned niggers!'"[69]

Other novels by Black writers similarly indict Southern Whites. James Weldon Johnson's *The Autobiography of an Ex-Colored Man* (1912) graphically describes how angry Whites capture and immolate a Black man. And while much of Dunbar's *The Sport of the Gods* (1902) is set in New York, the novel opens with a bitter denunciation of the prejudice of White Southerners who conspire to send an innocent African American to prison.

These novels challenge stereotypes by presenting a panoply of accomplished African Americans. Iola Leroy, who becomes a nurse, marries Frank Latimer, a doctor, who is also "a leader in every reform movement for the benefit of the community." The hero of Chesnutt's *The Marrow of Tradition* is William Miller, a Black physician educated in Paris and Vienna. Of all the doctors in the (fictional) town of Wellington, only he has the skills to save the son of Major Carteret—the leader of the campaign for disenfranchisement. *The Autobiography of an Ex-Colored Man* also includes a discussion of Black achievements, emphasizing music and dance. "In spite of the bans which musicians and music teachers have placed upon it," the narrator comments, "the people still demand and enjoy ragtime. One thing cannot be denied; it is music which possesses at least one strong element of greatness: it appeals universally."[70]

Finally, all these novels distinguish between educated, self-respecting African Americans, who are the natural leaders of their community, and lower-class Blacks, who are often shiftless and subservient. These books share the spirit of W. E. B. Du Bois's 1903 essay, "The Talented Tenth," which concludes, "The Negro race, like all other races, is going to be saved by its exceptional men."[71] In *The Autobiography of an Ex-Colored Man*, the narrator tours Washington, DC, with a Black physician, who comments, "You see those lazy, loafing, good-for-nothing darkies; they're not worth digging graves for; yet they are the ones who create the impressions of the race for the casual observer." The author, the text makes clear, shares those sentiments. In *The Marrow of Tradition*, Dr. Miller resents a group of farm laborers who enter the "colored only" car into which he has been forced: "personally, and apart from the mere matter of racial sympathy, these people were just as offensive to him as to the whites in the other end of the train." A note of ambiguity, however, shapes Johnson's novel. Susan Danielson comments that Miller is "discredited through a series of increasingly challenging reversals."[72] Perhaps. But at least a few of the lower-class Blacks are childish and subservient, while Miller and his dilemmas remain the author's focus. In *Iola Leroy*, some individuals rebuff Iola's efforts to teach literacy, complaining, "Oh, yer can't git dat book froo my head, no way you fix it. I know nuff to git to hebben, and dat's all I wants to know." *The Sport of the Gods* not only shows the many low-lifes in the Black community of New York, but also illustrates how quickly African Americans in the South turned against one of their own who ran afoul of White law. The narrator comments: "In the Black people of the town the strong influence of slavery was still operative."[73]

Even noting these distinctions within the Black community, novels by African American authors strongly criticized genteel assumptions about race. They too contributed to the unraveling of an orthodoxy in place since the 1870s.

VI

Similar changes were evident in the world of art. Two groups of painters, both inextricably tied to the new, bustling cities, joined the onslaught against genteel values. In the 1890s, the National Academy of Design in New York stood at the pinnacle of the art establishment, with its annual show serving as the arbiter of good taste. Approved canvases promoted sound morals and featured meticulously rendered scenes, often with classical allusions. The two finest artists of these years were marginalized figures: Winslow Homer was painting increasingly bleak seascapes at Prout's Neck, Maine, while in Philadelphia, Thomas Eakins, recently ousted from the Pennsylvania Academy, undertook penetrating portraits that rarely sold.[74]

The first set of dissidents, the Ashcan School, as modern critics call them, defied accepted norms by depicting the lives of the urban poor. Robert Henri, the

6.1. GEORGE BELLOWS, *CLIFF DWELLERS*, 1913.

6.2. MAX WEBER, *THE LIBERTY TOWER FROM THE SINGER BUILDING*, 1912.

leader of the group, declared, "In this country we have no need of art... as refined and elegant performance.... What we do need is art that expresses the *spirit* of the people of today."⁷⁵ Members of this coterie included George Luks, John Sloan, William Glackens, Everett Shinn, and George Bellows. Most had met as newspaper illustrators in Philadelphia, but soon after 1900, the group relocated to New York. When the National Academy rejected their canvases, they mounted independent shows in 1908 and 1910. The exhibitions attracted scoffers ("Is it fine art to exhibit our sores?") but also crowds of the curious, and a few purchasers.⁷⁶

These painters had common ground with naturalist authors—members of both groups explored the lives of the poorest city folk. The settings for paintings such as George Bellows's *Cliff Dwellers* (1913) (ptg. 6.1) resembled the scenes depicted by Crane, Dreiser, and Norris. Some canvases, much like contemporary novels, celebrated "primitive men," boxers, and wrestlers. And like their literary counterparts, these artists grew less interested in depicting hard times or the poor after 1913.

A second set of painters—American modernists—also challenged the art establishment. This group coalesced around Alfred Stieglitz's New York studio. Beginning in 1908, Stieglitz mounted a series of exhibitions of European avant-garde art, including works by Matisse, Picasso, Cézanne, and the Italian Futurist Gino Severini. Stieglitz's passion, reputation (as a leading photographer), and patronage attracted these talented individuals, some of whom were American born and others recent immigrants. Members of this coterie, including Arthur Dove, John Marin, Joseph Stella, Max Weber, and Marsden Hartley, had spent time in Europe admiring and absorbing recent developments.⁷⁷

Like shoppers at an exotic bazar, the American modernists selected from an enticing array of possibilities—the planarity and bright colors of the Fauves (like Matisse), the spatial reconstruction of the Cubists (like Picasso), the dynamic compositions of the Futurists (like Severini)—to reimagine the realities they saw around them. Stella, Weber, and Marin used these techniques to depict skyscrapers and bridges in innovative ways, as Weber's *The Liberty Tower from the Singer Building* illustrates (ptg. 6.2). Introducing abstract shapes, Dove recast images of the natural world, as did a newcomer to the group, Georgia O'Keeffe. When Stieglitz saw her work in 1916, he declared, "Finally a woman on paper!" (He fell in love with her as well as her art, and the two later married.) Although the modernists and the Ashcan School both rebelled against the art establishment, they denounced each other's work. The modernists labeled Henri's followers old-fashioned, while the Ashcan painters regarded Stieglitz's circle as elitist.⁷⁸

Emerging from this dissent and helping it coalesce was the 1913 Armory Show, which displayed a broad array of contemporary works. The newly formed

Association of American Painters and Sculptors organized the event, the most important exhibition of art ever staged in the United States. Perhaps half the thirteen hundred pieces featured at the New York Armory were European, largely French, and included a selection of paintings by Matisse, Gauguin, Cézanne, Van Gogh, and Picasso. Both Henri's and Stieglitz's circles were well represented. Visitors, sometimes puzzled or bemused, poured into the exhibit; almost three hundred thousand saw the show during its three-city tour in New York, Chicago, and Boston. The art establishment, however, was not amused. The *New York Times* labelled the modernists "cousins to the anarchists in politics," while students and teachers from the Chicago Art Institute, another bastion of the genteel, burned Matisse and the sculptor Brancusi in effigy. Still, in the aftermath of the Armory Show, new collectors of modern art emerged, new galleries opened, and new shows were regularly mounted. The annual exhibition by the National Academy of Design became not the gatekeeper for acceptable art, but simply another event in a crowded calendar.[79]

PART THREE
The Modern Era

Around 1920, American society and middle-class culture underwent still another far-reaching transformation. Two closely related changes birthed the new era. One was the rise of the great cities, whose dominance ended the grip that small towns had on the outlook of "middling folk." The other was the ascent of a business civilization that embodied hierarchy and preached conformity. The two developments, respectively, fostered freedom and encouraged repression, and together they shaped the culture of the modern era.

Cities, with their diverse populations, relative anonymity, and shrines to consumption, undermined the restraints of gentility and ignited a new sense of optimism. The rigid prescriptions of the genteel era could not long survive in this polyglot, raucous environment. From the 1920s to the early 1940s, these metropolises were, for middle-class Whites, places of excitement, economic advancement, and social diversity. Rich, poor, and "middling folk" lived together in seeming harmony. Approaching New York, Nick Carraway in *The Great Gatsby* (1925) observes, "The city seen from the Queensboro Bridge is always the city seen for the first time, in its first wild promise of all the mystery and the beauty in the world."[1]

With the city replacing the small town as the arbiter of culture, the earthen walls that had blocked powerful currents of change gave way. Language became more daring, even if from today's perspective the advances seem tame. The use of *damn* soared (fig. P3.1), while some novelists, like Ernest Hemingway, proffered dashes that allowed readers to fill in words not even alluded to in earlier novels. In *A Farewell to Arms* (1929), one soldier affirms, "To-morrow we'll sleep in the king's bed." His companion replies, "To-morrow maybe we'll sleep in——."[2] In *The Naked and the Dead* (1948), Norman Mailer introduced the word "fug" to show how real Americans spoke.

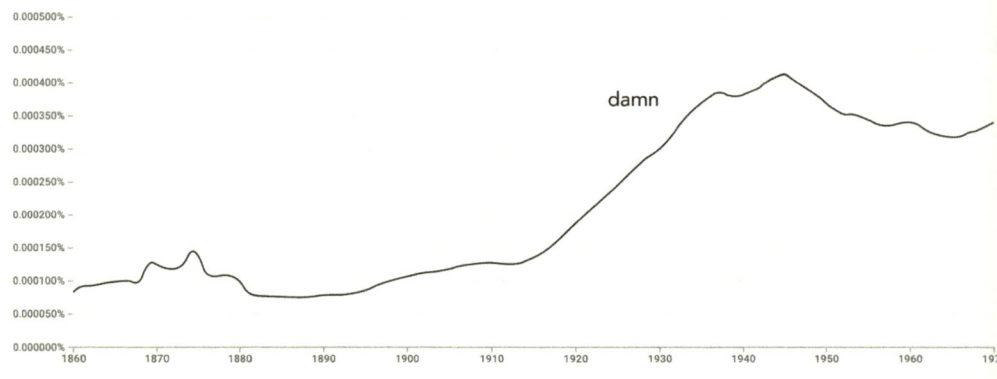

P3.1. FREQUENCY OF *DAMN* IN AMERICAN ENGLISH (2019) NGRAM DATABASE, 1860–1970.

Writers also discussed sex more openly. Terms such as *sex appeal*, *petting,* and *necking* became more common. F. Scott Fitzgerald's 1920 novel, *This Side of Paradise*, offers a fanfare for the era. The narrator observes that Amory Blaine "had come into constant contact with that great current American phenomenon, the 'petting party.' None of the Victorian mothers—and most of the mothers were Victorian—had any idea how casually their daughters were accustomed to be kissed."[3]

This newfound freedom, along with the affluence buoying the middle class, fostered a resurgent optimism. The genteel era had once nurtured such a positive outlook, but by 1890s, with factories and mills transforming the landscape, cheerful nostrums seemed

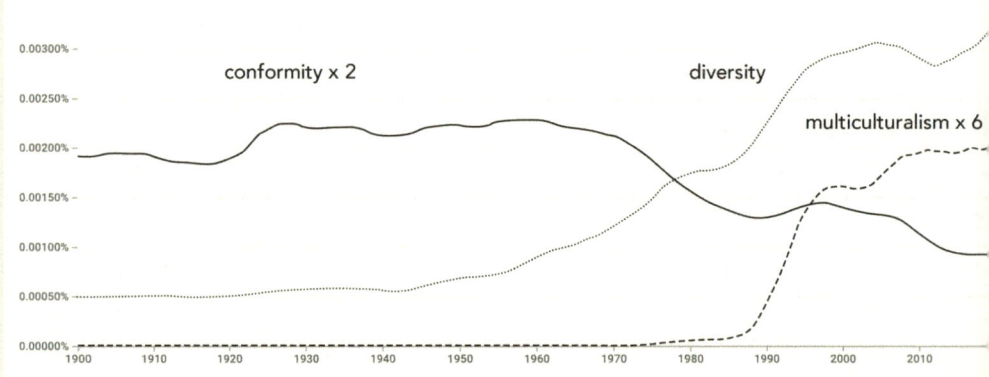

P3.2: FREQUENCY OF *CONFORMITY, DIVERSITY,* AND *MULTICULTURALISM* IN AMERICAN ENGLISH (2019) NGRAM DATABASE, 1900–2019.

MODERN ERA 133

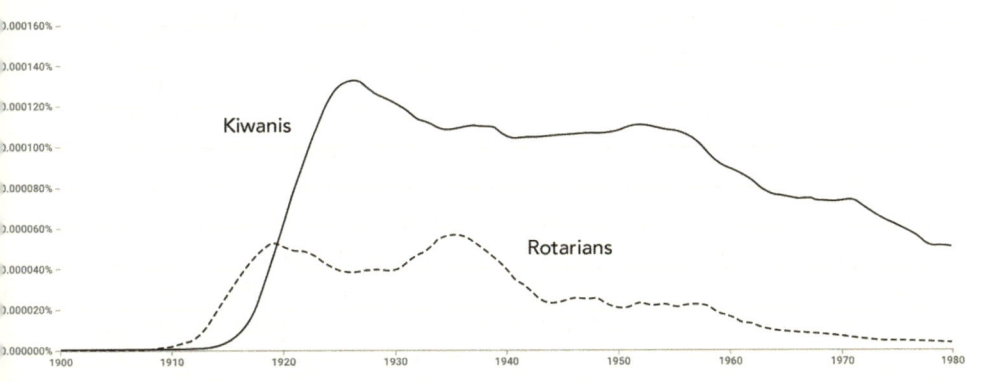

P3.3. FREQUENCY OF *KIWANIS* AND *ROTARIANS* IN AMERICAN ENGLISH (2019) NGRAM DATABASE, 1900–1980.

out of place. Now hope returned, evident in the 1920s in the romantic dreams of individuals like Jay Gatsby, the hero of Fitzgerald's 1925 novel. That sense of joy pervades the Harlem Renaissance, shaping the works of Zora Neale Hurston, Langston Hughes, and Claude McKay, although the racism that stained the 1920s hedged any celebration. Even the gloom of the Great Depression did not entirely squelch that upbeat outlook. Few authors regressed to the oppressive determinism evident at the turn of the twentieth century. Novelists of the 1930s depicted caring migrants, doughty unionists, and the occasional brave entrepreneur. This positive perspective continued into the early 1940s. In Betty Smith's *A Tree Grows in Brooklyn* (1943), the tough ailanthus tree flourishing behind the Nolans' tenement provides the metaphor for Francie Nolan's climb out of poverty. Only in the late 1940s and 1950s did the worldview of the much-expanded middle class darken. Prosperity was no longer a balm that soothed all ills; anxiety now replaced optimism—a development that presaged the end of an epoch.

Countering the optimism and freedom that came from the ascendancy of cities was the pressure of a business civilization that increasingly dominated the lives of middle-class Americans. The new ethos restrained the romantic dreams of the 1920s, darkened the visions of reformers in the 1930s, and narrowed the options offered in the early 1940s. *Conformity* became the watchword of this era; invocations of the term declined only after 1960 (fig. P3.2).

During the 1920s, the ascendant business culture reshaped small-town life. Service organizations like the Kiwanis, Rotarians, and chambers of commerce transformed these communities, promulgating shared values. References to these fraternal societies—few women were members—climbed sharply after 1920 (fig. P3. 3). Novels, such as those by Sinclair Lewis, scathingly document the pressure to conform. More than ever before, books and essays discussed *salaried employees* (as opposed to those who punched the time clock) as well as *managers*—two indicators of the new structure of work (fig. P3. 4).

After World War II, the impact of big business was particularly evident in the large cities (and nearby suburbs), where head offices and the white-collar workforce were concentrated. References to *executive* now soared (fig. P3.4) and the composition of the middle class changed once again. No longer were shopkeepers, independent businessmen and women, and professionals its mainstay. Now middle managers, clinging tightly to the rungs of the corporate ladder, characterized the stratum.[4] The clash between conformity and postgenteel freedom, a conflict that had defined the first part of the era, came to an end: business culture had triumphed. Members of the middle class, prosperous and more numerous than ever before, grumbled but acquiesced in the new dispensation.

One striking sign of the impact of the conformist culture was the shift from *character* to *personality*.[5] During the nineteenth century, and particularly before the Civil War, *character* embodied the finest qualities that a self-reliant, courageous, honest individual could display. References to that word, beloved by Emerson, fell to low levels in the twentieth century, elbowed aside by *personality*, a term that emphasized appearances rather than substance (fig. P3.5). In a society of conformists, superficial traits became all important. Discussing the steel titan Charles Schwab, Dale Carnegie observes, "Schwab's personality, his charm, his ability to make people like him, were almost wholly responsible for his extraordinary success; and one of the most delightful factors in his personality was his captivating smile."[6] References to *personality* peaked

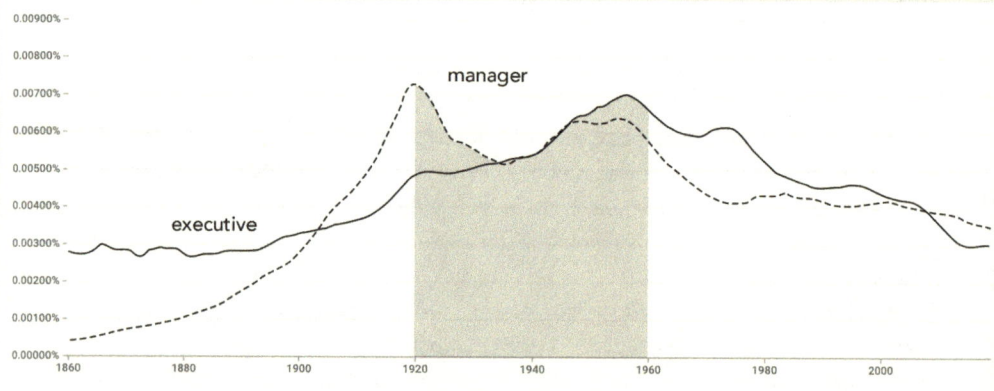

P3.4. THE TRIUMPH OF HIERARCHY IN THE MODERN ERA: *EXECUTIVE* AND *MANAGER* IN AMERICAN ENGLISH (2019) NGRAM DATABASE, 1860–2019.

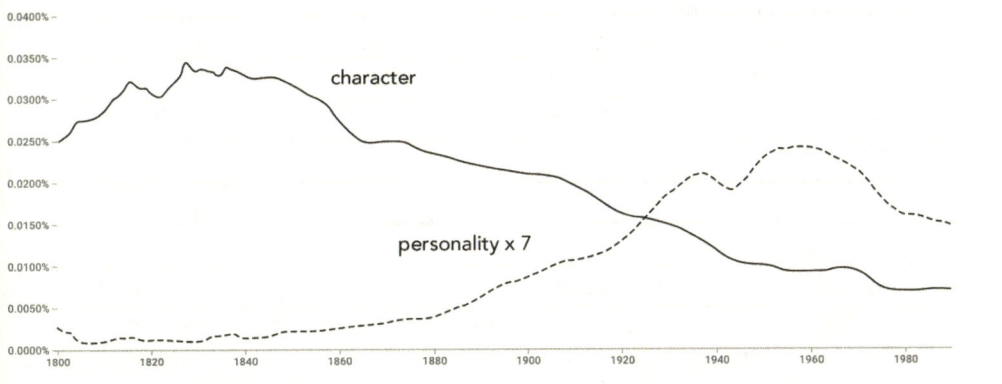

P3.5. *CHARACTER* AND *PERSONALITY* IN AMERICAN ENGLISH (2019) NGRAM DATABASE, 1800–1990.

in the mid-1950s, and then declined. In toppling the pillars of conformity, postmodern America dethroned personality as the ruler of worldly success.

Business ideology also affirmed traditional hierarchies: White over Black, men over women, straight over gay, Protestants over other faiths, native born over immigrants, and Americans over other "races," particularly people of color. Few White members of the middle class, even among those who pointed to the dangers of uniformity, distanced themselves from these racist and chauvinistic assumptions.

The magnetic poles of freedom and conformity aligned painting as well as literature. In the 1920s, some artists, like Charles Demuth and Charles Sheeler, sacralized factories, viewing them as America's cathedrals, while other observers, like Edward Hopper, depicted businessmen as sad and isolated. In the 1930s, important groups of painters exalted the people who worked with their hands and caricatured the wealthy as corrupt and overfed. After World War II, art confronted an increasingly affluent, conformist society. The abstract expressionists, like Jackson Pollock and Mark Rothko, must be understood in that context.

Finally, there is a need to determine the dates that defined the modern era. Efforts to establish this frame evoke no more scholarly consensus than do explorations of other periods. While this book opens the epoch in 1920, some critics suggest an earlier start. Norris Yates surveys the field and notes that various writers launch the era in 1893, 1910–16, or 1919–20. Yates contends that most of the criteria defining the modern period were in place "during or just before World War I."[7] The *Cambridge History of American Literature* begins modernism with the "cosmopolitan and experimental [stage] from 1910 through World War I."[8] Margot Norris in *The Columbia History of the American Novel* points to the Armory Show of 1913 and Ezra Pound's experimental poetry, 1912–15, as the opening knell of the epoch.[9] Other writers simply highlight the 1920s (and at times the 1930s) as the heyday of American literary modernism.[10]

Certainly, various dates can be defended: writers and painters delivered lethal blows to older values in the 1910s. But the argument here is that the modern era is defined not just by the breakdown of the old but also by the arrival of a new business civilization. Such a definition—as the previous graphs and discussion suggest—places the opening of this era around 1920.

Establishing a conclusion for the modern period (and a starting point for the postmodern era) is also challenging, but the change seems to occur around 1960. Carmen Holsberry, writing in 1981, labels William Faulkner and Fitzgerald "moderns," separating them from Thomas Pynchon, a "contemporary or post-modern" author.[11] Irving Howe titled his 1959 essay, "Mass Society and Post-Modern Fiction."[12] Harry Levin's article, "What Was Modernism?" first delivered as a talk in 1960, refers to the modern era in the past tense, and declares that "today we live in what has been categorized . . . as the Post-Modern Period."[13] Discussions about when postmodernism began are extensive, contentious, and explored later in this book. But most voices in that dissensus affirm the 1960s as the opening of a new era.

The developments that helped bring the modern era into existence also laid the groundwork for its demise. The great cities, which provided the foundation for the era, began to crumble. White middle-class families fled to the suburbs, whose population soared. For example, Nassau County, which borders Brooklyn and Queens, grew from 407,000 in 1940 to 1,300,000 in 1960. Similar exoduses transformed the areas surrounding virtually every US city. At the same time, poorer, non-White populations, particularly African Americans and Puerto Ricans, moved into these urban centers. During the 1950s, the non-White population in Washington, DC, rose from 35 to 55 percent; in Chicago, it climbed from 14 to 24 percent. Poor Whites from West Virginia and Kentucky migrated to Chicago and Cleveland.[14] More broadly, the proportion of the population living in the large cities declined, slightly but significantly. The percentage of Americans residing in centers of half a million or more had climbed steadily from 4 percent in 1870 to a peak of 18 percent in 1950 before falling off (as suburbs expanded) to 16 percent in 1960.

The delicate balance between conformity and freedom that had characterized the first decades of the epoch tipped toward a grudging conformity in the 1950s, and culminated after 1960 in a rejection of that social order. By 1960, the middle class, now much larger, salaried, and further removed from the products they produced, looked out upon an unsettled landscape. A pleasing personality no longer sufficed for advancement in this disordered world. The modern period yielded to the postmodern era.

7

Businessmen, Romantics, and Rebels, 1920–1940

In *Babbitt* (1922), Sinclair Lewis paints a harsh picture of the hero George Babbitt and the business culture he represents. "His name was George F. Babbitt," the opening lines inform the reader. "He was forty-six years old now, in April 1920, and he made nothing in particular, neither butter nor shoes nor poetry, but was nimble in the calling of selling houses for more than people could afford to pay." Babbitt's opinions, clothing, house, and even the furnishings in his bedroom, resemble those of his neighbors. ("Every second house in Floral Heights had a bedroom precisely like this."[1]) The book details Babbitt's boosterism and hypocrisies. Although self-righteously moral, he engages in shady land deals, misrepresents the properties he sells, and bribes local officials. Remarkably, despite Lewis's critical depiction, many in the business community identified with George Babbitt. Midwestern towns competed to be declared the model for the fictional city of Zenith, with Minneapolis announcing a "Babbitt week" to highlight its claim. Discussing the book, the *Kiwanis Magazine* stated, "It is of such men that substantial citizenship is made," while *Nation's Business*, a journal issued by the United States Chamber of Commerce, resolved, "Dare to be a Babbitt." The review added that the country would be "better off" with "more Babbitts."[2]

During the 1920s and 1930s, the newly ascendant business world with its push for conformity represented one side of a powerful dialogue shaping the outlook of the American middle class. The other side of that discourse emerged from the feeling of freedom that accompanied the rise of an urban, postgenteel society. Together, these opposing forces shaped novels and paintings. Along with that dialogue, the breathtaking swing from prosperity to depression molded the response of creative individuals.

Between 1920 and 1940, the US economy lurched from the best of times to the worst of times—with profound implications for the culture of the nation. For the middle class, the prosperity of the 1920s was genuine and unprecedented. In 1929, the Bureau of Labor Statistics announced that a family of four required $2,500 a year to maintain a "decent standard of living." Over 30 percent of families stood above that mark, with many in this group averaging more than $6,000 a year. Those in the upper tiers enjoyed a level of comfort that outpaced anything their forebears could have imagined. Their homes boasted electric refrigerators, vacuum cleaners, toasters, and radios. They drove sleek General Motors cars, the height of luxury compared to the rickety Fords that transported the less wealthy. Every day, if they chose, they could sample oranges and fresh lettuce. Their children completed high school, and almost half of them went to college. There had long been a middle class, but never a group that lived so well or been so large.[3]

The rising standard of living between 1920 and 1929 rested on a solid foundation. Urban construction and the automobile industry powered the growth in real incomes. New products—including aluminum goods, synthetic fibers, and plastics—spurred the expansion. Productivity soared as electric motors replaced steam power in manufacturing, and assembly lines grew more efficient.[4]

Still, dark clouds were gathering. Farming, which had expanded during the Great War, was hard hit by falling prices and excess capacity, as were coal mining and textiles. While a fourth of families lived comfortably, over half experienced hardship. Ominously, inequality increased during the decade, leading to a structural imbalance that meant workers could no longer buy the goods they produced. Diminished government outlays offered no counterweight to faltering consumer demand. And during the last years of the decade, the stock market alone drove growth. The result of the speculation and more fundamental problems was the Crash of 1929 and the ensuing depression.[5]

The Great Depression was the most severe downturn in US history. In 1932, the nadir of the slump, almost a fourth of the workforce was unemployed and manufacturing output dipped below 1913 levels. The stock market index plummeted from 452 in 1929 to 58. Falling prices and drought pummeled farmers who were already suffering. A million migrants, like the Joads in John Steinbeck's *The Grapes of Wrath* (1939), took to the roads. Farm protests spread like the clouds of dust that darkened counties and states. Farmers refused to deliver food when prices fell below their costs, and they blocked sheriff's auctions to protect their holdings. Field hands, with communist backing, protested in California and New Jersey, occasionally wresting gains from growers. Workers also demonstrated a newfound militance, with textile operatives stopping the looms in the east and longshoremen shutting down the docks in San Francisco. Backed by new labor laws, unions breached the seemingly insuperable bastions of General Motors and US Steel. Membership in these syndicates rocketed from 3.6 million in 1935 to 8.8 million in 1939.[6] Franklin Roosevelt's New Deal helped those hardest hit by the slump with a mix of direct assistance and public works projects. Still, those initiatives did not end the hard times—only the war did that. In 1940 almost 15 percent of the population remained unemployed.[7]

During the 1930s, the middle class shrank but did not disappear. Even during the worst years, three-fourths of the workforce remained employed, and at least a fourth of all families maintained incomes above $2,500 a year. Dale Carnegie's *How to Win Friends and Influence People*, with its advice about getting ahead in the world and its affirmation of social norms, sold over 250,000 copies in the first months after its publication in 1937—sales that far outpaced left-wing tracts.[8]

II

Authors and artists crafted their work within a social fabric defined by the warp and woof of an oppressive business culture and the freedoms that came from big city life. The repression that opened the era heightened the pressure to conform. In the Red Scare of 1919–1920, Attorney General Mitchell A. Palmer, assisted by J. Edgar Hoover from the Department of Justice, oversaw raids that ended in the arrest of six thousand persons, including labor leaders and radicals. Most were released but over five hundred individuals were deported, sending a clear message to dissenters.[9]

Novelists noted—and decried—the insistence on uniformity. In F. Scott Fitzgerald's *This Side of Paradise* (1920), Amory Blaine becomes increasingly critical of the behavior of the well-off stratum into which he is born. Initially, Amory accepts those values, attending a tony private school and entering Princeton, where he joins one of the elite "clubs." But while at Princeton, he begins to wonder about the life that awaits him, and in his first job—working at an advertising agency—he denounces the dreary workaday world. Tired of writing vapid copy, Amory quits, telling his boss: "It didn't matter a damn to me whether Harebell's flour was any better than any one else's." He spurns marriage, observing that when a man is married, "His wife shoos him on, from ten thousand a year to twenty thousand a year, on and on, in an enclosed treadmill that hasn't any windows." In the end, Amory appears ready to strike out on his own, announcing that he feels "sorry" for the "new generation dedicated more than the last to the fear of poverty and the worship of success."[10]

Edna Ferber's Pulitzer Prize–winning novel, *So Big* (1924), demonstrates a similar animus toward the business world. The story follows the life of an artistic schoolteacher, Selina Peake De Jong, who moves to a Dutch farming community west of Chicago, marries a farmer, and then after her husband's death, singlehandedly runs the farm and raises her son, Dirk. But that son, who gives up architecture to become a bond trader, gravely disappoints Selina—and the book makes clear the reader should share her point of view. When he tells her how successful he has been, she replies, "Yes, but there isn't much fun in it, is there? This selling things on paper? Now architecture, that must be thrilling." Dallas, the woman Dirk falls in love with, agrees with Selina: "'I'd rather,' Dallas said, slowly, 'plan one back door of a building that's going to help make this town beautiful and significant than sell all the bonds that ever floated.'" Rejected by his mother and Dallas, Dirk ends the novel in despair: "Inside Dirk something was saying, over and over, 'You're nothing but a rubber stamp, Dirk DeJong. You're nothing but a rubber stamp.'"[11]

Other novels echoed that criticism of the business world, but more fully embodied the dialectic that defined the 1920s: they presented characters who cherished romantic dreams but had their hopes dashed by the hard realities of a regimented society. References to *romantic*, as figure 3.3 illustrates, soared between 1918 and 1933. While these stories tantalize the reader with possibilities, they acknowledge that a coldly practical world left no space in which true love could triumph.

Fitzgerald's *The Great Gatsby* (1925) shines as the quintessential romantic novel of the period. From one vantage, Jay Gatsby is a disreputable figure; he associates with criminals, profits from illegal transactions, and lies about his past. But in his extraordinary love for Daisy and the purity of his dreams, Gatsby soars far above his peers. Strait-laced Nick Carraway, who like Dirk DeJong becomes a bond trader, narrates the tale and guides the reader. Carraway confesses that Gatsby "represented everything for which I have an unaffected scorn." Still, Carraway sets such criticism aside and praises his West Egg neighbor: "If personality is an unbroken series of successful gestures, then there was something gorgeous about him, some heightened sensitivity to the promises of life. . . . it was an extraordinary gift for hope, a romantic readiness such as I have never found in any other person and which it is not likely I shall ever find again." Gatsby's dream went far beyond obtaining the love of one woman; it involved the protective aura of wealth (Daisy was the "golden girl") and a return to a perfect past, a time untroubled by the cares of society. Carraway warns him, "You can't repeat the past." To which Gatsby responds, "'Can't repeat the past?' he cried incredulously. 'Why of course you can!'" Carraway was right, and the novel ends with the unraveling of Gatsby's world and his death.[12]

Fitzgerald's novel was only one of many during the 1920s shaped by such impossible longings. In Edith Wharton's *The Age of Innocence* (1920), both principal characters, Newland Archer and Countess Ellen Olenska, nurture unrealizable dreams for love and for a place that stands apart from quotidian problems. Newland, who is married to May Welland, passionately desires to unite with Ellen in a pure relationship. When she challenges him, "Is it your idea, then, that I should live with you as your mistress—since I can't be your wife?" he responds: "I want—I want somehow to get away with you into a world where words like that—categories like that—won't exist. Where we shall be simply two human beings who love each other, who are the whole of life to each other; and nothing else on earth will matter." The countess replies, "Oh, my dear—where is that country? Have you ever been there? ... I know so many who've tried to find it; and, believe me, they all got out by mistake at wayside stations." Ellen harbors her own implausible dream. When she returns from Europe, having fled an unhappy marriage, she imagines that New Yorkers comprise an idyllic society. "[T]his dear old place is heaven," she tells Newland. Only gradually does she awaken to the cruelty of her new circle. "I knew nothing of all this [malicious gossip] till Granny blurted it out one day," she explains. "New York simply meant peace and freedom to me: it was coming home. And I was so happy at being among my own people that every one I met seemed kind and good, and glad to see me."[13]

Hemingway's novels of the 1920s are driven by similar, unobtainable dreams. Close to the heart of *The Sun Also Rises* (1926) are two passionate, but unrealizable, love affairs. Jake Barnes, impotent from a war wound, is in love with Lady Brett Ashley, and she with him, but the impossibility of the relationship only causes both pain. She tells him, "You must know. I can't stand it, that's all. Oh, darling, please understand!" Equally in love with Brett is Robert Cohn, slandered by all for being Jewish and for his fawning personality. Jake notes Robert's infatuation with Brett: "She stood holding the glass and I saw Robert Cohn looking at her. He looked a great deal as his compatriot [Moses] must have looked when he saw the promised land." Brett sleeps with Robert, but soon rejects him.[14] *A Farewell to Arms* (1929) recounts another passionate, tragic love affair. The narrator, Frederic Henry, says simply about Catherine Barkley: "I loved her very much and she loved me."[15] But the story is a reminiscence, and Frederic in recounting these events knows that Catherine will die in childbirth. He observes, "The world breaks every one and afterward many are strong at the broken places. But those that will not break it kills. It kills the very good and the very gentle and the very brave impartially."[16]

Theodore Dreiser's *An American Tragedy* (1925) tells a similar tale, although presented in Dreiser's sometimes wooden prose and laced with determinist asides that seem a throwback to the heyday of naturalism. The story follows the ascent and fall of Clyde Griffiths, who is born poor, but eventually gets a job managing his uncle's shirt-collar factory. He falls in love with wealthy Sondra Finchley, who (like Daisy Buchanan in *Gatsby*) seems to promise unimaginable happiness. Clyde is transported: "At the sight of her now in her white satin and crystal evening gown, her slippered feet swinging so intimately near, a faint perfume radiating to his nostrils, he was stirred. In fact, his imagination in regard to her was really inflamed. Youth, beauty, wealth such as this—what would it not mean?" Sondra encourages him, but to make the relationship possible, Clyde resolves to kill the working-class girl who is carrying his child. He does, and is caught and executed.[17]

Finally, Willa Cather's *Death Comes for the Archbishop* (1927), which chronicles the adventures of two clerics in New Mexico of the 1850s, offers another tale of lovely, but fading, dreams. Bishop Jean Marie Latour leaves the already commercialized towns of Ohio for the expanses of the southwest. He recognizes that "the wooden figures of the saints, found in even the poorest Mexican homes" are "much more to his taste than the factory-made plaster images in his mission churches in Ohio." Latour and his friend Joseph Valliant face many challenges in the frontier territory, but their spirituality only grows stronger as do their ties with the Indigenous communities. Framing the story is the sense that the wonders Latour and Valliant observe are slipping from the earth. Latour thinks of retiring to France, but "Beautiful surroundings, the society of learned men, the charm of noble women, the graces or art, could not make up to him for the loss of those light-hearted mornings of the desert, for the wind that made one a boy again. He had noticed that this peculiar quality in the air of new countries vanished after they were tamed by man and made to bear harvests. . . . The air would disappear from the whole earth in time, perhaps; but long after his day."[18]

These novels embody haunting, quiet protests against the business society that dominated the 1920s. But as these authors knew, those dreams of true love and ideal communities could be realized only in a mythical past. Bishop Latour's lament for the fading air echoes the closing passages of *The Great Gatsby*. Carraway observes of Gatsby: "He had come a long way to this blue lawn, and his dream must have seemed so close that he could hardly fail to grasp it. He did not know that it was already behind him, somewhere back in that vast obscurity beyond the city, where the dark fields of the republic rolled on under the night." [19]

III

The downturn of the 1930s did not entirely erase the hopes that characterized postgenteel America. Although conditions in the Great Depression were in some respects worse than those at the turn of the twentieth century, authors did not revert to that earlier pessimism. Dreams persisted but faced extraordinary challenges with the hard times and the continuing, if attenuated, presence of the business ethos. The promise of better times came not from romantic love, but from the redemptive power of the soil, collective action, and caring communities.

One response to the Depression emphasized the strength Americans could draw from the land. The belief in a virtuous countryside and corrupt cities characterized the decade. In his 1933 inaugural address, Franklin Roosevelt stated, "we must frankly recognize the overbalance of population in our industrial centers" and the need for "a redistribution" of people on "a national scale."[20] Pearl S. Buck's bestseller, *The Good Earth* (1931), apotheosized these ideas in telling the story of a Chinese peasant, Wang Lung, defined by his love of the land. When drought sweeps his district and others flee, he cries defiantly, "I shall never sell the land!" The bond to the soil defines Wang, even as his wealth grows. After a fight with his concubine, "Wang Lung was healed of his sickness of love by the good dark earth of his fields and he felt the moist soil on his feet and he smelled the earthy fragrance rising up out of the furrows."[21]

The soil helps redeem Joe Christmas, the rootless hero of Faulkner's *Light in August* (1932). The novel follows him from his birth to his Christlike martyrdom. A tortured soul, Christmas is never quite sure whether he has a tincture of "black blood" that in the Southern code would make him a Black man. Only at the end, as a murderer fleeing the law, does he have an epiphany; it comes as he walks through the rich Mississippi farmland. The narrator explains, "It is as though he desires to see his native earth in all its phases for the first or last time. . . . For a week now he has lurked and crept among its secret places. . . . For some time as he walks steadily on, he thinks that this is what it is—the looking and seeing—which gives him peace and unhaste and quiet." The account continues: "Though during the last seven days he has had no paved street, yet he has travelled further than in all the thirty years before." He decides to turn himself in, and ultimately to meet his death. Christmas's awakening illustrates "the mystical oneness which can be absorbed from the earth," which Karl Zink identifies as a hallmark of Faulkner's work.[22]

For other fictional characters, the quest to possess the land is a chimera, that mythological being that stands forth as both an unrealizable dream and a deadly monster. In Erskine Caldwell's *Tobacco Road* (1932), the hapless Jeeter Lester refuses to leave his barren tract and follow his neighbors to the cotton mills of Augusta, Georgia. The narrator comments, "There was an inherited love of the land in Jeeter that all his disastrous experiences with farming had failed to take away." When he lights a fire to clear away brush, the conflagration engulfs his house, killing him and his wife.[23] Equally tragic is the ending of Steinbeck's novella, *Of Mice and Men* (1937), in which the dream of owning land plays a central role. Repeatedly, George reminds Lennie, his strong, but slow-witted, companion, about their plan to get a farm: "'Well, it's ten acres,' said George. 'Got a little win'mill. Got a little shack on it, an' a chicken run.'" Others at the ranch where they work are entranced by the same longings, but that hope proves illusory. After Lennie kills a woman who flirts with him, those plans simply become the litany that George repeats as he ends his friend's life rather than let him be captured.[24]

A second response to hard times highlights the promise of social change and the power of collective action. References to protestors and demonstrations are a commonplace in the novels of this era, as they were in the news of the day. In James T. Farrell's *Studs Lonigan,* Studs's father watches a protest march along with a policeman, who observes, "Most of them are poor people. That's the reason a lot of them are in the parade. It's being out of work and having no money that makes Communists out of them."[25] Mac McCreary, one of the twelve characters that John Dos Passos follows in the *U.S.A.* trilogy, takes part in revolutionary movements in the United States and Mexico. Monroe Stahr, the studio head in Fitzgerald's *The Last Tycoon,* is forced to strike a deal with a communist labor union. In Richard Wright's *Native Son* (1940), two communists are the only White men helping defend Bigger Thomas, an African American who has killed twice. Michael Gold's *Jews Without Money* (1930) closes with an apostrophe to revolution. Mikey, the narrator of this thinly disguised autobiography, claims to have been converted to radicalism by a soap-box orator. Mikey announces, "O workers' Revolution, you brought hope to me, a lonely, suicidal boy. You are the true Messiah. You will destroy the East Side when you come, and build there a garden for the human spirit." Still, this novel is more about Mikey's childhood in a New York tenement than about labor agitation.[26]

Other novels in the 1930s set the struggle against oppressive forces at the heart of the narrative. The strike at the Gastonia, North Carolina, textile mill in 1929 inspired many authors; six fictional accounts, appearing between 1930 and 1934, retold the story of hard times in the mill town and the failed uprising.[27] Grace Lumpkin's *To Make My Bread* (1932) is one of the most radical of these works. The novel follows the McClures from their impoverished lives in the Appalachian highlands to their resettlement in Leesburg (i.e., Gastonia), North Carolina. Apart from a brief spell during World War I, life is difficult at the mill and worsens in the years leading up to the strike. John and his sister Bonnie McClure Calhoun exhort the workers to resist, and are, in turn, instructed by a savvy union organizer, John Stevens, who teaches them about the Russian Revolution and the anarchists Sacco and Vanzetti. He tells the McClures: "We must go beyond the strike to the message . . . that we must join with all others like us and take what is ours. For it is our hands that have built, and our hands that run the machines and ours that dig the coal and keep the furnaces going."[28]

A third source of hope came from the belief in the value of caring communities. While John Steinbeck wrote about labor conflicts, his focus remained more on the participants' shared humanity than on political issues. On first reading, *In Dubious Battle* (1936) seems to be another left-leaning account of a strike. The story details the efforts of communists to organize a group of migrant apple pickers in California. The tale reveals the near-starvation wages the men were paid and the heavy-handed tactics of the Fruitgrower's Association. But the picture Steinbeck paints is not simply a struggle between good and evil. Warren French remarks that "the problem of interpretation begins with identifying the 'dubious battle' of the title"—a reference to a line in Milton's *Paradise Lost* and to the strike.[29] The communist organizers are callous in their approach to violence and death. One of the more admirable characters, Doc Burton, provides a counterpoint to the agitators. Burton states: "But in my little experience the end is never very different in its nature from the means. Damn it, Jim, you can only build a violent thing with violence."[30] While working on the book, Steinbeck explained to a friend, "I'm not interested in strike as means of raising men's wages, and I'm not interested in ranting about justice and oppression . . . [T]his self-hate which goes so closely in hand with self-love is what I wrote about."[31]

The same concern for a supportive community marks Steinbeck's masterpiece, *The Grapes of Wrath*. Like *In Dubious Battle*, this novel shows the difficult conditions the migrants face in California, the oppressive tactics of the landowners, and the efforts of courageous individuals to organize the pickers. But the lesson Steinbeck draws is less about organizing than about the need for individuals to help each other. Tom Joad, fleeing the police, tells his mother: "Wherever they's a fight so hungry people can eat, I'll be there. Wherever they's a cop beatin' up a guy, I'll be there."[32] In the closing scene, Rose of Sharon, whose baby has died, allows a starving man to suckle her milk. Jenn Williamson comments, "Thus the actions of the Joad family and the expansion of caretaking becomes a microcosm for the kind of social caretaking that Steinbeck envisions as necessary for human survival in a capitalist society which has previously (and harmfully) emphasized individual greed and self-advancement."[33]

Hemingway also shows his commitment to shared values in *For Whom the Bell Tolls* (1940). The heroes in his 1920s novels shunned such ideals. In *A Farewell to Arms*, Frederic Henry, who serves as a paramedic in the Italian army, declares, "I was always embarrassed by the words sacred, glorious, and sacrifice and the expression in vain."[34] But in this tale of the Spanish Civil War, the American Robert Jordan resolutely opposes the fascist forces attempting to overthrow the duly-elected republican government. The work is nuanced: it details atrocities committed by both sides and sharply criticizes the communists leading the republican forces. While acknowledging the republicans' shortcomings, Jordan (and the novel) remain vehemently anti-fascist. Referring to himself, Jordan presents his deep convictions, "You believe in Liberty, Equality and Fraternity. You believe in Life, Liberty and the Pursuit of Happiness. . . . If this war is lost all of those things are lost."[35] Hemingway knew the war as a reporter, and David Sanders notes that Jordan's "anti-fascism had the precise quality and intensity of Hemingway's as he articulated it in war dispatches."[36]

Finally, the fascination with business culture and entrepreneurs never wholly disappears during these dark years. Successful businessmen play a prominent role in Dos Passos's sprawling *U.S.A.* trilogy (1930–36) as well as in Farrell's *Studs Lonigan* trilogy (1932–1935). Margaret Mitchell's *Gone with the Wind* (1936) chronicles Scarlett's O'Hara's remarkable accomplishments in running lumber mills and a dry goods store. In Zora Neale Hurston's *Their Eyes Were Watching God* (1937), Jody Starks has the vision to invest in the all-Black community of Eatonville.

Two novels written in 1940 confirm the sustained interest in businessmen—and the mixed view authors took toward these individuals. *The Last Tycoon,* unfinished at Fitzgerald's death in December 1940 and published the next year, celebrates the talents of studio head Monroe Stahr. Faulkner takes a far more critical approach in *The Hamlet* (1940), which details how Flem Snopes, the epitome of the soulless proprietor, along with other members of his family gradually infest fictional Yoknapatawpha County, Mississippi. In a fanciful interlude, Faulkner imagines the devil bargaining with Flem, who offers up his soul in a matchbox. But when the devil opens the container, "there wasn't nothing in the matchbox but a little kind of dried-up smear under one edge." Emotionless and calculating, Flem outwits the locals, and the novel ends with his departure for the town of Jefferson, his next field of conquest.[37] After 1940, and particularly during the postwar years, the culture of business became still more important, while works that championed the land or a commitment to social change grew ever less common.

IV

The ideal of manhood changed during these decades, as men confronted an array of challenges. Most authors rejected any simple adherence to the business credo. George Babbitt was a pompous fool; Amory Blaine in *This Side of Paradise* denounces meaningless, well-paid work; neither Nick Carraway (in *Gatsby*) nor Dirk de Jong (in *So Big*) gain pleasure from selling bonds. Similarly, in *The Age of Innocence*, the legal profession bores Newland Archer. The narrator describes Archer's law office: "[N]one of these young men had much hope of really advancing in his profession . . . and over many of them the green mould of the perfunctory was already perceptibly spreading."[38]

Men labored during these years to remain the dominant figures in their relationships with women. Like a ship that had once seemed so stable and now was battered by contrary winds and in danger of capsizing, men struggled with new challenges: the emergence of rich women and, in the 1930s, widespread unemployment. Two of Fitzgerald's novels illustrate the dangers that came from entanglements with wealthy partners. Jay Gatsby first meets Daisy Fay when she is a debutante and he a poor army officer: "[H]e let her believe that he was a person from much the same stratum as herself—that he was fully able to take care of her."[39] His quest to make that pretense a reality, and the questionable means he pursues to achieve that end, led to their wondrous romance, but also to his demise. In *Tender Is the Night*, a similar imbalance shatters the relationship between Dick Diver, a psychoanalyst with a modest income, and the heiress Nicole Warren. Seduced by their luxurious lifestyle, Dick loses interest in his work—and his sense of self. As the marriage falls apart, he realizes, "he had been swallowed up like a gigolo, and somehow permitted his arsenal to be locked up in the Warren safety-deposit vaults."[40]

Hard times pummeled men who felt their natural role was breadwinner and head of the family. When Mikey's father in *Jews Without Money* loses his livelihood as a house painter, he laments to his wife, "Oh, my God, what shall I do now? I have no trade, no money, no courage left! I will kill myself, Katie! I have become a burden!"[41] In *Studs Lonigan*, the protagonist similarly despairs; he is unemployed, sick, impoverished because of his foolish stock speculation—and about to marry his pregnant girlfriend. He sighs, "Jesus Christ! Getting married on her money, after he had knocked her up, and wasted his own like an out-and-out chump."[42] His desperate search for a job ends with his illness and death. In *Grapes of Wrath*, when the family is forced from the farm, Ma Joad becomes the decision maker, much to Pa's chagrin: "Pa sniffled. 'Seems like times is changed,' he said sarcastically. 'Time was when a man said what we'd do. Seems like women is telllin' now. Seems like it's purty near time to get out a stick.'" Ma responds: "But you jus' get you a stick now an' you ain't lickin' no woman; you're a-fightin', 'cause I got a stick all laid out too."[43]

A few men asserted their independence when dealing with well-off women. In *Home to Harlem* (1928), by the African American author Claude McKay, Jake refuses to live "sweet" with Rose, that is, become a kept man. Rose accepts the relationship, but is upset by her loss of control: "She felt no thrill about the business when her lover was not interested in her earnings."[44] In *Gone with the Wind*, Rhett Butler, unlike Scarlett's previous husband, feels comfortable both asserting his dominance and letting her continue her business ventures: "'There's never going to be any doubt in anybody's mind about who wears the pants in the Butler family,' drawled Rhett. 'I don't care what fools say. In fact, I'm ill bred enough to be proud of having a smart wife. I want you to keep on running the store and the mills.'"[45]

With traditional roles under fire, novelists proffered an alternative: courageous manhood marked by "grace under pressure," a disdain for the pursuit of wealth, and an extraordinary competence when facing dangerous challenges. Hemingway's protagonists epitomize this outlook. "His heroes are not defeated except upon their own terms," notes Robert Penn Warren in his classic summary of Hemingway's work. "They are not squealers, welchers, compromisers, or cowards, and when they confront defeat they realize that the stance they take, the stoic endurance, the stiff upper lip mean a kind of victory."[46] For Hemingway, bullfighters epitomize these qualities. In *The Sun Also Rises,* Jake Barnes shares with Lady Brett his admiration for Pedro Romero: "She saw how close Romero always worked to the bull, and I pointed out to her the tricks the other bull-fighters used to make it look as though they were working closely.... Romero had the old thing, the holding of his purity of line through the maximum of exposition, while he dominated the bull by making him realize he was unattainable, while he prepared him for the killing."[47] Nor does death cow Hemingway's heroes. In *For Whom the Bell Tolls,* Robert Jordan knows he may not survive his mission to destroy a vital bridge: "So if your life trades its seventy years for seventy hours I have that value now and I am lucky enough to know it. And there is not any such thing as a long time, nor the rest of your lives, nor from now on, but there is only now, why then now is the thing to praise and I am very happy with it."[48]

The detective fiction of these decades displays similar virtues. "Hemingway's lean prose," Fred Marcus notes, "paves the way for a hard-boiled school of fiction—realistic, disillusioned, weary of false idealism, and unsentimental."[49] In Raymond Chandler's *The Big Sleep* (1939), Philip Marlowe shows a quiet courage and an indifference to bribery and threats, all for "twenty-five dollars a day and expenses." The district attorney asks, "And for that amount of money you're willing to get yourself in Dutch with half the law enforcement of this county?" Marlowe responds: "I don't like it.... But what the hell am I to do? I'm on a case. I'm selling what I have to sell to make a living. What little guts and intelligence the Lord gave me and a willingness to get pushed around in order to protect a client."[50] James M. Cain's *The Postman Always Rings Twice* (1934) presents a protagonist, Frank Chambers, with similar sangfroid. Chambers, who writes the tale as a memoir while he awaits his execution for murder, faces his end coolly, regretting only that his lover Cora has died: "There won't be any stay, and there won't be any commutation. I know that. I never kidded myself.... Here they come. Father McConnell says prayers help. If you've got this far, send up one for me, and Cora, and make it that we're together, wherever it is."[51]

African American novelists suggested that men dealt with hard times in still another way: humor—a topic discussed more fully in the following pages. The common note among these varying approaches to masculinity was the effort to respond to conditions that unsettled traditional roles. For some that meant struggling to reaffirm male dominance; for others, courage and detachment; and for still others, humor. All that would change as business culture became more pervasive in the 1940s and 1950s.

V

Novels reflect the limited progress women made during these years. Women secured the vote in 1920 but did not become a political force; fewer women than men went to the polls, and they typically voted as their husbands or fathers did. The proportion of women in the workforce increased, but only marginally, from 21 percent in 1920 to 24 percent in 1940. Overwhelmingly, female workers were relegated to low-status occupations: domestic service, nursing, teaching, sales, and clerical work. Few married women worked outside the home; only 15 percent did so in 1940.[52] References to *strong women*, which had risen steeply in the nineteenth century, were lower in the 1920s and 1930s than in the 1910s—and indeed would not climb until after 1965 (fig. 7.1).

Still, gains in a few areas hint at progress. With the crumbling of genteel values, women expressed their sexuality more freely. The 1920s were the decade of the "flapper," bobbed hair, the skyrocketing use of cosmetics, and the proliferation of beauty parlors.[53] Some women boldly advocated change. Alice Paul and the National Women's Party led a prolonged although ultimately unsuccessful campaign for a federal equal rights amendment. In the 1930s, First Lady Eleanor Roosevelt,

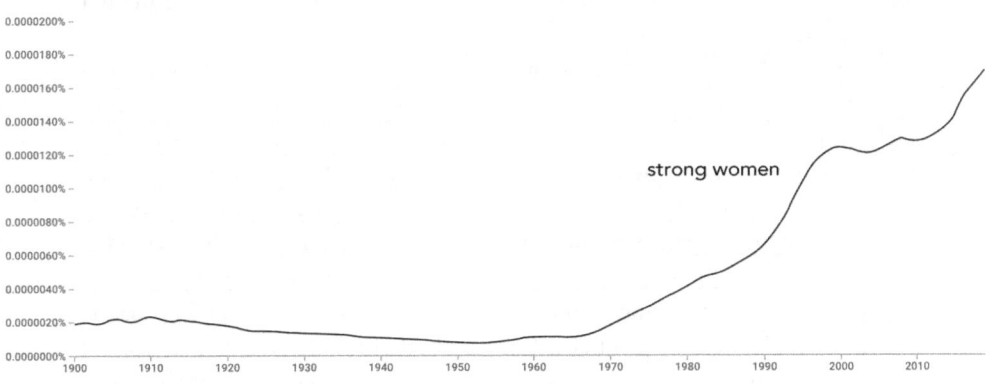

7.1. FREQUENCY OF *STRONG WOMEN* IN AMERICAN ENGLISH (2019) NGRAM DATABASE, 1900–2019.

Secretary of Labor Frances Perkins, and Mary McLeod Bethune, president of the National Association of Colored Women, were among the important female decision makers. Courageous, outspoken women contributed their autobiographical accounts to the collection, *I Am a Woman Worker* (1936).[54] Many women were well-educated; during the 1930s they received roughly 40 percent of all bachelor's and master's degrees.[55]

Even authors who resisted portraying independent women readily depicted the new sexual mores. In *Gatsby*, Tom Buchanan, who complains "women run around too much these days to suit me," had reason to be concerned. Here is his wife, Daisy, and Gatsby: "As he [Tom] left the room again she got up and went over to Gatsby and pulled his face down, kissing him on the mouth. 'You know I love you,' she murmured."[56] In Hemingway's *The Sun Also Rises*, Lady Brett Ashley is drawn to the bullfighter, Romero: "'My God! He's a lovely boy,' Brett said. 'And how I would love to see him get into those clothes. He must use a shoe-horn.'"[57]

Although some of the "proletarian" novels seem staid in their treatment of women's sexuality, the trend toward greater freedom continued in the 1930s.[58] In *Light in August*, Faulkner gives the reader a glimpse, through young Joe Christmas's eyes, of a woman masturbating. In Christmas's adult relationship with Joanna Burden, she is the aggressor, attacking him "in the wild throes of nymphomania."[59] Raunchy sex scenes punctuate Caldwell's *Tobacco Road* and noir novels like Cain's *The Postman Always Rings Twice*. Frank Chambers, the narrator in *Postman*, recounts Cora's passion: "'Bite me! Bite me!' I bit her. I sunk my teeth into her lips so deep I could feel the blood spurt into my mouth."[60] In Hemingway's *For Whom the Bell Tolls*, Maria tells Pilar, the guerilla leader and earth-mother figure, that the "earth moved" when she had intercourse with Robert Jordan. Pilar replies, "When I was young the earth moved so that you could feel it all shift in space and were afraid it would go out from under you."[61]

While comfortable portraying more open sexuality, male writers such as Fitzgerald, Faulkner, and Hemingway denigrated assertive women. In *Tender Is the Night*, Fitzgerald deals harshly with Nicole's sister, "Baby" Warren, who is wealthy, independent, and unmarried. The narrator comments: "She was a compendium of all the discontented women who had loved Byron a hundred years before, yet, in spite of the tragic affair with the guards' officer there was something wooden and onanistic about her."[62] Faulkner, who believed that fundamentally different principles governed men and women, had little sympathy for women like Joanna Burden (in *Light in August*), with her Calvinist background, unmarried status, and devotion to work. The novel describes her as a "coldfaced, almost manlike, almost middleaged woman who had lived for twenty years alone." The excessive sexuality she showed in her relationship with Joe Christmas came from her "frustrate and irrevocable years, which she appeared to attempt to compensate each night as if she believed that it would be the last night on earth by damning herself forever to the hell of her forefathers."[63] In *For Whom the Bell Tolls,* Pilar, the brave guerilla leader, is ugly and manlike: "Robert Jordan saw a woman of about fifty almost as big as Pablo, almost as wide as she was tall, ... with heavy wool socks on heavy legs ... and a brown face like a model for a granite monument."[64]

Steinbeck seemingly creates a strong woman in Ma Joad, but her limits are more striking than her power. Nellie McKay points out that Steinbeck "need give her no first name, for she is the paradigmatic mother, and this is the single interest of her life." McKay adds that Ma Joad's concerns do not "extend ... beyond the domestic sphere, other than that which has a direct relationship on the survival of the family."[65] Ma Joad does not engage in the larger dialogue of ideas, as do her son Tom and Jim Casy. Only once does she go into the fields to help pick. More generally, in both *Grapes of Wrath* and *In Dubious Battle,* Steinbeck minimizes the role of women as producers. To be sure, married women typically remained in the camps. But throughout the West many of the pickers and some of the union organizers were women. Steinbeck excludes those individuals, as he does the Mexicans and Filipinos, who made up a large portion of the migrant workers. His pickers and protesters are White men.[66]

A few male writers applaud independent women. In Gold's *Jews Without Money,* Mikey's mother repeatedly moves beyond her narrow domestic sphere; she organizes a rent strike in her building and gets a job when her husband loses his. Lena, Mikey's aunt, takes part in a garment workers' strike. Dos Passos's *U.S.A* trilogy profiles several women who pursue nontraditional careers, including an interior decorator, a journalist, and an actress. McKay's *Home to Harlem* and Hughes's *Not Without Laughter* (1930) extol determined Black women who are laundresses, maids, waitresses, cannery workers, as well as cooks, singers, and teachers.

Female novelists often depicted bold women, but even these characters bear the stamp of a society dominated by men. In Ferber's *So Big,* Selina becomes one of the most successful farmers in the Dutch community west of Chicago—but only after her husband dies. While married, she could not persuade her slow-witted mate to improve their run-down farm, nor would she dream of leaving him. In Lumpkin's *To Make My Bread,* Bonnie Calhoun is an outspoken strike leader. Modeled after Ella May Wiggins, the martyr of the Gastonia strike, Calhoun inspires the strikers with her singing, reaches out to Black workers, and is killed by the bosses. Still, the men in the novel do the heavy intellectual lifting. Her brother John and the organizer, John Stevens, are Calhoun's mentors, and the ones who craft a larger vision.[67] Mitchell's *Gone with the Wind* also features several very capable women, apart from the heroine. Scarlett's mother, Ellen, manages "Tara," just as Beatrice

Tarleton runs the large neighboring plantation, "Fairhill." Dolly Merriwether, a dowager, responds to the wartime devastation by opening a bakery. But these women, and others, work within a framework in which men make the larger decisions about buying and selling land and goods, and about waging war. In running sawmills and a general store, Scarlett breaks some of these taboos. But she is sharply condemned by her peers, and at least in part by Mitchell, who has created an unfeeling character. As Charles Beye notes, "Scarlett remains curiously untouched by the emotion of human kindness throughout the novel."[68]

VI

During the 1920s and 1930s, White and Black authors grappled with race, as Americans long had, but in new ways reflecting the changing society. For many Whites, particularly those in small towns and rural areas, the recent tides of immigration and the breakdown of genteel values heightened the fear of the "other." The twenties witnessed the reborn Klan, Prohibition, immigration restriction, and the Scopes trial. As figure 4.1 illustrates, the use of *nigger* soared during the 1920s, reaching a peak in 1934. (Hatred of Jews and Italians was also rampant. The frequency of *kike* and *dago* skyrocketed in these years.) Tensions moderated, however, in the 1930s; FDR's New Deal, the rise of industrial unions, and the growth of left-wing parties encouraged tolerance, even if discrimination against Blacks and other groups persisted.[69]

Racism tainted many of the novels by White authors. In *The Great Gatsby*, Fitzgerald certainly did not endorse Tom Buchanan's pompous pronouncements about "Coloured Empires." But it is Nick Carraway, the fair-minded narrator, who describes a nearby car with "three modish negroes, two bucks and a girl," adding, "I laughed aloud as the yolks of their eyeballs rolled toward us in haughty rivalry."[70] In Hemingway's *A Farewell to Arms*, Frederic Henry dismisses Catherine Barkley's reference to a Shakespearean hero with the curt observation, "Othello was a nigger."[71] The leader of a Jewish gang in Gold's *Jews Without Money* (1930) calls himself "Nigger" because his nose was smashed in.[72] Farrell's *Studs Lonigan* trilogy (1932–35) is filled with anti-Black (and antisemitic) invective as Studs, his Irish American family, and friends vent their frustrations. This racism may not be Farrell's outlook; but the trilogy offers no character whose presence or views counters such venom.

Other novels reinforce stereotypes, presenting African Americans who are timid and intellectually challenged. Crooks, the Black stable hand in Steinbeck's *Of Mice and Men*, lacks any sense of self-worth. Insulted by Curley's wife, "Crooks had reduced himself to nothing. There was no personality, no ego—nothing to arouse either like or dislike."[73] Mitchell's best-selling *Gone with the Wind* resurrects the century-old plantation myth. "Mammy," who is "black, pure African, [and] devoted to her last drop of blood to the O'Haras," presides in the Big House, as does Big Sam, who is strong and simple-minded, in the fields. Emancipation highlights the fawning character of the slaves. The narrator remarks: "The better class of them, scorning freedom, were suffering as severely as their white masters." But the "lowest in the black social order" were like "monkeys or small children turned loose among treasured objects whose value is beyond their comprehension."[74]

The same framework shapes Faulkner's works. The color line is absolute; a few "drops" of Black blood define Joe Christmas (whose parentage is uncertain) in *Light in August* and Charles Etienne Bon in *Absalom, Absalom!* During the Civil War, slaves remain loyal to their masters and dismissive of their freedom. Blacks may at times be surly, but they remain properly subservient. As scholars note, Faulkner depicts a few familiar characters, such as the faithful retainer and the "mammy." Edmond Volpe remarks, "Most of the Negroes with important roles are variations on members of a single Negro family."[75] George Kent observes that for Faulkner, Black women appeared as three types: "as sexual force, as faithful servant, and as mammy." Kent adds, "In the body of Faulkner's fiction [dealing with Blacks], we look in vain for the complexity of personality."[76]

Still, during the Depression years, some White authors raised concerns about the mistreatment of Blacks. Grace Lumpkin's *To Make My Bread*, which retells the story of the 1929 mill strike in Gastonia, North Carolina, highlights efforts to reach across the color line. Bonnie McClure denounces race baiting, telling her fellow workers, "The colored people work alongside of us. . . . And I can't see why they shouldn't fight alongside us, and we by them"—a message of solidarity she carries into the Black community.[77] In Hemingway's *For Whom the Bell Tolls*, Robert Jordan, who has come to Spain to fight fascism, reflects on the horrors at home and condemns the lynching of a Black man as "ugly and brutal."[78] Fitzgerald's views also evolved. In *The Last Tycoon*, Monroe Stahr deals sympathetically with labor leaders—and African Americans. On a Malibu beach, he encounters a Black man reading Emerson. When this stranger tells Stahr that none of the studio pictures appeal to him, Stahr gains a new perspective and decides to put into production a "difficult picture." The narrator comments, "He rescued it for the Negro man."[79]

For African American novelists, the 1920s and early 1930s were banner years, in large part thanks to the Harlem Renaissance. Alain Locke, editor of *The New Negro: An Interpretation* (1925), was among the many proclaiming this cultural awakening. Locke declared that the "life of the Negro community" had entered "a new dynamic phase." The catalyst was the migration to the North, and particularly the growth of Harlem, the community at the northern end of Manhattan Island.

Between 1900 and 1930, the proportion of Blacks living outside the South soared from 10 to 21 percent, with Harlem home to two hundred thousand African Americans. "In the very process of being transplanted," Locke explains, "the Negro is becoming transformed," adding that, "In Harlem, Negro life is seizing upon its first chances for group expression and self-determination."[80] Aided by the prosperity of the 1920s and the (slightly) more liberal sentiments of the North, Harlem provided the critical mass for an explosion of Black writing.

The novelists of the Harlem Renaissance were caustic in describing the racism Blacks experienced. That critique, not a new aspect of African American literature, provides a background for all else they wrote. In *Cane* (1923), a set of loosely connected stories about Blacks in the North and South, Jean Toomer recounts several horrific episodes, including the burning of one man and the killing of a pregnant woman. Langston Hughes's autobiographical novel, *Not Without Laughter* (1930), shows the many indignities inflicted upon the protagonist, Sandy Rogers, growing up in a small Kansas town. Although much of Hurston's *Their Eyes Were Watching God* (1937) takes place in an all-Black Florida village, mean-spirited Whites clearly shape the world of African Americans, just as discrimination provides the backdrop for Claude McKay's *Home to Harlem* (1928). In *Quicksand* (1928), Nella Larsen calls out the prejudice blighting the United States. The heroine, Helga Crane, like Larsen, part African American and part White and Danish, lives on both sides of the Atlantic and reflects ruefully on returning to the States: "Go back to America, where they hated Negroes! To America, where Negroes were not people. To America, where Negroes were allowed to be beggars only, of life, of happiness, of security."[81]

What was strikingly new about the authors of the Harlem Renaissance was their celebration of a vibrant, joyous community. Earlier African American novels had portrayed beleaguered groups (like Philadelphia Blacks in Webb's *The Garies and Their Friends* or the Wilmington, North Carolina, neighborhoods in Chesnutt's *The Marrow of Tradition*) or had viewed Black nightlife as corrupting (as in Dunbar's *The Sport of Gods*). Now, whether the setting was Harlem or another locale, authors saluted an exuberant African American society. *Their Eyes Were Watching God* recounts the parties that brought workers together in the Everglades: "The house was full of people every night.... Some were there to hear Tea Cake pick the box; some came to talk and tell stories, but most of them came to get into whatever game was going on or might go on."[82] *Home to Harlem* eulogizes that New York community: "Harlem ... Its hot desires. But, oh, the rich bloodred color of it! The warm accent of its composite voice, the fruitiness of its laughter, the trailing rhythm of its 'blues' and the improvised surprises of its jazz." In *Not Without Laughter*, Sandy leaves Kansas for the Chicago "blackbelt," where his sister is a singer.

He attends a show: "It was a typical Black Belt audience, laughing uproariously, stamping its feet to the music, kidding the actors, and joining in the performance, too."[83] In *Quicksand,* despite her reservations, Helga Crane returns to Harlem: "She liked the sharp contrast to her pretentious stately life in Copenhagen. It was as if she had passed from the heavy solemnity of a church service to a gorgeous carefree revel."[84]

One key aspect of that joy was humor. Shared laughter had long been part of Black culture, but was often missing in earlier novels. Now it was abundantly evident, and also suggested a new, more open approach to manhood. In *Their Eyes Were Watching God,* Tea Cake provides a refreshing contrast with Janie's two former husbands, who were dour, controlling businessmen. Here is where Janie learns about Tea Cake's name.

> "Now ain't you somethin'! Mr. er—er—You never did tell me whut yo' name wuz."
> "Ah sho didn't. Wuzn't expectin' fuh it to be needed. De name mah mama gimme is Vergible Woods. Dey calls me Tea Cake for short."
> "Tea Cake! So you sweet as all dat?" She laughed and he gave her a little cut-eye look to get her meaning.
> "Ah may be guilty. You better try me and see."[85]

In *Not Without Laughter,* Sandy, the narrator and voice of the author, Langston Hughes, underscores the importance of humor for Blacks—reinforcing the work's title: "That must be the reason, thought Sandy, why poverty-stricken old Negroes like Uncle Dan Givens lived so long—because to them, no matter how hard life might be, it was not without laughter."[86] Jake in McKay's *Home to Harlem* expresses similar sentiments. Noting the challenges of living in New York, he observes, "Yet even New York, passing its strange thousands through its great metropolitan mill, cannot rob Negroes of their native color and laughter."[87]

Harlem Renaissance novels also presented sex with a new frankness—in keeping with the times. Change did not come all at once. In a 1922 letter, Toomer laments that "we who have Negro blood in our veins, who are culturally and emotionally the most removed from the Puritan tradition, are its most tenacious supporters."[88] Four years later, Locke spoke more positively, pointing to the "revolt against Puritanism" as a source of the new openness.[89] The language in Toomer's 1923 novel, *Cane,* was (for that time) daring: "Cora glides up . . . squeezing his head into her breasts . . . Halsey grabs her arms and pulls her to him. She struggles. Halsey pins her arms and kisses her. She settles, spurting like a pine-knot afire."[90] In *Not Without Laughter,* Hughes describes without censure activities on the "wrong side of the tracks": "It was a gay place—people did what they wanted to do, or what they had to do, and didn't care—for in the Bottoms folks ceased to struggle against the boundaries between good and bad, or white and Black, and surrendered amiably to immorality."[91] Similarly, *Home to Harlem* is rich with sexual allusions. One character explains to the protagonist, Jake: "Susy ain't nothing to look at like you' fair-brown queen, but she's tur'bly sweet loving. You know when a ma-ma ain't the goods in looks and figure, she's got to make up foh it some. And that Susy does."[92]

The Depression ended the Harlem Renaissance, exacerbating the travails of a community in which poverty had never been absent and encouraging many to join left-wing groups. The Harlem Riot of 1935 left three dead and millions of dollars' worth of property destroyed. Claude McKay observed, "Their rioting was the gesture of despair of a bewildered, baffled, and disillusioned people."[93] The Communist Party attracted prominent African Americans. McKay had shown his interest in the Party in the 1920s; Langston Hughes was part of a group that went to the USSR in 1932. W. E. B. Du Bois and actor Paul Robeson voiced similar leanings. So did Richard Wright, who moved from the South to Chicago in 1927, and by the 1930s was involved in party activities. Wright's *Native Son* reflects those protests and the hard times gripping Black communities. The novel, set in Chicago, tells the story of a twenty-year-old African American, Bigger Thomas, who kills two women and is sentenced to death despite the eloquent pleas of his communist lawyer, Boris Max. The book shows Bigger's unreflective anger as well as the oppressive conditions that kept him and other Blacks in poverty. At the trial, Boris warns the court about the danger of "misreading the consciousness of the submerged millions."[94] There would be important Black authors in the ensuing decades, but not until the 1970s and the impact of the civil rights movement would another remarkable era of African American writing emerge.

VII

Painting too reflected the interplay of the new business ethos and the resistance to those values. In the 1920s, some painters, including Charles Demuth and Charles Sheeler, celebrated the corporations that were reshaping the landscape, figuratively and literally. Around 1920, these two men adopted a Cubist-influenced style called "Precisionism" that, with its straight lines and limited palette, suited the industrial structures they admired. Demuth depicted the grain elevators in his hometown of Lancaster, Pennsylvania, in a composition he called *My Egypt* (1927), suggesting such buildings were worthy successors to the pyramids.[95] Sheeler agreed to help publicize the Ford Motor Company's new River Rouge plant. He spent weeks photographing the buildings, observing, "The subject matter is incomparably the most thrilling I have to work with."⁹⁶ Along with the photographs, Sheeler produced a series of oil paintings, including *American Landscape* (1930). A towering smokestack and powerful machines dominate the canvas, which features only one human figure, barely visible (ptg. 7.1). Sheeler, who would later photograph Chartres cathedral, regarded the River Rouge plant as a modern temple. "Our factories," he pronounced, "are our substitute for religious expression." Absent in his paintings and photographs of the Ford plant is any reference to the dangerous, repetitive work to which many of the 75,000 employees were subjected.⁹⁷

With the Great Depression, artists more openly criticized corporate America, the blighted cities, and the dreariness of business culture. One group of painters, the Regionalists, disdained urban places and advocated, as did novelists, a return to the soil. Three Midwesterners led this school: Thomas Hart Benton from Missouri, John Steuart Curry from Kansas, and Grant Wood from Iowa. Wood's *American*

7.1. CHARLES SHEELER, *AMERICAN LANDSCAPE*, 1930.

Gothic, 1930, which portrays a farmer and his daughter, became an iconic American painting. Wood rejected the many satirical renderings of his composition. "These people had bad points," he remarked, "and I did not paint them under, but to me they were basically good and solid people. I had no intention of holding them up to ridicule."[98]

Benton, the most prominent and outspoken of the Regionalists, grew increasingly disenchanted with the cities. The ten panels of his *America Today* mural (1930–31), painted for the New School for Social Research in New York, seem even-handed in portraying industry and agriculture, cities and countryside. But his *The Arts of Life in America* mural (1932) is less balanced. One panel, *Arts of the West*, extols western virtues, with brave cowboys and plain folk enjoying themselves in a variety of pastimes. "I wanted to show, he remarked, "that the people's behaviors, their *action* on the opening land, was the primary reality of American life."[99] By contrast, his painting of the city has bootleggers, top-hatted capitalists, and gangsters. "The great cities are dead," he explained. "They offer nothing but coffins for the living and thinking."[100]

The Social Realists were the urban counterparts of the Regionalists, sharing a belief in the common folk; together, the two groups were called American Scene painters. Some of the Social Realists, like Ben Shahn, championed radical causes; in a series of panels, Shahn honored Sacco and Vanzetti, the anarchists executed in 1927. Another painter, Moses Soyer, advised his peers, "Do not glorify Main Street. Paint it as it is—mean, dirty, avaricious. Self-glorification is artistic suicide. Witness Nazi Germany."[101] Others portrayed the urban scene, though with less overt political content. Isabel Bishop provided sensitive renderings of "office girls," the women who worked in the New York towers.[102] In the late 1930s, the African American artist Jacob Lawrence was just beginning his career depicting themes from Black history; his masterpiece, *The Migration Series*, would be completed in 1941.[103]

Probably the most important artist of this era, and the one who provides the most incisive commentary on the business-inflected culture that shaped America after 1920, was Edward Hopper. Hopper's mature style emerged in 1925 and continued relatively unchanged until his death in 1967. Hopper's figures typically are middle class, isolated from each other, and joyless. He highlights that loneliness in his canvases with two or more figures, who typically turn away from each other. In *Room in New York* (1932), the man is buried in his newspaper; the woman touches a single key on the piano—but he does not look up. The viewer glimpses this unguarded moment through an apartment window, as if to say—this is what really goes on in such lives (ptg. 7.2). The individuals he depicts enjoy a modicum of comfort but live in a world that provides them with little spiritual sustenance. The unsatisfied individuals on Hopper's canvases might have stepped from the pages of Fitzgerald's *This Side of Paradise,* Ferber's *So Big,* or from Newland Archer's law office in Wharton's *The Age of Innocence.*[104]

Understanding how Hopper arrived at that outlook in the mid-1920s clarifies his view of American society. Hopper made three trips to Paris, in 1906–7, 1909, and 1910, fell in love with France, and was struck by the contrast with the United States. He observed, "The people here in fact seem to live in the streets, which are alive from morning until night, not as they are in New York with that never-ending determination for the 'long-green' [i.e., money] but with a pleasure loving crowd that doesn't care what it does or where it goes, so that it has a good time." The paintings and sketches of the Paris years reflect that spirit; people chat with each other, often an arm is placed on a friend's shoulder. Returning to New York was a

7.2. EDWARD HOPPER, *ROOM IN NEW YORK*, 1932.

shock. He later noted, "It seemed awfully crude and raw here when I got back. It took me ten years to get over Europe." Until about 1920, much of the artwork he exhibited either came from his Parisian days or was inspired by it.[105]

He also disliked his involvement in the business world. Because Hopper sold few paintings before 1924, he was forced to make his living as a commercial artist—a necessity he loathed. He did covers for employee magazines such as *Wells Fargo Messenger* and *The Dry Dock Dial,* and briefly worked for an advertising agency. He reflected on these years: "Illustrating was a depressing experience. And I didn't get very good prices because I didn't often do what they wanted."[106]

In the mid-1920s, Hopper consciously renounced his ties with Europe and determined to paint only the world around him, specifically New York, where he spent much of the year, and New England, where he and his wife summered. In a 1927 manifesto, Hopper announced that "American art should be weaned from its French mother." His new style, not incidentally, sold well and quickly established his reputation. In painting isolated, melancholy Americans, he captured an inner as well as an outer reality. In the catalogue for the 1933 retrospective exhibit at the Museum of Modern Art, Hopper observed, "I believe the great painters with the intellect as master, have attempted to force this unwilling medium of paint and canvas into a record of their emotions. I find any digression from this large aim leads me to boredom."[107] Although Hopper lived until the 1960s, after World War II other artists took the lead in responding to a society that was increasingly prosperous and ever more dominated by corporations.

8

Anxious Conformists, 1941–1960

"My personal maladies and malaises," Patricia Highsmith remarked in her notebook in 1950, "are only those of my own generation and of my time, heightened." Highsmith was right. Her novels and journals in the 1950s sound themes that her contemporaries found familiar, including a critique of corporate life, the anxieties of the prosperous, and the prevalence of externally defined, seemingly interchangeable individuals. In *The Blunderer* (1954), wealthy lawyer Walter Stackhouse, owner of a splendid Long Island home, complains about his work and neighbors. He "asked himself what he was doing there among these pleasant, smugly well-to-do and essentially boring people, what he was doing with his whole life." Highsmith's most famous work, *The Talented Mr. Ripley* (1955), turns on the fluid nature of what defines a person. After Tom Ripley kills his friend Dickie Greenleaf, he assumes his identity and, remarkably, manages to fool Dickie's girlfriend, father, and the police. Moreover, Ripley, like Walter Stackhouse, disdains the tedium of the business world. In praising Dickie's decision to move to Europe, he observes: "Why should Dickie want to come back to subways and taxis and starched collars and a nine-to-five job. Or even a chauffeured car and vacations in Florida and Maine?"[1]

After World War II, the nation grew wealthier and the middle class expanded, but affluence did not bring contentment. The battle between the business ethos and postgenteel freedoms, a clash that for many years had defined modernity, now ended: conformity carried the day. For most in the middle stratum, the only concern was how to deal with a society that threatened numbing uniformity. Despite broadcasting their grievances, chroniclers of the late modern era—with few exceptions—accepted a society that allowed so many to live so well. That note of grudging acceptance was evident even in fiction by African American writers such as Ralph Ellison and James Baldwin. The crossbeams of dissatisfaction and acquiescence provided the framework that shaped the novels and art of these years.

I

During the last decades of the modern era, the nature of work in the United States changed—enlarging the middle class and tightening the grip that business had on the nation's culture. Advances in productivity lessened the demand for people who worked with their hands. For example, during the 1950s, the proportion of the cotton crop mechanically harvested climbed from 8 to 51 percent, the number of sharecroppers plummeted, and total bales remained stable. More broadly, farmers declined from 34 percent of the labor force in 1900 to 25 percent in 1920 to 6 percent in 1960, while output rose. Similarly, more efficient factories reduced calls for new operatives. Between 1945 and 1960, auto plants halved the number of hours needed to assemble a car. Overall, from 1947 to 1957, the number of factory workers fell by 4 percent, while production soared.[2]

The counterpart to the decline in manual labor was the increase in white-collar employment. In 1956, for the first time, there were more white- than blue-collar workers. In the chemical sector, operatives rose 3 percent between 1947 and 1952, while salaried workers (as distinct from those who punched a time clock) jumped 50 percent. Corporations grew in size and complexity, creating more levels of management to oversee their far-flung activities. While in 1917, the top two hundred firms accounted for less than 25 percent of goods produced, by 1947 they claimed 47 percent of a much larger output. Further spurring the demand for educated workers was the rise of the service sector. By 1950, services, which included finance, education, health, law, and transportation, constituted fully half the national product. The confluence of these trends transformed the United States from a proletariat-based economy to one—using Daniel Bell's term—driven "by a salariat." These white-collar workers occupied the neatly drawn boxes in complex organization charts; they were David Riesman's "outer-directed" men (few were women) and William Whyte's "organization men."[3]

Prosperity raised the standard of living, dramatically expanding the middle class. Between 1945 and 1960, income per person climbed 35 percent, and significantly, these benefits were widely distributed. Income inequality, which had peaked in 1929, declined during World War II with full employment and overtime wages. The favorable distribution achieved in 1945 would continue into the 1970s. Affluence enlarged the middle stratum, those earning between $3,000 and $10,000. This group, which had claimed 31 percent of the population just before the Depression, embraced almost 60 percent of Americans in the mid-1950s. The "middling folk" now included not only much of the "salariat" but also the better-paid (and often unionized) production workers.[4]

The transformation of the middle class had profound implications. This group had evolved since Ben Franklin's time from well-off farmers and craftspeople to (by the 1920s) small proprietors and professionals, and now to salaried employees who occupied the middle ranks of towering hierarchies. Never before had bureaucracies been so important or kept such a tight rein on members of this class; never before had these individuals been so removed from the products and services they produced. Corporations offered security, and in return for those guarantees expected employees to march in lock step. If you worked at IBM, you wore a dark suit and were grateful for lifetime employment. While references to *conformity* were heightened throughout the modern era, they inched still higher in the 1950s (fig. P3.2).

These newly comfortable (if anxious) citizens left their mark on the 1940s and 1950s by buying homes in record numbers, moving to the suburbs, and having babies. With strong support from the Veteran's Administration and Federal Housing Authority, home ownership soared. In 1945, 40 percent of Americans lived in their own homes; by 1960 that percentage had climbed to 60 percent. Overwhelmingly, the houses that middle-class Americans now purchased were in the suburbs, which grew six times as fast as the cities in the 1950s. A remarkable eighteen million people moved to the 'burbs during that decade. Tract homes, while small, were a great improvement over the cramped apartments available at the end of the war. Women and men now married earlier and had more children, a "baby boom" that spanned the years from 1946 to the early 1960s. This surge in births temporarily reversed the long-term decline in fertility that marked US history and included not just White middle-class families but African Americans as well.[5]

Although most Americans prospered, many did not. Over 20 percent of families earned less than $3,000 in 1960. Michael Harrington's *The Other America: Poverty in the United States* (1962) estimated that forty to fifty million Americans lived in Depression-like conditions even at the end of 1950s. Most individuals over sixty-five had incomes of less than $1,000 in 1958. Racist practices excluded African Americans from the funds that helped White homeowners, dovetailing with the determination of developers to keep the suburbs lily White. And while the government assisted White home buyers, it provided little aid for the inner cities, which increasingly were scarred by poverty.[6]

II

The novels and art of the 1940s and 1950s portray a prosperous, but troubled, middle-class society. After the war, the demands for uniformity became ever more insistent—a climate of opinion reinforced by the crusade against communism. The House Un-American Activities Committee, confirmed as a permanent body in 1945, and Joseph McCarthy, whose anticommunist crusade began in 1950, scourged left-leaning thinkers. The new inquisition targeted scientists, actors, writers, government officials, teachers, and a variety of dissenters. Corporate rules also insisted on conformity, while the increasing wealth of the middle class argued for accepting the social order. Still, even with repression and the unprecedented high standard of living, complaints about postwar society grew louder. The result? Novels and painting—and the analysis here begins with literature—embody a seeming contradiction: they bitterly criticize society, but in the end willingly and often happily accept that world. Anger reverberates within a closed system.

The clash between criticism and acceptance of a conformist, hierarchical society defines Herman Wouk's bestseller *The Caine Mutiny* (1951). The first part of this World War II novel provides overwhelming evidence why an incompetent boss should be removed, even if extreme measures—a mutiny at sea—are required. Captain Philip Queeg is deceitful, vengeful, and cowardly, endangering the *Caine* and its crew. Thanks to the skills of lawyer Barney Greenwald, the ensuing court-martial accepts the mutineers' actions. But the last part of the book radically changes the message, affirming the sanctity of ranks. At a celebratory party, Greenwald tells the defendants he was sickened by the need to attack Queeg and declares the captain a hero who for many years "was standing guard on this fat dumb and happy country of ours." A review board reverses much of the court-martial, effectively ending the careers of the protesters. Most significantly, Ensign Willie Keith, whose perspective shapes the book, now agrees their actions were a mistake. He writes to May, the woman he loves: "The idea is, once you get an incompetent ass of a skipper—and it's a chance of war—there's nothing to do but serve him as though he were the wisest and the best, cover his mistakes, keep the ship going, and bear up."[7]

Not all critics are comfortable with the twist that shapes Wouk's novel. James R. Browne notes the "puzzling distortion introduced by the author toward the end of the story. . . . The final result is a picture of Queeg widely at variance with the Queeg who has been consistently presented throughout the book. It is with this latter problem, the Queeg-as-victim problem, that I am concerned with here."[8] Browne may be right aesthetically. But in the late modern era, most readers would have nodded knowingly at the concept of the boss as inviolable.

Another bestseller of 1951, J. D. Salinger's *The Catcher in the Rye*, shows the same uneasy yoking of condemnation and acquiescence. Few fictional individuals denounce middle-class conformity more vituperatively than Holden Caulfield. Looking around at a New York restaurant, he observes, "All those Ivy League bastards look alike. My father wants me to go to Yale, or maybe Princeton, but I swear, I wouldn't go to one of those Ivy League Colleges, if I was dying, for God's sake." Later, during a theater intermission, he remarks, "You never saw so many phonies in all your life, everybody smoking their ears off and talking about the play so that everybody could hear and know how sharp they were." Holden dreams of escaping to a cabin in Vermont or out West. But in the end, he has an epiphany watching his younger sister, Phoebe, on a carousel and casts off his despair: "I felt so damn happy all of sudden, the way old Phoebe kept going around and around. I was damn near bawling." He receives treatment for his psychological problems at a California institution, and the book strongly suggests he will return to society and accept his role in it.[9]

Jack Kerouac's *On the Road* (1957) provides still another example of a caustic social critique coupled with acceptance of middle-class life. In this autobiographical novel, Sal Paradise (the name Kerouac gives himself) takes a series of road trips with Dean Moriarty (the pseudonym for Neal Cassady). The two glorify those living on the fringes of society and mock the bourgeoisie with their quotidian cares. Sitting in the back seat of a shared ride, Dean tells Sal, "Now you just dig them in front.... [T]hey need to worry and betray time with urgencies false and otherwise, purely anxious and whiny, their souls really won't be at peace unless they can latch onto an established and proven worry."[10] But at the end, Sal gains a modicum of wealth from the sale of his book, and rejects Dean and his dissolute life. In a remarkably callous turn, Sal refuses on a cold New York evening to let Dean ride in the Cadillac taking him to a concert. Sal remarks, "Dean, ragged in a motheaten overcoat he brought specially for the freezing temperatures of the East, walked off alone, and the last I saw of him he rounded the corner of Seventh Avenue, eyes on the street ahead, and bent to it again."[11]

It is easy to lengthen the list of late modern-era novels shaped by the tension between criticism of the business world and its affirmation. Scholars often consider Sloan Wilson's *The Man in the Gray Flannel Suit* (1955) the quintessential depiction of corporate and suburban malaise. Tom Rath is dissatisfied with his job, his small home, and his family ties. But he surmounts those problems, and at the end tells his wife, "'I've been remembering a line from a poem that used to sound ironic and bitter. It doesn't sound that way any more." She asks, "What is it?" He replies, "God's in his heaven, . . . all's right with the world."[12] In Robert Penn Warren's *All the King's Men* (1946), Jack Burden grows increasingly disgruntled with his life, the corruption he sees in politics, and his complicity in that deceit. But the book ends with him marrying his childhood sweetheart and his decision to assist a politician he admires.[13] Similarly, Neil Klugman, the hero of Philip Roth's *Goodbye, Columbus* (1959), is critical of striving, middle-class conformists, and particularly his girlfriend's family, the Patimkins. But Neil too accepts the restraints imposed by society, and the closing sentence of the work reads: "I was back in plenty of time for work."[14]

Surveying the dreary adult world of the late 1940s and 1950s, authors suggested a counterweight: the purity of children. Only occasionally and briefly, were kids, like the Buchanans' daughter in *Gatsby,* visible in the novels of the 1920s. When present in the 1930s, they often belonged to desperate families trying to make ends meet. But after World War II, in the era of the baby boom, they amble onto center stage as avatars of the virtues adults lack. In *The Catcher in the Rye,* Holden's delight in children is as palpable as his scorn for grown-ups. He likes the way they put on skates or puzzle over a museum exhibit. Until the end of the narrative, when he accepts the inevitability of adult society, Holden wants to protect them from the corrupt world. He imagines himself in a field of rye with thousands of children: "What I have to do, I have to catch everybody if they start to go over the cliff."[15] In Bellow's *The Adventures of Augie March* (1953), Augie has a similar dream. He tells a friend he'd like to set up a rural school: "I'd love to have my own little children. I long for little children. And these kids from institutions who have had it rough." He continues: "I'd fix up a shop for woodwork. . . . My brother George could be the shoemaking instructor. Maybe I'd study languages so I could teach them." Like Holden, Augie abandons this dream once he has settled into the adult world.[16]

Other late modern novels similarly ennoble children. In *Goodbye, Columbus,* Neil Klugman, a library worker, becomes a "catcher" when he protects a young Black boy who comes regularly to look at a book of Gauguin paintings. Neil encourages the boy and keeps the book from other patrons. He enjoys other children as well: "Alongside me at the fence were dozens of kids; they giggled and screamed when the deer licked the popcorn from their hands."[17] In Harper Lee's *To Kill a Mockingbird* (1960), racial conflicts are seen through the eyes of ten-year-old "Scout" Finch. The opening chapters reveal that her classmates have more wisdom and compassion than their teachers. Later in the story, Scout's innocent questions help disperse a lynch mob. She and her friend Dill become the sole confidants of Dolphus Raymond, a White man who has an African American wife and pretends to be a drunk. When she asks him "why had he entrusted us with his deepest secret," he replies, "Because you're children and you can understand it."[18]

III

Along with their critique of conformist society, late modern–era novels detail the debilitating anxieties that characterize these years. The German-born philosopher Erich Fromm, who fled to the United States in 1934, points to this burden in his 1947 book, *Man for Himself*. Fromm observes, "[T]he *problem of production*—which was the problem of the past—is, in principle, solved." Nonetheless, "modern man feels uneasy and more and more bewildered. He works and strives, but he is dimly aware of a sense of futility with regard to his activities. While his power over matter grows, he feels powerless in his individual life and in society."[19] Disconnected from their jobs, housed in cookie-cutter suburban homes, "middling folk" felt increasingly distressed.

Wilson's *The Man in the Gray Flannel Suit* amply illustrates middle-class angst. Betsy Rath, wife of the protagonist Tom Rath, reflects on their suburban neighborhood: "Dull. That was the word she usually used for Greentree Avenue, but tonight she rejected it. If this were just a dull place, I wouldn't mind it so much, she thought. The trouble is, it's not dull enough—it's tense and it's frantic. Or, to be honest, Tom and I are tense and frantic, and I wish to heaven I knew why." Tom worries about losing his job and house, and about his former mistress making problems. Drawing little pleasure from his work, he reflects on his plight, "It's absurd to think of these things, he thought. I could get a job in an advertising agency. I'll write copy telling people to eat more corn flakes and smoke more and more cigarettes and buy more refrigerators and automobiles, until they explode with happiness."[20]

Eugene Henderson, the hero of Saul Bellow's *Henderson the Rain King* (1959), similarly finds life oppressive, despite his wealth and education. He explains why he decides to escape to Africa:

> When I think of my condition at the age of fifty-five when I bought the ticket, all is grief. The facts begin to crowd me and soon I get a pressure in the chest. A disorderly rush begins—my parents, my wives, my girls, my children, my farm, my animals, my habits, my money, my music lessons, my drunkenness, my prejudices, my brutality, my teeth, my face, my soul! I have to cry, "No, no, get back, curse you, let me alone!" But how can they let me alone? They belong to me. They are mine. And they pile into me from all sides. It turns into chaos.

That anguish, he recognizes, is widely shared. Henderson notes: "I tried every cure you can think of. Of course, in an age of madness, to expect to be untouched by madness is a form of madness." His trip to Africa helps him turn his life around. Henderson (like Tom Rath) surmounts his problems and at the end of the book emerges as a joyous individual, ready to rejoin the society he once cursed.[21]

Harry "Rabbit" Angstrom, hero of John Updike's *Rabbit, Run* (1960), experiences the same concerns, although unlike most late modern heroes he finds no solution for his ills. Harry is burdened by his marriage and children, by his relationship with a prostitute he briefly lives with, and by his low-level jobs demonstrating kitchen appliances and selling used cars. He too rehearses his troubles: "What held him back all day was the feeling that somewhere there was something better for him than listening to babies cry and cheating people in used-car lots and it's this feeling he tries to kill, right there on the bus. . . . The kink in his stomach starts to take the form of nausea and he clings to the icy bar bitterly as the bus swings around the mountain."[22]

IV

The novels of the 1940s and 1950s highlight still one more layer of the conformist middle-class culture: the turn toward religion. During these years, church attendance and membership increased sharply; 97 percent of Americans declared they believed in God.[23] Along with those indications of piety came an outpouring of religious bestsellers that crowded both the fiction and non-fiction lists. From 1920 to 1939 those surveys featured a total of only five Christian novels and eight faith-based advice books (counting books each time they appeared on the annual tallies). By contrast, from 1940 to 1959 twenty-five religious novels stood among the bestsellers, as did twenty-two volumes of Christian nonfiction.[24]

Not only were many more religious novels read in the late modern period than during the preceding two decades, but also the tone of these works changed in ways that suggest an intriguing fit with the anxieties of the 1940s and 1950s. Lloyd Douglas, the most successful religious novelist of this era, illustrates the transition. In Douglas's work of the 1920s and 1930s, faith leads to worldly success and demands no belief in other-worldly agency. Carl Bode explains that, before 1940, Douglas "pays little attention to the miraculous in Christian theology and tries to explain anything that is not normal in psychological terms."[25] But all that changed after 1940. Douglas's two blockbuster works, *The Robe* (1942) and *The Big Fisherman* (1948), highlight Jesus's miracles and denounce materialism. *The Robe*, which sold three million copies, retells the story of the crucifixion and its aftermath. The central character, a young Roman soldier, Marcellus, learns that "Jesus had much to say about a man's responsibility as a possessor of material things. Hoarded things might easily become a menace; a mere fire-and-theft risk; a breeding-ground for destructive insects; a source of worry. Men would have plenty of anxieties, but there was no sense in accumulating worries over THINGS!"[26] Douglas's books, and similar works by other religious authors, served a valuable function for middle-class readers, even if few recast their acquisitive lives. Like Washington Irving's *Sketch Book*, written during another time of turbulent change, anxious members of the middle class found comfort in hearing about higher values and the need to move away from accumulating more goods.[27]

V

The gains women made during the war, and their setbacks after 1945 and in the 1950s, were reflected in novels. Wartime advances were short-lived: while more than six million women entered the workforce in the early 1940s, with the return of peace, more than half of those individuals were laid off or left voluntarily. More particularly, they were pushed out of the better-paid positions, and their relative pay declined. In 1945, women in manufacturing earned two-thirds of what men did; by 1950, their pay was just over half. Female employment climbed again during the late 1940s and the 1950s, even while salaries remained comparatively low. Many of the service industries, such as banking, insurance, and advertising, demanded secretaries and other female staffers. By 1960, 40 percent of women over sixteen held a job, a striking rise from the 27 percent employed in 1940. Few, however, were in executive positions. While more married women worked than ever before, the majority remained at home taking care of their baby-boom families.[28] The Ngram graph of *strong women* sounded its lowest levels of the twentieth century during the 1940s and 1950s (fig. 7.2).

With only a few exceptions (in the early 1940s), novelists depicted weak women. In Wilson's *The Man In the Gray Flannel Suit*, Betsy Rath tells her husband, "Don't keep telling me I'm pretty. . . . If you want to compliment me, tell me I'm something I'm not. Tell me I'm a marvelous housekeeper, or that I don't have a selfish bone in my body."[29] In short, Betsy Rath was neither a good housekeeper nor a generous person—and could claim few other accomplishments. The offices Tom Rath worked in had two secretaries: one hired for her looks and the other for her efficiency. Ralph Ellison's *Invisible Man* (1952) addresses racism, but not sexism; none of the women in the novel is independent-minded.[30] The same holds true for the two women, Hella and Sue, who have a relationship with David, the bisexual protagonist of James Baldwin's *Giovanni's Room* (1956). In Steinbeck's *Sweet Thursday* (1954), the best women are sweet but ignorant.

Authors minimize even those women with accomplishments. In Lillian Smith's *Strange Fruit* (1944), Nonnie and her sister Bess are college-educated African American women who return to their small Southern town to work as maids. When her White boyfriend upbraids Nonnie for asking so little of life, she replies, "You're ambitious. I'm not. Sometimes I don't think contented people ever are."[31] In John Steinbeck's *Cannery Row* (1945), the "captain," whose wife is in the state assembly, bitterly mocks her accomplishments, observing, "My wife is a wonderful woman, . . . Most wonderful woman. Ought to of been a man."[32] Sadie Burke, a key figure in Warren's *All the King's Men*, is an adviser to Governor Stark and "a very smart cooky." But she is hopelessly in love with the governor and cursed with poor skin:

"Her features were good, if you noticed them, which you were inclined not to do, because her face was pocked."[33] Even the faculty wives and female English professors in Mary McCarthy's *The Groves of Academe* (1952) are quirky souls who demonstrate little boldness in academic battles. In Bellow's *The Adventures of Augie March*, the reader learns that Charlotte Magnus was "an excellent businesswoman" only many pages after her body is described: "She had remarkably handsome eyes . . . they were warm. So was her bosom, which was abundant, and she had large hips."[34] The list of novels with women whose abilities are undercut, or simply lacking, easily could be extended.

A few novels stand out because they present stronger women. None of these individuals is a feminist demanding equal status with men. If literature provides the touchstone, the "first wave" of the woman's rights movement had subsided in the 1880s, and the "second wave" would not emerge until the 1970s. Still, several works of the late modern period contain, for the times, uncharacteristically spunky women. Significantly, two of these books come from the early 1940s, before the heavy hand of conformist society settled on the middle class. Douglas's 1942 religious bestseller, *The Robe*, features several impressive women. Marcellus's sister, Lucia, is an outspoken critic of the empire. Theodosia, an innkeeper's daughter whom Marcellus encounters in Greece, draws a man's bow, and condemns the society that keeps her down. And before her martyrdom, Diana, Marcellus's wife, upbraids the emperor in front of his servitors: "These wise men all know that the Empire is headed for destruction—and they know why!"[35] Another book from the early 1940s, Betty Smith's *A Tree Grows in Brooklyn* (1943), presents determined women, often pairing them with weak men. Smith's novel, set in the early twentieth century, follows the childhood and adolescence of Francie Nolan. Because her father is a drunk and eventually dies of alcoholism, Francie's mother, Katie, has to keep the family together and raise her three children. Remarkably brave, Katie on one occasion grabs her husband's gun and kills a child molester. Katie's two sisters are equally bold. Evy, for example, takes over her husband's delivery business after he mismanages it. And Francie, through her ability and resolve, lands a series of increasingly well-paid jobs, and eventually enters college.[36]

Carson McCullers' novels *The Member of the Wedding* (1946) and *The Ballad of the Sad Café* (1951) are cautionary tales about the forces that overwhelm women who dare to defy social codes. Referring to the two protagonists, Frankie Addams in *Wedding* and Amelia Evans in *Sad Café*, literary critic Constante Groba observes, "Both of them resist being classified into the gender roles assigned them by tradition."[37] Frankie is a tall, twelve-year-old tomboy growing up in a small Southern town. She is conflicted about becoming feminine, although she sees that society demands she assume that role. The idea of sexual relations with men puzzles and

ANXIOUS CONFORMISTS, 1941-1960   171

frightens her. Instead, she hopes to join her brother and his bride as a member of a new family—an impossible fantasy. When she dresses up as a woman, the only person accepting her as an adult is a soldier who tries to rape her until she clobbers him with a pitcher. Amelia in *Sad Café* is a physically strong individual, who wears "overalls and gum boots," and is "the richest woman for miles around."[38] When a hunchback, Cousin Lymon, enters her life, her heart warms, and she opens a café that brings the townsfolk together. But Amelia cannot maintain her tradition-defying role. Her ex-husband, Macy, returns to town and, together with Lymon, who now turns on her, beats her mercilessly. Amelia closes the café and retreats into spinsterhood. Groba comments, "No longer an anomalous figure with a woman's name and masculine physique and behavior, she at last fits a role (the old maid) the town can safely relate to."[39]

Finally, Edna Ferber's *Giant* (1952) sets its female protagonist in that middle ground Ferber is so fond of—women who are independent-minded but not willing to openly challenge the male-dominated world. Leslie Lynnton of Virginia marries wealthy Texas rancher Bick Benedict—an unabashed chauvinist. He reminds Leslie, "In Texas the cattle come first, then the men, then the horses and last the women." Still, Leslie stands up for the causes she believes in, particularly the mistreatment of Mexican workers. She also criticizes the rich housewives who visit the ranch: "'They lack confidence,' she had said in tones of one who has made a discovery after long search. 'That's it. Unsure and sort of deferential. Like oriental women.... Even their voices go up at the end of a declarative sentence, instead of down.'"[40] In sum, most of the fictional women in the 1940s and 1950s were weak and subordinate. And even those who were exceptions to this rule, particularly after the early 1940s, accepted male dominance.

VI

The pressures of the late modern era also narrowed the range of acceptable roles for men. The novels of these two decades suggest that society no longer encouraged men to be dreamers (like Gatsby), rebels (like Tom Joad), or even unflinching heroes (like Robert Jordan).[41] *The Old Man and the Sea* (1952) closes Hemingway's decades-long chronicle of men who excelled at their craft, disdained money-making, and defied death. Santiago, the "old man," tells the fish he fights for days: "Never have I seen a greater, or more beautiful, or a calmer or more noble thing than you, brother. Come on and kill me. I do not care who kills who." But after sharks devour the fish's carcass, Santiago brings only its skeleton back to shore, and the narrative ends with him alone, tired, old, and near death.[42]

The most admirable individuals, the novels of the 1950s tell us, triumph over their discontents and become happy, well-adjusted employees and family men. *The Man in the Gray Flannel Suit* favorably contrasts Tom Rath with his hard-driving boss, Ralph Hopkins. Hopkins loses his wife and daughter to his obsession with work, while Rath settles into a comfortable niche at the firm, foregoing a lucrative promotion that would have entailed longer hours and less time with his family. Many other men fit Rath's mold and demonstrate their willingness, despite any grumbling, to accept their allotted role in society. These men include Augie March, Eugene Henderson, Jack Burden, Atticus Finch, Ensign Willie Keith, Sal Paradise, and very probably Holden Caulfield.[43]

Underlining the narrowing roles for men was the postwar demonization of homosexuality. The praiseworthy men of the late modern era were not only cheerful, reliable breadwinners, but also heteronormative. Nineteenth-century literature had shown few concerns about male bonding, even when unclothed men slept side by side. Leslie Fiedler's cheekily-entitled essay, "Come Back to the Raft Ag'in, Huck Honey!" reflects on such encounters, including Huck and Jim lying naked as they drift down the Mississippi.[44] In *Intimate Matters*, John D'Emilio and Estelle B. Freedman suggest a new openness to gay and lesbian relations in the 1920s, 1930s, and early 1940s. They remark that for many Americans leaving home for the first time, World War II "created a setting in which to experience same-sex love, affection, and sexuality."[45]

Literature during the 1920s and 1930s had embodied that same tolerance. For example, *The Great Gatsby* (1925) presents without censure the encounter between Nick Carraway and Mr. McKee, "a pale feminine man." Nick recollects, matter-of-factly: "I was standing beside his bed and he was sitting up between the sheets, clad in his underwear."[46] Similarly, John Dos Passos's *The 42nd Parallel* (1930) views a gay couple favorably: "Maurice and Eric seemed to be thoroughly happy. They slept in the same bed and were always together. Eleanor used to wonder about them sometimes but it was so nice to know boys who weren't horrid about women."[47] The lack of invective directed against gays in Dos Passos's work is noteworthy, particularly because the novel derogates other groups, including Blacks and Jews.

After the war, that tolerance was replaced by a crusade against gays and lesbians, a shift evident in both society and literature. Beginning in 1950, Congress launched a campaign to drive homosexuals out of government; local law enforcement raided gay clubs in cities across the country.[48] Negative references to gays became commonplace in literature. In *The Catcher in the Rye*, Holden Caulfield remarks on the scene at a hotel: "The other end of the bar was full of flits. They weren't too flitty-looking—I mean they didn't have their hair too long or anything—but you could tell they were flits anyway."[49] His acquaintance Carl Luce is gay, as is a teacher, Mr. Antolini, who tries to molest him. In *On the Road*, Sal Paradise, while friendly to hoboes and drifters, has no time for homosexuals: "There were plenty of queers. Several times I went to San Fran with my gun and when a queer approached me in a bar john I took out the gun and said, 'Eh? Eh? What's that you say?' He bolted."[50] Harry in *Rabbit, Run* remembers an early job unpacking crates with "Chandler the fairy mincing in every hour on the hour telling him to wash his hands so he wouldn't foul the furniture."[51] Although Patricia Highsmith was herself a lesbian, her portraits of gays in *Ripley* are not flattering. One is Marc Priminger, who had a "hobby of helping out young men in temporary financial difficulties by putting them up in his two-storey, three-bedroom house." Tom Ripley felt "the sooner he could forget Marc's stupid, piglike eyes, his massive jaw, his ugly hands with the gaudy rings (waving through the air, ordering this and that from everybody), the happier he would be."[52]

Two important novels by gay authors appeared in these decades, but even these books present a conflicted portrait of the homosexual community. Gore Vidal's *The City and the Pillar* (1948) was one of the first major American novels about homosexuality. The hero, Jim Willard, a tennis player, is straight-acting and condemns effeminate gay men as "strange womanish creatures."[53] Vidal, an established writer at the time, enraged many with this work. In *Giovanni's Room*, by the African American novelist James Baldwin, the hero, David, is White and bisexual. Growing up in America, David is frightened and depressed when he discovers his homosexual leanings. He flees to France, and falls in love, at least briefly, with Giovanni, a young bartender from Italy. Despite this romance, David has only acerbic comments about the gays, young and old, whom he meets in Parisian bars.[54] More broadly, the vilification of gays in postwar literature narrowed the space in which men defined themselves.

VII

During these years, discussions of race intertwined with the pressure to conform. Despite landmark advances—the integration of the armed forces and professional sports, *Brown vs. Topeka Board of Education*, and the beginning of the civil rights movement—derogatory stereotypes marred many White-authored books. Racial slurs pepper conversations in Norman Mailer's war novel, *The Naked and the Dead* (1948). The African American mess boys in Herman Wouk's *The Caine Mutiny* tremble when Captain Queeg confronts them: "The Negro's eyes were rounded in fright; perspiration rolled down his long, narrow cheeks, and his tongue flickered across his lips."[55] In *On the Road*, Kerouac's alter ego, Sal Paradise, envisions Blacks as a joyful counterpoise to reviled bourgeois society. He remarks, "I was only myself, Sal Paradise . . . wishing I could exchange worlds with the happy, true-hearted, ecstatic Negroes of America."[56] James Baldwin labels Kerouac's proposal to trade places, "absolute nonsense, of course, objectively considered, and offensive nonsense at that."[57]

Even Harper Lee's acclaimed 1960 novel, *To Kill a Mockingbird*, presents a questionable view of Blacks. In "Why It's Time Schools Stopped Teaching *To Kill a Mockingbird*," Naa Baako Ako-Adjei points out that Lee portrays African Americans as "mostly happy contented people," while dismissing the Klan as a "farcical group." Tom Robinson, the Black man falsely accused of rape, is frightened and humble, never defiant. African Americans appear as supplicants, not leaders, when they honor Atticus Finch by quietly standing as he leaves the courthouse. More broadly, the book, written against the background of the newly awakened civil rights movement, argues for gradualism guided by upper-class Whites.[58]

African American novels of the 1950s pointedly criticize discrimination while sharing with other fiction of this conformist era the pairing of rebellion and acceptance. Ralph Ellison's *Invisible Man* (1952) takes aim at a lengthy list of targets. The book opens with the powerful metaphor of "invisibility," an apt metaphor for the absence of Blacks in novels, movies and TV, and corporate boardrooms. The unnamed narrator announces: "I am invisible, understand, simply because people refuse to see me." The book turns a harsh light on racism in the South as well as Booker T. Washington's philosophy of "accommodation." Much of the work skewers the hypocrisies of the Communist Party, called the "Brotherhood" in the book. Ellison had been attracted to the party, and then renounced his ties. Ellison also attacks unions, White liberals with their goal of "uplifting the race," and Black nationalist rabble-rousers.[59]

But the book closes with the narrator resolving to return to society. He announces, "I've overstayed my hibernation, since there's a possibility that even an invisible man has a socially responsible role to play." His fervent hope is to do so, while retaining his Black identity. "Whence all this passion toward conformity anyway?" he asks, and continues: "Must I strive toward colorlessness? But seriously, and without snobbery, think of what the world would lose if that should happen. America is woven of many strands; I would recognize them and let it so remain." The ending disappoints some critics. As Barbara Foley notes, these readers "have complained of the unproblematic celebration of American democracy in the closing pages of a novel that has yielded scant basis for such loyalty."[60] Those scholars may have a point. But viewed in the broader context, *Invisible Man* fits well with the novels of the late modern era that combine criticism and acceptance.

James Baldwin's *Go Tell It on the Mountain* (1953) strikes a similar balance, combining a scathing critique of society with the surprisingly optimistic hope of succeeding in that world. The story, loosely autobiographical, focuses on John Grimes, a teenager in Harlem of the 1930s. Baldwin shows that for Black people life in New York was difficult, while the lengthy backstories of John's family members make clear that conditions were still more brutal in the South, with rape and mob violence commonplace. John's stepfather is a bitter man, mean to John, and angry at all White people. Despite such adversity, John demonstrates great resilience. A religious conversion provides him with new strength (and links the novel to the upsurge in faith-based fiction in the late modern era). Equally important, the praise John receives in school for his intellect heightens his confidence: "he apprehended totally . . . that he had in himself a power that other people lacked; that he could use this to save himself, to raise himself; and that, perhaps, with this power he might one day win that love which he so longed for." He challenges his father's assertion that all White people are evil, and envisions himself living a comfortable bourgeois life: "Behind him stood his house, great and rambling and very new, and in the kitchen his wife, a beautiful woman, made breakfast, and the smoke rose out of the chimney, melting into the morning air."[61] Thus fiction by Black writers both stood apart from and shared common themes with the White-authored literature of the era.

VIII

During these years, the leading school of art, abstract expressionism, exhibited the same balance as mainstream literature: it pointedly challenged but, in the end, affirmed conformist society. The large abstract canvases by Jackson Pollock, Mark Rothko, Lee Krasner, Robert Motherwell, and others puzzled, and in some cases infuriated, middle-class observers. Michigan congressman George Dondero, chairman of the House Committee on Public Works, declared that "Modern art is Communistic because it is distorted and ugly, because it does not glorify our beautiful country, our cheerful and smiling people, and our material progress." Dondero and like-minded lawmakers sought to ban abstract paintings from government-sponsored exhibitions.[62] Two presidents shared this disdain. Reviewing the exhibit, "Advancing American Art," Truman remarked of one canvas, "If that's art, I'm a Hottentot." Nor was Eisenhower any more enthusiastic. Discussing a show earmarked for government support, he observed that his favorite painting in the group was by the realist Andrew Wyeth. Ike suggested that in the future the committees arranging such shows include "one or two people that, like most of us here . . . are not too certain exactly what art is, . . . but know what we like and what America likes."[63]

8.1. JACKSON POLLOCK, *ONE: NUMBER 31, 1950* (1950).

Far more pleasing to middle Americans were realists like Norman Rockwell, whose sentimental depictions of happy families made him the best-known American artist of these years. Crowds also lined up to see Anna Mary Robertson Moses's country scenes. In 1949, Truman awarded the painter, better known as "Grandma Moses," a medal for her outstanding work. Viewers similarly acclaimed Wyeth and his depictions of rural folk in Pennsylvania and Maine.[64]

Even as the abstract expressionists seemed out of step with middle-class America, they supported its values and would become, in their own way, the leading representatives of the "American Way of Life." Abstract art was a reaction against the left-leaning social realism of the 1930s. A remarkable number of these painters, including Pollock, Rothko, Krasner, Willem de Kooning, and Arshile Gorky, had been part of the Federal Arts Project, and their early paintings typically had been representational. But they turned against that approach. Gorky labelled the work of the social realists "Poor art for poor people."[65] Pollock had studied with regionalist Thomas Hart Benton, and his early works tracked his master's style—but not for long. "I'm damn grateful to Tom," Pollock wrote in 1950, "He drove his kind of realism at me so hard I bounced right into non-objective painting." Benton agreed: "I don't think Jack ever adopted my ideas about the function of art in society. I don't think they even interested him."[66] Ben Shahn, a social realist whose art celebrated workers and protesters, was still more disappointed by the turn to abstraction. "Not only was the social dream rejected, but any dream at all," he explained in lectures delivered at Harvard in 1956–57. Referring to the paintings of Clyfford Still, Mark Rothko, and Ad Reinhardt, Shahn observed, "The work of these three painters is perhaps as content-less as anything to be seen currently."[67]

Instead of exploring social and political ills, abstract expressionists focused on the personal, revealing on their canvases the anxieties that were the mark of the late modern period. In 1947, painter Adolph Gottlieb explained, "Today when our aspirations have been reduced to a desperate attempt to escape from evil, and times are out of joint, our obsessive, subterranean and pictographic images are the expression of the neurosis which is our reality." Robert Motherwell concurred, noting that his fellow painters were "rebellious, individualistic, unconventional, sensitive, irritable . . . this attitude arose from a feeling of being ill at ease in the universe."[68] Hence, abstract expressionists were interested in Jungian archetypes, ancient myths, and the art of Indigenous peoples—influences that helped them channel their feelings into visual representations. These artists also recognized that size intensified the emotional impact of their work, a discovery that came in part from their admiration of Mexican muralists. Their canvases were often enormous; Pollock's *One: Number 31, 1950* measures 17' 6" by 8' 10" (ptg. 8.1).

In the Cold War battle of ideas, abstract expressionism, which was daring but apolitical at its core, became, as Eva Cockcroft notes, "the ideal style for these propaganda activities. It was the perfect contrast to the 'regimented, traditional, and narrow' nature of 'socialist realism.'"[69] Thomas W. Braden, who from 1951 to 1953 was the CIA's supervisor for cultural activities, sent these modern art works to exhibits around the world. Recognizing that congressional funding for these shows was "as likely as the John Birch Society's approving Medicare," he used a variety of CIA front organizations to disseminate the art. New York's Museum of Modern Art similarly brought these works to international audiences.[70] Serge Guilbaut's thoughtful study of abstract expression summarizes the contradictory relationship these paintings had with American society: "The rebellion of the artists, born of frustrations within the left, gradually changed its significance until ultimately it came to represent the values of the majority, but in a way (continuing the modernist tradition) that only a minority was capable of understanding."[71]

PART FOUR
The Postmodern Era

For many young people in the early 1960s, Paul Goodman's *Growing Up Absurd* (1960) struck with the same force that J. D. Salinger's *The Catcher in the Rye* (1951) had a decade earlier. But the gulf between the two bestsellers was enormous and embodied the differences between the late modern and postmodern eras. Salinger's hero, Holden Caulfield, condemns "phonies" but ultimately, after some counseling, prepares to return to the society that breeds such individuals. For Goodman, that world is rotten, and accommodation foolish. He begins by noting the "two subjects . . . brought together in this book, the disgrace of the Organized System of the semimonopolies, government, advertisers, etc., and the disaffection of the growing generation." "My stratagem in this book is a simple one," Goodman explains, "I assume that the young *really* need a more worth-while world in order to grow up at all, and I confront this real need with the world that they have been getting."[1]

As Goodman's book suggests, the outlook of many middle-class Americans shifted dramatically in the early 1960s. Discontent became denunciation. Three far-reaching changes provided the basis for the new epoch; together they shattered the veneer of harmony that marked modernity and pointed to a new framework for society. The first was the movement of the middle class from vibrant, heterogenous cities to sterile suburbs. Life in cookie-cutter houses on cul-de-sacs proved disconcerting, leading middle-class families to question the value of traditional goals. Second, many individuals, like Goodman, now decided that a society dominated by corporate behemoths no longer merited their approbation and loyalty. Beliefs that had served as the bedrock of the modern era crumbled. Those critiques would become still harsher as inequality soared at the end of the century.[2]

The third transforming force was the waves of revolt roiling the 1960s. In 1960, college students from Greensboro, North Carolina, reinvigorated the civil rights protests begun in the 1950s with their sit-in at Woolworth's. The Freedom Rides on interstate buses in 1961, and a variety of demonstrations, including the 1963 March on Washington for Jobs and Freedom and the Mississippi Freedom Summer of 1964, intensified the demand for change. Agitation burst out on other fronts. The free speech movement at University of California, Berkeley, erupted in 1964–65, about the same time resistance to the Vietnam war quickened. In 1967, one hundred thousand antiwar protestors rallied at the Lincoln Memorial. Toward the end of the decade, women began organizing "consciousness raising" groups. Longer hair, the freer use of drugs, and more open attitudes toward sex revealed the breadth of the youth revolt.

The 1960s were admittedly a special time: in no subsequent decade did so many young, middle-class individuals take part in the resistance. But the damage had been done; the high walls of the modern era had been breached. Many Americans remained conservative and excoriated those who attacked established beliefs. But like the warming that melts glaciers, seemingly impregnable customs and practices slowly gave way in the ensuing years. The results included changes in lifestyle, language, and religion. This revolt was never simply an attack on older values. Rather, it pointed to a new social order, one that emphasized compassion and respect for groups that had long been subject to discrimination.[3]

These developments, taken together, created the two sides of the postmodern era: the destruction of accepted norms on the one hand and, on the other, the demand for a more caring and just nation. The clash between (and sometimes the intermingling of) chaos and rebuilding shaped the period, its literature and art.

How did creative individuals respond to this unsettled universe—and the warring imperatives of postmodernity? Analysis starts with literature and a crucial question: just who were the postmodern writers? One set of critics restricts the label to a coterie of experimental novelists, such as William Gaddis, Donald Barthelme, William Gass, Thomas Pynchon, Don DeLillo, and John Barth. Those authors share a variety of traits, explains Robert McLaughlin, such as "wordplay for the sake of wordplay," "skepticism toward narrative as a meaning-providing structure," and "irony and self-referentiality."[4] Other observers dissent, insisting that a broad range of novelists writing after 1960 deserve to be called postmodernists. Wendy Steiner notes the ambiguity in the term *postmodern:* "It means both the stylistically innovative writing from the 1960s to the 1990s, such as that by Pynchon or Barth, and the literature of the period as a whole." Steiner leaves no doubt which side of this divide she stands on. "The purist argument," she observes, "leads to a main line of aesthetic activity that is utterly male and white." Steiner continues: "These works by women, blacks, homosexuals and other nonaesthetically defined groups ... embody the assumptions of postmodernism every bit as fully as the more obvious, esoteric, and largely unread 'neomodernists' do."[5] While literary debates brook no absolutes, there are good reasons to second Steiner's conclusions and broaden the postmodern canon. Inclusivity moves the field away from privileging White males. It emphasizes the shared qualities characterizing works by women, minorities, popular authors, *and* experimental writers. It helps link fiction to changes in America.

Postmodern writers (using the broader definition of that group) document the forces of disruption. Fragmentation was evident in the shattered conventions strewn across the literary landscape. The ghosts wandering through these works are not Halloween phantasmas, but complex characters who fully share the narrative with their flesh-and-blood counterparts. Such specters populate William Kennedy's *Ironweed* (1983), Toni Morrison's *Beloved* (1987), Edward Jones's *The Known World* (2003), and George Saunders's *Lincoln in the Bardo* (2017). Other novels unsettle the reader's solid footing like a temblor rumbling beneath a California town. In John Irving's *A Prayer for Owen Meany* (1989), the protagonist accurately predicts the timing and circumstances of his death; streets rearrange themselves, and a five-hundred-year-old man demonstrates superhuman strength in Karen Tei Yamashita's *The Tropic of Orange* (1997). In Colson Whitehead's *Underground Railroad* (2016), the metaphorical escape route becomes a literal train, with tunnels drilled deep under the Southern states. Postmodern novels also overflow the high levees of propriety and spew language once judged impermissible for mainstream literature. As figure P4.1 illustrates, terms such as *shit, fuck*, and *asshole* appeared in mainstream works after 1960, and became increasingly common in the new century.

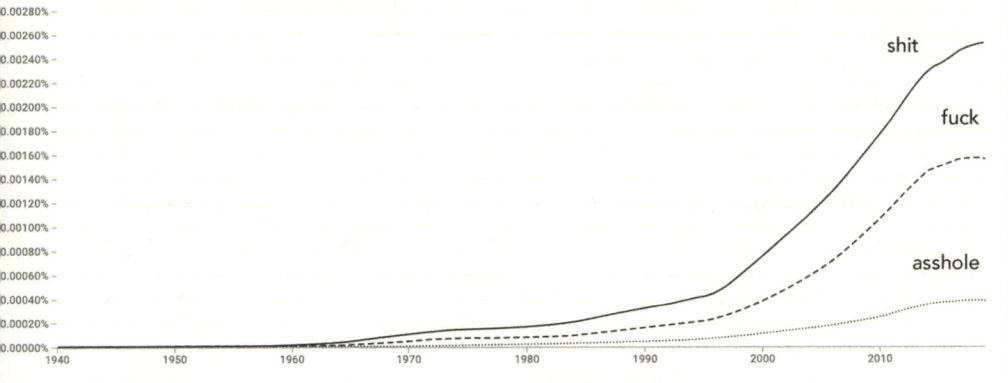

P4.1. FREQUENCY OF *SHIT, FUCK,* AND *ASSHOLE* IN AMERICAN ENGLISH (2019) NGRAM DATABASE, 1940–2019.

Changes in the substance as well as the form of postmodern fiction highlight the breakdown of norms within middle-class America. Authors who write traditional novels acknowledge that their protagonists have been expelled from the garden of contentment that marked the 1950s. In 1961, Philip Roth recognized the widening fissure that separated current writing from late modern works. Reviewing the fiction of the 1950s, he observes, "If the world is as crooked and unreal as I think it is becoming, day by day; if one feels less and less power in the face of this unreality, day by day; if the inevitable end is destruction, if not of all life, then of much that is valuable and civilized in life—then why in God's name is the writer pleased? . . . Why is it, in fact, that so many of our fictional heroes . . . wind up affirming life?"[6]

The form and content of postmodern art also challenged long-held conventions. Traditionally, the most important visual technique was painting, while other approaches remained mere rivulets beside that torrent. After 1960, painting became simply one mode of expression among many. Alternatives included Andy Warhol's silkscreens, Romare Bearden's collages and photomontages, Betye Saar's mixed-media assemblage, and Jean-Michel Basquiat's graffiti. Like novels, art illustrates the violence, class conflict, and racism unsettling society.

Alongside that fragmentation, the quest for a new social order also was unmistakable. The desire to build a compassionate, progressive world was evident in the novels that exalted peaceful communities, celebrated the bonds between parent and child, opposed racism, and supported the demands of feminists, immigrants, and the LGBTQ community. Visual media shared these goals.

An examination of postmodernity must also explore two closely related issues: Should the epoch be split in two? And how best can we date the era? Many critics divide the years after 1960 into two segments, with the point of demarcation typically reflecting an important event: 1991 (fall of the Soviet Union), 2001 (destruction of the Twin Towers), or 2008 (the financial crisis). While all observers label the first period "postmodernism," the second is often called "post-postmodernism" but also "postmodernism 2.0," "digimodernism," and "technomodernism." The substantive explanations scholars put forth also range widely. Rachel Adams declares the second period the "globalization of American literature."[7] For Andrew Hoberek, the "salient event in post-postmodern fiction is the rise (or rather, return) of popular genres to literary respectability."[8] In his book *Post-Postmodernism,* Jeffrey Nealon declares recent American culture "an intensified version of yesterday."[9] Finally, in a 1993 essay that is as much prescription as reporting, novelist David Foster Wallace declares that postmodern irony "tyrannizes us" and demands a literature that presents "old untrendy human troubles and emotions in U.S. life with reverence and conviction." Picking up on those themes, some writers suggest that the hallmark of post-postmodernism is "sincerity" or "sentimental posthumanism."[10]

There are problems with these formulations both individually and collectively.

Typically, they rest on a small evidentiary base. Adams's essay contrasts two books: Pynchon's *The Crying of Lot 49* (1966) and Yamashita's *Tropic of Orange*. Hoberek's emphasis on the return of genre privileges a small set of works. Nealon's book never makes clear what "intensification" means for contemporary fiction. Novelists did not grant Wallace's wish for the end of irony.[11]

Viewed more broadly, the arguments for dividing postmodernism into distinct periods seem unconvincing. Certainly, important changes altered society, literature, and art between 1960 and 2020. That was true for all four eras discussed in the book—but in each case the overall unities transcend any segmentation. For example, during the sentimental era, which stretched from 1789 to 1869, society evolved dramatically, but still works like Stowe's *Uncle Tom's Cabin* (1852) and Alcott's *Little Women* (1868–69), appealed to emotions much as did Brown's *The Power of Sympathy* (1789). Similarly, the fragmentation and disorder that mark novels of the 1960s, such as Joseph Heller's *Catch-22* (1961) or Pynchon's *The Crying of Lot 49*, also characterize works of the 2010s, for example, Whitehead's *The Underground Railroad* and Saunders's *Lincoln in the Bardo*. There is a unity to postmodernity, stretching across these six decades, that binds the period together and distinguishes it from the preceding era.

The dates assigned to postmodernity are also a source of contention. This discussion has quietly assumed that the period began around 1960, but not all scholars agree. Critics propose starting points ranging from the 1930s to 2001. Among the frequently mentioned years are 1966 (because of the publication of Pynchon's *The Crying of Lot 49* and Beatlemania) and 1973 (thanks to Watergate). Still, most observers locate Day One around 1960. Advocates for that periodization include the commentators who focus on the experimental authors, since their novels typically appeared after 1960.[12] Although not part of that set of critics, Frederic Jameson, in his landmark study *Postmodernism: Or, the Cultural Logic of Late Capitalism* (1991), suggests a similar time frame, pointing to a "radical break or *coupure*, generally traced back to the end of the 1950s or the early 1960s." Jameson argues that changes in literature, art, and society highlight this dividing line.[13] As for the terminus of the era, those who contend for post-postmodernism conclude that postmodernity ended in the 1990s or early in the new millennium. This discussion suggests no such division but rather posits an era that is ongoing. It will end one day, as every epoch does—but just not yet.[14]

9
New Realities, 1961–1990

For many postmodern writers, like E. L. Doctorow, reality is not what it used to be. Doctorow's 1975 novel, *Ragtime*, offers a fanciful take on events at the beginning of the twentieth century. In a wholly invented scene, J. P. Morgan invites Henry Ford to the Morgan Library and expounds on reincarnation. Ford responds that he knows all about rebirth from a twenty-five-cent book he purchased. Most noteworthy is Doctorow's view of the text. "I'm under the illusion that all of my inventions are quite true," he told an interviewer. "For instance, in *Ragtime*, I'm satisfied that everything made up about Morgan and Ford is true, whether it happened or not. Perhaps truer because it didn't happen. And I don't make any distinction any more—and can't even remember—what of the events and circumstances in *Ragtime* are historically verifiable and what are not."[1] Doctorow, a talented writer, is neither delusional nor joking; rather, he sees the world differently from those who wrote in earlier eras.

Around 1960, American middle-class culture, and its reflection in the work of novelists and artists, changed dramatically. The shift was every bit as momentous as those demarcating earlier eras. To be sure, the "middling" stratum—and its worldview—were never monolithic. While some individuals applauded works, like Doctorow's, that toyed with reality, others preferred books and paintings that took more traditional approaches. Demands for social justice, one of the key drivers of change, met hostility as well as affirmation. Still, the advent of postmodernity signaled the beginnings of a profound transformation, one that reshaped the world for individuals with widely differing views. The first dominoes in a lengthy row had fallen. Time-honored hierarchies of race and gender experienced withering attacks. Verities from the 1950s and earlier decades were cast aside. In the 1953 hearings to become a member of Eisenhower's cabinet, a business leader, Charles Wilson, stated his long-held conviction, that "what was good for our country was good for General Motors, and vice versa."[2] That was no longer the American credo.

Understanding the initial decades of the postmodern era involves carefully tracking contrary winds. On the one hand, the swirl of destruction was unmistakable. Novelists and artists defied hallowed assumptions about society—and, in some instances, about reality. A contagion of amorality, evident in books, opinion pieces, and works of art, undercut old-fashioned rectitude. Violence erupted in literature and artworks as well as on city streets. On the other hand, calls for a new ordering—one that fostered compassion and justice—became ever louder. Books and art suggested new, more positive roles for women, men, and, more broadly, African Americans. Other works affirmed the ties between a parent and child. These contrary torrents, the antipodal gales of destruction and rebuilding, defined the first decades of the epoch.

I

Analysis of the economy sheds light on the years from 1960 to 1990. A paradox, puzzling but crucial to any understanding of the era and its literature and art, lies at the heart of the relationship between the middle class and the corporate world. To begin, changes in society and the economy alienated many middle-class Americans. They found unsettling the move from the city to the suburbs, which in these years were sterile, dreary communities segregated by wealth and race. They resented the increasing control that big businesses, with their mainframe computers and ubiquitous punch cards, exercised over employees. ("Everyone feared IBMification," Lee Konstantinou remarks about these years.) In 1955, the first year for the Fortune 500 list of the largest corporations, IBM stood 61st. By 1960, with the demand for its services soaring, the data processing giant had climbed to 27th, and by 1970 to 5th place, a position it would maintain in the ensuing decades. Rebellious, middle-class youth amplified these concerns. They denounced a system that discriminated against people of color, made war in faraway lands, and reduced students to digits on punch cards.[3]

But there was another side to this paradox: in many respects, the early years of the postmodern era were extraordinarily favorable ones for "middling folk." During the 1960s and the first half of the 1970s, strong growth, the relative equality of incomes, and a bevy of large, highly profitable, well-regarded corporations characterized the American economy. The biggest employers, such as General Motors, Ford, and General Electric, paid unionized workers solid middle-class salaries, and for the moment the lack of innovation that characterized many factories proved no hindrance to success. John Kenneth Galbraith celebrated this system in *The New Industrial State* (1967), the rare economic treatise that was also a bestseller. Surveying the postwar era, Galbraith observed that "the production of goods ... has been notably high and remarkably reliable." Perched at the pinnacle of this edifice was the corporation: "A rich society owes its productivity and income, at least in part, to large scale organization—to the corporation." Galbraith declared that, since the pursuit of efficiencies argued for ever-larger companies, there was "no clear upper limit to the desirable size."[4]

However, in the mid-1970s, that vaunted structure crumbled and slowly crashed to earth. The flaw in the corporate system, unremarked by Galbraith, was its smugness, an outlook nurtured during years that earnings were high and foreign competition absent. Auto plants fought the introduction of front-wheel-drive cars; tire factories spurned the shift to radials; electronics companies questioned the value of printed circuit boards. By 1970, European and Far Eastern producers had recovered from the war and barreled back onto the world stage, championing innovation, and emerging as the low-cost, high-quality producers of steel, autos, tires, appliances, and electronic goods. American consumers voted for these wares with their pocketbooks, in 1979 buying $38 worth of imports for every $100 spent on domestic wares (compared to $14 worth in 1969)—a proportion that continued to rise. US companies responded not with innovation, but by shedding workers, shuttering plants, and relocating production overseas. Between 1979 and 1986, the northern states lost 1.6 million manufacturing jobs. Union membership plummeted. Workers found new positions but at much lower salaries, say, fixing refrigerators rather than making them.[5]

For many, the consequences were dire and deepened the alienation that had been present even in the prosperous years. Inequality increased, a social fissure that widened during the ensuing decades. The sharp increase in oil prices in the 1970s, the rise in leveraged buyouts, and the Reagan tax cuts of the 1980s accelerated this trend. The expansion of the "middling orders" screeched to a halt, as wages stagnated and job prospects dimmed. References to the *middle class,* which had skyrocketed during the preceding decades, declined after 1970 (fig. IN. 1). Although most individuals, when asked, continued to identify with this cohort, the welcome mat had been snatched away. Meanwhile, the foundation stones for a less welcoming economy were being set. That new order was marked by the decline of manufacturing, the expansion of entry-level jobs, and the emergence of a fantastically wealthy elite that owned, managed, and financed the largest companies. These trends, which date from the mid-1970s, became ever more visible after 1990.

The changing economy had a mixed impact on African Americans. Thanks to the prosperity of the 1960s and early 1970s and the Great Society programs, the

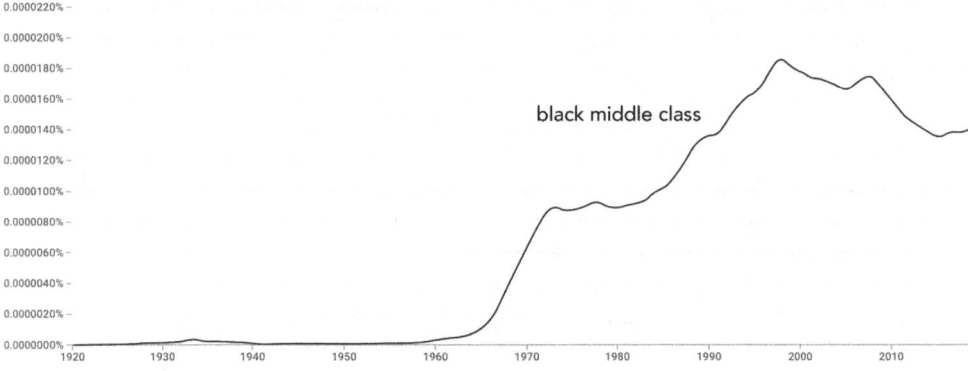

9.1. FREQUENCY OF *BLACK MIDDLE CLASS* IN AMERICAN ENGLISH (2019) NGRAM DATABASE, 1920–2019.

Black poverty rate declined from over 50 percent in 1960 to about 30 percent in 1974. The proportion of Black families earning more than $10,000 (in constant dollars) rose from 3 percent in 1947 to over 30 percent in 1971. While the Black middle class has its origins in the nineteenth century, the group now dramatically expanded; after 1990, its presence in society and literature would be unmistakable. References to the *Black middle class* illustrate that rise (fig. 9.1). Most persons of color, however, fared less well. The movement of well-off African Americans out of the cities, often to segregated suburbs, left behind impoverished communities. Deindustrialization hit African Americans particularly hard. They were the last hired and first fired. The riots of the 1960s testify to the anger and despair of the inner-city residents who did not share in the prosperity of these years.[6]

II

During the first decades of the postmodern period, authors and artists broke with the orderly world of late modern America. Even the most traditional novels made clear they no longer accepted a discredited social order. More daring works introduced ghosts, fractured time, suggested shadowy conspiracies, and posed irresolvable conundrums. The transformation of literature, art, and society involved fashioning a new order as well as shattering the old. This account begins with the unsettling of long-accepted norms.

Moral ambiguity—or at times, amorality—now shaped many novels, a weak-kneed relativism decried by many critics. Writing in *Time* magazine after the 2001 attack on the Twin Towers, Roger Rosenblatt lamented, "For some 30 years ... the good folks in charge of America's intellectual life have insisted that nothing was to be believed in or taken seriously."[7] While such blanket condemnations are questionable (as were the pious wishes that 9/11 would end such wobbling), many authors seemed almost indifferent to atrocities and acts of cruelty.

Joseph Heller's *Catch-22* (1961), a World War II novel that examines a bomber command on a small Mediterranean island, illustrates the new amorality. For the protagonist Yossarian, Hitler is just another person to despise, no worse than the army brass or entrepreneur Milo Minderbinder. Literary critic Sanford Pinsker notes the "conspicuous absence of any acknowledgement that the *real* enemy was not Milo Minderbinder or ex-PFC Wintergreen or even General Dreedle, but Hitler. A World War II novel that leaves this crucial fact out begs for moral reassessment." Pinsker continues: "And what about the Holocaust, a part of history that doesn't fit into Heller's aesthetic plan and that he simply sweeps under the rug?"[8] As Pinsker suggests, Heller's absurdist vision makes no room for crimes against humanity.

Similarly, a deep moral ambivalence characterizes Vonnegut's *Slaughterhouse-Five* (1969), which focuses on the fire-bombing and destruction of Dresden. On the one hand, the protagonist Billy Pilgrim agrees with the (fictional) historian Bertram Rumfoord that the bombing *"had* to be done" to achieve victory in a brutal war. On the other hand, Billy's philosophy and, more broadly, the narrative undercut normative judgements. The Tralfamadorians, the aliens who kidnap Billy, teach him that all events are predestined and free will is illusory. Billy tells Rumfoord, "It was all right.... *Everything* is all right, and everybody has to do exactly what he does. I learned that on Tralfamadore." Billy expounds on that viewpoint: "Now, when I myself hear that somebody is dead, I simply shrug and say what the Tralfamadorians say about dead people, which is 'So it goes.'" The expression appears 106 times in the novel, muting every horror. For example, the narrator remarks, "And Billy had seen the greatest massacre in European history, which was the fire-bombing of Dresden. So it goes."[9]

Morality teeters as well in Don DeLillo's novels. In *End Zone* (1972), Gary Harkness matter-of-factly tells a classmate about his interest in nuclear war: "I like to read about mass destruction and suffering. I spend a lot of time reading stuff that concerns thermonuclear war and things that pertain to it." Striking the same placid tone, his friend Taft Robinson discusses his obsession with the Shoah: "I like to read about atrocities. I can't help it. I like to read about the ovens, the showers, the experiments, the teeth, the lampshades, the soap."[10] *White Noise* (1985) demonstrates a similar moral blindness. The protagonist, Jack Gladney, who is a professor of Hitler studies, makes no mention of Hitler's racial views or the Holocaust in his discussions with students and colleagues. Instead, Gladney humanizes the German dictator, comparing him to Elvis and noting his troubled childhood: "Hitler was a lazy kid. His report card was full of unsatisfactorys. But Klara loved him, spoiled him, gave him the attention his father failed to give him."[11]

Cormac McCarthy's *Blood Meridian* (1985), a novel set on the Mexican border around 1850, flouts traditional values of right and wrong. The novel details the unchecked sadism of Glanton's gang with its wanton slaughter of people and animals. Judge Holden, whose erudition and commanding presence place him at the heart of the narrative, declares, "Moral law is an invention of mankind for the disenfranchisement of the powerful in favor of the weak." The other principal character, the "kid" (we are never given his full name) provides at best a weak counterforce, at times refusing to follow the Judge's lead. But his resistance is passive and his reasoning unspoken—while the Judge expounds loudly on the virtues of lawlessness.[12]

Similarly, Clay, the spoiled college student and central figure in Bret Easton Ellis's *Less Than Zero* (1985), registers only the mildest dissent at his friends' sadism. The novel chronicles the activities of Clay and his circle during one winter break. Occasionally Clay turns his gaze away or mentions that his hands are shaking. More often he watches, remarking, "I cannot take my eyes off the dead boy." When a twelve-year-old girl is stripped and tied to a bed, Clay simply reports: "Someone's put a lot of makeup on her.... Spin digs the syringe into her arm. I just stare. Trent says 'Wow.' Rip says something."[13]

Although irony would continue after 1990 (alive in the banter in works such as Richard Ford's *Independence Day* [1995] or Ben Fountain's *Billy Lynn's Long Halftime Walk* [2012]), novels fraught with deep moral ambivalence became less common. The increasing extremes in wealth created a moral dimension that reshaped much of the literary world and made clearer the distinctions between good and evil.

III

The spread of lawlessness compounded the sense of disorder marking the first decades of the postmodern era. Between 1960 and 1990, violence in literature reflected national trends that showed a sharp rise in murders and robberies. After 1990, the crime rate subsided and references to violence suggest a different source—mounting apocalyptic fears—a change discussed in the next chapter. Figure 9.2 shows the rising concern for *violence* throughout this epoch as well as, after 1990, the decline in *robbery* and the more frequent mentions of *apocalypse*.

During the first postmodern decades, novels highlight urban crime, creating a sharp contrast with the late modern era. Saul Bellow's works of the 1950s, like *The Adventures of Augie March* (1953) and *Henderson the Rain King* (1959), while

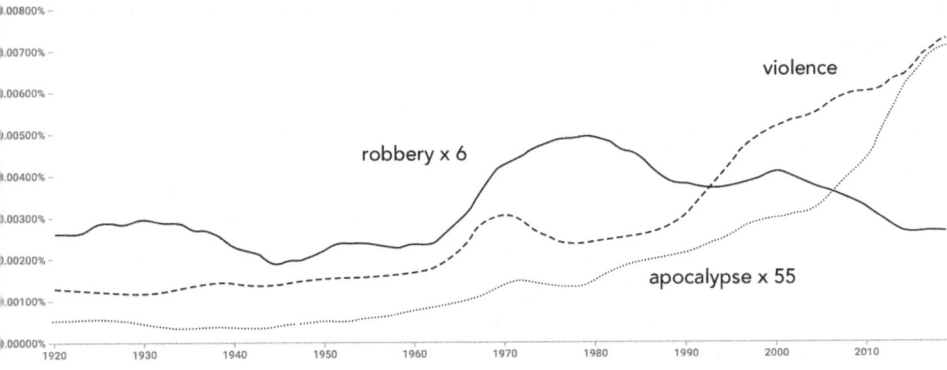

9.2. FREQUENCY OF *VIOLENCE, ROBBERY,* AND *APOCALYPSE* IN AMERICAN ENGLISH (2019) NGRAM DATABASE, 1920–2019.

exploring personal problems, present an America in which disorder is kept in check. After 1960, the city in Bellow's novels grows more menacing. Moses Herzog, hero of *Herzog* (1964), obsessively composes, but does not send, a series of letters complaining about the breakdown of society. For example, he tells the Chicago police commissioner: "I have a small daughter who lives near Jackson Park, and you know as well as I do the parks are not properly policed. Gangs of hoodlums make it worth your life to go in." While waiting in court for his divorce proceedings, Herzog catalogues the despicable crimes and individuals he observes. In *Mr. Sammler's Planet* (1970), Bellow's vision of urban decay is distilled in his repeated (and racist) depiction of a Black pickpocket who exposes himself. As Sander Gilman notes, Bellow "uses the exposed member of the Black pickpocket as a sign for the potency of those pathological forces that claim the city for themselves."[14]

Other novels highlight the prevalence of crime. Maria Wyeth, protagonist of Joan Didion's *Play It as It Lays* (1970), examines the FBI posters on a post office wall: "Wandering the country somewhere were Negro Females Armed with Lye, Caucasian Males posing as Baby Furniture Representatives, Radio Station Employees traveling out of Texas with wives and children and embezzled cash."[15] Felonies so are commonplace in Carl Hiaasen's *Double Whammy* (1987) that news reports barely mention the homicides that detective R. J. Decker is investigating. The narrator observes, "[They] probably would have gotten better play had it not been for the biannual mass murder in Oklahoma: this time it was twelve motorists shot by a disgruntled toll-booth operator who was fed up with people not having the exact change."[16]

Violence drives story lines. Walker Percy's *Love in the Ruins* (1971) establishes a parallel universe, one that heightens the conflicts troubling America. The narrator remarks, "For our beloved old U.S.A. is in a bad way. Americans have turned against each other; race against race, right against left, believer against heathen."[17] In William Kennedy's *Ironweed* (1983), the protagonist, Francis Phelan, who is by turns a baseball player, labor agitator, and hobo, rarely restrains his anger. When he sees non-union drivers piloting trolleys during a strike, he "wound up his educated right arm, and let fly that smooth round stone the weight of a baseball, and brained the scab working as the trolley conductor."[18] The landscape in Cormac McCarthy's *Blood Meridian* becomes a vast charnel house. The campaign undertaken by Glanton's gang begins with attacks on the Apaches, but soon becomes indiscriminate slaughter.[19] Lawlessness is pervasive as well in Charles Portis's *True Grit* (1968), a novel set in Indian Territory (later to be Oklahoma) in the 1870s. Even "Rooster" Cogburn, the US marshall who helps Mattie Ross track down the man who killed her father, had robbed banks before he became a lawman. Ellis's *Less than Zero* presents an unsettling vision of sadistic, unchecked individuals. In Pat Conroy's *The Prince of Tides* (1986), a horrific episode lies at the core of the narrative. Escaped convicts rape several members of the Wingo family, and then are murdered by Tom Wingo and his brother Luke.

IV

Balancing the drift toward fragmentation, amorality, and violence was the affirmation of caring relationships and the respect given individuals and groups that had long been subject to discrimination. No aspect of the desire to seek order in a world tilting toward chaos was more intriguing than authors' grudging recognition of the benefits provided by large companies. In the later decades of the postmodern period such positive notes would be replaced by scathing critiques. Figure 9.3 maps the change within this era. It shows the ascent of *corporate power* during the first part of the era and *corporate greed* after 1990. Still, affirming that big business contributed to society did not mean a return to the values of the 1950s and acceptance of the established order. Early postmodern novels paired an unsettling fragmentation with kind words about large firms.

Thomas Pynchon's *The Crying of Lot 49* (1966) illustrates these crosscurrents. The shattering of social norms is unmistakable. The story follows Oedipa Maas, a California housewife, into a Wonderland of secretive organizations and nefarious deeds. She stumbles upon Trystero, a centuries-old alternative mail service, now the courier of choice for social outcasts. She reflects: "For here were God knew

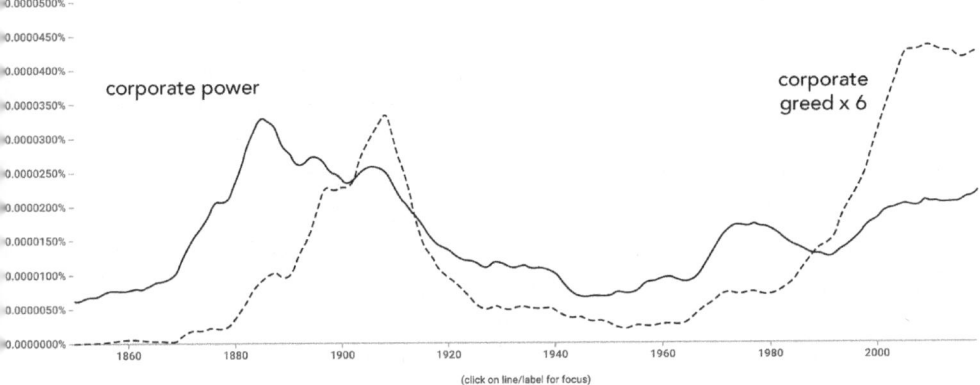

9.3. FREQUENCY OF *CORPORATE POWER* AND *CORPORATE GREED* IN AMERICAN ENGLISH (2019) NGRAM DATABASE, 1850–2019.

how many citizens, deliberately choosing not to communicate by U.S. Mail.... [I]t was a calculated withdrawal, from the life of the Republic, from its machinery."[20]

These activities play out against Oedipa's investigation—and generally favorable view—of Pearce Inverarity, a business mogul and former lover, now deceased, for whom she serves as executor. Yoyodyne, an aerospace company in which Inverarity invested heavily, is the largest employer in the fictional town of San Narcisco. Oedipa praises Inverarity's far-flung real estate developments, noting a seniors' home he erected and the aesthetic charm of his developments. His upbeat outlook buoys her: "'Keep it bouncing,' he'd told her once, 'that's all the secret, keep it bouncing.'" His vision, as Oedipa comes to realize, had no small element of grandeur: "She had dedicated herself, weeks ago, to making sense of what Inverarity had left behind, never suspecting that the legacy was America." His worldview, while positive, was complex. Oedipa acknowledges Inverarity's "need to possess, to alter the land, to bring new skylines, personal antagonisms, growth rates into being."[21]

Four other books written during the early postmodern decades present the same balance: a rejection of older norms coupled to an acknowledgement that the largest corporations are more beneficial than evil. Heller's dark comedy, *Catch-22*, suggests that the US military, and indeed all such hierarchical organizations, rests on a foundation of absurd rules and procedures. Heller's own comments are apt: "*Catch-22* is about the contemporary regimented business society depicted against the background of universal sorrow and inevitable death that is the lot of all of us."[22]

The conundrum signaled in the title exemplifies the lunacy that hides behind long-accepted rules. According to Catch-22, the doctor at the airbase had the power to ground aviators, because as the number of missions demanded of individuals rose, flying sorties became the mark of insanity. But to get that relief, you had to ask, and anyone who requested a discharge clearly was rational and had to keep flying.

In *Catch-22*, the largest organizations—the army and IBM, which handled personnel matters for the military—are foolish but not evil. In one instance, a private with the unlikely name of Major Major is elevated to the rank of major, four days after his enlistment. The narrator explains, "Major Major had been promoted by an I.B.M. machine with a sense of humor." In another case, IBM intervenes when a colonel is dying: "There was a . . . cystologist for his cysts, and a bald and pedantic cetologist from the zoology department at Harvard who had been shanghaied ruthlessly into the Medical Corps by a faulty anode in an I.B.M. machine and spent his sessions with the dying colonel trying to discuss *Moby-Dick* with him." The army's worst failings lie with its absurd rules and bumbling bureaucracy. One general confesses: "Nothing we do in this large department of ours is really very important, and there's never any rush. On the other hand, it is important that we let people know we do a great deal of it." Heller reserves his harshest criticism for Milo Minderbinder, a mess officer, who stands apart from such established institutions and builds a far-flung organization to profit from wartime shortages.[23]

Richard Yates's *Revolutionary Road* (1961) shows the same break with older ways along with a tacit acceptance of the "New Industrial State." The novel retells the story of Sloan Wilson's *The Man in the Gray Flannel Suit* (1955), but without the happy ending of that quintessentially late modern work. In Wilson's novel, Tom and Betsy Rath overcome challenges and contentedly assume their place in a conformist society. But in *Revolutionary Road* (the title comes from their suburban neighborhood), Frank and April Wheeler meet a different fate. Frank's work at Knox Business Machine remains unsatisfying, the marriage collapses, and April self-aborts their third child, knowing that she will kill both the fetus and herself. Although Frank finds his work at Knox (an IBM-like company) "hopelessly dull," the firm clearly provides the business community with useful products. The Knox "500" Electronic Computer could "perform the lifetime work of a man with a desk calculator in thirty minutes."[24]

Doctorow's *Ragtime* similarly shatters norms and affirms capitalism. The book provides a mashup of famous people and events, and further subverts the text by not naming two of the three families who drive the narrative, instead discussing Mother, Father, and Younger Brother along with Mameh, Tateh, and The Little Girl. *Ragtime* also glorifies the industrial state. Tateh starts off as an artist and a socialist, takes part in the 1912 strike in Lawrence, Massachusetts, but soon realizes labor's paltry gains make little difference. He abandons the workers' struggle and goes to Hollywood, where he succeeds as a movie mogul. The narrator comments: "Thus did the artist point his life along the lines of flow of American energy." The book celebrates financier J. P. Morgan, "that classic American hero," and Henry Ford, who was a brilliant industrialist, despite his grave flaws. Ford was an anti-Semite and an employer who did not value his workers, but in perfecting mass production, "he experienced an ecstasy greater and more intense than that vouchsafed to any American before him, not excepting Thomas Jefferson." Much of the narrative turns on the destruction and reassembling of a Model T.[25]

Finally, DeLillo's wonderfully inventive *White Noise* presents the same balance: loosening the reader's grip on reality while presenting large firms that are more bumbling than mean. The book plays with language. The release of noxious chemicals goes from "a feathery plume," to "a black billowing cloud," to "the airborne toxic event"—and the symptoms experienced, including déjà vu, change with each iteration. The two companies profiled in this 1985 book (a time when the economy was already changing) are not important contributors to society, but neither are they the callous, self-interested firms evident in the literature after 1990. The first response to the noxious cloud comes from Advanced Disaster Management, a firm that "conceives and operates simulated evacuations." Its goal, preparing for the "real thing" is sensible, although the company uses the "airborne toxic event" only to refine its simulations. Later the narrative turns on the quest by Babette, the wife of the protagonist Jack Gladney, to acquire Dylar, a drug developed by a "secret research group" supported by "a multinational giant." Dylar, designed to counter the fear of death, does not work, instead producing strange side effects. Still, that multinational firm responds to a real need, and is far more virtuous than Valupro, the drug company profiled in Gary Shteyngart's *Lake Success* (2018). Valupro hikes the price of a life-saving drug with no concern for the murderous implications of its quest for profits.[26]

V

Writers also demonstrated a new respect for individuals who had often been regarded with prejudice and condescension. The emergence of a growing cohort of confident, assertive women helped recast fiction. The graph for *strong women*, which soars beginning in the 1970s, illustrates the impact of second-wave feminism (fig. 7.1). Intellectual, legal, and social developments provided the foundations for the movement. Simone de Beauvoir's *The Second Sex* (1949) and Betty Friedan's *The Feminine Mystique* (1963) became foundational texts for the second wave, which gathered strength in the late 1960s as "consciousness raising groups" spurred many to denounce discrimination. References to *women's liberation,* a rallying cry in these early years, surged between 1965 and 1974 (fig. 10.2). Federal legislation and a series of court cases complemented the newfound militancy, as did women's gains in the economy. An ever-larger proportion of women attended college, by 1981 equaling then surpassing the number of men enrolled. Women also entered traditionally male professions. In 1970, women earned 1 percent of the degrees in dentistry, 8 percent in medicine, and 5 percent in law. By 1990, those numbers had increased, respectively, to 31 percent, 34 percent, and 42 percent. The proportion of women gainfully employed climbed from 38 percent in 1960 to 59 percent in 1990. Still, most women clustered in traditional activities: teaching, nursing, clerical work, and sales. And the pay gap narrowed only slightly: women earned about 60 percent of what men did in 1960 and about 70 percent in 1990. Change was evident, but easily can be overstated.[27]

Only after the mid-1970s were these advances unmistakable in fiction. Novels published before 1975 document the persistence of older values. April Wheeler in *Revolutionary Road* is a suburban housewife with limited abilities; her efforts to distinguish herself in a local theater production fail badly. The women in *Catch-22* are sexy, intellectually challenged, and remarkably open to male groping. General Dreedle's nurse, the narrator remarks, was "succulent, sweet, docile and dumb, and she drove everyone crazy but General Dreedle."[28] Similarly, none of the women Vonnegut depicts in *Slaughterhouse-Five* is particularly smart. Maggie White, whom Billy meets at a party, "was a dull person, but a sensational invitation to make babies."[29] The three women who pursue Tom More in Walker Percy's *Love in the Ruins* are fawning, weak individuals. Jordan Dominy comments, "Fully developed, strong or admirable female characters are lacking in Percy's body of fiction, and *Love in the Ruins* is no exception."[30]

Other novels in these years similarly show few signs of the strides that would be made. Oedipa Maas, the heroine of Pynchon's *The Crying of Lot 49,* is a suburban housewife who comes from the world of Tupperware parties and conservative politics. She is curious and bold enough to explore the conspiracies that swirl around her, but repeatedly wonders if she is imagining these plots. She visits her psychiatrist: "'I came,' she said, 'hoping you could talk me out of a fantasy.'"[31] In Erich Segal's *Love Story,* Jenny plays the piano and harpsichord but lacks real talent; she teaches school only until Oliver becomes a lawyer. Mattie Ross, who narrates Portis's *True Grit,* is a spunky fourteen-year-old, implacable in her search for her father's killer; but in concluding her story, she notes that she never marries and is viewed by her neighbors as "a cranky old maid."[32] The women in Bellow's *Herzog* and *Mr. Sammler's Planet* are also flawed creatures. They hold university degrees but lack a deep understanding of the subjects they discuss. Some like Ramona and Sono in *Herzog* worship the male protagonist for his deep intellect. Sammler approvingly cites a friend who "taught at Hunter College—taught women. Charming, idiotic, nonsensical girls, he used to say."[33] Both books sexualize women who should be valued for their ideas.

Beginning around 1975, as the women's movement gathered strength, novels present more assertive female characters. The works of this second-wave feminism, unlike those written during the first wave in the nineteenth century, were not overtly political. Many of the most oppressive laws and practices had disappeared. Now the personal was political. Doctorow's *Ragtime* is a good example of this new female identity. Although *Ragtime* is set in the early twentieth century, the resonances of the 1960s and 1970s—including the woman's movement—are abundant. When Father leaves for a polar expedition, Mother changes from a modest, deferential individual to a savvy businesswoman: "As for the business during Father's absence, it seemed to have got on well. Mother could now speak crisply of such matters as unit cost, inventory and advertising. She had assumed executive responsibilities."[34] Pat Conroy's *The Prince of Tides* depicts Dr. Susan Lowenstein as a capable, empathetic New York psychiatrist. She helps Tom Wingo, the protagonist, understand himself better so he can reunite with his family, and guides Tom's sister, Savannah, in her recovery from psychosis.

Many of the strongest women appear in novels by authors of color. Alice Walker's *The Color Purple* celebrates powerful Black women who affirm their selfhood despite pervasive racism and misogyny. Shug Avery is a glamorous blues singer, who takes male and female lovers, and comes and goes as she pleases. Celie, the protagonist, begins as a timid girl and gradually, with Shug's help, becomes a self-confident woman. Sofia does not allow her husband, Harpo, to control her, and bloodies him when he tries to beat her. She knocks down the town's White mayor after he slaps her, but then is badly beaten and jailed. Even "Squeak," who marries Harpo after Sofia leaves him, grows more assertive and eventually pursues a singing career.

Toni Morrison's novels similarly present accomplished Black women. In *Song of Solomon*, Pilate is a remarkable figure. Part witch-woman, Pilate lacks a navel, makes voodoo dolls, and brews potions, one of which leads to Milkman's conception. She is compassionate but also fearless, using a knife to chase off a man molesting her daughter. *Beloved* too features several strong women. Sethe, who stands at the heart of the novel, escapes from slavery despite being on the verge of giving birth. She withstands the censure of the Black and White communities for her infanticide. At the end, with Beloved exorcised by the community of women, she slowly recovers, perceiving the wisdom in the statement made by her lover Paul D: "You your best thing Sethe. You are." Other female characters in *Beloved* also impress.

Baby Suggs, Sethe's mother-in-law, though old and lame, becomes a charismatic lay preacher. Denver, Sethe's daughter, seeing her mother overwhelmed by Beloved, seeks help from the community—and grows stronger in the process. Lady Jones, a schoolteacher, aids Denver and brings together other women to save Sethe.[35]

Two other novels round out this survey of works reflecting second-wave feminism. Louise Erdrich's *Love Medicine* (1984) follows the lives and loves of two resilient Indigenous women: Marie Lazarre Kashpaw and Lulu Lamartine. They raise children, get involved in tribal affairs, fight over the love of Nector Kashpaw, and eventually move to the same senior's home, where they become friends. Both retain a remarkable vitality. An elderly Lulu reflects on why men were attracted to her: "I was never any looker. It was just that I kept my youth. They couldn't take that away. Even bald and half blinded as I am at present, I have my youth and my pleasure. I still let in the beauty of the world."[36] Another strong woman is Princess Quaw Quaw Tralaralara in Ishmael Reed's *Flight to Canada* (1976). A Native American of remarkable accomplishments, Quaw Quaw crosses Niagara Falls on a tightrope, and stands up to her husband, Yankee Jack, when she discovers he exploits Indians, and to Raven Quickskill, who seeks to define her.[37]

VI

Literature also mapped changes in men's behavior, but only gradually, novels suggest, did positive roles emerge. With the advent of postmodernity, men faced a "crisis of masculinity." In the late modern period, the path for men had been straightforward: they could grumble about their work and neighbors, but in the end, they accepted their place in a prosperous society and settled into their role as breadwinners. The literary avatars of this outlook range from Willie Keith in *The Caine Mutiny* (1951) and Holden Caulfield in *Catcher in the Rye* (1951) to Bellow's heroes in *The Adventures of Augie March* and *Henderson the Rain King* and Tom Rath in *The Man in the Gray Flannel Suit*. After 1960, the carefully constructed foundations of this high road dissolved in a deluge of changes. Long-term employment in a large organization no longer bred contentment. Men discovered they were not the sole breadwinners at home, nor the sole possessors of professional credentials at work. Women's calls for equality threatened patriarchy, while African American demands struck at White male privilege. The distress was comparable to the 1850s, when the ethos of the self-made man faded, and individuals cast about for new approaches.[38]

Most of the male characters in the novels of the period from 1960 to 1990 illustrate the problem, not the solution. Frank Wheeler, hero of *Revolutionary Road*, resents his marriage and his job, and fails at both. Yossarian in *Catch-22* also falls short. He responds to the insanity of war with his own craziness, for example, attending an award ceremony buck naked. Billy Pilgrim in *Slaughterhouse-Five* is weak and mocked by the other soldiers. In *The Crying of Lot 49*, Oedipa's husband, Wendell "Mucho" Maas, cuts a sorry figure, first as a used-car salesman, then as a disk jockey. The narrator comments, "He had believed too much in the [car] lot, he believed not at all in the station."[39] In *White Noise,* Jack Gladney worries about the poor image he projects and frets about the diagnosis he receives after encountering the "airborne toxic event." Bellow's protagonists in *Herzog* and *Mr. Sammler's Planet* kvetch incessantly, angered by assertive women and emboldened criminals. Alexander Portnoy, of Roth's *Portnoy's Complaint,* shares a seemingly endless stream of problems with his psychoanalyst. The men in Alice Walker's *The Third Life of Grange Copeland* (except for Grange in his "third life") and *The Color Purple* are violent and misogynistic. In Wallace Stegner's *The Spectator Bird* (1976), Joe Allston complains repeatedly about the infirmities of old age. John Updike's hero, Harry "Rabbit" Angstrom, is no happier in *Rabbit Redux* (1979) or in *Rabbit Is Rich* (1981) than he was in *Rabbit, Run* (1960). He remains, as earlier, troubled by his work, marriage, and libido, and now also by unruly Blacks, angry youth, and the drug culture.[40]

Still, a few authors during the early postmodern decades suggest how men might play a more positive role in a disordered society. Oliver Barrett IV, hero of the romantic novella *Love Story,* embodies one favorable mix of qualities. He is an athlete, a star on Harvard's hockey team. He's smart, magna cum laude as an undergraduate, and third in his Harvard law class. His ripostes with his fellow jocks are quick, cynical, and facetious. Oliver greets his roommates, "Hello, animals," and notes, "They responded with appropriate grunts." Like others who learn to navigate an absurdist world, Oliver wears a mantle of wry detachment, while caring deeply about a few things. Family is at the top of that list. He is a loving husband and deeply involved with his father; his anger at his father at the beginning of the novel and the love he shows at the end are two facets of the same passion. After Jenny dies, he is not ashamed to cry in his father's arms.[41]

Although Conroy's *The Prince of Tides* stands many removes from *Love Story* in tone and subject matter, its hero, Tom Wingo, shares many qualities with Oliver. Both are athletes; Tom has a brilliant turn as a college football player and becomes a high school football coach. Tom has the same detachment and cutting wit Oliver displays. When his mother tells him, "If I had known how all of you were going to turn out, I would have murdered you in your sleep when you were babies," Tom replies, "Considering our childhood, that sounds like an act of mercy." And like Oliver, Tom manifests a deep love for his family. His psychological problems lead to a temporary separation from his wife; both have affairs. But he is determined to reunite with Sallie and his daughters. He reflects on his time away: "I had spent the summer writing love songs to my daughters and love letters to my wife. I missed my daughters terribly and the mere mention of their names could wound me. But they could not cast me out of their lives." In the end, he comes back together with his wife and children, and even reconciles with his sometimes tyrannical father.[42]

Very different in some respects, Paul D in *Beloved* provides a third example of a positive male presence in early postmodern fiction. Paul D's courage is unquestionable. He endures Schoolteacher, the vicious slaveholder on Sweet Home plantation, and survives imprisonment in Alfred, Georgia. Even with those brutal experiences, he retains a remarkable sense of joy. When Paul D, Sethe, and Denver visit a carnival, "there was something about him ... that made the stares of other Negroes kind, gentle, something Denver did not remember seeing in their faces. Several even nodded and smiled at her mother, no one, apparently, able to withstand sharing the pleasure Paul D was having." He is tender and loving toward Sethe—except when Beloved's witchery intervenes. Seeing him as a rival for her mother's affection, Beloved forces Paul D out of the house and, it seems, temporarily turns him against Sethe. But in the end, with Beloved driven out, Paul D and Sethe come together in a strong, supportive relationship.[43]

These three examples suggest the positive identities men would carve out amid the turmoil of the postmodern era. The three men share physical courage (or athletic prowess), resilience, a sense of humor, and a deep love of family.

VII

Also countering the chaos that churned in the frothy wake of postmodernism was the more positive depiction of African Americans. Still, change was slow here too, and many White authors remained mired in older attitudes, with Saul Bellow's work a case in point. In *Herzog*, crime often has a Black face. Sitting in a courtroom, Herzog was "able to make out the defendant in this case. He was the Negro in filthy brown pants." The plaintiff was equally unappealing—Black, drunk, and inarticulate in his accusations ("He said he given me a drink").[44] In *Mr. Sammler's Planet*, a work peppered with racist asides, the menacing Black pickpocket is a recurring presence. At the toy store F.A.O. Schwartz, "Nigger minstrels had fallen in price." Sammler laments that "the sexual ways of the seraglio and of the Congo bush [had been] adopted by the emancipated masses."[45]

Other novels by White authors perpetuate stereotypes. In Roth's *Portnoy's Complaint*, Alexander Portnoy declares his opposition to racism. But the book describes the shiftless Blacks who refuse to pay insurance premiums to his father. Portnoy notes his mother scrubs the silverware "that had passed between the *schvartze's* thick pink lips," and remarks that "the body odor of Negroes fills me with compassion."[46] In Walker Percy's *Love in the Ruins*, African Americans threaten suburbia; they are, the narrator explains, "ferocious black Bantus who use the wilderness both as a refuge and a guerilla base."[47] One of the few African Americans mentioned in Segal's *Love Story* is a drug dealer, pedaling his wares in Harvard Square. Skeeter, a principal character in John Updike's *Rabbit Redux*, is a foul-mouthed, homophobic criminal, who at times spews Black power rhetoric. Rabbit judges Skeeter "a pit of scummed stench impossible to see the bottom of."[48]

Beginning around the mid-1970s, White novelists adopted a more enlightened stance. In *Ragtime*, Doctorow makes clear his belief in the legitimacy of Black grievances and the loutishness of their antagonists. Much of the narrative focuses on Coalhouse Walker, the talented, dignified African American piano player who demands restitution and an apology when Irish firemen vandalize his Model T. Only after the legal system, riddled with bias, fails him does Coalhouse resort to violence. The narrator intones, "[E]ven at this date we can't condone the mayhem done in his cause but it is important to know the truth insofar as that is possible."[49] Cormac McCarthy's *Blood Meridian* also has strong Black characters. When a bartender tells an African American, Jackson, to sit in another part of the room, Glanton, leader of the irregular force, responds: "Mr. Owens, if you was anything at all other than a goddamn fool you could take one look at these men and know for a stone fact aint a one of em goin to get up from where they're at to go set somewheres else." When Owens persists, Jackson blows his brains out, much to the delight of the other soldiers.[50] In Carl Hiaasen's *Double Whammy*, the Black state trooper, Jim Tile, clearly has the author's sympathy, while the White Floridians who taunt him are dim-witted hicks. John Grisham's first novel, *A Time to Kill* (1988), also portrays Blacks favorably; this courtroom drama set in Mississippi pits the Klan against the African American community.

Pat Conroy's novels similarly highlight this more positive view of Blacks. In *Lords of Discipline* (1980), Will McLean is a liberal-minded outsider attending the Carolina Military Institute in Charleston. The Commandant asks Will to look out for Tom Pearce, the school's first Black cadet. In supporting Pearce, Will battles with a racist, homophobic, and often violent group of cadets. *The Prince of Tides* tells a similar tale. Tom Wingo describes his personal transformation: "I grew up in South Carolina, a white southern male, well trained and gifted in my hatred of blacks when the civil rights movement caught me outside and undefended along the barricades and proved me to be both wicked and wrong." Like McLean, Wingo stands up for the Black student who is integrating his tradition-bound high school.[51]

The work of Black authors also tracks the changes in society. One such development was the soaring number of Black families led by single unmarried women—

and the weakening of traditional male roles. Births to unwed African American mothers rose from about a quarter of all pregnancies in 1960 to over two-thirds in 1990. (Illegitimacy rose more slowly for White women, climbing during this span from about 5 to 18 percent.) The diminished importance of Black fathers and breadwinners reflected, in turn, other disturbing trends. With deindustrialization in the 1970s, Black unemployment soared, surpassing 20 percent in the early 1980s, double the level for Whites. Black incarceration rates skyrocketed, starting in the mid-1970s. Black males were more than eight times as likely to be jailed as Whites. Scholarly research shows little correlation with increases in crime, but rather "the use of prisons as a means of social control" of Blacks. Nixon's war on drugs, along with disparities in sentencing and enforcement, filled the prisons with Black men.[52]

Reflecting the troubled realities of the postmodern era, African American novels portray families in which angry men physically and mentally abuse their wives. The 1965 Moynihan Report ascribes these problems to slavery, but in fact this dysfunction was of more recent origin.[53] Earlier African American novels provide few examples of such violent misogyny, often depicting loving families, as in *The Garies and Their Friends* (1857), *Iola Leroy* (1892), and *The Marrow of Tradition* (1901).

Alice Walker's work illustrates this violence. In *Grange Copeland,* Grange's son lashes out at his wife, Mem: "Brownfield beat his once lovely wife now, regularly, because it made him feel, briefly, good." Eventually, he kills Mem and is jailed. Grange is little better, treating his wife with scorn while cavorting with other women. After he abandons her, she kills herself and her baby. In an "Afterword" written in 1987, Walker remarks: "It was an incredibly difficult novel to write, for I had to look at, and name, and speak up about violence among black people in the black community at the same time that all black people (and some whites)—including me and my family—were enduring massive psychological and physical violence from white supremacists in the Southern states, particularly Mississippi."[54] Abusive men also fill the pages of *The Color Purple*. Alphonso, Celie's stepfather, repeatedly rapes her, then forces her into a marriage with an older, violent man, Albert. Eventually, Celie leaves and establishes her own female-headed household. Black male critics vigorously debate these works, with some like filmmaker Spike Lee complaining that Walker depicts Black men as "one-dimensional animals."[55]

Toni Morrison's novels also highlight female-headed families that confront difficult times. In *The Bluest Eye* (1970), Cholly Breedlove violates his daughter Pecola, then flees, leaving his hard-pressed wife, Pauline, to raise a child who is now pregnant. In *Song of Solomon*, Pilate heads a household with her daughter and granddaughter—and no men. *Beloved* shares that framework. When Sethe escapes to freedom, she leaves her husband, Halle, behind, and sets up a household with her mother-in-law, who had been freed earlier, and daughter Denver. Her two sons run away from a house haunted by a malicious ghost.[56]

These novels touch on a second development: the intensifying dialogue about what it meant to be an African American in a racist society. These were the decades of Black Power and Black Is Beautiful. Two novels of 1970 open this discourse by showing how Blacks internalized White values. In Morrison's *The Bluest Eye*, Pecola accepts the White standard of beauty: "Each night, without fail, she prayed for blue eyes." Her mother, Pauline, idolizes White movie stars and cares more for the children in the family where she is a maid than she does for Pecola. Not every character in the novel shares these longings, but many do.[57] In *The Third Life of Grange Copeland*, Brownfield feels inferior when confronted by a White landowner: "He made as if to straighten all the way up but managed to stand stooped a little so that he felt small and black and bug-like, and Captain Davis, with his sparse white hair, seemed a white giant that could step on him."[58]

That subservience disappears in subsequent novels, replaced by the confidence and empathy of a close-knit Black community. When Pilate (in *Song of Solomon*) plays up to White police officers, she is clearly manipulating them. The same holds for Uncle Robin in Reed's *Flight to Canada*. His Uncle Tom act is a sham, used to fool the wealthy Arthur Swille into signing over his entire estate. Both *Beloved* and *The Color Purple* feature a Black community that draws together in times of need. In *Beloved*, with one glaring exception (when Schoolmaster came for Sethe), African Americans assist each other, offering Paul D a home and exorcising Beloved. In *The Color Purple*, Shug Avery, Sofia, and other women help Celie stand on her own.

These novels explore still another question: how pervasive is White racism? Ever since the 1850s, Black-authored novels had detailed the oppressive nature of White society. What was new in the postmodern era was a broader dialogue over whether any Whites were commendable. Grange tells his granddaughter Ruth that Whites "are your natural enemy." But Ruth is not entirely convinced, even though her schoolbooks and teachers expound prejudice. The White civil rights workers who enter the narrative at the end soften the novel's critique.[59] In *The Bluest Eye*, a Black girl, Claudia McTeer, tries to help Pecola by planting flowers. When the attempt fails, Claudia observes, "I even think now that the land of the entire country was hostile to marigolds that year."[60] *Flight to Canada* suggests the ubiquity of White racism. In this postmodern mashup of twentieth- and nineteenth-century figures, Reed depicts Lincoln as racist and shows that the "promised land" of Canada is tainted. "And don't let the Prime Minister fool you," Quickskill tells Quaw Quaw. "He sees himself as a white man in a white man's country."[61] In *Beloved*, Sethe's mother-in-law, Baby Suggs, observes, "There is no bad luck in the world but white-folks." The book bears out that adage: the "good" slaveholders, the Garners, turn over their plantation to their sadistic relative, the Schoolteacher. Even Edward Bodwin, the abolitionist, who helps get Sethe out of jail after she kills her baby, displays a statuette of a Black boy with bulging eyes and a wide red mouth. Used as a coin holder, the figure has the words, "At Yo Service" on its pedestal. James Berger comments, "Bodwin apparently has no comprehension of African American culture apart from stereotypes."[62] Taken together, these texts scathingly indict White attitudes.

VIII

Another important facet of reimagining society during these years was the renewed emphasis on the bonds between parent and child. While mid-nineteenth-century writers had depicted such ties, postmodern pairings were more frequent, sustained, and central to the narratives. In *The Scarlet Letter,* Hester Prynne defends her right to raise her daughter, Pearl. The novel, however, focuses less on that relationship than on the interactions among Hester, Dimmesdale, and Chillingworth. And while Eliza's escape with her son, Harry, animates the first part of *Uncle Tom's Cabin* (1852), their journey remains at best a minor strand in the rest of the novel. By contrast, in *Beloved* the deep passions lacing together Sethe and her daughter Beloved comprise the book's core. Several Ngram graphs, with curves that turn upward after 1960 and particularly after 1980, testify to the importance of these ties in postmodern America. These charts track references to *mother* and *father* (fig. 3.1), *childhood* (fig. 4.3), *loving mother* (fig. 6.1), and *grandparents, nurturing, toddler,* and *babysitter* (fig. 9.4).

Single parents loom large in these pairings. During these years the nuclear family weakened, along with other institutions. The rate of divorce climbed steadily

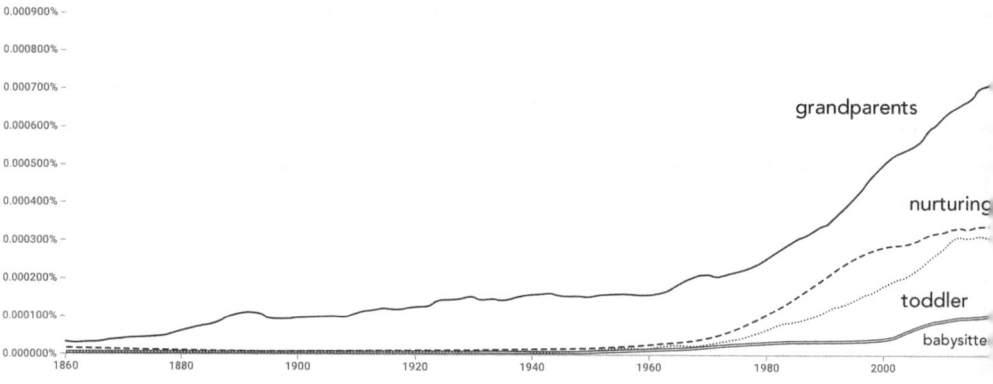

9.4. FREQUENCY OF *GRANDPARENTS, NURTURING, TODDLER,* AND *BABYSITTER* IN AMERICAN ENGLISH (2019) NGRAM DATABASE, 1860–2019.

in the 1970s, reaching a new high-water mark around 1980. The slowing pace of separations after 1980, however, was not a sign of connubial bliss. Rather, it reflected the plummeting rate of marriage—a free fall that would (eventually) drop even below the depths recorded in the Great Depression. Grandparents often assumed a larger role in these disassembled families. For many kids, childhood was no longer the joyous time it had been in the mid-nineteenth century. In the earlier period, the COHA database links *childhood* to *innocence, sunny,* and *sports,* now the collocates were *unhappy, trauma,* and *abuse.*[63] Still, the evidence for that grimness must be read carefully. The COHA database ends in 2000, and the Ngram curve for *happy children,* which had been falling since the sentimental era, turns upward in the new millennium.

A series of works illustrates the importance of affection between parent (or grandparent) and child. Two novels with troubled, sometimes aimless, protagonists show how such ties countered anomie. In Didion's *Play It as It Lays,* Maria Wyeth shuns friends, endlessly drives the Los Angeles freeways, and finally has a mental breakdown and is committed to a psychiatric hospital. What puts Maria on the road to recovery is her determination to rescue her four-year-old daughter Kate, who also has been placed in an institution. Maria reflects: "Why bother, you might ask. I bother for Kate ... Carter [Maria's ex] put Kate in there and I am going to get her out." Critic Chip Rhodes comments: "But to say that Maria believes in nothing would not be accurate. Her love of Kate remains her one powerful motive, one that requires no defense and knows no boundaries."[64] In Ellis's *Less Than Zero,* Clay's fondness for his grandmother, who dies of cancer, and his lyrical reminiscences of her stand in sharp contrast to his disdain for most people.

Alice Walker's novels similarly highlight the role of family. Much of *The Third Life of Grange Copeland* profiles dysfunctional homes. Grange Copeland mistreats his son Brownfield, who in turn is cruel to his wife and daughters, including the youngest, Ruth. But as Grange ages (his "third life"), he bonds with Ruth, and resolves to protect her from her abusive father. The last part of the book reveals the growing affection between Grange and Ruth: "Ruth and her grandfather became inseparable. They did not plan it this way; but always they were together; where Grange went, Ruth went, what he did, Ruth did."[65] *The Color Purple* also examines the disruption and reestablishment of family ties. Celie, the principal character, dreams of reuniting both with her children, who were taken from her as babies, and with her younger sister Nettie, who was driven from their home. The book ends with a joyous reunion.

Toni Morrison's *Song of Solomon* (1977), like *Beloved,* centers on family. The book follows the odyssey of Macon Dead III (also known as Milkman), who begins as an angry, self-centered young man, raised by distant, unloving parents. He comes to appreciate his aunt, Pilate, who in an homage to *her* father keeps his bones in her house. Milkman travels from Chicago to Virginia to learn about Solomon, the progenitor of the Dead family and a "flying African," who reportedly (and fittingly for a postmodern novel) flew back to Africa. Barbara Cooper notes Milkman's personal journey and the "complete awareness" he has on the edge of a vertiginous cliff: "On Solomon's Leap, he understands how little value there is in property and how priceless are family relationships and connections."[66]

Erdrich's *Love Medicine* looks at the tangled, intense bonds that bring together two families—the Kashpaws and Lamartines—on a Chippewa reservation in North Dakota during the 1970s and early 1980s. Maternal and filial passions abound. Marie Kashpaw describes adopting an abandoned girl, June Morrisey: "So I took the girl. I kept her. It wasn't long before I would want to hold her against me tighter than any of the others." With equal warmth, Lulu Lamartine speaks of her sons: "Time went fleetingly by until every one of my boys was a grownup man. Some did me grief, though I was proud of them. Gerry was one. In and out of prison, yet inspiring the Indian people, that was his life. Like myself he could not hold his wildness in."[67]

Other postmodern novels similarly foreground the relationships between parents and children. Bobbie Ann Mason's *In Country* (1985) tracks the efforts of Samantha ("Sam") Hughes to learn about her father, Dwayne, who died in Vietnam a month before she was born. She draws closer to Dwayne's parents, who share their son's Vietnam journal with her. In Kennedy's *Ironweed*, Francis Phelan, returning to Albany after many years, is stirred by his ties with his deceased parents and infant son; those three enter the narrative as ghosts. He also reunites with the living—his ex-wife, two grown children, and a grandson—who slowly come to accept him. Much of Philip Roth's *Portnoy's Complaint* (1969) focuses on Portnoy's relationship with his parents, and particularly with his overbearing mother. In Erich Segal's *Love Story* (1970), the main narrative follows Oliver's relationship with Jennifer, who dies prematurely. But also noteworthy is the second story line: Oliver's evolving ties with his wealthy father, who at first rejects his son and bride but at the end has a complete change of heart.

IX

Like novelists, painters broke decisively with the past around 1960. During the next decades, artists embodied in their work the tension between fragmentation and the creation of a new, more progressive social order. Many now cast aside time-honored forms. Before the 1960s, most visual artists worked in customary ways, applying pigment to canvas. Painting continued in the postmodern era, but creative individuals now viewed it as only one medium among many. For example, in 1962, Andy Warhol, founder of Pop art, switched from painting to silkscreens. Printmaking allowed Warhol to introduce and enlarge photographic images to create his wall-size posters. Warhol also taught silk-screening to Robert Rauschenberg, recasting his art; Rauschenberg's mixed-media "combine paintings" in the 1950s had been a precursor to the experiments of the 1960s.

Artists drew upon techniques that had long remained on the margins of the established art world. African American painter Romare Bearden, who had been a social realist and then an abstract expressionist, created a series of powerful collages and photomontages in the early 1960s. The show, *The Art of Assemblage*, mounted at New York's Museum of Modern Art in 1961, inspired Bearden as it did other artists. Some individuals blurred the line between painting and sculpture, fashioning mixed-media creations, which might be mounted on a wall, but could include neon signage, cloth, and metal fabrications. In examining the period after 1960, this work expands the rubric *painting* to include these diverse media.[68]

Changes in the content of art also signaled a rending with the past. Reflecting on the early 1960s, art historian Arthur Danto observes that "it was as though some deep transformation in artistic consciousness had taken place." For Danto, 1960 marks "The End of Art" and the advent of "post-historical artmaking." From the Renaissance to the abstract expressionists, Danto contends, paintings sought to represent an external reality, whether an image or emotions. After 1960, paintings became objects themselves, the detritus of a consumer society.[69] Danto's argument is intriguing, if overstated—representational art continued during the postmodern era.

Still, Danto has a point: many artists now created works that were artifact rather than reference. The minimalist art of Frank Stella and Ad Reinhardt is an example. Some of these paintings present large black canvases with only a few discernable lines. Rosalind Krauss comments that, in these works "Meaning would no longer be a function of illusion, of an imagined 'inside' or 'behind' the surface. Meaning, since it could form nowhere but on the surface itself, would be an effect of that surface: a meaning-effect."[70] Warhol similarly viewed his creations as manufactured objects rather than as personal reflections. He refused to sign his silkscreen posters, explaining: "I turned toward the idea of a rubber stamp signature because I wanted to get away from style. I feel an artist's signature is part of style, and I don't believe in style."[71] Roy Lichtenstein took a similar stance to his large-scale paintings, which were influenced by comics, and linked his creations to the banal consumer society around him. Lichtenstein remarked, "[I]f you ask me how one can love moronization, how one can love the mechanization of work, how one can love bad art, I answer: I see it, it's here, it's the world."[72]

9.1. BETYE SAAR, THE LIBERATION OF AUNT JEMIMA, 1972.

Like literature, artworks revealed the struggle between fragmentation and renewal. Warhol illustrates the violence and amorality of the period. In the 1960s, he created what he called the *Death and Disaster* series—"the Car Crashes, the Disasters, the Electric Chairs." "When you see a gruesome picture over and over again," he observed, "it doesn't really have any effect."[73] Moral ambiguity also marks Philip Guston's postmodern studies of Ku Klux Klan members. "The KKK has haunted me since I was a boy in LA" in the 1920s, he remarked. In the 1930s, his portrayals of Klansmen were harshly realistic, showing, for example, hooded nightriders lynching an African American. After 1960, Guston's Klansmen transmogrify into cartoonish, comical figures with big cigars coming out of their hoods. "They're obviously based on Ku Klux Klan figures," he explains, "but I didn't mean to make a story of the Klan, I am using them as, what would you call them, a symbol."[74]

Unlike the artwork that would appear after 1990, but like the novels of these years, artistic creations supported rather than criticized corporations. Absent were the critiques of the rich that would become a staple of paintings and assemblages in the late postmodern period. Instead, Warhol celebrated corporate productivity. He called his studio *The Factory* and turned out replicas of consumer goods, such as the stacks of Campbell soup cans that he created for a 1964 exhibit, *American Supermarket*.

Art also suggested a more positive vision of society. The civil rights and women's movements influenced many creative individuals, with Black painters becoming increasingly militant. Shortly before the 1963 March on Washington, Romare Bearden and other African American artists formed a new group, Spiral, with the goal of supporting the mounting protests. During the ensuing years, African Americans came together in other alliances, including the Black Emergency Cultural Coalition, which denounced the Museum of Modern Art's *Harlem on My Mind* (1969), a show that featured no Black painters. The Black Arts Movement, which flourished for a decade beginning in 1965, encouraged individuals to direct their artistic energies toward the liberation struggle. Because many of these groups were overwhelmingly male, African American women formed their own organizations. Prominent among these outspoken artists was the Californian Betye Saar. Her shoe-box size, mixed-media assemblage, *The Liberation of Aunt Jemima* (1972) transforms a familiar stereotype into a militant warrior. Jemima holds a broom and a rifle, and stands behind a large, clenched, Black power fist (ptg. 9.1).[75]

In the 1980s, the best-known Black American artist was Jean-Michel Basquiat, who was of Haitian and Puerto Rican descent. Basquiat first drew public attention for his graffiti, reinvigorating another art form that had little importance before the postmodern era. His rise from poverty to fame and riches was spectacular; before his death from a heroin overdose in 1988 at age twenty-seven, major galleries had acquired his paintings. Critics group Basquiat's figurative if stylized canvases with the neo-expressionists, an art movement that countered minimalism. Much of Basquiat's work, as Laurie Rodrigues notes, "illustrates a concern with the experience of being black in America—both in and before the twentieth century." His paintings examine slavery as well as the co-option of Black performers by the media.[76]

Demands for change also energized the female arts community—including both scholars and painters. Linda Nochlin's 1971 essay, "Why Have There Been No Great Women Artists?" was a tocsin that roused many individuals. Nochlin did not propose female equivalents of Leonardo or Picasso, but rather contended that the "fault lies ... in our institutions and our education—education understood to include everything that happens to us from the moment we enter this world."[77] Beginning in the 1970s, women opened feminist art galleries and formed collectives. Shows and books honored individuals such as Mary Cassatt and Georgia O'Keeffe as well as the abstract expressionists Lee Krasner and Helen Frankenthaler. A debate raged whether female painters should celebrate women's values, or simply paint as they pleased. Judy Chicago's large installation, *The Dinner Party* (1974–79) highlights the contributions of thirty-nine famous women with place settings around a large triangular banquet table.[78] O'Keeffe, however, rejected feminist dictates, announcing "I am not a woman painter!" Pat Mainardi, who wrote extensively on women's art, agreed: "The only feminine aesthetic worthy of the name is that women artists must be free to explore the entire range of art possibilities." Such big-tent thinking was evident also in Susan Rothenberg's ethereal horses and in Elizabeth Murray's colorful, cartoon-influenced abstracts.[79] After 1990, artists, female and male, would respond to an American society growing increasingly unequal.

10
Beset on All Sides, 1991–2020

In a 2010 interview, Jennifer Egan discusses the fractured, uncertain—and increasingly unequal—world she inhabits. "I don't experience time as linear," she tells the interviewer, the aspiring writer Heidi Julavits. "I experience it in layers that seem to coexist." That view cannot surprise readers of her Pulitzer Prize-winning *A Visit from the Goon Squad* (2010), which blithely bounces around the past, present, and future. Reflecting on American society, Egan urges Julavits to study Jaron Lanier's *You Are Not a Gadget* (2010), a work that decries "online elites" and "digital serfdom." Egan comments: "He was a true believer in the power of the Internet and the bounteous possibilities that it held. But now he's talking about how many of the people who were so ecstatic about the Internet are basically unemployed because of it."[1]

As Egan is well aware, the decades after 1990 were marked by growing extremes in wealth, with an ever more powerful elite and an expanding number of precariously employed individuals. For the middle class, still the largest stratum, these changes spell trouble; the group is beset on all sides. A fundamental break with the past had occurred in 1960, with many abandoning their faith in the "system" and demanding radical changes. Now the storms disrupting society intensified, as did efforts to create a more compassionate, just world. That dialectic pervaded society, literature, and art. The chapter begins with the howling winds of change: soaring inequality and its significance for the arts.

I

During the three decades after 1990, the US economy underwent a far-reaching restructuring—further unsettling the once secure lives of middle-class Americans.

To understand these troubling times, one must go beyond the glowing reports posted during these years. After leaving office in 2001, the Clinton administration boasted, "unemployment and core inflation are at their lowest levels in more than 30 years, and America is in the midst of the longest economic expansion in our history." In a similar vein, Obama's 2017 *Economic Report of the President* declares, "As of November 2016, the economy has added 14.8 million jobs over 74 months, the longest streak of total job growth on record." Even President Trump's bitterest foes acknowledge that during his first three years in office, unemployment declined and the stock market boomed.[2]

The problem with this compendium of encomiums is not simply that it leaves out the 2007–2008 recession and the far more serious crash that accompanied the Covid-19 pandemic in 2020. More significantly, it avoids crucial questions: What sort of jobs were these workers filling? Who benefits from growth? The answers demand a focus on the changing economy.

Shape-shifting began with deindustrialization in the mid-1970s. Far Eastern and European firms, excelling in both quality and price, cut into the market share of American producers, throwing millions out of work. But that shock was only the first stage in reconfiguring the economy. Economist Joseph Schumpeter exalts "creative destruction": economies surge because they cast off the outmoded and embrace the new.[3] So it was with the United States, which got back on the highway of growth by the 1980s and raced ahead in the new millennium. Productivity and the gross national product rose; the Internet and the spread of personal computers were among the developments fostering new efficiencies.

The problem? Only the few reaped the benefit of this expansion. Waves of mergers and acquisitions remade the economy. Finance capitalists loaded the new companies with debt, forcing them to keep wages low and close or sell off divisions. Some of these unwieldly conglomerates, like AOL-Time Warner, assembled in 2000, collapsed. In other cases, debt-burdened if venerable institutions, like Sears, were forced to close their doors, even while demand for their products and services continued. Such failures seemed incidental to the Wall Streeters who earned princely incomes from these deals.[4]

Economic transformation pounded the folk in the middle. The new owners of corporate America severed the long-standing links between the rise in productivity and wage gains. The ratio of the pay of CEOs to the earnings of the average worker soared, with the most striking increases recorded in the 1990s. While in 1970 25:1 was the norm, by 2000 the average chief executive in the largest corporations earned well over three hundred times the pay of his (rarely, her) workers, with the new fixed points $20,000,000 versus $48,000. Real wages stagnated. Unions, which had traditionally comprised a counterweight to rapacious corporations, declined in importance, battered by the drop in manufacturing and hostile corporate policies. Governments accelerated these trends. They lowered taxes on the rich, undercut protections for unions, and loosened regulations on business. Unsurprisingly, inequality increased. By the mid-2010s the wealthiest 1 percent earned 20 percent of all pre-tax income, twice the proportion recorded in 1975; the top 10 percent received fully as much as the remaining 90 percent, again a sizeable increase in its share.[5]

For the bottom 90 percent, which now had just half the pie to divvy up, life has grown harder. In the early 1970s, the largest employers included General Motors, Ford, and General Electric, firms that provided unionized workers with middle-class incomes. In 2018, the leading employers were Walmart, Amazon, Kroger, Yum China Holdings (Taco Bell, KFC, Pizza Hut), and The Home Depot, businesses that bestow fortunes upon the few and pay minimum wages to much of their workforce.[6] Conditions are even more difficult for the roughly 14 percent of Americans living below the poverty line. The group is disproportionately people of color, with Blacks and Hispanics experiencing indigency at twice the rates of Whites. For these individuals, the safety net, put in place with the New Deal programs in the 1930s and the Great Society legislation of the 1960s, has frayed. Measured in constant dollars, support has declined significantly since the 1970s. The economic freefall in 2020, caused by the pandemic and lax government response, at least initially, made this bad situation worse.[7]

Finally, it is important to emphasize that these changes are the product not of new technologies or trade patterns, but of cowboy capitalism that allows gunslingers to assert their dominance in a Wild West where the sheriff sits quietly complicit. In the mid-1970s, the United States had roughly the same level of inequality as other industrialized nations. By the 2010s, however, America stood apart from its competitors, with wealth far more skewed than a long list of countries, including Japan, France, Germany, and Italy. Once the poster child for upward social mobility, the United States now trails those formerly stodgy Old World countries.[8]

II

Growing inequality intensified the sense of disorder, a crucial component of the narrative shaping postmodern literature. Novelists now portrayed velociraptor-like firms that were many removes from the lumbering beasts who dominated the economy in the 1960s and early 1970s. If literary accounts are credited, few relished working in firms such as GM, Ford, and IBM, but at least those businesses offered secure, well-paid jobs and did not destroy communities or the environment. *Corporate greed* became the watchword for the late postmodern period—just as *corporate power* had marked the earlier postmodern decades (fig. 9.3).

Jonathan Franzen's *The Corrections* (2001) sets the tone for these years of avarice and inequality. The novel examines the fortunes of the Lambert family, against the background of the economic turmoil of the 1990s. Chip, the youngest son and a failed English professor, agrees to work for a Lithuanian entrepreneur. Eastern Europe proves oddly familiar: "Chip was struck by the broad similarities between black-market Lithuania and free-market America. In both countries, wealth was concentrated in the hands of a few; . . . ordinary citizens lived in ceaseless fear of being fired . . . and the economy was fueled largely by the elite's insatiable demand for luxury." Paralleling Chip's adventures is Orfic Midland's takeover of Midpac, the Midwestern railroad company where Alfred Lambert, the family patriarch, worked for many years. The new conglomerate "eliminated train service to much of rural Kansas," and concentrated on "prison-building, prison management, gourmet coffee, and financial services." Its tentacles reached even to Lithuania, where it closed the port of Kaunas.[9]

Some novels skewer particular industries. Ann Pancake's *Strange as this Weather Has Been* (2009) targets the coal companies that devastated West Virginia with their open pit, dragline mining. One of the characters, Bant, climbs to the summit of a nearby mountain: "What I saw punched my chest. Knocked me back on my heels. . . . . Whole top of Yellowroot amputated by blast, and that dragline hacking into the flat part left. Monster shovel clawed the dirt, and you felt it in your arm, your leg, your belly, and how lucky Grandma died, I thought." The result was nightmarish floods and ruined communities.[10] Richard Powers's *Gain* (1998) tells the intertwined stories of the Clare Corporation, originally a maker of soap and candles, and Laura Bodey, who develops ovarian cancer after exposure to Clare's pesticides. The company blandly denies all charges: "[W]e would like to take a moment to address these concerns and to reassure the residents living near our plants of their complete and unqualified safety." Eventually, without admitting guilt, Clare settles with Laura and other claimants.[11] Critic Ralph Clare (no relation to the fictional company) notes a world grown grimmer since DeLillo's *White Noise* (1985): "The amusing exposure of Jack Gladney to Nyodene Derivative is replaced, in *Gain*, by the sobering diagnosis of Laura Bodey's ovarian cancer."[12]

The music business suffers from similar pressures, as Egan's *A Visit from the Goon Squad* makes clear. After predatory capitalists acquire Bennie Salazar's record company, he "worked tirelessly, feverishly, to get things right, stay on top, make songs that people would love . . . above all, to satisfy the multinational crude-oil extractors he'd sold his label to five years ago. But Bennie knew that what he was bringing into the world was shit. . . . the problem was *digitization,* which sucked the life out of everything that got smeared through its microscopic mesh."[13]

In Gary Shteyngart's *Lake Success* (2018), the dangers come from financiers and drug companies—and the collusion between the two. The protagonist, Barry

Cohen, a hedge fund manager, uses insider information to buy Valupro, a pharmaceutical firm notorious for raising the price of life-saving drugs. A friend whose father needed that medication gives Barry an earful: "'A month's supply went from thirty bucks to seven hundred as soon as Valupro bought the company that made the drug.' Jeff Park paused, as if to let that figure register, but Barry had heard it all before. Prices went up. Shareholders profited. What part of 'capitalism' didn't Jeff Park understand?"[14]

Many businessmen portrayed in late postmodern literature are mean, self-centered individuals. In *Billy Lynn's Long Halftime Walk* (2012), by Ben Fountain, a celebrated company of soldiers, including Billy, is brought back from Iraq in 2004 for a victory tour—the high point of which is their introduction at a Dallas Cowboys game. They meet the Cowboys' owner Norm Oglesby and his oil-rich friends—individuals Billy studies closely: "All the fakeness just rolls right off them, maybe because the nonstop sales job of American life has instilled in them exceptionally high thresholds for sham, puff, spin, bullshit, and outright lies, in other words for advertising in all its forms. Billy himself never noticed how fake it all is until he'd done time in a combat zone."[15]

The works of authors active before and after 1990 highlight the changed portrayal of businessmen. In Bret Easton Ellis's *Less Than Zero* (1985), eighteen-year-old Clay and his friends are aimless, amoral, and at times, sadistic. But Clay's father, a movie producer, and others in the industry, are guilty of venial rather than mortal sins: they are irresponsible parents and unfaithful spouses but not horrid people. Compare those Hollywood moguls to the smug, young Wall Streeters who populate Ellis's *American Psycho* (1991). Patrick Bateman and his circle are self-indulgent, narcissistic, racist, homophobic, misogynistic individuals who mock the poor. Patrick relates a pertinent anecdote: "Back at our table Reeves is telling Hamlin about how he taunts the homeless in the streets, about how he hands a dollar to them as he approaches and then yanks it away and pockets it when he passes the bums."[16] Thomas Pynchon's novels offer the same contrast. In *The Crying of Lot 49* (1966), Pierce Inverarity, examined more fully in the last chapter, was a flawed individual, but also a builder with an uplifting vision of American growth. In *Inherent Vice* (2009), Mickey Wolfmann, whose disappearance lies at the heart of the story, is a reprehensible real estate developer. One person summarizes her views of the appropriately named Wolfmann: "[S]ome of these developers, they make Godzilla look like a conservationist." Wolfmann ruins the landscape, erases a traditionally Black neighborhood, and, although Jewish, hires Aryan brotherhood bikers to protect him.[17]

Along with depicting the very rich, novels illuminate the rise in homelessness. The poor had long been part of the American scene but during the nineteenth and much of the twentieth century, geographical mobility offered a sliver of hope. References to *tramps* surged in hard times, with the peak coming around 1900. In the late twentieth century, with much of the nation urbanized or suburbanized, hitting the road made less sense. The numbers of men, women, and children who slept in doorways, on park benches, and over grates soared after 1980, elevated by cuts in welfare, the continuing deinstitutionalization of the mentally ill, and growing extremes in wealth. That change is reflected in novels and the Ngram data for *homeless* (fig. 10.1).[18]

Ellis's *American Psycho* illustrates the new prominence of homelessness. The beggars who seemingly inhabit every corner in New York are the object of Patrick Bateman's scorn—and homicidal urges. (In this postmodern novel, the reader is left unsure if Bateman commits the murders he describes.) The contrast with his earlier work, *Less than Zero*, is striking. In the 1985 book, the terms *homeless, beggar,* and *bum* (referring to a poor person) turn up in only three instances; in the 1991 novel, they appear 77 times.

While the homeless are rarely sighted in the novels of the early postmodern era, they frequently confront readers after 1990. In Karen Tei Yamashita's *Tropic of Orange* (1997), a novel shaped by magic realism and largely set in Los Angeles, the indigent take over empty luxury cars when mysterious catastrophes close the freeways.[19] Street people are a recurrent presence in David Foster Wallace's *Infinite Jest* (1996), a sprawling novel set partly in and around a Boston addiction center. In warm weather, there are "Homeless vets and twisted figures in wheelchairs with hand-lettered signs outlining entitlement," while in the winter, "Homeless men hunched nearly drift-covered in doorways."[20] Displaced people are a focus of the charitable activities undertaken by the Black middle-class women profiled in Terry McMillan's *Waiting to Exhale* (1992). In Shteyngart's *Lake Success,* hedge fund man-

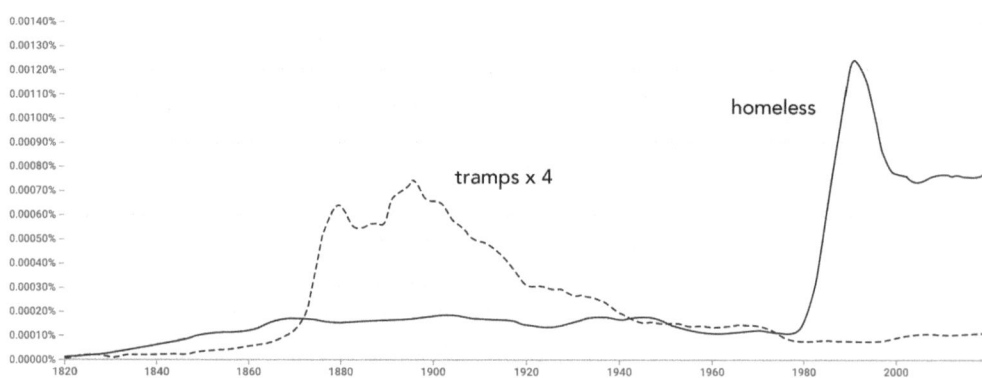

10.1. FREQUENCY OF *TRAMPS* AND *HOMELESS* IN AMERICAN ENGLISH (2019) NGRAM DATABASE, 1820–2019.

ager Barry Cohen encounters the poor during a bus trip he takes across the South to discover himself and his country. Robbed, he gets off the bus and sits down at a luncheonette: "He remembered all the homeless men he had seen in the last two months of travel and the signs they had attesting to the state of their lives." He pens his own sign which reads in part: "THEY STOLE ALL MY MONEY./ I HAVE AN AUTISTIC SON./ PRAYING FOR A MIRACLE./ ANY LITTLE BIT HELPS!"[21]

III

The rise of apocalyptic literature underscores the disorders afflicting society. References to *apocalypse* soar during these years (fig. 9.2). In his 2011 essay, "Apocalypse: What Disasters Reveal," novelist Junot Diaz links catastrophes to the course of American society. "[D]isasters don't just happen," Diaz explains. "They are always made possible by a series of often invisible societal choices." He describes the coming apocalypse: "[W]hat we will be left with will be . . . a future out of a sci-fi fever dream where the super-rich will live in walled up plantations of impossible privilege and the rest of us will wallow in unimaginable extremity, staggering around the waste and being picked off by the hundreds of thousands by 'natural disasters' and 'acts of god.'"[22]

As Diaz suggests, the surge in chiliastic visions emerges from the conflicts riving postmodern America. While much of Pancake's *Strange as This Weather Has Been* focuses on the dire present—the ruination that coal mining has brought to West Virginia, one character, Avery Taylor, propounds an unsettling view of the future. He realizes, "This disaster is cumulative, is governed by a different scale of time. . . . Kill the ground and trees by blasting out the coal, . . . and then, by burning the coal . . . heat up the climate and kill everything left." Avery sees that "the end times his mother obsesses about won't arrive with a trumpet and Jesus come back all of a sudden and everybody jump out of their graves. No. It is a glacial-pace apocalypse. The end of the world in slow motion. A de-evolution, like the making of creation in reverse."[23]

Similar forebodings haunt other late postmodern books. In Diaz's *The Brief, Wondrous Life of Oscar Wao* (2007), a work that oscillates between the horrors of the Trujillo-era Dominican Republic and the rigors of growing up in Paterson, New Jersey, the principal character, Oscar, is fascinated by the apocalypse: "as the eighties marched on, [he] developed a growing obsession with the End of the World. (No apocalyptic movie or book or game existed that he had not seen or read or played.)"[24] Similarly, Yamashita's *Tropic of Orange*, which depicts both the homeless and super rich, touches on final times. A superhuman character, Arcangel, announces that in 2012 *"The end of the world as we know it is coming!"*[25]

Elliott Holt's *You Are One of Them* (2013) looks back on the dangers of the Cold War in reimagining the story of Samantha Smith, the schoolgirl who wrote to the head of the Soviet Union. Sarah Zuckerman, who narrates the story, also drafts a letter to Yuri Andropov, though it is never sent: *"My mother says that after a nuclear bomb, everything will be dark . . . She says that there will be ashes everywhere, so the world will be gray."*[26] Wallace's *Infinite Jest* presents a dystopia set in the near future, where cities are filled with the homeless, powerful corporations name years ("Year of the Perdue Wonderchicken"), and an underground video empties the minds of all who watch it. Meanwhile, Maine, Vermont, and New Hampshire have become a dumping ground for nuclear waste—the "Great Concavity." At an elite tennis camp, the focus of much of the novel, children play an elaborate game involving scenarios for a nuclear holocaust.[27]

Cormac McCarthy's *The Road* unfolds in a post-apocalyptic world—a dystopia with resonances that tie it to the early twenty-first century. A father and son wander a barren landscape after an unspecified disaster has wiped out most humans, plants, and animals. The extent of devastation suggests a nuclear war or an extreme change in climate—two postmodern fears. But the lack of radiation poisoning and sudden advent of the catastrophe leave any full explanation unresolved. Like the hordes of the homeless in the big cities, packs of ragged men and some women range across the countryside in a desperate effort to survive. The challenge for the father and son, along with finding food, is maintaining their goodness in a society with so many evil individuals.

Unquestionably the bestselling apocalyptic novels are the twelve volumes of the *Left Behind* series by Tim LaHaye and Jerry Jenkins. This collection, which begins with *Left Behind: A Novel of the Earth's Last Days* (1995), sold over forty million copies by the early 2000s. Although based on the Bible, these works also embody the deep concerns White, evangelical Americans have about their changing world. The Antichrist, an eastern European named Nicolae Carpathia, uses the power of the United Nations to override the sovereignty of nation states. He pushes for "proper legislation concerning abortion, assisted suicide, and the reduction of expensive care for the defective and handicapped." When the American military supports Carpathia, "patriotic militia forces" are among the few that stand resolute against evil. Here as elsewhere writing about the apocalypse turns on present discontents as well as fears for the future.[28]

IV

Against that background of growing inequality and grim forebodings, novelists offered another narrative, one that affirmed a caring, progressive re-ordering of society. No book, to be sure, was suffused with pure optimism; even the most cheerful tales acknowledge the difficult environment. Among the most upbeat were the works that transported readers to small, harmonious communities—places that stood apart from the troubles afflicting the nation. In providing succor for harried individuals, these stories resemble Washington Irving's "Legend of Sleepy Hollow" (1819–20), a dreamy tale that appeared as the United States entered a period of breakneck growth.

E. Annie Proulx's *The Shipping News* (1993) traces the saga of Quoyle, who, abandoning an unhappy marriage and precarious employment in upstate New York, moves to his ancestral home, the welcoming, friendly town of Killick-Claw, Newfoundland. There he finds love and a respected position on the local newspaper, draws closer to his young daughters, and becomes part of a vibrant, warmhearted community. The townsfolk get together for wild, drunken parties and pack the auditorium for a Christmas celebration at the local school: "It was not what he thought. Yes, children lisped comic or religious poems to thunderous applause. But it was not just schoolchildren. People from the town and the outlying coves came onstage as well." Meanwhile, friends back in the United States rehearse the problems they confront, with one individual in Los Angeles telling Quoyle: "It's like the whole country got infected with some rage virus, going for their guns like it used to be you'd look at your watch."[29]

Haddam, the New Jersey town where Frank Bascombe, a realtor and hero of Richard Ford's *Independence Day* (1995), lives is another irenic community. The opening lines set the scene: "In Haddam, summer floats over tree-softened streets like a sweet lotion balm from a careless, languorous god, and the world falls in tune with its own mysterious anthems." Violence, such as a murder at a motel where Frank spends the night, typically happens outside the town limits. Frank delights in the pleasures of Haddam, distributing free hot dogs to the Independence Day crowd and applauding the parade: "The trumpets go again. My heartbeat quickens. I feel the push, pull, the weave and sway of others." As Kathy Knapp notes, the novel concludes "with Frank basking in the warmth of a sustaining community he helped build."[30]

Similarly, whatever problems trouble the good folk of Crosby, Maine, the town where Elizabeth Strout's *Olive Kitteridge* (2008) is set, they pale in comparison to the ills afflicting big cities. In one of the interwoven stories that make up the book, Kevin Coulson, who grew up in Crosby, comes back to commit suicide. He had lived in Dallas, West Hartford, Chicago, and New York, but "they all became places that sooner or later, one way or another, assured him that he didn't, in fact, fit." Returning to Crosby with its familiar houses and meeting up with Olive, who had been his seventh-grade math teacher, leads him to embrace life again. In these tales, the nastiest folk come from out of town, like the Philadelphia family of the woman who marries Olive's son, Christopher.[31]

In Barbara Kingsolver's *Pigs in Heaven* (1993), the ideal community is the appropriately named Heaven, a Cherokee town in Oklahoma. Taylor Greer and her mother, Alice, travel to that village to help sort out the future of Turtle, a six-year-old Cherokee girl whom Taylor had adopted. Heaven is remarkable for the many generations of family members who live together harmoniously. The ceremonies the Greers witness have a wonderful effect on sixty-one-year-old Alice: her "life and aloneness and the things that have brought her here all drop away, as she feels herself overtaken by uncountable things. She feels a deep, tired love for the red embers curled in the center of this world."[32] Kathleen Godfrey suggests Kingsolver deals in stereotypes: "Kingsolver's Indians thrive in spite of poverty and place their community first, characteristics which Kingsolver holds up as model for Anglo-America. She envisions the American Indian community as the solution to U.S. selfishness."[33]

Whatever critical problems these books might have, they struck a resonant chord with readers and prize juries. *The Shipping News, Independence Day,* and *Olive Kitteridge* won Pulitzers. All four provide straightforward, "realistic" narratives, and except for *The Shipping News* became part of multi-novel series.[34]

V

As in the first decades of the postmodern era, authors celebrated the ties that brought together parent and child. These bonds created a sturdy lifeboat that kept the two individuals afloat in turbulent seas.[35] In several instances such links form the heart of the novel. In Kingsolver's *Pigs in Heaven*, Taylor Greer and her adopted daughter, Turtle, draw together with a powerful, almost desperate affection. As Turtle sees it, "She's been marked in life by a great many things, and Taylor's odd brand of maternal love is by far the kindest among them."[36] Deep feelings between Abraham Lincoln and his son Willie, who was trapped in the netherworld of the Bardo, pervade Saunders's *Lincoln in the Bardo*. Speaking to what he thinks is an unhearing corpse, the president laments: "We have loved each other well, dear Willie, but now, for reasons we cannot understand, that bond has been broken. But our bond can never be broken. As long as I live, you will always be with me, child."[37] Close, almost worshipful, ties mark the relationship between father and son in McCarthy's *The Road*. At one point in the journey, the father "sat beside him and stroked his pale and tangled hair. Golden chalice, good to house a god."[38] In Jeanine Cummins's 2020 bestseller, *American Dirt*, Lydia draws close to her eight-year-old son, Luca, as the two flee from a murderous Acapulco cartel to the safety of the United States. Lydia emotes: "[S]he would staple him to her, sew him into her skin, affix her body permanently to his now, if she could. . . . She would forgo a private thought in her head for the rest of her life, if she could keep him safe."[39]

Even when parental ties are not key to the storyline, their role remains important. In Richard Russo's *Empire Falls*, Miles Roby and his teenage daughter Christina, "Tick," care deeply for each other. At the end of the book, when Tick slashes a homicidal classmate with her Exacto knife, Miles scoops up his near-catatonic daughter and carries her off to Martha's Vineyard to recover. One of the delights of Proulx's *The Shipping News* comes from watching Quoyle draw closer to his young daughters. In Pancake's *Strange as This Weather Has Been,* the protagonist, Bant, cherishes her mother and grandmother and learns the ways of the woods from them. In Amor Towles's *A Gentleman in Moscow* (2016), the charming, erudite Count Alexander Ilyich Rostov draws great pleasure from his ties with Nina Kulikova, whom the Count meets first when she is nine, and then from his wardship of Nina's daughter, Sofia, after her mother (who flees into exile) entrusts the five-year-old to the Count's care.

In other cases, the strands lacing together parent and child are tested by almost unbearable tensions. In Dorothy Allison's *Bastard Out of Carolina* (1992), Anney, the mother of the protagonist, Ruth Ann "Bone" Boatwright, is devoted to a man, Glen, who physically abuses and then rapes Bone. In a pivotal scene, Anney tells her, "You don't know how much I love you.... How much I have always loved you." The reader hears Bone's response: "My heart broke all over again. I wanted my life back, my mama, but I knew I would never have that."[40] In Philip Roth's *American Pastoral* (1997), the world of Seymour "Swede" Levov is turned upside down when his daughter, Meredith, protesting the Vietnam War, blows up a local post office, killing a bystander, and then flees. Much of the book turns on the Swede's quest to find his daughter and, when he does, to understand her anger. In Strout's *Olive Kitteridge*, Olive deeply loves her son Christopher, but time and again drives him away with her overbearing manner. Diaz's *The Brief, Wondrous Life of Oscar Wao* depicts the love-hate relationship between Oscar's sister, Lola, and their mother. Lola confesses: "I was my mother's daughter. Her hold on me stronger than love."[41]

VI

Writers—and middle-class Americans—had still another way of finding comfort in difficult times: they reaffirmed their relationship with God. The approaches taken are wide-ranging. Some regard the deity as a bulwark against disorder, while others gain an odd reassurance from a celestial sphere that mirrors the uncertainties of a troubled world. Only a few assert their independence by avowing atheism. In the twenty-first century, the United States stands apart from other wealthy nations for the high proportion of its citizenry who believe in a deity. For most people, faith remains a key component of their lives.

A good starting point is with the works directed toward evangelical Protestants, a group that in 2014 accounted for about 25 percent of the population. Religious novels, including such bestsellers as Susan Warner's *The Wide, Wide World* (1850), Lew Wallace's *Ben-Hur* (1880), and Lloyd Douglas's *The Robe* (1942), had long been part of mainstream American fiction. Major presses published these works and their appeal was broad. During the last decades of the twentieth century, as society grew increasingly divided, Christian publishing surged and focused more particularly on evangelicals. These believers were overwhelmingly White, disproportionately Southern, and ever more alienated from a society that tolerated abortion, same-sex couples, and recreational drugs. The changing economy, which lessened chances for advancement, deepened these resentments. Evangelical anger, however, was directed not at the elite but at the non-White groups they felt were undeserving beneficiaries of government programs.[42]

Evangelicals viewed their god as a mighty fortress, a comfort in difficult times. That fortress, however, was a redoubt that excluded non-believers. Illustrative of this outlook was the wildly popular *Left Behind* series, which focuses on the Rapture, the lifting up of godly souls to heaven. These volumes are ethnocentric works, with little mention of African Americans or other non-White groups. Although describing global events, the volumes rarely mention Islam or other non-Western faiths. Jews play a prominent role, largely because biblical prophecy regards their conversion as the prelude to the Second Coming. In these books, Christ is a ruthless avenger, destroying those, including recalcitrant Jews, who refuse to accept his supremacy.[43]

Other authors, while not evangelicals, exalt God and prayer. The Christy Award (given to works written "from a perspective of faith") named Lori Benton's *Burning Sky* (2013) as the 2014 "Book of the Year." A romance novel set in war-ravaged New York state in the 1780s, the story presents a beautiful, independent woman, a handsome Scottish botanist, and a noble Indian—all of whom rely on God for guidance at crucial moments. In Tayari Jones's *An American Marriage* (2018), a novel about middle-class Blacks and the unusual strains that imprisonment puts on a relationship, the principal characters make clear their strong faith and belief in conventional Christianity.

Several novels revere a Christian deity, but with a postmodern twist—the rumblings of a disordered world are now audible in the celestial firmament. George Saunders's *Lincoln in the Bardo* (2017) features heaven, hell, and angels, but also the *bardo*, an intermediate state drawn from the *Tibetan Book of the Dead*. Here the souls of the deceased who do not fully accept their deaths remain in horribly distorted forms. The story turns, in part, on the efforts of various spirits to release

Lincoln's deceased son, Willie, from that limbo. In Jesmyn Ward's *Sing, Unburied, Sing* (2017), individuals who die violently, linger as ghosts, visible to a few mortals. One character remarks about those horrid deaths: "[S]ometimes it's so awful even God can't bear to watch, and then half your spirit stays behind and wanders, wanting peace the way a thirsty man seeks water."[44] Characters in Cormac McCarthy's *The Road* speculate on the existence of God in that post-apocalyptic world. While the landscape is described as "Barren, silent, godless," the father tells his son, "My job is to take care of you. I was appointed to do that by God." An old man they meet remarks cryptically, "There is no God and we are his prophets," adding, "Where men cant live gods fare no better."[45]

Reflecting that prayers so often go unanswered, authors with a note of postmodern whimsy suggest God might be too busy or simply absent-minded. In Richard Russo's *Empire Falls* (2001), the narrator explains, "We want Him to be there, ready to receive our call in the moment of our need . . . Whereas God, for reasons of His own, sometimes chooses to let the machine answer. *The Supreme Being is unavailable to come to the phone at this time, but He wants you to know that your call is important to Him.*"[46] In Edward P. Jones's *The Known World* (2003), a novel about Black slaveholders, a White man encourages the protagonist, Henry Townsend, to buy land and slaves: "You might as well step in and take what they ain't takin. Why not? God is in his heaven and he don't care most of the time. The trick of life is to know when God does care and do all you need to do behind his back."[47] Hal in Wallace's *Infinite Jest* explains to his brother Mario: "I'll say God seems to have a kind of laid-back management style I'm not crazy about."[48] In Pancake's *Strange as this Weather Has Been*, Dane is reluctant to pray, "because he knows if God listens to prayers at all anymore, He listens only to a certain number of them. You better be careful, ration them out."[49]

Finally, some works openly reject evangelical appeals or simply make no reference to a Supreme Being—although few of these novels hint at atheism. A fourth of Americans are now unaffiliated with any religion, although most in that group acknowledge a higher power. After an initial meeting, a preacher hounds Billy Lynn, the young soldier at the center of Fountain's *Billy Lynn's Long Halftime Walk*. The narrator captures Billy's thoughts: "The guy is relentless, he is a used-car salesman in sheep's clothing. Billy deletes the text, wondering if it's bad luck to dis a preacher, even a worthless one."[50] In Allison's *Bastard Out of Carolina*, Bone is similarly unmoved by evangelical appeals: "The magic I knew was supposed to wash over me with Jesus' blood was absent, the moment cold and empty."[51] Still, for many writers, belief in God, even in an eccentric, postmodern deity, offers a semblance of stability in a troubled society.

VII

Another part of the effort to construct a more loving world was the welcome extended to immigrants, a development that marked US society as well as its literature and art. Arrivals to the United States had fallen off sharply in the 1920s with legislation that closed the gates to eastern and southern Europeans; earlier, in 1882, the Chinese Exclusion Act had blocked Asians. All that changed with the Immigration and Nationality Act of 1965, which ended national quotas. The number of Mexicans, other Latin Americans, as well as persons from South and East Asia soared. In 1960, those regions had accounted for less than 15 percent of immigrants; in the new millennium, they provided three-quarters of all newcomers, with overall totals skyrocketing. Since the turn of the twenty-first century, arrivals have averaged over a million people a year, four times the level of the 1950s. In 2015, the US population included 47 million immigrants, comprising 14 percent of the total—compared to only 6 percent in the 1950s. References to *diversity* and *multiculturalism* climbed—reflecting the new heterogeneity of the US population (fig. P3.2).[52]

Although literature by immigrants from Latin America and Asia has important progenitors, the explosion of novels by these newcomers dates from the 1980s. While these diverse voices reflect many cultures, they also share postmodern concerns. Magic realism helps shape Dominican-American Junot Diaz's *Oscar Wao*, Japanese American Yamashita's *The Tropic of Orange*, and *The Gangster We Are All Looking For* (2003) by Vietnamese American writer lê thi diem thúy. In *The Gangster*, the narrator labors to free a butterfly whose wings she can hear beating inside a glass paperweight. The young Chicana narrator of Sandra Ciscernos's *The House on Mango Street* (1983) notes the homeless in her Chicago neighborhood and looks longingly at the grand homes where her father works as a gardener. Homeless shelters are a presence as well in Korean American Chang-Rae Lee's *Native Speaker* (1994). Lee even contributes a post-apocalyptic novel, *On Such a Full Sea* (2014), in which class distinctions are stark, pollution has rendered cities uninhabitable, and the Chinese take over the United States.[53]

Still, these novels stand out from other works of the period, marked by the efforts of their protagonists to sort out their identity as hyphenated Americans. That quest shapes characters' lives in *Native Speaker, The House on Mango Street, Oscar Wao, The Tropic of Orange,* and *The Gangster We Are All Looking For*. It also informs the narrative in Gish Jen's *Typical American* (1991), which follows two Chinese immigrants, Ralph and Helen Chang, who pursue success and riches in the United States. These personal odysseys affect the relationship between parent and child, where often the two are separated not just by years but by the divergent outlooks of different generations.

VIII

Literature and art also portrayed (and promoted) women's advancement. Social change provided the underpinnings for the upsurge in feminism. By the 1990s, three-fourths of women were in the workforce, including over 60 percent of those married; more women than men now earned bachelor's degrees—numbers that represented significant advances over earlier decades.[54] Many viewed equality as their birthright. One young woman noted, "For our generation feminism is like fluoride. We scarcely notice that we have it—it's simply in the water."[55] More women entered state and national legislatures. The proportion of women in the US House and Senate rose from 5 percent in 1987–89 to nearly 28 percent in 2021–23. Feminists also organized the March on Washington in January 2017, the largest women-led protest in history.[56] Figure 10.2 shows the early, widespread acclaim for *women's liberation,* which was linked to the first years of the second wave as well as the broad acceptance of *feminism* after 1990.

Still, any hosannas celebrating progress must be muted. Right-wing Christians, always a sizeable group, reject feminists' assumptions. The salary gap persists, even while women's earnings rose from 60 percent of men's income in 1975 to 80 percent in 2017. Although the glass ceiling showed myriad cracks, it did not

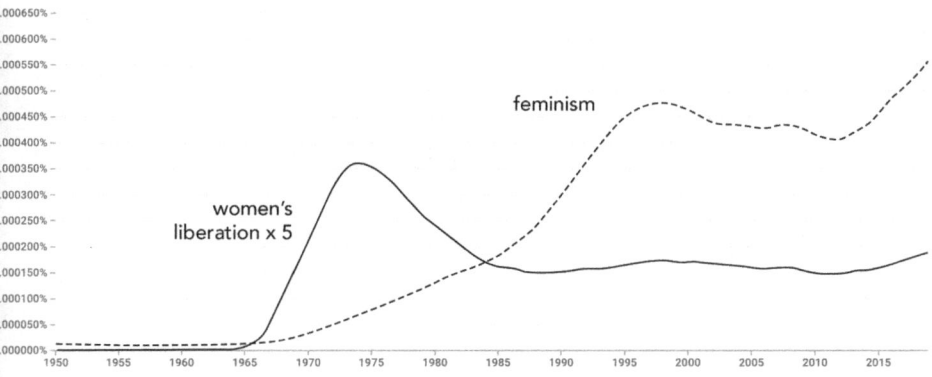

10.2. FREQUENCY OF *WOMEN'S LIBERATION* AND *FEMINISM* IN AMERICAN ENGLISH (2019) NGRAM DATABASE, 1950–2019.

shatter. In 2016, women comprised 45 percent of employees in S&P 500 companies but only 11 percent of the top earners and 5 percent of CEOs. The rise in women's participation in the workforce stalled after the 1990s.[57]

Hopes that enlightenment had won the day also must acknowledge the many novels, typically by men, that condescend to women or relegate them to minor roles. The unbridled misogyny expressed by Patrick Bateman and his circle in *American Psycho* is unsettling. In LaHaye and Jenkins's *Left Behind* series, men lead while women follow. Similarly, Saunders's *Lincoln in the Bardo* and McCarthy's *The Road* are stories about men, with few outspoken women. Wallace's *Infinite Jest* focuses on the challenges men face, while a surprising number of the women profiled are physically disfigured. Michael Chabon's *The Amazing Adventures of Kavalier & Clay* (2000) is similarly a story about men (and boys), with the one important female artist, Rosa, repeatedly described in sexual terms. Many of the women in Pynchon's *Inherent Vice* strut about in revealing clothing or simply are prostitutes. The female characters in Roth's *American Pastoral* are more often described in terms of their bodies than their minds. When one night the Swede has a vision of the Black activist Angela Davis, he remarks "Her legs are long and she wears colorful minidresses to expose them."[58]

If the postmodern era was not marked by feminists striding arm-in-arm into Valhalla, nonetheless progress was genuine. Expressions of sisterhood, with groups of women helping each other, became more common. Nineteenth-century novelists like Louisa May Alcott and Sarah Orne Jewett had noted such support, but cooperation became less common in the twentieth century—until its resurgence

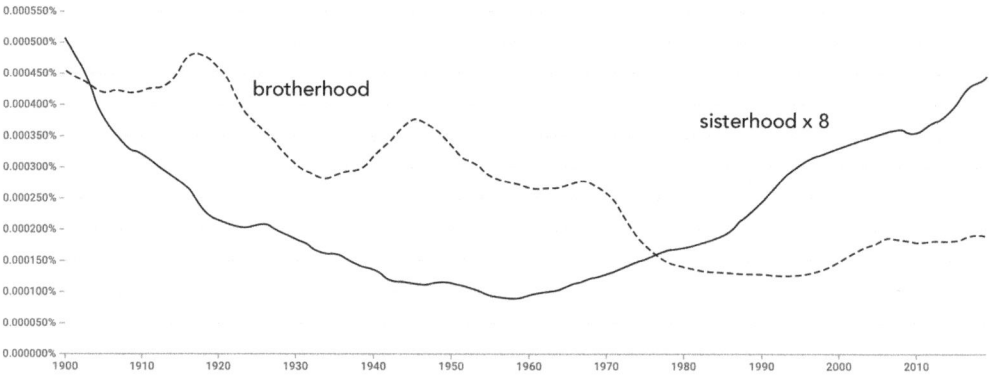

10.3. FREQUENCY OF *BROTHERHOOD* AND *SISTERHOOD* IN AMERICAN ENGLISH (2019) NGRAM DATABASE, 1900–2019.

with the woman's movement in the 1960s. The divergent trend lines for *sisterhood* and *brotherhood* illustrate the bonding that women, but not men, enjoyed in the postmodern period (fig. 10.3).

Beginning in the 1980s, works such as Alice Walker's *The Color Purple* (1982) and Toni Morrison's *Beloved* (1987) highlight the strength of women working together. Sisterhood pervades Allison's *Bastard Out of Carolina*. Note the response to Wade, the uncle of the protagonist, Bone, when he declares, "A man has needs," to justify his tomcatting (pursued while his wife was pregnant). The narrative continues: "Wade's woeful complaint was a joke to all the aunts. 'A man has needs,' they'd laugh each time they got together. 'So what you suppose a woman has?' 'Men!' one of them would always answer in a giggling roar. Then they would all laugh till the tears started running down." Bone comments: "I liked being one of the women with my aunts, like feeling a part of something nasty and strong and separate from my big rough boy-cousins."[59] The same fellowship is evident in Pancake's *Strange as This Weather Has Been*, in which Bant bonds with her mother and grandmother, and they in turn cooperate with other women fighting the coal industry. Bant remarks, *"So the women are tougher, because they take it from the industry, the government, and the men."*[60] When African American women come together in a small Oklahoma community in Toni Morrison's *Paradise* (1997), their independence angers a fractious group of Black men who attack the settlement in a murderous rage. The four Black women in McMillan's *Waiting to Exhale* form a strong support group but are hardly feminist icons. Although they pursue their careers, they put more energy into relationships with untrustworthy and often abusive men.

More than ever before, novels during the late postmodern era feature strong women. The opening sentence sets the tone for Kingsolver's *Pigs in Heaven*: "Women on their own run in Alice's family." The independent women include not only Alice, her mother, and grandmother, but also the Cherokee lawyer, Annawake Fourkiller.[61] McCarthy's *All the Pretty Horses* profiles Dueña Alfonsa who battles Mexican machismo, remarking, "The societies to which I have been exposed seemed to me largely machines for the suppression of women."[62] Resolute women fill the pages of Jones's *The Known World*. They include slaves like Alice, who fools everyone into thinking she is daft until she leads an escape party, and Black slaveowner Fern Elston, who was "known throughout Manchester [County] as a formidable woman."[63] Several female characters stand out in Diaz's *Oscar Wao*, including La Inca, who goes to great lengths to rescue a young cousin, whom she adopts as her granddaughter. Hilola Bigtree in Karen Russell's *Swamplandia* (2011) performs with alligators in the family's amusement park, and after her death continues to inspire her daughter. In Powers's *Gain*, Julia Hazelwood Clare guides the Clare corporation during much of the nineteenth century. In Russo's *Empire*

Falls, Francine Whiting runs the town mills, while Bea, Miles's mother-in-law, chastises local racists. Olive Kitteridge, the eponymous heroine of Strout's book, is independent, outspoken—and irascible. Cora, the hero of Colson Whitehead's *The Underground Railroad* (2016), twice fights off and escapes from slave catchers. In Cummins's *American Dirt,* Lydia Perez stands out as a brave, resourceful individual. This list too can be lengthened.

Lesbians are now viewed more positively. In *Bastard Out of Carolina,* Bone draws close to her Aunt Raylene, who earlier "had worked for the carnival like a man, cutting off her hair and dressing in overalls." Raylene tells Bone, "And I ain't never wanted to marry nobody. I like my life the way it is."[64] In *The Shipping News,* Quoyle's warm-hearted, independent aunt, Agnis Hamm, lived for many years with a woman, Irene Warren. In *The Corrections,* Denise Lambert, who is bisexual, has passionate relations with both men and women.

Finally, the evolution of romance novels confirms the new mindset. The genre had long been dominated by escapist fare, with White, heterosexual protagonists pursuing Mr. Right. In 1970, Germaine Greer condemned Harlequin readers as "women cherishing the chains of their bondage." As if touched by a sorcerer's wand, these paperbacks underwent a remarkable transformation after 1990. Books about lesbian romances, African Americans, women with disabilities, and interracial liaisons now crowd bookshelves alongside more traditional fare. In 2004, Harlequin launched a series featuring "kick-ass women." Glen Thomas observes, "Romance is continually being updated as tastes within the wider culture change." Willa Oberchain, the heroine in Lori Benton's *Burning Sky* is strong both physically and mentally. In this novel, set in the aftermath of the American Revolution, Willa cultivates and defends her farm, sympathizes with Native people, and just incidentally, it seems, pursues her love interest. Only in the romances directed toward evangelical readers is the lack of change noticeable.[65]

IX

As in the first decades of the postmodern era, men's progress was more incremental than dramatic. The signs of change were mixed. Men undertook more housework during these years, a response not only to changing values but also to the surge of married women in the workforce. Women still did more at home, but the level of men's participation places the United States ahead of most other wealthy countries (apart from Scandinavia).[66] Homosexuality became more acceptable, again reflecting evolving norms—a trend confirmed by the 2015 Supreme Court decision approving gay marriage. Tougher times, however, made some individuals more resentful and less accommodating. Michael Kimmel observes, "It is those American men—White, native-born, middle and lower-middle class—who were the rank and file of our historical march of self-made masculinity who have become the angriest." The divergence in voting patterns between men and women testified to this malaise: far more men than women were attracted to President Trump and his angry, often misogynistic, rhetoric.[67]

In various novels, women lament how little men have changed. The men in Allison's *Bastard Out of Carolina* are good-natured but irresponsible. Bone, who narrates the story, explains: "My aunts treated my uncles like overgrown boys—rambunctious teenagers whose antics were more to be joked about than worried over—and they seemed to think of themselves that way too."[68] Not far removed are the men in Pancake's *Strange as This Weather Has Been*. Bant relates her mother's comments: *"They never have to grow up,* Lace would say, *stay babified. Never have to because the women always take care of them, first their mothers, then their wives, and then they die. The women always wait and die later."*[69] In Terry McMillan's *Waiting to Exhale* (1992), the four single, middle-class Black women whose stories intertwine find the men they date, with only a few exceptions, self-centered and inconsiderate. Savannah notes how few good men there are: "When you get right down to it, we're talking five, maybe ten percent. What about the rest?" Her question leads the four to riff on men's flaws: *"They're ugly." "Stupid." "In prison." "Unemployed." "Liars." "Unreliable." "Shallow." "Boring." "Arrogant." "Childish."* And more.[70]

Most of the men depicted in late postmodern novels have grave shortcomings. In Kingsolver's *Pigs in Heaven,* Alice Greer leaves her husband, observing, "he's a good enough man but a devotee of household silence. His idea of marriage is to spray WD-40 on anything that squeaks."[71] Along with being misogynistic and cruel, Patrick Bateman, in Ellis's *American Psycho,* feels hollow inside: "[T]hough I can hide my cold gaze and you can shake my hand and feel flesh gripping yours and maybe you can even sense our lifestyles are probably comparable: *I simply am not there."*[72] Keith Neudecker, the protagonist in Don DeLillo's *Falling Man* (2007), a novel about the aftermath of 9/11, gets little satisfaction from his job, his relationships, and his son. He leaves New York for Las Vegas to become a professional gambler: "He was also going home periodically, three or four days, love, sex, fatherhood, home-cooked food, but was lost at times for something to say."[73] Both Lambert sons in Franzen's *The Corrections* are flawed. Gary quarrels with his wife, children, and father. Chip has trouble maintaining a relationship and a job. Only a happy ending, which descends into the narrative like a *deus ex machina,* suggests improvement. Frank Bascombe in Ford's *Independence Day* too often is sharp with his son and ironic and evasive with the women in his life. Barry Cohen, the protagonist of Shteyngart's *Lake Success,* is self-centered, arrogant, dishonest in business, and heartless in abandoning his wife and autistic son. Despicable men are rife in the literature of these years.

But there are exceptions. John Grady, the hero of Cormac McCarthy's *All the*

Pretty Horses (1992), is courageous when tested in a knife fight and caring toward both the woman he falls in love with and an erring friend, whom he could have easily abandoned. River in Ward's *Sing, Unburied, Sing,* which portrays a conflict-ridden Black family in Mississippi, is another loving individual. He looks after his grandson when the boy's parents prove incapable of doing so and protects a young inmate when the two are together in prison. Miles Roby, in Russo's *Empire Falls* is another good, thoughtful man. At first the reader learns of his shortcomings: physically weak, indecisive, not much of a lover. His mother-in-law describes him as "about the nicest, saddest man in all of Empire Falls, a man so good-natured that not even being married to her daughter, Janine, had ruined him." Miles, who draws close to his brother and daughter, becomes more resolute as the narrative progresses, settling scores at the end with those who crossed him.[74] Quoyle in Proulx's *The Shipping News* is another individual who grows in ability and love. He begins with a disastrous marriage and a dismal part-time job, and he ends—after moving to Killick-Claw, Newfoundland—by becoming a talented reporter and a warm-hearted father, lover, and friend. Successful men in the postmodern era differ from those admired in earlier periods. They are not seekers after higher truths, or dreamers, or employees willing to accept their role in a corporate society. But they possess skills that suit the times: love for family and friends, a sense of humor, resilience in the face of adversity (or absurdity), and tolerance for those who are different.

Many late postmodern novels are more accepting of homosexuality. Homophobia clearly persists. It stains Patrick Bateman's views in *American Psycho* and mars the banter in *Infinite Jest*. Gay bashers insult Dane, one of the less macho characters in *Strange as This Weather Has Been*. Such slurs may not be the authors' views, but none of those books offers a countermotion—a positive gay character or a critical voice. Still, the shift toward tolerance in post-1990 novels is unmistakable. In some instances, gays are matter-of-factly included in narratives where twenty years earlier they would not have appeared. In *Lincoln in the Bardo*, one of the principal ghosts, roger bevins iii, is homosexual. In Jones's *The Known World*, Calvin, the son of a well-off Black slaveholder, also cares for men. In the upbeat ending to *The Corrections*, Enid Lambert, the family matriarch and someone who had nursed a variety of prejudices, defends gay rights. In Michael Chabon's *The Amazing Adventures of Kavalier & Clay*, a novel loosely based on the lives of the creators of the early superhero comics, one of the two principal characters, Sammy Clay, discovers he loves men. Chabon's *Mysteries of Pittsburgh* (1988) and *Wonder Boys* (1995) similarly feature gay or bisexual protagonists. D. G. Meyers notes, "Each of Chabon's first three novels assumes the form of a coming-out story."[75] As a group, however, men have a long way to go in casting off older, self-centered ways.

X

The progress in race relations was another crucial aspect of postmodern culture and an important counterweight to narratives that emphasized fragmentation and decline. Although the gains for African Americans were genuine, for many—such as those who took to the streets in 2020—advances seem paltry while racism remains pervasive. At best the picture is a mixed one, an uneasy collage of victories and setbacks. Even in the late postmodern era, some mainstream White authors disparage African Americans. Ellis's *American Psycho*, the poster boy for so many biases, unsurprisingly falls short in this area. Wallace's *Infinite Jest* has few admirable Black characters, but many who are described with harsh epithets. Similarly, Franzen's *The Corrections* presents blatantly racist individuals, like Alfred Lambert, but few countervailing voices. The African Americans depicted in Shteyngart's *Lake Success*, like the drug dealer Barry meets in Baltimore, are stereotypes. In Roth's *American Pastoral*, Swede Levov and his father bitterly complain about the work ethic of the Blacks employed in their Newark glove factory. Margaret Wrinkle's *Wash* (2013), a novel about slavery, reprises antiquated attitudes, with Whites cleverer than Blacks. On the ship coming from Africa, the captain outwits Rufus, a rebellious slave: "What Rufus does not realize is that the captain reads each of these thoughts as they cross his mind, no matter how closed he keeps his expression." Richardson, the principal slaveholder in the story, similarly outthinks his servants. Most slaves in the book are content, but on occasion they invite whippings. Wash reflects, "And you bet I made Richardson give me the stripes. I wanted to make sure he'd have trouble selling me and he did."[76]

Other White authors now take a more progressive stance. Bone, in *Bastard Out of Carolina*, distances herself from the hateful comments made by her cousins and wants to play with a Black girl who refuses to come outside: "Her mama had probably told her all about what to expect from trash like us."[77] *Lincoln in the Bardo* highlights the violence directed toward African Americans, whose spirits initially are confined in a separate graveyard. As part of the effort to save the president's son, one of the Black phantasms melds into Lincoln, saying, "Sir, if you are as powerful as I feel you are, and as inclined toward us as you seem to be, endeavor to *do* something for us, so that we might do something for ourselves."[78] In Russell's *Swamplandia*, Ava and her sister are homeschooled, and learn a very untraditional Florida history: "Black laborers had drowned by the thousands in the vegetable fields, and, because they were black, the laborers' deaths never got recorded in the official tallies."[79] James Patterson, the bestselling American author (with over 400 million books in print) centers his long-running crime and thriller series around the African American detective and psychologist Alex Cross. Cross first appeared in 1993 in *Along Came a Spider*. *The Shipping News*, *A Visit from the Goon Squad*, and *Billy Lynn's Long Halftime Walk* also depict impressive African Americans, who often are uncoded when first introduced.[80]

Divisions within Black society shape the perspectives of African American writers. The small Black middle class that had emerged by the 1980s (fig. 9.1) coexisted uneasily with a much larger group of impoverished African Americans.[81] All observers accept two antithetical propositions—racism persists and doors once nailed shut have been pried opened at least for the few—but balance these realities differently. In *Who's Afraid of Post-Blackness?* (2011), TV personality and journalist Touré emphasizes opportunities awaiting determined individuals: "If Obama succeeded at a massive task that almost everyone thought was impossible, then what smaller mountains can we climb that are currently deemed insurmountable.... Let's be like Barack. Let's get what we want from America in spite of racism."[82] Others, like literary critic Thabiti Lewis, reject such optimism, observing, "Although an elite minority has arrived the other ninety to ninety-five percent of black folk are still waiting for deliverance.... [R]acial progress, while noticeable, is quite shallow if the black majority live in horror and squalor."[83]

Novelists stand on both sides of this divide. Several writers sharing Touré's outlook emphasize possibilities while passing lightly over racist indignities. Tayari Jones's *An American Marriage* focuses on three, successful college-educated African Americans and their personal travails. Roy and Celestial's marriage breaks down when Roy, falsely accused of rape, is sentenced to twelve years in a Louisiana penitentiary. While Roy is in prison, Celestial falls in love with Roy's college roommate, Andre, and when Roy is released (after five years) Celestial ends the marriage. There are references to discrimination. Andre, for example, notes the problems he faces driving his high-end vehicle: "The truck—Mercedes M-Class—had gotten me pulled over a half-dozen times in the last three years, and once I was even slammed against the hood." But the silences are still more striking. Although Roy spends five years in a Louisiana penitentiary, part of a system notorious for its warring gangs, the novel makes no mention of racial conflict within the prison. Nor does the reader learn the race of the woman who accuses Roy of rape or of bias in the courts. By contrast, the narrative is expansive in discussing Celestial's entrepreneurial success in selling handcrafted dolls.[84]

McMillan's *Waiting to Exhale* similarly emphasizes broadly shared concerns—the problems that any single, professional woman might face—rather than the challenges of being Black in America. In a few instances, the novel highlights prejudice—Gloria's son is expelled from school because the principal is "a real die-hard racist." But such moments are infrequent: most of the book deals with the quest of four African American women to find true love. Complaints about racism are gently deflected. When Savannah complains about her low salary, Robin replies: "Don't tell me. Because you're black." Savannah explains: "That's only part of it. Of all the areas in broadcasting, public relations is the least respected. It's full of women, that's why."[85]

Edward Jones's *The Known World* also seems to embody those middle-class values: it focuses on a small group of Black slaveholders in (fictional) Manchester County, Virginia. More conflicted in its ideology than the novels by Tayari Jones and Terry McMillan, *The Known World*, nonetheless, shifts the locus of evil away from a White power structure to a society in which property-owning Blacks and Whites are partners in oppression. For Shauna Kirlew, the novel "illustrates how the nascent Black middle class was complicit in part with the system of U.S. American Capitalism that would further suppress blacks in the United States."[86] A pall of moral ambivalence hangs over this work. The novel portrays many of the Black slave lords in sympathetic tones. The truly evil characters, in keeping with long-standing tropes, are the lower-class White slave patrollers.

Other African American authors direct their criticism squarely at White racism. Set in Mississippi, Ward's *Sing, Unburied, Sing* depicts White terror stretching over many decades. After a Black man, walking with his wife, brushes up against a White woman, angry locals (according to one observer) "beat them so bad they eyes disappeared in they swollen heads. . . . The man was missing his fingers, his toes, and his genitals. The woman was missing her teeth." A fight with Whites in a juke joint sends River (also known as "Pop") and his brother to the state penitentiary at Parchman. Unlike the sanitized version in *An American Marriage*, the prison in *Sing, Unburied, Sing* is a brutal, racist institution—and the nearby communities are equally hostile. When a young, Black inmate escapes, Pop kills the boy rather than allowing a vicious mob to dismember and burn him. In scenes reminiscent of *Beloved*, the ghost lingers, asking Pop why he took a child's life.[87]

Whitehead's *The Underground Railroad*, a postmodern novel about slavery, presents a litany of horrors. Cora shudders when a boy spills a drop of wine on the master's shirt: "She had seen men hung from trees and left for buzzards and crows. Women carved open to the bones the with cat-o'-nine tails. Bodies alive and dead roasted on pyres. Feet cut off to prevent escape and hands cut off to stop theft. She had seen boys and girls younger than this beaten and had done nothing." Cora escapes from that Georgia plantation and takes the underground railroad (a real train in this book) to South Carolina. At first the slaveholders there seem more humane, until she learns that they are using Blacks for medical experiments. She then travels to North Carolina, which, she discovers, has become a nightmarish dystopia: a state determined to be free of all Blacks. As she rides, hidden in a wagon, from the station to town, she glimpses the horror: "The corpses hung from trees as rotting ornaments. Some of them were naked, others partially clothed, the trousers black where their bowels emptied when their necks snapped." Cora's adventures continue with her recapture, another escape, refuge in an Indiana community, another recapture, and escape.[88] A survey of this literature reflects, but does not resolve, the different perspectives in the African American community.

XI

Like novelists, artists documented both the fracturing of society and the determination to build a more loving and just world. Artwork now embodied many forms: techniques ranged from painting to mixed media to installations. Arthur Danto notes the "extreme pluralism of contemporary art," while Erika Doss remarks, "No single style, medium, or subject dominates American art today."[89] Still, within such multiplicity, familiar themes emerge.

No less than novelists, artists depict the inequalities afflicting the United States, a theme that Jules de Balincourt, a French-born, Brooklyn-based painter highlights in his work. His *People Who Play and People Who Pay* (2004) presents Whites lounging poolside in a Florida resort and people of color serving them, while his *U.S. World Studies III* (2005) brings together a list of Republican corporate donors and a map of the United States. Matthew Branson's stylized paintings of snakes feature titles such as *Other People's Money* (2006) and *People Who Divide People* (2006). Chicano artist Juan Capistran created a scathing series, including *Sympathy for the Devil (I Eat the Rich) or 13 point program to destroy America*. The caption on Kelley Walker's 2001 painting of a broken bridge reads, "Fight capitalism, support failure." In his mixed-media piece, *Supreme Court* (2004), African American artist Rodney McMillian presents a crumbling structure to illustrate an institution that favors the well-to-do and the religious right.[90]

Art also celebrates a more inclusive world and the new multiculturalism. Artists from many countries now reside in cities across the United States, particularly in New York and Los Angeles.[91] Hispanic art has become increasingly important. Cheech Marin (of Cheech and Chong fame) organized *Chicano Visions: American Painters on the Verge*, a travelling exhibit that opened at the Smithsonian in 2002. Other presentations of Chicanx works include the Los Angeles County Museum of Art's *Phantom Sighting: Art after the Chicano Movement* (2008) and the Getty's *Pacific Standard Time LA/LA* (2017–2018). Tribal art similarly has a new prominence. The Cherokee multimedia artist Jimmie Durham launched the installation *Building a Nation* (2006) in a London gallery. The show features, along with an original sculpture, writings by Davy Crockett and other Whites who attacked native societies. The Smithsonian National Museum of the American Indian mounted a

10.1. KARA WALKER, *ALABAMA LOYALISTS GREETING THE FEDERAL GUNBOATS*, 2005.

major show of recent Indigenous art in 2007, as did the Crocker Art Museum, in Sacramento, California, in 2019.[92]

African American artists debate "post-Blackness" much as novelists do, with some rejecting demands that Black art support the liberation struggle. "The cult of the individual is something that is going to be a rescuing point for Black people," the painter Kehinde Wiley asserts. He continues: "You have to be able to say I'm gonna try something that my group has never tried before.... Because the white boys have always been given that free run to be individuals."[93] While Wiley's heroic paintings of African American men, including his portrait of Obama, eschew references to oppression, other Black artists highlight the pain inflicted by a racist society. Glenn Ligon's text-heavy creations present biting critiques: one picture quotes extensively from Ralph Ellison's *Invisible Man,* another features a faux advertisement for a runaway slave who appears to be Ligon. Michael Ray Charles mocks Sambo figures and the Klan, while Hank Willis Thomas uses G.I. Joe figures to depict the killing of his cousin. Kara Walker introduces silhouettes, in some instances as part of wall-sized panoramas, to show the horrors of slavery. In *Alabama Loyalists Greeting the Federal Gunboats* (2005), she overlays the outline of a slave fleeing bondage on a print from the 1866 edition of *Harper's Pictorial History of the Civil War* (ptg. 10.1).[94]

Despite signs of progress, women remain woefully unrepresented in the galleries. A 2019 study undertaken of twenty-six leading American museums found that during the preceding decade only 11 percent of acquisitions and 14 percent of exhibitions involved female artists. For Black women, the numbers are worse: just 3 percent of the works by women that museums purchased were by African Americans. "These numbers are a little heart-wrenching," African American artist Mickalene Thomas observes, "But they are also awakening. This is not about who you are as an artist—there is a system that you aren't a part of. It's still a boys' game." Several major museums recognize the need for change and are working to rebalance their collections. As earlier, women form no "school," nor does it seem possible to read a feminist agenda into the diverse work they produce.[95]

CONCLUSION

For many years at York University in Toronto, I taught a fourth-year history seminar, "The US Novel as a Historical Document." That odd-sounding title was my way of smuggling into the history curriculum materials that I greatly enjoyed. Most of the books assigned were "canonical" novels like *Huckleberry Finn* and *Beloved*, although a few like Richard Russo's *Empire Falls* were slightly off the beaten track. Works came and went on the syllabus. For me, one of the saddest departures occurred when I bade farewell to *Moby-Dick*, my candidate for the Great American Novel, but a book that the students almost uniformly disdained. I allowed Ahab, the *Pequod*, and the white whale to sink beneath the waves, and introduced other, more likeable, visitors. The class focused on the issues that eventually led to this study. But before plunging into those discussions, I always opened with a simple question, "How did you like this week's reading?" Opinions varied widely, depending on students' backgrounds, and those responses often provided links to the more substantive analysis.

So, one fringe benefit of this study, I would hope, is expanding readers' knowledge of the wonderful treasures that comprise American literature. Like the individuals in my seminar, many students of US novels have a brush with the canonical works. But there's a pleasure that comes from paddling away from those well-mapped shores to sample the fiction in what some might view as *terra incognita*. Here are a handful of gems from the nineteenth century and one from the early twentieth. None of these novels is particularly obscure; all are well-known to specialists (and discussed in the preceding chapters), but only occasionally do they find their way onto reading lists. Frank Webb's *The Garies and Their Friends* (1857), one of the earliest African American novels, provides a vivid picture of conflicts in Philadelphia; E.D.E.N. Southworth's *The Hidden Hand: Or, Capitola the Madcap* (1859) is a rollicking melodrama with strong feminist overtones; George Washington Cable's *The Grandissimes: A Story of Creole Life* (1880) is Faulknerian in its portrayal of the clash of cultures and the oppressive weight of past generations; my favorite Henry James novel is *The Princess Casamassima* (1886), a story of revolution, conspiracy, and love; Sara Orne Jewett's *The Country of the Pointed Firs* (1896) offers a moving account of a world where women's voices dominate; Willa Cather's *Death Comes for the Archbishop* (1927) is a charming, lyrical tale.[1]

Still, the larger point of this book has been to trace the changing outlook of "middling" Americans, with fiction, art, and quantitative data as the principal sources. *A Mirror for History* argues that the arc of middle-class culture reflects the evolution of the economy from the near-subsistence agriculture of the 1750s to the extraordinarily unequal society of the twenty-first century. In this story the successive transformations of the economy provide the dynamic for change. Literature, painting, and Ngrams reveal this process and highlight the shifts in values. Fiction provides the key for much of this analysis. By delving deep into the souls of characters and creating complex worlds, novels shed light on an array of issues, including the dreams, hopes, and goals of middle-class individuals as well as the role of women, men, and more broadly, African Americans.

A few examples, drawn from these chapters, underscore how fiction and painting document changes in society. The novels of James Fenimore Cooper, Nathaniel Hawthorne, and Herman Melville during the 1830s, 1840s, and early 1850s trumpet the exalted possibilities of these antebellum years. Characters commune with God and tangle with the devil—a worldview revealed as well in Thomas Cole's canvases. Such works mirror an era of reform and perfectionism, a period when growth accelerated, enterprises remained small, and White people in much of the nation enjoyed a rough-hewn equality. Similarly, the good-natured villages that characterize the literature and art of the 1870s illuminate the opening decade of the genteel era, a time before an industrializing society judged these locales backward and beleaguered. St. Petersburg, where Mark Twain's *Tom Sawyer* takes place, epitomizes such settlements, and similar communities flourish in the writings of Harriet Beecher Stowe, William Dean Howells, and Sarah Orne Jewett. The paintings of Winslow Homer and Thomas Eakins also illustrate these joyous years, an artistic vision that would darken noticeably in the next decade. The towns depicted, it must be emphasized, shared the same limitations: their warm welcome was extended only to White, Anglo-Saxon Protestants.

In the 1920s, the dashed romantic dreams that weave through various novels and paintings point to warring values: the clash between the freedom that came with the end of gentility and the conformity demanded by the world of business.

F. Scott Fitzgerald's *The Great Gatsby* embodies that tension, while a similar dialectic animates works by other White authors, including Edith Wharton, Ernest Hemingway, Theodore Dreiser, and Willa Cather. Paintings by Charles Demuth, Charles Sheeler, and Edward Hopper further document these sensibilities. Joy and hope also course through the novels of the Harlem Renaissance, but for Black writers the cruel realities of racism even more than the pressure of conformity kept expansive visions in check.

The fiction and art of the 1970s and 1980s embody the crosscurrents of the early postmodern era. Sterile suburbs, overbearing firms, mounting violence, and a youth rebellion, led writers and artists to abandon their faith in institutions and in a rational, orderly universe. A Cambrian explosion of literary and artistic innovations reflected this shattering of norms. But countering the narrative of fragmentation was an effort to reimagine a more caring and progressive society, one that respects the rights of women, Blacks, and members of the LGBTQ+ community. The result, in works by authors such as E. L. Doctorow, Toni Morrison, and Cormac McCarthy, was fiction that unsettled literary conventions, acknowledged endemic violence, but accorded new respect to individuals long the objects of prejudice. The same powerful currents are present in the creations of artists such as Andy Warhol and Betye Saar. These works and many others serve as Sherpas for anyone wishing to scale the heights of US social history.

This study also underscores the value of examining quantitative data. Social scientists vigorously debate the utility of tabulations, with essays touting the wonder-working abilities of numeracy balanced by screeds condemning such nostrums.[2] The Ngram and COHA databases that inform this work are not magical elixirs. But taken in small doses, they deepen our understanding of changing worldviews.

Still, novels and painting comprise the principal source for this work. The richness of that material is inexhaustible—and besides, a delight. This book suggests a particular benefit from exploring those creations: a deeper understanding of the evolution of Americans' outlook. That story does not conclude with these pages, but continues with each new enjoyable, intriguing work of fiction and art.

ACKNOWLEDGMENTS

During the fourteen years I spent writing this book, I've incurred a small mountain of debts to my readers and others who assisted in this work. My York University colleague and friend Art Redding read every chapter, offering suggestions while we lingered over lunches. Other specialists examined particular sections or commented on the articles and conference papers I quarried from this work. Like the eighteenth-century "republic of letters," this community of engaged individuals has helped elevate scholarly discourse—and has kept writing from becoming the solipsistic activity it might be. I extend my thanks to Rebecca Bedell, Rita Bode, Kenneth Carpenter, Leonard Cassuto, David Cowart, William Decker, Paul Downes, Sandra Gustafson, Andrew Hartman, Joy Kasson, Mary Kelley, Joan Rubin, Betty Sabiston, Merinda Simmons, Jewel Spangler, Wendy Steiner, Carole Stewart, Tamara Thornton, and Jamie Zeppa. I'm grateful to another group of readers, drawn from friends and family, who suggested ways to make this work clearer and more accessible. This support team includes Jamie Cameron, Nancy Case, Susanna Coates, Ron Knowles, Allen Koretsky, Steve Mitchell, and Tim Nau.

I also want to thank Thomas Wells, the acquisition editor at the University of Tennessee Press, for his unwavering support for this unusual book. He persisted in finding readers and gaining board approval even as the manuscript underwent several revisions.

My best reader, as always, has been my wife, Judith Humphrey, herself the author of four books. Her comments, which guided me as I wrote and rewrote these chapters, were invariably frank and on the mark. And somehow, all that give-and-take works. The year 2021 marked not only the completion of a near-final draft but also our fiftieth wedding anniversary.

My younger son, Ben, an art director in the advertising world, created the graphs. He and my older son, Bart, their wives, respectively Fang Yu and Emily Mather, and our four grandchildren (to whom this work is dedicated) are not the reason this book took more than a decade to complete; but they added joy to those years and set my scholarship in perspective. This book, I hope, will have resonances for that next generation. Writing history, I believe, should never be a purely "academic" exercise. It should always deepen our understanding of where we've been and help us decide where we are going.

SOURCES FOR ARTWORK

My thanks to the following museums and collections for granting permission to use works from their holdings.

1.1. Robert Feke, *Isaac Royall and Family* (Harvard Law School Collection)
1.2. Charles Willson Peale, *The Peale Family* (New-York Historical Society)
2.1. Washington Allston, *Elijah in the Desert* (Boston Museum of Fine Arts)
3.1. Thomas Cole, *The Oxbow* (Metropolitan Museum of Art, New York)
4.1. Thomas Cole, *Niagara Falls* (Art Institute of Chicago)
4.2. Frederic Church, *Niagara* (National Gallery of Art, Washington, DC)
4.3. Albert Bierstadt, *The Rocky Mountains, Landers Peak* (The Metropolitan Museum of Art, New York)
5.1. Winslow Homer, *Snap the Whip* (The Metropolitan Museum of Art, New York)
5.2. Winslow Homer, *The Life Line* (Philadelphia Museum of Art)
5.3. Thomas Eakins, *The Courtship* (Fine Arts Museums of San Francisco)
5.4. Thomas Eakins, *Portrait of Walt Whitman* (Pennsylvania Academy of the Fine Arts)
6.1. George Bellows, *Cliff Dwellers* (Los Angeles County Museum of Art)
6.2. Max Weber, *The Liberty Tower from the Singer Building* (Boston Museum of Fine Arts)
7.1. Charles Sheeler, *American Landscape* (The Museum of Modern Art, New York)
7.2. Edward Hopper, *Room in New York* (Sheldon Museum of Art, University of Nebraska, Lincoln)
8.1 Jackson Pollock, *One: Number 31, 1950* (The Museum of Modern Art, New York)
9.1 Betye Saar, *The Liberation of Aunt Jemima* (Art Museum and Pacific Film Institute, Berkeley, CA, from National Endowment for the Arts; courtesy of the artist and Roberts Projects, Los Angeles, CA.)
10.1 Kara Walker, *Alabama Loyalists Greeting the Federal Gunboats* (The Museum of Modern Art, New York)

NOTES

Introduction

1. John Guillory, *Professing Criticism: Essays on the Organization of Literary Study* (Chicago: The University of Chicago Press, 2022), 44–78.

2. Christopher Ingraham, "The Long, Steady Decline of Literary Reading," *The Washington Post*, September 7, 2016; Christopher Ingraham, "Leisure Reading in the U.S. is at an All-Time Low," *The Washington Post*, June 29, 2018; Seth Studer and Ichiro Takayoshi, "Franzen and the 'Open-Minded but Essentially Untrained Fiction Reader,'" *Post45*, July 8, 2013, http://post45.research.yale.edu/2013/07/franzen-and-the-open-minded-but-essentially-untrained-fiction-reader/, discusses the decline in fiction reading, 1982–2008. See also Jeffrey Jones, "Americans Reading Fewer Books Than in Past," January 10, 2022, *Gallup News*, https://news.gallup.com/poll/388541/americans-reading-fewer-books-past.aspx.

3. Three foundational works that explore the interaction between individual genius and social context are T. S. Eliot, "Tradition and the Individual Talent," first published in *The Egoist* (1919), https://www.poetryfoundation.org/articles/69400/tradition-and-the-individual-talent; M. H. Abrams, *The Mirror and the Lamp: Romantic Theory and the Critical Tradition* (New York: Oxford University Press, 1953); and Frederic Jameson, *The Political Consciousness: Narrative as a Socially Symbolic Act* (London: Methuen, 1981). Although the approaches vary (Abrams was influenced by "New Criticism" and Jameson by Marxism), all three acknowledge this dialectic.

4. Philip Roth, "My Life as a Writer," *New York Times*, March 2, 2014.

5. See the still-pertinent discussions of these issues in R. Gordon Kelly, "Literature and the Historian," *American Quarterly* 26, no. 2 (1974): 141–59; Leo Marx, "American Studies: Defense of an Unscientific Method," *New Literary History* 1 (1969): 75–90.

6. *The Cambridge History of American Literature*, vol. 1: *1590–1820*, ed. Sacvan Bercovitch (New York, 1994), 4; Dana D. Nelson, "Rooting for a Better World: American Literary

History Today," *American Literary History* 33, no. 3 (2021): 691–701. For a spirited exchange on "historically oriented scholarship" (575), see the essays in *New Literary History* 42, no. 4 (2011), and particularly Rita Felski, "Context Stinks!" 573–91.

7. Raymond Williams, *Culture and Materialism: Selected Essays* (London: Verso, 2005), 34. See also the valuable discussion in T. J. Jackson Lears, *No Place of Grace: Antimodernism and the Transformation of American Culture, 1880–1920* (Chicago: The University of Chicago Press, 1983, 1994), xi–xx.

8. Richard F. Teichgraeber III, *Building Culture: Studies in the Intellectual History of Industrializing America, 1867–1910* (Columbia: University of South Carolina Press, 2010), 1–23, discusses how the concept of "culture" helps bring coherence to the "pluralist approach"; Hayden White, "Literature and Social Action: Reflections on the Reflection Theory of Literary Art," *New Literary History* 11, no. 2 (1980): 363–80, supports, with some qualifications, the idea that literature reflects social structures.

9. Scholars who engage the "new historicism" discuss this issue. See Jeffrey Insko, "Anachronistic Imaginings: *Hope Leslie*'s Challenge to Historicism," *American Literary History* 16, no. 2 (2004): 179–207; Harold Aram Veeser, *The New Historicism* (New York: Routledge, 1989).

10. I have read far more novels and looked at many more paintings than are referenced in the text. For example, I have read almost all of John Irving's novels but mention only one (*A Prayer for Owen Meany*) in these pages. These works silently inform the arguments about middle-class culture. My question has always been, do *any* of these books or artworks point to the need to modify conclusions?

11. Ronald J. Zboray and Mary Sarcino Zboray, "The Novel in the Antebellum Book Market," in *The Cambridge History of the American Novel*, ed. Leonard Cassuto (Cambridge: Cambridge University Press, 2011), 67–70; Cassuto, General introduction to *Cambridge History of the American Novel*, 1; Matthew Wilkens, "Contemporary Fiction by the Numbers," *Post45: Contemporaries*, March 11, 2011, http://post45.research.yale.edu/2011/03/contemporary-fiction-by-the-numbers/.

12. For valuable discussions of the evolution of the canon, see "Forum: The End of the Canon?" *J19: The Journal of Nineteenth-Century Americanists* 4, no. 1 (2016): 125–79; John Alberti, ed., *The Canon in the Classroom: The Pedagogical Implications of Canon Revision in American Literature* (New York: Routledge, 1995); Dana D. Nelson, "We Have Never Been Anti-Exceptionalists," *American Literary History* 31, no. 2 (2019): e1–e17, https://doi.org/10.1093/alh/ajz017.

13. Ellen Dupree, "'Usually the Reward of Tosh': Edith Wharton's Business Education," *Edith Wharton Review* 17, no. 2 (2001): 1, 3–14.

14. Michael Denning, *Mechanic Accents: Dime Novels and Working-Class Culture in America* (New York: Verso, 1987); David S. Reynolds, *Beneath the American Renaissance: The Subversive Imagination in the Age of Emerson and Melville* (New York: Knopf, 1988); Daryl Jones, *The Dime Novel Western* (Bowling Green, OH: Popular Press, 1978); Ron Goulart, *Cheap Thrills: An Informal History of the Pulp Magazines* (New Rochelle, NY: Arlington House, 1972); Lawrence W. Levine, *Highbrow / Lowbrow: The Emergence of*

Cultural Hierarchy in America (Cambridge, MA: Harvard University Press, 1988). Frank Felsenstein and James J. Connolly, *What Middletown Read: Print Culture in an American Small City* (Amherst: University of Massachusetts Press, 2015), studies library borrowing in Muncie, Indiana, at the end of the nineteenth century and shows the different tastes of social classes.

15. Donald A. Ringe, *The Pictorial Mode: Space & Time in the Art of Bryant, Irving & Cooper* (Lexington: The University Press of Kentucky, 1971), ix, quotes James.

16. David Lubin, *Picturing a Nation: Art and Social Change in Nineteenth-Century America* (New Haven, CT: Yale University Press, 1994), uses "identity politics" to link painting to changes in US society.

17. Franco Moretti, *Distant Reading* (New York: Verso, 2013), 48–49; Jonathan Arac and Holly Yanacek, "Keywords, Structures of Feeling, and the Novel," *Novel: A Forum on Fiction* 54, no. 1 (2021): 121–29; "The Digital in the Humanities: An Interview with Ted Underwood," August 10, 2016, *Los Angeles Review of Books*, https://lareviewofbooks.org/article/digital-humanities-interview-ted-underwood/; Steven Ruggles, "The Revival of Quantification: Reflections on Our New Histories," *Social Science History* 45, no. 1 (2021): 1–25.

18. Jean-Baptiste Michel et al., "Supporting Online Material for Quantitative Analysis of Culture Using Millions of Digitized Books," *Science*, December 2010, www.sciencemag.org/cgi/content/full/science.1199644.DCI; Jean-Baptiste Michel et al., "Quantitative Analysis of Culture Using Millions of Digitized Books," *Science* 331 (January 2011) 176–82; "What Happened to Google's Effort to Scan Millions of University Library Books," *EdSurge*, August 10, 2017, https://www.edsurge.com/news/2017-08-10-what-happened-to-google-s-effort-to-scan-millions-of-university-library-books.

19. https://books.google.com/ngrams.

20. For the Keywords Project, see http://keywords.pitt.edu; Jonathan Arac and Holly Yanacek, "Keywords, Structures of Feeling, and the Novel," *Novel: A Forum on Fiction* 54, no. 1 (2021): 121–29, builds on Raymond Williams's insights into keywords.

21. Mark Davies, "Expanding Horizons in Historical Linguistics with the 400-Million Word Corpus of Historical American English," *Corpora* 7, no. 2 (2012): 121–57; Corpus of Historical American English, http://corpus.byu.edu/coha/.

22. "Books Ngram Viewer," http://ngrams.googlelabs.com/info; Patricia Cohen, "In 500 Billion Words, New Window on Culture," December 17, 2010, *New York Times Online*, http://www.nytimes.com/2010/12/17/books/17words.html?pagewanted'1&_r'1; Robert Lee Hotz, "New Google Database Puts Centuries of Cultural Trends in Reach of Linguists," December 17, 2010, *Wall Street Journal* Online, http://online.wsj.com/article; Michael Pettit, "Historical Time in the Age of Big Data: Cultural Psychology, Historical Change, and the Google Books Ngram Viewer," *History of Psychology* 19, no. 2 (2016): 141–53.

23. For the spirited debate over the use of data in literary analysis, see Gary Hall, "Towards a Postdigital Humanities: Cultural Analytics and the Computational Turn to Data-Driven Scholarship," *American Literature* 85, no. 4 (2013): 781–809; Nan Z. Da, "The

Computational Case against Computational Literary Studies," *Critical Inquiry* 45, no. 3 (2019): 601–39; Matthew L. Jockers, *Macroanalysis: Digital Methods and Literary History* (Champaign: University of Illinois Press, 2003).

24. Myra Jehlen, "The Novel and the Middle Class in America," in *Ideology and Classic American Literature*, ed. Sacvan Bercovitch and Myra Jehlen (New York: Cambridge University Press, 1986), 125–44; Amy Schrager Lang, *The Syntax of Class: Writing Inequality in Nineteenth-Century America* (Princeton, NJ: Princeton University Press, 2003), 6–9. Arguing that most novels reflected middle-class values does not deny the existence of social conflict. Many of the books examined in this work detail those clashes. Joe Shapiro, *The Illiberal Imagination: Class and the Rise of the U.S. Novel* (Charlottesville: University of Virginia Press, 2017), highlights class conflict.

25. Debby Applegate, "Henry Ward Beecher and the "Great Middle Class": Mass-Marketed Intimacy and Middle-Class Identity," in *The Middling Sorts: Explorations in the History of the American Middle Class*, ed. Burton J. Bledstein and Robert D. Johnson (New York: Routledge, 2001), 107.

26. Ibid.; C. Hartley Grattan, "The Middle Class, Alas!" *Harper's Magazine*, February 1951, 39–47.

27. Stuart Blumin, *The Emergence of the Middle Class: Social Experience in the American City, 1760–1900* (New York: Cambridge University Press, 1989), 13; Stuart Blumin, "The Hypothesis of Middle-Class Formation in Nineteenth-Century America: A Critique and Some Proposals," *American Historical Review* 90, no. 2 (1985): 299–338; Maris A. Vinovskis, "Stalking the Elusive Middle Class in Nineteenth-Century America: A Review Article," *Comparative Studies in Society and History* 33, no. 3 (1991): 582–87; Melanie Archer and Judith R. Blau, "Class Formation in Nineteenth-Century America: The Case of the Middle Class," *American Review of Sociology* 19 (1993): 17–41; Mary P. Ryan, *Cradle of the Middle Class: The Family in Oneida County, New York, 1790–1865* (New York: Cambridge University Press, 1981), xiii, 5; Paul E. Johnson, *A Shopkeeper's Millennium: Society and Revivals in Rochester, New York, 1815–1837* (New York: Hill and Wang, 1978).

28. Jackson Turner Main, *The Social Structure of Revolutionary America* (Princeton, NJ: Princeton University Press, 1969), 273. For other works with a similar point of view, see Dallett Hemphill, "Middle Class Rising in Revolutionary America: The Evidence from Manners," *Journal of Social History* 30, no. 2 (1996): 317–44; Jennifer L. Goloboy, "The Early American Middle Class," *Journal of the Early Republic* 25, no. 4 (2005): 537–45; Ronald Schultz, *The Republic of Labor: Philadelphia Artisans and the Politics of Class, 1720–1830* (New York: Oxford University Press, 1993), 44–45, 51–60; Robert E. Brown, *Middle-Class Democracy and the Revolution in Massachusetts, 1690–1780* (Ithaca, NY: Cornell University Press, 1955); Konstantin Dierks, "Middle-Class Formation in Eighteenth-Century North America," in *Class Matters: Early North America and the Atlantic World*, ed. Simon Middleton and Billy G. Smith (Philadelphia: University of Pennsylvania Press, 2008), 99–108; Thomas Doerflinger, *A Vigorous Spirit of Enterprise: Merchants and Economic Development in Revolutionary Philadelphia* (Chapel Hill: University of North Carolina Press, 1986), 16–17; Carroll Smith-Rosenberg, "Black Gothic: The Shadowy Or-

igins of the American Bourgeoisie," in *Possible Pasts: Becoming Colonial in Early America*, ed. Robert Blair St. George (Ithaca, NY: Cornell University Press, 2000), 243–69.

29. Emma Hart, "Work, Family, and the Eighteenth-Century History of a Middle Class in the American South," *Journal of Southern History* 78, no. 3 (2012): 551–78, quotation on 555. See also Jennifer L. Goloboy, *Charleston and the Emergence of Middle Class Culture in the Revolutionary Era* (Athens: University of Georgia Press, 2016).

30. *Poor Richard Improved*, 1757, *The Papers of Benjamin Franklin*, ed. Leonard W. Labaree et al. (New Haven, CT: Yale University Press, 1959), 7: 344; *Poor Richard Improved, 1756, Franklin Papers*, 6: 321; *Poor Richard*, 1746, *Franklin Papers*, 3: 63; William Pencak, "Politics and Ideology in *Poor Richard's Almanack*," *Pennsylvania Magazine of History and Biography* 116, no. 2 (1992): 197, quotes the quatrain about Pennsylvania. See also Patrick Sullivan, "Benjamin Franklin, the Inveterate (and Crafty) Public Instructor: Instruction on Two Levels in 'The Way to Wealth,'" *Early American Literature* 21, no. 3 (1986/1987): 248–59; Todd N. Thompson, "Representative Nobodies: The Politics of Benjamin Franklin's Satiric Personae, 1722–1757," *Early American Literature* 46, no. 3 (2011): 449–80; Marc Egnal, "The Politics of Ambition: A New Look at Benjamin Franklin's Career," *Canadian Review of American Studies* 6 (1975): 151–64.

31. Franklin, *Plain Truth*, 1747, *Franklin Papers*, 3: 201; Walter Isaacson, *Benjamin Franklin: An American Life* (New York: Simon & Schuster, 2003), 123–26.

32. Quoted in Blumin, *Emergence of the Middle Class*, 34.

33. *Pennsylvania Gazette* and *Pennsylvania Chronicle*, quoted in Sarah Knott, *Sensibility and the American Revolution* (Chapel Hill: University of North Carolina Press, 2009), 48–49; [Melancton Smith?], Letter 5, October 13, 1787, *Empire and Nation: Letters from a Farmer in Pennsylvania, Letters from the Federal Farmer*, ed. Forrest McDonald (Indianapolis, IN: Liberty Fund, 1999); Saul Cornell, *The Other Founders: Anti-Federalism and the Dissenting Tradition in America, 1788–1828* (Chapel Hill: University of North Carolina Press, 1999), 38–39, 88–94.

34. Charles Brockden Brown, "Alliance Between Poverty and Genius," *Literary Magazine* 3 (May 1805): 333, quoted in Steven Watts, *The Romance of Real Life: Charles Brockden Brown and the Origins of American Culture* (Baltimore, MD: Johns Hopkins University Press, 1994), 146.

35. Blumin, *Emergence of the Middle Class*, 73–74.

36. Quoted in Applegate, "Henry Ward Beecher," 110.

37. Eric Foner, *Free Soil, Free Labor, Free Men: The Ideology of the Republican Party before the Civil War* (New York: Oxford University Press, 1970), 11–39; Amy Schrager Lang, *The Syntax of Class: Writing Inequality in Nineteenth-Century America* (Princeton, NJ: Princeton University Press, 2003), discusses the tension between gender and class in mid-nineteenth-century novels.

38. Whitman quoted in Blumin, *Emergence of the Middle Class*, 1.

39. Lydia Maria Child to Sarah Shaw, August 25, 1877, in *Lydia Maria Child: Selected Letters, 1817–1880*, ed. Milton Meltzer and Patricia G. Holland (Amherst, MA: University of Massachusetts Press, 1982), 544; Burton J. Bledstein, "Introduction: Storytellers to

the Middle Class," in *Middling Sorts,* 10; Blumin, "Hypothesis of Middle-Class Formation," 335.

40. Theodore Dreiser, *Sister Carrie* (1900; Oxford: Oxford University Press, 1998), 2, 83; Theodore Dreiser, *The Financier* (New York: Harper & Brothers, 1912), 776; Bledstein, "Introduction," 14, 295.

41. Thelma Herman, "Pragmatism: A Study in Middle Class Ideology," *Social Forces* 22, no. 4 (1944): 405–10; Mary Bosworth Treudley, "An Ethnic Group's View of the American Middle Class," *American Sociological Review* 11, no. 6 (1946): 715–24; Robert E. L. Faris, "The Middle Class from a Sociological Viewpoint," *Social Forces* 39, no. 1 (1960–61): 1–5.

42. See discussion in chapter 9.

43. Alissa Quart, *Squeezed: Why Our Families Can't Afford America* (New York: Ecco/Harper Collins Publishers, 2018); Frank Levy, "The Middle Class: Is It Really Vanishing?" *The Brookings Review* 5, no. 3 (1987): 17–21.

44. Frank Newport, "Americans' Identification as Middle Class Edges Back Up," *Gallup,* December 15, 2016, https://news.gallup.com/poll/199727/americans-identification-middle-class-edges-back.aspx. Identification with the middle class rose in 2106. For different figures, see Richard Morin and Seth Motel, "A Third of Americans Now Say They Are in the Lower Class," September 10, 2012, *Pew Social & Demographic Trends,* http://www.pewsocialtrends.org/2012/09/10/.

45. The dating of these eras and of chapters usually reflects landmark books. So Louisa May Alcott's *Little Women / Good Wives* (1868–69) signals the end of the sentimental era, and Herman Melville's *Moby-Dick* (1851) closes chapter 3. While change was gradual, particular works announce a break (or the end of a period) much as cooling water suddenly turns to ice.

46. Bercovitch, *Cambridge History of American Literature;* Elliott, *Columbia History of the American Novel;* Cassuto, *Cambridge History of the American Novel;* Ted Underwood, *Why Literary Periods Mattered: Historical Contrast and the Prestige of English Studies* (Stanford, CA: Stanford University Press, 2013); Christopher Hager and Cody Marrs, "Against 1865: Reperiodizing the Nineteenth Century," *The Journal of Nineteenth-Century Americanists* 1, no. 2 (2013): 259–84; John L. Rowlett, "Ralph Cohen on Literary Periods: Afterword as Foreword," *New Literary History* 50, no. 1 (2019): 129–39. See also the broad range of views expressed in Hager and Marrs, eds., *Timelines of American Literature* (Baltimore, MD: Johns Hopkins University Press, 2019).

47. For a classic statement of the splitter/lumper conflict, see J. H. Hexter, "The Burden of Proof," *Times Literary Supplement,* October 24, 1975.

Chapter 1

1. Walter Isaacson, *Benjamin Franklin: An American Life* (New York: Simon & Schuster, 2003), 246–47; Carl Van Doren, *Benjamin Franklin* (London, 1939), 9–13; Marc Egnal, "The Politics of Ambition: A New Look at Benjamin Franklin's Career," *Cana-*

dian Review of American Studies 6 (1975): 151–64; Benjamin Franklin, *Autobiography* in *The Autobiography and Other Writings*, ed. L. Jesse Lemisch (New York: New American Library, 1961), 74.

2. On the emergence of the middle class, see the discussion in the introduction.

3. Gary B. Nash, *The Urban Crucible: Social Change, Political Consciousness, and the Origins of the American Revolution* (Cambridge, MA: Harvard University Press, 1979), 387–401, 407–9; Marc Egnal, *New World Economies: The Growth of the Thirteen Colonies and Early Canada* (New York: Oxford University Press, 1998), 3–45, 55–56; Thomas M. Doerflinger, *A Vigorous Spirit of Enterprise: Merchants and Economic Development in Revolutionary Philadelphia* (Chapel Hill: University of North Carolina Press, 1986), 11–69; Lorena Walsh, "The Standard of Living in the Colonial Chesapeake," *The William and Mary Quarterly* 45, no. 1 (1988): 144; Richard L. Bushman, *The Refinement of America: Persons, Houses, Cities* (New York: Knopf, 1992), 110–40; Daniel Vickers, "Competency and Competition: Economic Culture in Early America," *The William and Mary Quarterly* 47, no. 1 (1990): 3–29; David Jaffee, *A New Nation of Goods: The Material Culture of Early America* (Philadelphia: University of Pennsylvania Press, 2010), 14–18.

4. On long-term trends, see Marc Egnal, "The Economic Development of the Thirteen Continental Colonies, 1720 to 1775," *The William and Mary Quarterly* 32, no. 3 (1975): 191–222; T. H. Breen, "'Baubles of Britain': The American and Consumer Revolutions of the Eighteenth Century," in *Of Consuming Interests: The Style of Life in the Eighteenth Century*, ed. Cary Carson, Ronald Hoffman, and Peter J. Albert (Charlottesville: University of Virginia Press, 1994), 444–82; Marc Egnal, *A Mighty Empire: The Origins of the American Revolution* (Ithaca, NY: Cornell University Press, 1988), 126–29; Egnal, *New World Economies*, 37–117.

5. John Wayles to Farrell & Jones, Aug. 30, 1766, John M. Hemphill II, ed., "John Wayles Rates His Neighbors," *Virginia Magazine of History and Biography* 66, no. 3 (1958): 305.

6. Cadwallader Colden to Board of Trade, August 9, 1764, New York Historical Society *Collections* 9 (1876): 341–42.

7. *Poor Richard Improved, 1758, The Papers of Benjamin Franklin*, ed. Leonard W. Labaree et al. (New Haven, CT: Yale University Press, 1959), 7: 349; Egnal, *New World Economies*, 37–77; Egnal, *A Mighty Empire*, 126–49; Egnal and Joseph A. Ernst, "An Economic Interpretation of the American Revolution," *The William and Mary Quarterly* 29, no. 1 (1972): 3–32.

8. Richard Buel Jr., *In Irons: Britain's Naval Supremacy and the American Revolutionary Economy* (New Haven, CT: Yale University Press, 1998); Doerflinger, *Vigorous Spirit*, 197–356.

9. Franklin, "Advice to a young Tradesman, written by an Old One," July 21, 1748, *Franklin Papers*, 3: 308. On the earlier use of these terms, with an emphasis on their ethical and spiritual dimensions, see J. E. Crowley, *This Sheba, Self: The Conceptualization of Economic Life in Eighteenth-Century America* (Baltimore, MD: Johns Hopkins University Press, 1974), 1–49; Darrett B. Rutman, *Husbandmen of Plymouth Farms and Villages in the Old Colony, 1620–1692* (Boston: Beacon Press, 1967), chap. 2.

10. *Poor Richard Improved, 1758, Franklin Papers*, 7: 340–50.

11. Benjamin Rush, *The Autobiography of Benjamin Rush*, ed. George W. Corner (Princeton, NJ: Greenwood Press, 1948), 83–84.

12. Dallett Hemphill, "Middle Class Rising in Revolutionary America: The Evidence from Manners," *Journal of Social History* 30, no. 2 (1996): 318–20; Egnal, *Mighty Empire*, 161–66, 185–89, 208–12; Crowley, *Sheba, Self*, 125–46; *Poor Richard Improved, 1758, Franklin Papers*, 7: 350; Egnal, *New World Economies*, 37–45; Drew R. McCoy, *The Elusive Republic: Political Economy in Jeffersonian America* (Chapel Hill: University of North Carolina Press, 1980), 48–104.

13. Nicole Eustace, *Passion Is the Gale: Emotion, Power, and the Coming of the American Revolution* (Chapel Hill: University of North Carolina Press, 2008), 158–59.

14. Franklin, *Plain Truth*, 1747, *Franklin Papers*, 3:187.

15. Kathleen M. Brown, *Good Wives, Nasty Wenches and Anxious Patriarchs: Gender, Race, and Power in Colonial Virginia* (Chapel Hill: University of North Carolina Press, 1996), 319–28; Eustace, *Passion Is the Gale*, 107–46, 286–319; Jan Lewis, "Domestic Tranquility and the Management of Emotion among the Gentry of Pre-Revolutionary Virginia," *The William and Mary Quarterly* 39, no. 1 (1982): 136–49.

16. Margaretta A. Lovell, "Reading Eighteenth-Century American Family Portraits: Social Images and Self-Images," *Winterthur Portfolio* 22, no. 4 (1987): 252; Richard McLanathan, *The American Tradition in the Arts* (New York: Harcourt, Brace & World, 1968), 76–81; Robert Hughes, *American Visions: The Epic History of Art in America* (New York: Alfred A. Knopf, 1997), 64–65; Jules David Prown, *John Singleton Copley: In America, 1738–1774* (Cambridge, MA: Harvard University Press, 1966), 10–11.

17. Karin Calvert, "Children in American Family Portraiture, 1670–1810," *The William and Mary Quarterly* 39, no. 1 (1982): 87–113.

18. Eustace, *Passion Is the Gale*, 10.

19. Sarah Knott, *Sensibility and the American Revolution* (Chapel Hill: University of North Carolina Press, 2009), 14–15; Brown, *Good Wives*, 327–28.

20. Fliegelman, *Prodigals and Pilgrims*, 34.

21. Edgar P. Richardson, "Charles Willson Peale and His World," in *Charles Willson Peale and His World*, ed. Edgar P. Richardson, Brooke Hindle, and Lillian B. Miller (New York: H.N. Abrams, 1983), 34–68; Lillian B. Miller, "Charles Willson Peale: A Life of Harmony and Purpose," in *Charles Willson Peale and His World*, 192; Darrel Sewall, "Charles Willson Peale's Portraits of the Cadwallader Family," *Philadelphia Museum of Art Bulletin* 91 (1996): 24–34; Jules David Prown, "Charles Willson Peale in London," in *New Perspectives on Charles Willson Peale: A 250th Anniversary Celebration*, ed. Lillian B. Miller and David C. Ward (Pittsburgh, PA: University of Pittsburgh Press, 1991), 43–44; Charles C. Sellers, "Charles Willson Peale's Career as a Painter," *Proceedings of the American Philosophical Society* 92 (1948): 105–6.

22. Calvert, "Children," 108.

23. Eustace, *Passion Is the Gale*, 409.

24. Thomas Paine, *Common Sense*, 1776, http://www.ushistory.org/PAINE/commonsense/sense1.htm.

25. Hannah Foster, *The Coquette* (1797; New York: Oxford University Press, 1993), 38; Herbert Ross Brown, *The Sentimental Novel in America, 1789–1860* (Durham, NC: Duke University Press, 1940), chaps. 1–3. Franco Moretti, *Graphs, Maps, Trees* (London: Verso, 2007), 14–17, presents graphs showing that the production of epistolary novels peaked in Britain around 1780 and had fallen off sharply by 1789, when the first American epistolary novels appeared.

26. Defoe, *Robinson Crusoe*, chapter 20; Ian Watt, *The Rise of the Novel: Studies in Defoe, Richardson and Fielding* (1957; Berkeley, CA: University of California Press, 1965), 60–82; Christopher Hill, "Robinson Crusoe," *History Workshop* 10 (1980): 6–24; Wolfram Schmidgen, "Robinson Crusoe, Enumeration, and the Mercantile Fetish," *Eighteenth-Century Studies* 35, no. 1 (2001): 19–39; David W. Spielman, "The Value of Money in *Robinson Crusoe, Moll Flanders*, and *Roxana*," *The Modern Language Review* 107, no. 1 (2012): 65–87.

27. Nancy Armstrong, "Fiction and the Making of the Modern Middle Class," in *Clarissa and Her Readers: New Essays for the Clarissa Project*, ed. Carol Houlihan Flynn and Edward Copeland (New York: AMS Press, 1999), 19–44; Nancy Armstrong, *Desire and Domestic Fiction: A Political History of the Novel* (New York: Oxford University Press, 1987), 3–50; Scott P. Gordon, "Disinterested Selves: *Clarissa* and the Tactics of Sentiment," *ELH* 64, no. 2 (1997): 473–502; Tom Keymer, *Richardson's* Clarissa *and the Eighteenth-Century Reader* (Cambridge, UK: Cambridge University Press, 1992); Watt, *Rise of the Novel*, 135–232; Christopher Hill, "Clarissa Harlowe and her Times," *Essays in Criticism* 5 (1955): 315–340; Thomas Keymer and Peter Sabor, eds., *The Pamela Controversy: Criticisms and Adaptations of Samuel Richardson's Pamela, 1740–1750*, 6 vols. (London: Pickering & Chatto, 2001).

28. Judith Frank, "'A Man Who Laughs is Never Dangerous': Character and Class in Sterne's *A Sentimental Journey*," *ELH* 56, no. 1 (1989): 97–124; Keryl Kavanagh, "Discounting Language: A Vehicle for Interpreting Laurence Sterne's *A Sentimental Journey*," *The Journal of Narrative Technique* 22, no. 2 (1992): 136–44; Katherine Turner, *British Travel Writers in Europe, 1750–1800: Authorship, Gender and National Identity* (Burlington, VT: Ashgate Press, 2001), chap. 3.

29. Gregory L. Ulmer, "*Clarissa* and *La Nouvelle Héloïse*," *Comparative Literature* 24, no. 4 (1972): 289–308; Alexander Gelley, "The Two Julies: Conversion and Imagination in *La Nouvelle Héloïse*," *MLN* 92, no. 4 (1977): 749–60; Robert Darton, *The Great Cat Massacre and Other Episodes in French Cultural History* (New York: Basic Books, 1984), 215–56.

30. Caroline Wellberry, "From Mirrors to Images: The Transformation of Sentimental Paradigms in Goethe's *The Sorrows of Young Werther*," *Studies in Romanticism* 25, no. 2 (1986): 231–49.

31. Alexander Graydon to John Lardner, December 3, 1784, quoted in Knott, *Sensibility and the American Revolution*, 27. Kevin J. Hayes, *A Colonial Woman's Bookshelf* (Knoxville: University of Tennessee Press, 1996), 101–22, explores the response to romance novels.

32. Catherine Snell Crary, "The Tory and the Spy: The Double Life of James Rivington," *The William and Mary Quarterly* 16, no. 1 (1959): 61–72.

33. Knott, *Sensibility and the American Revolution*, 27–29; Stephen Botein, "The Anglo-American Book Trade before 1776: Personnel and Strategies," in *Printing and Society in Early America*, ed. William L. Joyce et al. (Worcester, MA: American Antiquarian Society, 1983), 59, 78–81; Hayes, *Colonial Woman's Bookshelf*, 11–16.

34. Arthur M. Schlesinger, *The Colonial Merchants and the American Revolution, 1763–1776* (1918; New York: Atheneum, 1968), 169–70, 178–78; Merrill Jensen, *The Founding of a Nation: A History of the American Revolution, 1763–1776* (New York: Oxford University Press, 1968), 359–62, 368; David Kaser, *A Book for a Sixpence: The Circulating Library in America* (Pittsburgh, PA: Beta Phi Mu, 1980), 31.

35. Kaser, *Book for a Sixpence*, 29–30, quotations on 30.

36. Ibid., 31. Kaser indicates that "literature and fiction" comprised 25 percent of the collection. Robert Winans, "The Growth of a Novel-Reading Public in Late Eighteenth-Century America," *Early American Literature* 9, no. 3 (1975), 270–71, suggests that "fiction" accounted for only 10 percent of the works in Mein's 1765 catalogue.

37. Knott, *Sensibility and the American Revolution*, 29–51, 68, quotations on 43, 44; Kaser, *Book for a Sixpence*, 39. Much of Bell's printing ventures can be traced in *Eighteenth Century Collections Online*, provided by the Gale Group.

38. Knott, *Sensibility and the American Revolution*, 31, 44, 52.

39. Ibid., 30, 42, 48, 51.

40. Robert B. Winans, "Bibliography and the Cultural Historian: Notes on the Eighteenth-Century Novel," in *Printing and Society*, 177–79. Still, some of the popular novels were not sentimental ones. The bestsellers include Miguel de Cervantes's *Don Quixote* (1605–1615); *Gil Blas* (1715–1735) by the French author Alain René Lesage; Samuel Johnson's philosophical work, *Rasselas* (1759); and Defoe's *Robinson Crusoe*.

41. Ibid., 178–81.

42. Kaser, *Book for a Sixpence*, 44–56, quotation on 48.

Part 1: The Sentimental Era

1. William Hill Brown, *The Power of Sympathy* (1789; Albany, NY: New College and University Press, 1970), letter 36; Dana M. McClain, "Regulating Feeling in the First American Novel: Sympathy, Sensibility, and Sentiment in William Hill Brown's *The Power of Sympathy*," *Studies in American Fiction* 45, no. 2 (2018): 143–64.

2. Shirley Samuels, Introduction to *The Culture of Sentiment: Race, Gender, and Sentimentality in Nineteenth-Century America*, ed. Shirley Samuels (New York: Oxford University Press, 1992), 4.

3. Benedict R. Anderson, *Imagined Communities: Reflections on the Origin and Spread of Nationalism* (London: Verso, 1991); U.S. Bureau of the Census, *Historical Statistics of the United States, Colonial Times to 1970* (Washington, DC: US Government Printing Office, 1975), 12.

4. Cindy Weinstein, "Sentimentalism," in *The Cambridge History of the American Novel*, ed. Leonard Cassuto, Clare Virginia Eby, and Benjamin Reiss (New York: Cambridge University Press, 2011), 209, 213; Samuels, Introduction to *The Culture of Sentiment*, 5.

5. David S. Reynolds, *Beneath the American Renaissance: The Subversive Imagination in the Age of Emerson and Melville* (Cambridge, MA: Harvard University Press, 1989), 337, 338; Jane Tompkins, *Sensational Designs: The Cultural Work of American Fiction, 1790–1860* (New York: Oxford University Press, 1985), 151; Laura Wexler, "Tender Violence: Literary Eavesdropping, Domestic Fiction, and Educational Reform," in *Culture of Sentiment*, 15.

6. Samuels, Introduction to *The Culture of Sentiment*, 5; Cindy Weinstein, *Family, Kinship, and Sympathy in Nineteenth-Century American Literature* (New York: Cambridge University Press, 2004), 8; Ashley Reed, *Heaven's Interpreters: Women Writers and Religious Agency in Nineteenth-Century America* (Ithaca, NY: Cornell University Press, 2020), 42–123.

7. Another famous example is John Vanderlyn, *The Murder of Jane McCrea* (1804). Precursors for this approach include such paintings as Benjamin West, *The Death of General Wolfe* (1770), and John Singleton Copley, *Watson and the Shark* (1778).

8. Reynolds, *Beneath the American Renaissance*, 337; Ann Douglas, *The Feminization of American Culture* (New York: Anchor Press/Doubleday, 1988), 62; Samuels, *Culture of Sentiment*, 4.

9. Cathy N. Davidson, *Revolution and the Word: The Rise of the Novel in America*, expanded ed. (New York: Oxford University Press, 2004), 30.

10. Douglas, *Feminization*, 87; Herbert Ross Brown, *The Sentimental Novel in America, 1789–1860* (Durham, NC: Duke University Press, 1940); Philip P. Gura, *Truth's Ragged Edge: The Rise of the American Novel* (New York: Farrar, Strauss and Giroux, 2013) suggests a different overview of the period from 1789 to 1870, arguing that literature traced an "arc from traditional religion to self-consciousness" (xiv).

11. Henry Nash Smith, "The Scribbling Women and the Cosmic Success Story," *Critical Enquiry* 1, no. 1 (1974): 50, quotes James; Nina Baym, *Woman's Fiction: A Guide to Novels by and about Women in America, 1820–1870*, 2nd ed. (Chicago: University of Illinois Press, 1993), xxxiv.

12. William Dean Howells, *The Rise of Silas Lapham* (1885; New York: Collier Books, 1962), 194.

Chapter 2

1. Steven Watts, *The Romance of Real Life: Charles Brockden Brown and the Origins of American Culture* (Baltimore, MD: The Johns Hopkins University Press, 1994), 27–31, 131–32, 164–66, quotations on 130, 166; "Charles Brockden Brown," *American National Biography*; Elizabeth Hewitt, Stephen Shapiro, and Karen A. Weyler, "Introduction to 'Symposium on Scholarly Editing and the New Charles Brockden Brown Studies,'" *Early American Literature* 57, no. 2 (2022): 531–35.

2. Douglass C. North, *The Economic Growth of the United States, 1790–1860* (New York: W. W. Norton & Co., 1966), 17–52; Gordon S. Wood, *Empire of Liberty: A History of the Early Republic, 1789–1815* (New York: Oxford University Press, 2009), 202, 620–25; Drew R. McCoy, *The Elusive Republic: Political Economy in Jeffersonian America* (Chapel Hill: University of North Carolina Press, 1980), 76–119, 209–35.

3. North, *Economic Growth*, 53–58; Wood, *Empire of Liberty*, 620–58.

4. Wood, *Empire of Liberty*, 708, quotes Niles.

5. Henry Clay, Mar. 31, 1824, *Annals of Congress*, 18th Congress, 1st session, 1977, 1966.

6. George Rogers Taylor, *The Transportation Revolution, 1815–1860* (New York: Harper and Row, 1951), 75–103; Erik F. Haites, James Mak, and Gary M. Walton, *Western River Transportation: The Era of Early Internal Development, 1810–1860* (Baltimore, MD: The Johns Hopkins University Press, 1975).

7. Robert F. Dalzell Jr., *Enterprising Elite: The Boston Associates and the World They Made* (Cambridge, MA: Harvard University Press, 1987), 5–25; Nathan Appleton, *Introduction of the Power Loom and the Origin of Lowell* (Lowell, MA: B. H. Penhallow, 1858), 7–9, 14–15; Taylor, *Transportation Revolution*, 229–31, 301–2; North, *Economic Growth*, 122–34.

8. Charles Brockden Brown, *Ormond; or, The Secret Witness* (1799; Peterborough, ON: Broadview, 1999); Brown, *Edgar Huntly; or, Memoirs of a Sleep-Walker* (1799; Charleston, SC: BiblioBazaar, 2006); Susanna Rowson, *Reuben and Rachel; or, Tales of Old Times* (1798; Peterborough, ON: Broadview, 2009); Hannah W. Foster, *The Coquette* [issued in one volume with William Hill Brown's *The Power of Sympathy*] (1797; Albany, NY: New College and University Press, 1970); Charles Brockden Brown, *Jane Talbot* (1801; Charlottesville: University of Virginia, 2000); Isaac Mitchell, *Alonzo and Melissa, or, The Unfeeling Father. An American Tale* (1811; Boston: Printed for the Publisher, 1851); Susanna Rowson, *Charlotte Temple* (1791, 1794; New York: Oxford University Press, 1986); Royall Tyler, *The Algerine Captive, or, The Life and Adventures of Doctor Updike Underhill* (1797; New York: The Modern Library, 2002). Henri Petter, *The Early American Novel* (Columbus: Ohio State University Press, 1971), although more encyclopedic than analytic provides illustrative material on other similar works.

9. Brown, *Edgar Huntly*, 136–37.

10. Rowson, *Reuben and Rachel*, 247

11. Mitchell, *Alonzo and Melissa*, 9–10.

12. Jeffrey Rubin-Dorsky, "The Early American Novel," in *The Columbia History of the American Novel*, ed. Emory Elliott (New York: Columbia University Press, 1991), 6; Paul Giles, "Transatlantic Currents and the Invention of the American Novel," in *The Cambridge History of the American Novel*, ed. Leonard Cassuto, Clare Virginia Eby, and Benjamin Reiss (New York: Cambridge University Press, 2011), 34.

13. Michael T. Gilmore, "The Literature of the Revolutionary and Early National Periods," in *The Cambridge History of American Literature*, ed. Sacvan Bercovitch, vol. 1: *1590–1820* (New York: Cambridge University Press, 1994), 646.

14. Cathy N. Davidson, *Revolution and the Word: The Rise of the Novel in America*, expanded edition (1986; New York: Oxford University Press, 2004), 20–21, 236–38, 260–67, 282–305; Gilmore, "Literature of the Revolutionary and Early National Periods," 637–39.

15. Charles Brockden Brown, *Wieland; or, The Transformation* (1798; New York: Harcourt Brace & Co., 1926); David Zimmerman, "Charles Brockden Brown and the Conundrum of Complicity," *American Literature* 88, no. 4 (2016): 665–93.

16. Brown, *Edgar Huntly*; Wayne M. Reed, "Sleepwalking, Class Mobility, and the Search for the Social Origins of Populism in Charles Brockden Brown's *Edgar Huntly*," *Journal of American Studies* 56, no. 4 (2022): 635–60.

17. Charles Brockden Brown, *Arthur Merwyn; or, Memoirs of the Year 1793* (1799; Philadelphia: David McKay, 1889).

18. Jane Tompkins, *Sensational Designs: The Cultural Work of American Fiction, 1790–1860* (New York: Oxford University Press, 1985), 87.

19. Brown, *Ormond*, 131.

20. Davidson, *Revolution and the Word*, 36.

21. Carroll Smith-Rosenberg, "Domesticating 'Virtue': Coquettes and Revolutionaries in Young America," in *Literature and the Body: Essays on Populations and Persons*, ed. Elaine Scarry (Baltimore, MD: The Johns Hopkins University Press, 1988), 160–84, quotation on 169.

22. Foster, *Coquette*, 152–53; Davidson, *Revolution and the Word*, 22, 75–76, 215, 230; Anna Mae Duane, "Susanna Rowson, Hannah Webster Foster, and the Seduction Novel in the Early US," in *The Cambridge History of the American Novel*, 37–39.

23. Kenneth A. Lockridge, *Literacy in Colonial New England: An Enquiry into the Social Context of Literacy in the Early Modern West* (New York: Norton, 1974), 13–71; Joel Perlmann and Dennis Shirley, "When Did New England Women Acquire Literacy?" *The William and Mary Quarterly* 48, no. 1 (1991): 50–67; Miriam H. Berlin, "The Education of Women: A Tale of Developing Autonomy and Expanding Choices," *Change* 18, no. 2 (1986): 50–55; Sally Schwager, "Educating Women in America," *Signs* 12, no. 2 (1987): 333–72.

24. William Hill Brown, *The Power of Sympathy* (1789; Albany, NY: New College and University Press, 1970), 52.

25. Enos Hitchcock, *Memoirs of the Bloomsgrove Family*, 2 vols. bound together (1790; Upper Saddle River, NJ: The Gregg Press, 1970), 2: 19. For similar passages, see Brown, *Power of Sympathy*, letters 11, 12; Rowson, *Reuben and Rachel*, 20–21, 117, 143; and Brown, *Ormond*, 62–63. Broader discussions are presented in Rust, *Prodigal Daughters*, 88–94, 125–31; Davidson, *Revolution and the Word*, 128–32, 200–209.

26. Brown, *Ormond*, 205–6.

27. Bryan Waterman, *Republic of Intellect: The Friendly Club of New York City and the Making of American Literature* (Baltimore, MD: The Johns Hopkins University Press, 2007), 107–29. Some of the captivity narratives display the courage of colonial women, such as Hannah Duston. See Cotton Mather, "A Notable Exploit," 1702, in Gordon M. Sayre, ed., *American Captivity Narratives* (New York: Houghton Mifflin, 2000), 183–85.

28. Davidson, *Revolution and the Word*, 266–75.

29. Talia Argondezzi, "The Haitian Revolution and the Limitations of White Feminism: A Comparison of *Zelica, the Creole* and Leonora Sansay's *Secret History*," *Studies in American Fiction* 47, no. 1 (2020): 1–22.

30. Kristin M. Comment, "Charles Brockden Brown's *Ormond* and Lesbian Possibility in the Early Republic," *Early American Literature* 40, no. 1 (2005): 61.

31. Marion Rust, *Prodigal Daughters: Susanna Rowson's Early American Women* (Chapel Hill: University of North Carolina Press, 2008), 7.

32. Brown, *Power of Sympathy*, 34; Rubin-Dorsky, "Early American Novel," 16. Once Harrington falls in love with Harriet, he changes his mind about marriage—but other complications ensue. Joe Shapiro, *The Illiberal Imagination: Class and the Rise of the U.S. Novel* (Charlottesville: University of Virginia Press, 2017), emphasizes the conflict of classes in these novels.

33. Foster, *Coquette*, 158.

34. Leonora Sansay, *Secret History; or, The Horrors of St. Domingo* and *Laura*, ed. Michael J. Drexler (1808; Peterborough, ON: Broadview Editions, 2007); Jennifer Desiderio, "Cultivating Cultural Cohesion in *Reuben and Rachel*," *Studies in American Fiction* 38, nos. 1–2 (2011): 77–97; Melissa Adams-Campbell, "Romantic Revolutions: Love and Violence in Leonora Sansay's *Secret History, or The Horrors of St. Domingo*," *Studies in American Fiction* 39, no. 2 (2012): 135–46.

35. The increasing tolerance for women's "transgressions" evident in the late genteel period, and discussed in chapter 6, focuses on *adultery* not *seduction*.

36. Christopher Grasso, "A 'Great Awakening'?" *Reviews in American History* 37, no. 1 (2009): 13–21; Paul E. Johnson, *A Shopkeeper's Millennium: Society and Revivals in Rochester, New York, 1815–1837* (New York: Hill and Wang, 1978); Roger Finke and Rodney Stark, "Turning Pews into People: Estimating 19th Century Church Membership," *Journal for the Scientific Study of Religion* 25, no. 2 (1986): 180–92; Finke and Stark, *The Churching of America: Winners and Losers in Our Religious Economy* (New Brunswick, NJ: Rutgers University Press, 1992), 22–44; Jon Butler, *Awash in a Sea of Faith: Christianizing the American People* (Cambridge, MA: Harvard University Press, 1990), 1–2, 164–65, 180–93; Nathan O. Hatch, *The Democratization of American Christianity* (New Haven, CT: Yale University Press, 1989); Christine L. Heyrman, *Southern Cross: The Beginnings of the Bible Belt* (Chapel Hill: University of North Carolina Press, 1997). The figures for "churched" are for total population. In 1776, the about 20 percent of the White population had an active religious affiliation. See Finke and Stark works cited above.

37. Brown, *Wieland*, 24; Watts, *Romance of Real Life*, 67–69, 91, 124; Emory Elliott, *Revolutionary Writers: Literature and Authority in the New Republic, 1725–1810* (New York: Oxford University Press, 1982), 11–18, 272–76.

38. Brown, *Ormond*, 183.

39. Brown, *Jane Talbot*, letter 34.

40. Watts, *Romance of Real Life*, 139.

41. Tyler, *Algerine Captive*, 131.

42. Davidson, *Revolution and the World*, 285–305, quotation on 302.

43. Hugh Henry Brackenridge, *Modern Chivalry* (1792–1815; Indianapolis, IN, 2009), 255–59, 333–36.

44. Hitchcock, *Bloomsgrove Family*, letter 32.

45. William Cronon, "The Trouble with Wilderness, or Getting Back to the Wrong Nature," *Environmental History* 1, no. 1 (1996): 7.

46. Gombrich quoted in Dennis Berthold, "Charles Brockden Brown, *Edgar Huntly*, and the Origins of the American Picturesque," *The William and Mary Quarterly* 41, no. 1 (1984): 67.

47. Quoted in Henry Nash Smith, *Virgin Land: The American West as Symbol and Myth* (Cambridge, MA: Harvard University Press, 1950), 4.

48. Berthold, "Charles Brockden Brown," 67, quotes Gilpin.

49. Brown, *Edgar Huntly*, 92.

50. Mitchell, *Alonzo and Melissa*, 37–38.

51. Brown, *Edgar Huntly*, 7, 160; Timothy Sweet, "American Land, American Landscape, American Novels," in *Cambridge History of the American Novel*, 88–102; Berthold, "Charles Brockden Brown," 62–84.

52. Barbara Novak, *American Painting of the Nineteenth Century: Realism, Idealism, and the American Experience*, 2nd ed. (New York: Westview Press, 1969, 1979), 44–59, quotation on 45; William H. Gerdts and Theodore E. Stebbins Jr., *"A Man of Genius:" The Art of Washington Allston (1779–1843)* (Boston: Museum of Fine Arts, 1979), 9–13, quotation on 19; Edgar Preston Richardson, *Washington Allston: A Study of the Romantic Artist in Letters of Washington Allston* (Chicago: University of Chicago Press, 1948).

53. Gerdts and Stebbins, *"Man of Genius,"* 19; Clayton Zuba, "Apess's Eulogy on King Philip and the Politics of Native Visualcy," *Early American Literature* 52, no. 3 (2017), 651–77; John T. Spike, "'Salvator Rosa in America' at Wellesley College Museum," *The Burlington Magazine* 121, no. 917 (1979): 542–44.

Chapter 3

1. Alexis de Tocqueville, *Democracy in America*, trans. George Lawrence (1835, 1840; New York: Harper & Row, 1966), 453.

2. Ralph Waldo Emerson, "Nature," 1836, in Emerson, *Selected Essays* (New York: Penguin, 1982), 41.

3. Simon Kuznets, "Notes on the Pattern of U.S. Economic Growth," in *The Reinterpretation of American Economic History*, ed. Robert William Fogel and Stanley L. Engerman (New York: Harper & Row, 1971), 17–24; Marc Egnal, *New World Economies: The Growth of the Thirteen Colonies and Early Canada* (New York: Oxford University Press, 1998), 3–4, 42–45.

4. George Rogers Taylor, *The Transportation Revolution, 1815–1860* (New York: Rinehart, 1951), vii.

5. Tocqueville, *Democracy in America*, 554; D. W. Meinig, *Continental America, 1800–1867*, vol. 2 of *The Shaping of America: A Geographical Perspective on 500 Years of History* (New Haven, CT: Yale University Press, 1993), 221–374; Christopher Clark, "The Agrarian Context of American Capitalist Development," in *Capitalism Takes Command: The Social Transformation of Nineteenth-Century America*, ed. Michael Zakim and Gary J. Kornblith (Chicago: University of Chicago Press, 2012), 13–31; Robert A. Gross, *The Transcendentalists and Their World* (New York: Farrar, Straus and Giroux, 2021), chaps. 5, 16.

6. Taylor, *Transportation Revolution*, 15–103, 132–75, 207–28; Daniel Walker Howe, *What Hath God Wrought: The Transformation of America, 1815–1848* (New York: Oxford University Press, 2007), 211–36, 536–46; Marc Egnal, *Divergent Paths: How Culture and Institutions Have Shaped North American Growth* (New York: Oxford University Press, 1996), 12–20, 88–101; Jeremy Atack and Peter Passell, *A New Economic View of American History*, 2nd ed. (New York: Norton, 1994), 143–74.

7. Taylor, *Transportation Revolution*, 229–49; Atack and Passell, *Economic View*, 175–211; Howe, *What Hath God Wrought*, 546–52; Lance Newman, *Our Common Dwelling: Henry Thoreau, Transcendentalism, and the Class Politics of Nature* (New York: Palgrave Macmillan, 2005), 25–27.

8. Washington Irving, *The Sketch Book* (1819–20; New York: Signet Classic, 1961), 331.

9. James Fenimore Cooper, *The Pioneers, or the Sources of the Susquehanna; A Descriptive Tale* (1823; New York: Rinehart & Co., 1959), 1–2.

10. James Fenimore Cooper, *The Prairie* (1827; Charleston, SC: BiblioBazaar, 2007), 415.

11. Marvin Meyers, *The Jacksonian Persuasion: Politics and Belief* (Stanford, CA: Stanford University Press, 1957, 1960), vii.

12. Cooper, *Pioneers*, 324–25.

13. William Gilmore Simms, *Guy Rivers: A Tale of Georgia* (1834; Chicago: Donohue, Henneberry & Co., 1890), 69; Lawrence P. Spingarn, "The Yankee in Early American Fiction," *The New England Quarterly* 31, no. 4 (1958): 484–95.

14. For painting, see particularly the work of the genre artist William Sidney Mount.

15. Cathy N. Davidson and Jessamyn Hatcher, introduction to Davidson and Hatcher, eds., *No More Separate Spheres! A Next Wave American Studies Reader* (Durham, NC: Duke University Press, 2002), 8, 22; Nancy F. Cott, *The Bonds of Womanhood: "Woman's Sphere" in New England, 1780–1835* (New Haven, CT: Yale University Press, 1977), 70. Jeanne Boydston, *Home and Work: Housework, Wages, and the Ideology of Labor in the Early Republic* (New York: Oxford University Press, 1990); Barbara J. Berg, *The Remembered Gate: Origins of American Feminism. The Woman and the City, 1800–1860* (New York: Oxford University Press, 1978); Aileen S. Kraditor, ed., *Up from the Pedestal: Selected Writings in the History of American Feminism* (Chicago: Quadrangle Books, 1968), 9–14; Gerda Lerner, "The Lady and the Mill Girl: Changes in the Status of Women in the Age of Jackson," *Midcontinent American Studies Journal*, 10 (1969), 5–15.

16. Barbara Welter, "The Cult of True Womanhood, 1820–1860," *American Quarterly* 18, no. 2, Part 1 (1966), 151–74, quotation on 151.

17. Jane Tompkins, *Sensational Designs: The Cultural Work of American Fiction, 1790–1860* (New York: Oxford University Press, 1986), 124.

18. Suggesting such a balance are Lora Romero, *Home Fronts: Domesticity and Its Critics in the Antebellum United States* (Durham, NC: Duke University Press, 1977), 8–9; Susan K. Harris, *Nineteenth-Century American Women's Novels: Interpretative Strategies* (New York: Cambridge University Press, 1990).

19. Amy Kaplan, "Manifest Domesticity," *American Literature* 70, no. 3 (1998), 584.

20. Boydston, *Home and Work*, 150.

21. Mary Kelley, "Commentary," in *Locating American Studies: The Evolution of a Discipline*, ed. Lucy Maddox (Baltimore, MD: The Johns Hopkins University Press, 1999), 67.

22. Romero, *Home Fronts*, 23.

23. Catharine Beecher, *A Treatise on Domestic Economy, for the Use of Young Ladies at Home, and at School* (1841; New York: Harper, 1846), 27, 33, 37.

24. James Fenimore Cooper, *Notions of the Americans* (1828; Philadelphia: Carey, Lea & Blanchard, 1838), 106.

25. Ira Gershwin, "But Not for Me," from *Girl Crazy*, 1930.

26. Nathan O. Hatch, *The Democratization of American Christianity* (New Haven, CT: Yale University Press, 1989), 87–96, 195–201, quotations on 199–200; Jon Butler, *Awash in a Sea of Faith: Christianizing the American People* (Cambridge, MA: Harvard University Press, 1990), 241, 283; Mark A. Noll, *America's God: From Jonathan Edwards to Abraham Lincoln* (New York: Oxford University Press, 2002), 168–69, 182–85, 188–91, 200, 293–95, 341–44, 364; Christine L. Heyrman, *Southern Cross: The Beginnings of the Bible Belt* (Chapel Hill: University of North Carolina Press, 1997), 194–201; Roger Finke and Rodney Stark, *The Churching of America: Winners and Losers in Our Religious Economy* (New Brunswick, NJ: Rutgers University Press, 1992), 15–102.

27. Susan Warner, *The Wide, Wide World* (1850: New York: A. L. Burt, n.d.), 31; Butler, *Awash in a Sea of Faith*, 277–78; Noll, *America's God*, 198, 371–77; Hatch, *Democratization of American Christianity*, 125–26, 141–45, 179–84; Ann Douglas, *The Feminization of American Culture* (New York: Anchor Press/Doubleday, 1988), 109, quotes Warner.

28. Cooper, *Pioneers*, 130, 149; Alan Taylor, *William Cooper's Town: Power and Persuasion on the Frontier of the Early American Republic* (New York: Random House, 1995), 18–20.

29. James Fenimore Cooper, *The Pathfinder, or The Inland Sea* (1840; New York: Penguin Books, 1989), 440.

30. James Fenimore Cooper, *The Deerslayer, or The First War-Path* (1841; New York: New American Library, 1963), 443.

31. James Fenimore Cooper, *The Wing-and-Wing, or, Le feu-follett*, 2 vols. (Philadelphia: Lea & Blanchard, 1842), 2: 196–97.

32. Judith Fetterley, "My Sister, My Sister!": The Rhetoric of Catharine Sedgwick's *Hope Leslie*," *American Literature* 70, no. 3 (1998), 495–97.

33. Lucy Maddox, *Removals: Nineteenth-Century American Literature and the Politics of Indian Affairs* (New York: Oxford University Press, 1991), 103.

34. James L. Machor, *Reading Fiction in Antebellum America: Informed Response and Reception Histories, 1820–1865* (Baltimore, MD: The Johns Hopkins University Press, 2011), 221. Machor also quotes both Fetterley and Maddox.

35. Tocqueville, *Democracy in America*, 590.

36. Sarah M. Grimké, *Letters on the Equality of the Sexes and the Condition of Woman--Addressed to Mary S. Parker, President of the Boston Female Anti-Slavery Society* (Boston: Isaac Knapp, 1838); Margaret Fuller, *Woman in the Nineteenth Century* (1845; New York: W.W. Norton & Co., 1998), 20.

37. Sally G. McMillen, *Seneca Falls and the Origins of the Women's Rights Movement* (New York: Oxford University Press, 2008).

38. Nathaniel Hawthorne, *The Scarlet Letter* (1850; Boston: Houghton Mifflin Company, 1960), 163, 164; Monika M. Elbert, "Hester's Maternity: Stigma or Weapon?" *ESQ* 36, no. 3 (1990): 175–207.

39. Hawthorne, *Scarlet Letter*, 74; Ellen Moers, "*The Scarlet Letter*: A Political Reading," *Prospects* 9 (1984): 54; Suzan Last, "Hawthorne's Feminine Voices: Reading *The Scarlet Letter* as a Woman," *The Journal of Narrative Technique* 27, no. 3 (Fall 1997): 349; David Leverenz, "Mrs. Hawthorne's Headache: Reading *The Scarlet Letter*," *Nineteenth-Century Fiction* 37, no. 4 (1983): 560.

40. Barbara Bardes and Suzanne Gossett, *Declarations of Independence: Women and Political Power in Nineteenth-Century American Fiction* (New Brunswick, NJ: Rutgers University Press, 1990), 81.

41. James Fenimore Cooper, *The Ways of the Hour* (New York: George P. Putnam, 1850), 308; Wayne Franklin, *James Fenimore Cooper: The Later Years* (New Haven, CT: Yale University Press, 2017), 484–96.

42. Milette Shamir, "Manhood and the Early American Novel," in *The Cambridge History of the American Novel*, ed. Leonard Cassuto, Clare Virginia Eby, and Benjamin Reiss (New York: Cambridge University Press, 2011), 195; David Leverenz, *Manhood and the American Renaissance* (Ithaca, NY: Cornell University Press, 1989), 72–107; E. Anthony Rotundo, *American Manhood: Transformations in Masculinity from the Revolution to the Modern Era* (New York: Basic Books, 1993), 19–25.

43. Ralph Waldo Emerson, "Self-Reliance," 1841, in *Selected Essays*, 185.

44. See the discussion of *character* and *personality* in the introduction to part three of this book; Warren I. Susman, "'Personality' and the Making of Twentieth-Century Culture," in Susman, *Culture as History: The Transformation of American Society in the Twentieth Century* (New York: Pantheon Books, 1984), 271–85; Judy Hilkey, *Character is Capital: Success Manuals and Manhood in Gilded Age America* (Chapel Hill: University of North Carolina Press, 1997).

45. Emerson, "Self-Reliance," 178. Catherine L. Albanese, *Corresponding Motion: Transcendental Religion and the New America* (Philadelphia: Temple University Press, 1977), 31–55; Philip F. Gura, *American Transcendentalism: A History* (New York: Hill and Wang, 2007), 180–239, sets Emerson's views within the spectrum of Transcendental thought.

46. Michael J. Hoffman, "The Anti-Transcendentalism of *Moby-Dick*," *The Georgia Review* 23, no. 1 (1969): 11.

47. Victor Strandberg, "The Artist's Black Veil," *The New England Quarterly* 41, no. 4 (1968): 570; Hoffman, "Anti-Transcendentalism," 3; Claudia D. Johnson, "Hawthorne and Nineteenth-Century Perfectionism," *American Literature* 44, no. 4 (1973): 585–95; Larry J. Reynolds, "Hawthorne and Emerson in 'The Old Manse,'" *Studies in the Novel* 23, no. 1 (1991): 60–81.

48. Hawthorne, *Scarlet Letter*, 194.

49. Hawthorne, *Mosses from an Old Manse* (1846; New York: The Modern Library, 2003), 28–43 ("The Birthmark"), 71–99 ("Rappaccini's Daughter"); Hawthorne, *The*

Celestial Railroad and Other Stories (New York: New American Library, 1963), 271–87 ("Ethan Brand").

50. Herman Melville, *Moby-Dick, or The White Whale* (1851; New York: New American Library, 1961), 167; Allen Austin, "The Three-Stranded Allegory of *Moby-Dick*," *College English* 26, no. 5 (1965): 348; T. Walter Herbert Jr., "Calvinism and Cosmic Evil in *Moby-Dick*," *PMLA* 84, no. 6 (1969): 1613–19.

51. Melville, *Moby-Dick*, 398.

52. Emerson, "Nature," 1836, in *Selected Essays*, 39.

53. Cooper, *Pioneers*, 299; James D. Wallace, *Early Cooper and His Audience* (New York, 1986), 63–116; Donald A. Ringe, *The Pictorial Mode: Space & Time in the Art of Bryant, Irving & Cooper* (Lexington: The University of Kentucky Press, 1971), 28.

54. Cooper, *Pathfinder*, 24, 92.

55. Cooper, *Deerslayer*, 255.

56. Simms, *Guy Rivers*, 147.

57. Lydia Maria Child, *Hobomok* (1824) in Child, *Hobomok and Other Writings on Indians*, ed. Carolyn L. Karcher (New Brunswick, NJ: Rutgers University Press, 1986), 34.

58. Cooper, *Deerslayer*, 267.

59. Cooper, *Pioneers*, 1.

60. James Fenimore Cooper, *The Last of the Mohicans* (1826; New York: The Modern Library, 2001), 41.

61. The words associated with *romantic* changed dramatically from the 1820s to the 1920s. In the earlier period, *wild, picturesque,* and *scenery* often appeared alongside *romantic*; in the 1920s *temperament* was linked to that term. See the discussion of the Corpus of Historical American English in the introduction.

62. Judith A. Ruskin, "Thomas Cole and the White Mountains: The Picturesque, the Sublime, and the Magnificent," *Bulletin of the Detroit Institute of Arts* 66, no. 1 (1990): 18–25, quotations on 20, 23.

63. Ringe, *Pictorial Mode*, 29.

64. David Bjelajac, "Thomas Cole's *Oxbow* and the American Zion Divided," *American Art* 20, no. 1 (2006): 60–83; Ellwood C. Parry III, "Overlooking the Oxbow: Thomas Cole's *View from Mount Holyoke* Revisited," *American Art Journal* 34/35 (2003/2004): 6–61.

Chapter 4

1. James R. Mellow, *Nathaniel Hawthorne in His Times* (Boston: Houghton Mifflin Company, 1980), 372, quotes Melville; Michael Davitt Bell, "Conditions of Literary Vocation," in *The Cambridge History of American Literature*, vol. 2: *1820–1865*, ed. Sacvan Bercovitch (New York: Cambridge University Press, 1995), 122; David S. Reynolds, *Beneath the American Renaissance: The Subversive Imagination in the Age of Emerson and Melville* (Cambridge, MA: Harvard University Press, 1989), 259, quotes Hawthorne.

2. Jane Tompkins, *Sensational Designs: The Cultural Work of American Fiction, 1790–1860* (New York: Oxford University Press, 1985), 17–18; John T. Frederick, "Hawthorne's 'Scribbling Women,'" *The New England Quarterly* 48, no. 2 (June 1975): 231–40, quotation on 231.

3. Jonathan Levy, "The Mortgage Worked the Hardest: The Fate of Landed Independence in Nineteenth-Century America," in *Capitalism Takes Command: The Social Transformation of Nineteenth-Century America*, ed. Michael Zakim and Gary J. Kornblith (Chicago: The University of Chicago Press, 2012), 42–43; Henry David Thoreau, *Walden, or Life in the Woods* [1854] in *Thoreau: Walden and Other Writings*, ed. Joseph Wood Krutch (New York: Bantam Books, 1962), 129.

4. Alan Olmstead, "The Mechanization of Reaping and Mowing in American Agriculture, 1833–1870," *The Journal of Economic History* 35, no. 2 (1975): 327–52; Levy, "Mortgage Worked the Hardest," 48.

5. Alfred D. Chandler Jr., *The Visible Hand: The Managerial Revolution in American Business* (Cambridge, MA: Harvard University Press, 1977), 82–93; Robert E. Wright, "Capitalism and the Rise of the Corporate Nation," in *Capitalism Takes Command*, 149–65.

6. Michael Zakim, "Producing Capitalism: The Clerk at Work," in *Capitalism Takes Command*, 223–47.

7. George Rogers Taylor, *The Transportation Revolution, 1815–1860* (1951; New York: Harper& Row, 1968), 284–88.

8. Marc Egnal, *A Clash of Extremes: The Economic Origins of the Civil War* (New York: Hill and Wang, 2009), 309–25.

9. Chandler, *Visible Hand*, 122–44, 240–314.

10. Patricia Pulham, "'Of marble men and maidens': Sin, Sculpture, and Perversion in Nathaniel Hawthorne's *The Marble Faun*," *The Yearbook of English Studies* 40, no. 1/2 (2010): 83–102.

11. The possible exception is George Shelby, who is moved by Uncle Tom's death and frees his slaves. See also Cynthia Griffin Wolff, "'Masculinity' in Uncle Tom's Cabin," *American Quarterly* 47, no. 4 (1995): 595–618; Amy Shrager Lang, "Slavery and Sentimentalism: The Strange Career of Augustine St. Clare," *Women's Studies* 12 (1986): 31–54.

12. Tim Prchal, "The Bad Boys and the New Man: The Role of Tom Sawyer and Similar Characters in the Reconstruction of Masculinity," *American Literary Realism* 36, no. 3 (2004): 187–205, quotation on 187; David E. Shi, *Facing Facts: Realism in American Thought and Culture, 1850–1920* (New York: Oxford University Press, 1995), 104–11; Stacey M. Robertson, "'Aunt Nancy Men': Parker Pillsbury, Masculinity, and Women's Rights Activism in the Nineteenth-Century United States," *American Studies* 37, no. 2 (1996): 33–60, suggests that at least some men accepted feminist doctrines.

13. Steven M. Gelber, "Working at Playing: the Culture of the Workplace and the Rise of Baseball," *Journal of Social History* 16, no. 4 (1983): 3–22; E. Anthony Rotundo, *American Manhood: Transformations in Masculinity from the Revolution to the Modern Era* (New York: Basic Books, 1993), 200–73; Milette Shamir, "Manhood and the Early American Novel," in *The Cambridge History of the American Novel*, 192–208; George B. Kirsch, *Baseball and Cricket: The Creation of American Team Sports, 1838–1872* (Urbana: University of Illinois Press, 2007), 3–84; Mark C. Carnes, "Middle-Class Men and the Solace of Fraternal Ritual," in *Meanings for Manhood: Constructions of Masculinity in Victorian America*, ed. Mark C. Carnes and Clyde Griffen (Chicago: University of Chicago Press,

1990), 37–52; Gail Bederman, *Manliness and Civilization: A Cultural History of Gender and Race in the United States, 1880–1917* (Chicago: University of Chicago, 1995).

14. John Ernest, "Stowe, Race and the Antebellum American Novel," in *The Cambridge History of the American Novel*, 255–57; Catharine Juanita Starke, *Black Portraiture in American Fiction: Stock Characters, Archetypes, and Individuals* (New York: Basic Books, 1971), 29–45; Thomas M. Allen, "South of the American Renaissance," *American Literary History* 16, no. 3 (2004): 496–508, discusses Simms and race.

15. Harriet Beecher Stowe, *Uncle Tom's Cabin* (1852; New York: Signet Classics, 2008), 3, 448.

16. Ernest, "Stowe," 253.

17. Nancy Bentley, "White Slaves: The Mulatto Hero in Antebellum Fiction," *American Literature* 65, no. 3 (1993): 503–14, quotation on 508; Starke, *Black Portraiture*, 89–90; Evan Brandstadter, "Uncle Tom and Archy Moore: The Antislavery Novel as Ideological Symbol," *American Quarterly* 26, no. 2 (1974): 160–75.

18. H. Jordan Landry, "Of Tricks, Tropes, and Trollops: Revisions to the Seduction Novel in E. D. E. N. Southworth's *The Hidden Hand*," *The Journal of the Midwest Modern Language Association* 38, no. 2 (2005): 31–44, quotation on 35; Vicki L. Martin, "E.D.E.N. Southworth's Serial Novels *Retribution* and *The Mother-in-Law* as Vehicles for the Cause of Abolition in the *National Era*: Setting the Stage for *Uncle Tom's Cabin*," in *E.D.E.N. Southworth: Recovering a Nineteenth-Century Popular Novelist*, ed. Melissa J. Homestead and Pamela T. Washington (Knoxville: University of Tennessee Press, 2012), 1–24.

19. Eleanor E. Simpson, "Melville and the Negro: From *Typee* to 'Benito Cereno,'" *American Literature* 41, no. 1 (1969): 19–38, quotation on 20.

20. Herman Melville, *Moby-Dick, or the White Whale* (1851; New York: Vintage Books, 1961), 65, 489; Donald Pease, "Pip, *Moby-Dick*, Melville's Governmentality," *Novel: A Forum on Fiction* 45, no. 3 (2012): 327–42; Fred V. Bernard, "The Question of Race in *Moby-Dick*," *The Massachusetts Review* 43, no. 3 (2002): 384–404.

21. Jean Fagan Yellin, "Black Masks: Melville's 'Benito Cereno,'" *American Quarterly* 22, no. 3 (1970): 687–89; quotation on 687.

22. Timothy Marr, "'Out of this World': Islamic Irruptions in the Literary Americas," *American Literary History* 18, no. 3 (2006): 540.

23. Kay L. Chiles, "Blake; or the Huts of America," *Encyclopedia Virginia*, http://www.encyclopediavirginia.org/Blake_or_the_Huts_of_America_1859–1861; Hanna Crafts, *The Bondwoman's Narrative*, ed. Henry Louis Gates (c. 1855–59; New York: Warner Books, 2003), xxi–xcii.

24. Frederick Douglass, *The Heroic Slave* (1853; Another Leaf Press, 2013).

25. Frank J. Webb, *The Garies and Their Friends* (1857; Baltimore, MD: Johns Hopkins University Press, 1997), 121–22.

26. Martin R. Delany, *Blake; or, The Huts of America: A Novel* (1859–1862; Boston: Beacon Press, 1970), 16.

27. Ann duCille, "Where in the World is William Wells Brown? Thomas Jefferson, Sally Hemings, and the DNA of African American Literary History," *American Literary*

History 12, no. 3 (2000): 443–62; Christopher Mulvey, "Freeing the Voice, Creating the Self: the Novel and Slavery," in *Cambridge Companion to the African American Novel*, ed. Maryemma Graham (Cambridge, UK: Cambridge University Press, 2004), 25, quotes the 1864 version; Christopher Stampone, "Are We Reading the Right *Clotel (le)*? Revolutions in Early African American Literature," *Studies in American Fiction* 45, no. 2 (2018): 191–211.

28. Delany, *Blake*, chapter 2.

29. Harriet E. Wilson, *Our Nig; or, Sketches from the Life of a Free Black* . . . (1859; New York: Vintage Books, 1983), 25.

30. duCille, "William Wells Brown," 455.

31. *The Elite of our People: Joseph Willson's Sketches of Black Upper-Class Life in Antebellum Philadelphia*, ed. Julie Winch (University Park: Pennsylvania State University Press, 2000).

32. William Wells Brown, *Clotel; or, the President's Daughter: A Narrative of Slave Life in the United States* (London: Partridge & Oakey, 1853), 28–32.

33. Webb, *Garies*, chapter 4; Samuel Otter, "Frank Webb's Still Life: Rethinking Literature and Politics through *The Garies and Their Friends*," *American Literary History* 20, no. 4 (2008): 728–52.

34. Anna Mae Duane, "Remaking Black Motherhood in Frank J. Webb's *The Garies and their Friends*," *African American Review* 38, no. 2 (2004): 201–12, quote from Blyden Jackson on 201; Addison Gayle, Jr., *The Way of the New World: The Black Novel in America* (Garden City, NY: Anchor Press/Doubleday, 1975), 1–25, is sharply critical of novelists who advocate assimilation; duCille, "William Wells Brown," 454–58.

35. Elizabeth Stordeur Pryor, "The Etymology of Nigger: Resistance, Language, and the Politics of Freedom in the Antebellum North," *Journal of the Early Republic* 36, no. 2 (2016): 203–45; Samuel Otter, "Frank Webb's Still Life: Rethinking Literature and Politics through *The Garies and Their Friends*," *American Literary History* 20, no. 4 (2008): 728–52.

36. Delany, *Blake*, 291; Gregory Pierrot, "Writing over Haiti: Black Avengers in Martin Delany's *Blake*," *Studies in American Fiction* 41, no. 2 (2014): 175–99; Andy Doolen, "When Mammy Lies: The Everyday Resistance of Slave Women in Martin Delany's *Blake*," *Studies in American Fiction* 45, no. 1 (2018): 1–17.

37. Webb, *Garies*, chapter 11.

38. During these decades, White authors depicted another group—Native Americans—that they judged inferior. Broadly viewed, descriptions of tribal people evolved from the cruel savages found in Puritan writings and the novels of Charles Brockden Brown to the "noble savages" found in James Fenimore Cooper's books and Henry Wadsworth Longfellow's poetry. Compounding those stereotypes was the myth of the "vanishing American"—the confident belief that, in the face of a superior civilization, Indians were on the path to extinction. Among the works on this topic are Lora Romero, "Vanishing Americans: Gender, Empire, and New Historicism," *American Literature* 63, no. 3 (1991): 385–404; Jennifer Dyar, "Fatal Attraction: The White Obsession with Indianness," *The Historian* 65, no. 4 (2003): 817–36; Wynette L. Hamilton, "The Correlation

between Societal Attitudes and Those of American Authors in the Depiction of American Indians, 1607–1860," *American Indian Quarterly* 1, no. 1 (1974): 1–26; Brian W. Dippie, *The Vanishing American: White Attitudes and U.S. Policy* (New York: Columbia University Press, 1982).

39. Tompkins, *Sensational Designs*, 124.

40. Lora Romero, *Home Fronts: Domesticity and Its Critics in the Antebellum United States* (Durham, NC: Duke University Press, 1997), 70.

41. Elizabeth Ammons, "Heroines in *Uncle Tom's Cabin*" in *Critical Essays on Harriet Beecher Stowe*, ed. Elizabeth Ammons (Boston: G.K. Hall, 1980), 154; Tompkins, *Sensational Designs*, 124–45.

42. Lang, "Slavery and Sentimentalism," 38; Stowe, *Uncle Tom's Cabin*, 93; Ann Douglas, *The Feminization of American Culture* (New York: Anchor Press/Doubleday, 1988), 3–12; Bell, "Conditions of Literary Vocation," 111–14; Cindy Weinstein, *Family, Kinship, and Sympathy in Nineteenth-Century American Literature* (New York: Cambridge University Press, 2004), 1–7.

43. Nina Baym, *Woman's Fiction: A Guide to Novels by and about Women in America, 1820–1870*, 2nd ed. (Urbana: University of Illinois Press, 1993), 136. Frank Felsenstein and James J. Connolly, *What Middletown Read: Print Culture in an American Small City* (Amherst: University of Massachusetts Press, 2015), 130–31, notes that in Muncie, Indiana, in the 1890s, Hentz's novel was borrowed from the library far more often than Stowe's.

44. Susan Warner, *The Wide, Wide World* (1850; New York: A. L. Burt Co., n.d.), 585.

45. Maria Susanna Cummins, *The Lamplighter*, ed. Nina Baym (1854; New Brunswick, NJ: Rutgers University Press, 1988), 420.

46. Douglas, *Feminization of American Culture*, explores the links between conservative Protestantism and women's subordination.

47. Lori D. Ginzberg, *Women and the Work of Benevolence: Morality, Politics, and Class in the Nineteenth-Century United States* (New Haven, CT: Yale University Press, 1990), 98–213; Sally G. McMillen, *Seneca Falls and the Origins of the Women's Rights Movement* (New York: Oxford University Press, 2008), 104–228.

48. Frank Luther Mott, *Golden Multitudes: The Story of Best Sellers in the United States* (New York: R. R. Bowker Company, 1947), 307–8. Mott lists thirty bestsellers by American authors written during these two decades. However, five of them, including *Moby-Dick* and *Walden* sold more than two hundred thousand copies only in the twentieth century when "rediscovered." For information on sales, see also Linda Naranjo-Huebl, "The Road to Perdition: E. D. E. N. Southworth and the Critics," *American Periodicals* 16, no. 2 (2006): 140; Ammons, *Critical Essays on Harriet Beecher Stowe*, 117.

49. E.D.E.N. Southworth, *The Discarded Daughter; or, The Children of the Isle: A Tale of the Chesapeake* (Philadelphia: A. Hart, 1852), 206; Barbara Bardes and Suzanne Gossett, *Declarations of Independence: Women and Political Power in Nineteenth-Century American Fiction* (New Brunswick, NJ: Rutgers University Press, 1990), 88–94.

50. E.D.E.N. Southworth, *The Hidden Hand, or Capitola the Madcap*, ed. Joanne Dobson (1859; New Brunswick, NJ: Rutgers University Press, 1988); Lynette Carpenter,

"Double Talk: the Power and Glory of Paradox in E.D.E.N. Southworth's *The Hidden Hand*," *Legacy* 10, no. 1 (1993): 17–30; Joanne Dobson, "The Hidden Hand: Subversion of Cultural Ideology in Three Mid-Nineteenth-Century American Women's Novels," *American Quarterly* 38, no. 2 (1986): 223–42; Robert Y. Rabiee, "'The Little Mistress': Chivalry, Autonomy, and Domestic Relations in E.D.E.N. Southworth's *The Hidden Hand*," *J19: The Journal of Nineteenth-Century Americanists* 6, no. 1 (2018): 147–65, argues that "Capitola's liberation" was "frustratingly limited" (164) because of her lack of concern for slavery.

51. Naranjo-Huebl, "Road to Perdition," 132–33, notes that these negative critiques ended around 1855, but does not suggest why. Perhaps since many other writers now shared Southworth's views, her work seemed less shocking.

52. Baym, *Woman's Fiction*, 116.

53. Nathaniel Hawthorne, *The Blithedale Romance* (1852; New York: W. W. Norton & Company, 1958), 137; Mary Suzanne Schriber, "Justice to Zenobia," *The New England Quarterly* 55, no. 1 (March 1982): 75; Nina Baym, "*The Blithedale Romance*: A Radical Reading," *The Journal of English and Germanic Philology* 67, no. 4 (October 1968): 545–69, disputes Zenobia's feminism.

54. Fanny Fern, *Ruth Hall, A Domestic Tale of the Present Time* (1855; New York: Penguin Books, 1997), 17.

55. Mary Kelley, *Private Woman, Public Stage: Literary Domesticity in Nineteenth-Century America* (New York: Oxford University Press, 1984), 155; Gale Temple, "A Purchase on Goodness: Fanny Fern, *Ruth Hall*, and Fraught Individualism," *Studies in American Fiction* 31, no. 2 (2003): 132, suggests the importance of Ruth Hall's "prowess as a consumer."

56. Kelley, *Private Woman*, 188.

57. Earl Yarington, "Mary Jane Holmes (1825–1907)," *Legacy* 25, no. 1 (2008): 142–50.

58. William Gilmore Simms, *Woodcraft, or, Hawks About the Dovecote: A Story of the South at the Close of the Revolution* (1852; New York: W. W. Norton & Co., 1961), 513.

59. Susan K. Harris, *19th-Century American Women's Novels: Interpretative Strategies* (New York: Cambridge University Press, 1990), 73.

60. Augusta J. Evans, *St. Elmo* (New York: A. L. Burt, 1866), chap. 37; Kelley, *Private Woman*, 154–55; Felsenstein and Connolly, *What Middletown Read*, 112–13, notes that Evans's novel was one of the dozen most borrowed books in the library of Muncie, Indiana, in the 1890s. Almost all the others in that elite group were children's fiction.

61. Richard H. Brodhead, "The American Literary Field, 1860–1890," in *The Cambridge History of American Literature*, vol. 3: *Prose Writing, 1860–1920*, ed. Sacvan Bercovitch (New York: Cambridge University Press, 2005), 19; Gregory Jackson, "Religion and the Nineteenth-Century American Novel," in *The Cambridge History of the American Novel*, ed. Leonard Cassuto (New York: Cambridge University Press, 2011), 171–73.

62. Barbara Sicherman, *Well-Read Lives: How Books Inspired a Generation of American Women* (Chapel Hill, NC: The University of North Carolina Press, 2010), 18–19.

63. Louisa May Alcott, *Little Women* (1868–69; New York: Penguin Books, 1989).

64. Corpus of Historical American English. See the introduction for more on this database.

65. Steven Mintz, *Huck's Raft: A History of American Childhood* (Cambridge, MA: Harvard University Press, 2004), 76, quotes Amos Bronson Alcott.

66. Bell, "Conditions of Literary Vocation," 90.

67. Daniel T. Rogers, "Socializing Middle-Class Children: Institutions, Fables, and Work Values in Nineteenth-Century America," in *Growing Up in America: Children in Historical Perspective*, ed. N. Ray Hiner and Joseph M. Hawes (Urbana: University of Illinois Press, 1985), 119–23.

68. Peter N. Stearns, "Girls, Boys, and Emotions: Redefinitions and Historical Change," *The Journal of American History* 80, no. 1 (1993): 36–74; Miriam Formanek-Brunell, *Made to Play House: Dolls and the Commercialization of American Girlhood, 1830–1930* (New Haven, CT: Yale University Press, 1993), 15.

69. Thomas Bailey Aldrich, *The Story of a Bad Boy* (1869; New York: Houghton, Mifflin, 1897); Tim Prchal, "Bad Boys," 188–91.

70. James Jackson Jarves, *The Art-Idea: Sculpture, Painting, and Architecture in America*, 2nd ed. (New York: Hurd and Houghton, 1965), 281.

71. John I. H. Baur, "American Luminism: A Neglected Aspect of the Realist Movement in Nineteenth-Century America," *Perspectives USA* (1954): 91–98; J. Gray Sweeney, "Inventing Luminism: 'Labels are the Dickens,'" *Oxford Art Journal* 26, no. 2 (2003): 95–120; John Wilmerding, Introduction to *American Light: The Luminist Movement, 1850–1875—Paintings, Drawings, Photographs*, ed. John Wilmerding (New York: Harper & Row, 1980), 11–18.

72. Barbara Novak, *American Painting of the Nineteenth Century: Realism, Idealism, and the American Experience*, rev. ed. (New York: Oxford University Press, 2007), 76.

73. John Howat, *Frederic Church* (New Haven, CT: Yale University Press, 2005), 44–46.

74. Sweeney, "Inventing Luminism," 107–8, also discusses critiques of Novak's efforts to link luminism and Transcendentalism.

75. Howat, *Church*, 72.

76. David C. Huntington, "Frederic Church's *Niagara*: Nature and the Nation's Type," *Texas Studies in Literature and Language* 25, no. 1 (1983): 100–38, quotes Adam Badeau on 100.

77. Linda S. Ferber, "Albert Bierstadt: The History of a Reputation," in *Albert Bierstadt: Art & Enterprise*, ed. Nancy K. Anderson and Linda S. Ferber (New York: Hudson Hills Press, 1990), 25.

78. Henry T. Tuckerman, *Book of the Artists: American Artist Life, comprising biographical and critical sketches . . .* 2nd ed. (1867: New York: J. H. Carr, 1966); Ferber, "Albert Bierstadt," 21–29.

79. Tuckerman, *Book of the Artists*, 375.

80. Samuel Clemens to Orion Clemens, March 16, 1860, quoted in Howat, *Church*, 86.

81. Kelly, "Nature Distilled," 11, quotes Gifford; Theodore E. Stebbins, Jr., *The Life and Works of Martin Johnson Heade* (New Haven, CT: Yale University Press, 1975): 37–42, 87; Tuckerman, *Book of Artists*, 389–96, 510–13, 524–26.

82. Ferber, "Albert Bierstadt," 40–64; Franklin Kelly, "Nature Distilled: Gifford's Vision of Landscape," in *Hudson River School Visions: The Landscapes of Sanford R. Gifford*,

ed. Kevin J. Avery and Franklin Kelly (New Haven, CT: Yale University Press, 2003), 16–18; Eleanor Jones Harvey, "Tastes in Transition: Gifford's Patrons," in *Hudson River School Visions*, 75; Theodore E. Stebbins, Jr., "Luminism in Context: A New View," in *American Light*, 213–19.

Part 2: The Genteel Era

1. Stanley Coben, "The Assault on Victorianism in the Twentieth Century," *American Quarterly* 27, no. 5 (1975): 604–25; Eric H. Monkkonen, "A Disorderly People? Urban Order in the Nineteenth and Twentieth Centuries," *The Journal of American History* 68, no. 3 (1981): 539–59, shows that drunk and disorderly behavior declined significantly during the genteel era. Henry James, "The Manners of American Women," 1907, in James, *The Speech and Manners of American Women*, ed. E. S. Riggs (Lancaster, PA: Lancaster House Press, 1973), 51–95, provides a classic statement of the importance of manners. See also Peter Brooks, "Visions of Waste," *New York Review of Books* 69, no. 5 (2022): 4–6.

2. George Santayana, "The Genteel Tradition in American Philosophy," 1911, in Santayana, *The Genteel Tradition*, ed. Douglas L. Wilson (Cambridge, MA: Harvard University Press, 1967), 39–40, 61.

3. Harold E. Stearns, ed., *Civilization in the United States: An Inquiry by Thirty Americans* (New York: Harcourt, Brace and Company, 1922), 148, 163, 179.

4. *Historical Statistics of the United States: Millennial Edition Online*, ed. Susan B. Carter et al. (New York: Cambridge University Press, 2006), tables Aa684–698, Aa699–715, Aa728, Aa740, Aa2244–6550.

5. Richard Lehan, *Realism and Naturalism: The Novel in an Age of Transition* (Madison: The University of Wisconsin Press, 2005), 61, quotes Twain. Hartford's population passed the fifty thousand mark in the 1880s.

6. Edith Wharton, *A Backward Glance*, intro. by Louis Auchincloss (1933; New York: Charles Scribner's Sons, 1964), 7.

7. Coben, "Assault on Victorianism," 604–25; *Historical Statistics*, tables Aa684–698, Aa699–715, Aa728, Aa740, Aa2244–6550.

8. Charles Johanningsmeier, "Realism, Naturalism, and American Public Libraries, 1880–1914," *American Literary Realism* 48, no. 1 (2015): 1–24, shows that libraries also were reluctant to acquire controversial realist novels such as Crane's *Maggie*, Chopin's *Awakening*, and Dreiser's *Sister Carrie*.

9. Dillingham, "Frank Norris," 15–24.

10. Wharton, *Backward Glance*, 147–48.

11. Ibid., 176.

12. Ibid., xi, 127.

13. Frederic I. Carpenter, "The Genteel Tradition: A Re-Interpretation," *The New England Quarterly* 15, no. 3 (1942): 434; Henry Nash Smith, *Democracy and the Novel: Popular Resistance to Classic American Writers* (New York: Oxford University Press, 1978), 6.

14. William B. Dillingham, "Frank Norris and the Genteel Tradition," *Tennessee Studies in Literature* 5 (1960): 15. Among the works focusing on the last third of the century

are Leslie Butler, *Critical Americans: Victorian Intellectuals and Transatlantic Liberal Reform* (Chapel Hill: University of North Carolina Press, 2007); John Tomsich, *Genteel Endeavor: American Culture and Politics in the Gilded Age* (Stanford, CA: Stanford University Press, 1971); James Kloppenberg, *Uncertain Victory: Social Democracy and Progressivism in European and American Thought, 1870–1920* (New York: Oxford University Press, 1986); Daniel Walker Howe, "American Victorianism as a Culture," *American Quarterly* 27, no. 5 (1975): 507–32; John G. Sproat, *"The Best Men": Liberal Reformers in the Gilded Age* (New York: Oxford University Press, 1968).

15. Katrina E. Bachinger, "Years of Ferment: American Literary Criticism Enters the Twentieth Century," *American Studies International* 20, no. 4 (1982): 31.

16. Henry F. May, *The End of American Innocence: The First Years of Our Own Time, 1912–1917* (New York: Knopf, 1964), xi; Ellery Sedgwick III, "The American Genteel Tradition in the Early Twentieth Century," *American Studies* 25, no. 1 (1984): 49–67.

Chapter 5

1. William Dean Howells, *Years of My Youth* (New York: Harper & Brothers, 1916), 16.

2. Nancy Bentley, "Literary Forms and Mass Culture, 1870–1920," in *The Cambridge History of American Literature*, vol. 3: *Prose Writing, 1860–1920*, ed. Sacvan Bercovitch (New York: Cambridge University Press, 2005), 132, quotes Howells.

3. Robert W. Wiebe, *The Search for Order, 1877–1920* (New York: Hill and Wang, 1967), xiii, 2.

4. Alfred D. Chandler Jr., *The Visible Hand: The Managerial Revolution in American Business* (Cambridge, MA: Belknap Press, 1977), 122–41; Alan Trachtenberg, *The Incorporation of America: Culture & Society in the Gilded Age* (New York: Hill & Wang, 1982), 38–41.

5. Chandler, *Visible Hand*, 171–90; *Historical Statistics of the United States, Colonial Times to 1970*, ed. Susan B. Carter et al. (New York: Cambridge University Press, 2006), series Df882-Df885, Df874–Df881, accessed on-line.

6. Chandler, *Visible Hand*, 287–320.

7. Vicki Howard, *From Main Street to Mall: The Rise and Fall of the American Department Store* (Philadelphia: University of Pennsylvania Press, 2015), 9, 59; John W. Ferry, *A History of the Department Store* (New York: Macmillan, 1960), 2–4, 20, 126, 183; Edd Applegate, *Rise of Advertising in the United States: A History of Innovation to 1960* (Lanham, MD: Scarecrow Press, 2012), 71–78, 111–14.

8. *Historical Statistics*, Ser. Ba1033–1043, Ba4954–4964, Dd1–Dd12; Trachtenberg, *Incorporation of America*, 87–95, 134–36.

9. Mark Twain, *The Adventures of Tom Sawyer* (Hartford, CT: American Publishing Company, 1876), 144, 146–47.

10. Sarah Orne Jewett, *Deephaven* (Boston: James R. Osgood and Co., 1877), 41.

11. Harriet Beecher Stowe, *Pink and White Tyranny: A Society Novel* (Boston: Roberts Brothers, 1871), 86.

12. James W. Tuttleton, "The Early Years" in *A Companion to Henry James Studies*, ed. Daniel Mark Fogel (Westport, CT: Greenwood Press, 1993), 109–10.

13. Stowe, *Pink and White Tyranny*, 93.

14. William Dean Howells, *The Lady of the Aroostook* (Boston: Houghton, Osgood and Co., 1879), 182.

15. Twain, *Tom Sawyer*, 168.

16. Stowe, *Pink and White Tyranny*, 155.

17. Henry James, *The American* (Boston: Houghton Mifflin Co., 1877), 94–95; Alide Cagidemetrio, "Henry James and the American Evolution of the Snob," in *The American Bourgeoisie: Distinction and Identity in the Nineteenth Century*, ed. Sven Beckert and Julia B. Rosenbaum (New York: Palgrave Macmillan, 2010), 52–53.

18. Stowe, *Pink and White Tyranny*, 33.

19. Mark Twain, *The Prince and the Pauper* (Boston: James R. Osgood and Co., 1881), 401.

20. Arthur Lawrence Vogelback, "*The Prince and the Pauper*: A Study in Critical Standards," *American Literature* 14, no. 1 (1942): 48–54, quotation on 53; John Daniel Stahl, "American Myth in European Disguise: Fathers and Sons in *The Prince and the Pauper*," *American Literature* 58, no. 2 (1986): 203–16; Justin Kaplan, *Mr. Clemens and Mark Twain: A Biography* (New York: Simon and Schuster, 1966), 238–41.

21. Kaplan, *Mr. Clemens*, 268, quotes Alcott; Mark Twain, *Adventures of Huckleberry Finn* (1884; New York: Airmont Books, 1962), 236.

22. Richard Hill, "Overreaching: Critical Agenda and the End of *Adventures of Huckleberry Finn*," *Texas Studies in Literature and Language* 33, no. 4 (Winter 1991): 493.

23. Albert E. Stone Jr., *The Innocent Eye: Childhood in Mark Twain's Imagination* (New Haven, CT: Yale University Press, 1961), 151.

24. Amy Kaplan, *The Social Construction of American Realism* (Chicago: The University of Chicago Press, 1988), 26.

25. William Dean Howells, *A Modern Instance* (Boston: James R. Osgood and Co., 1882), 33.

26. Ibid., 223.

27. Robie Macauley, "Let Me Tell You About the Rich . . . ," *Kenyon Review* 27, no. 4 (1965): 656–59; Patrick Dooley, "Nineteenth-Century Business Ethics and *The Rise of Silas Lapham*," *American Studies* 21, no. 2 (1980): 79–93; Dooley, "Ethical Exegesis in Howells's *The Rise of Silas Lapham*," *Papers on Language and Literature* 35, no. 4 (1999): 363–90.

28. William Dean Howells, *The Rise of Silas Lapham* (Boston: Ticknor and Co., 1885), 273.

29. John W. Crowley, "An Introduction to *The Rise of Silas Lapham*," *American Literary Realism* 42, no. 2 (2010): 159–69, quotation on 160; Kermit Vanderbilt, *The Achievement of William Dean Howells: A Reinterpretation* (Princeton, NJ: Princeton University Press, 1968), 101–3.

30. William Dean Howells, *A Hazard of New Fortunes* (1889; New York: Boni and Liveright, 1917), 253–54.

31. Howells, "Editor's Study," *Harper's New Monthly Magazine*, September 1887, 639; Michael A. Elliott, "Realism and Radicalism: The School of Howells," in *The Cambridge History of the American Novel*, ed. Leonard Cassuto, Clare Virginia Eby, and Benjamin Reiss (New York: Cambridge University Press, 2011), 298–99; Kaplan, *Social Construc-*

tion, 21–25, 46–63; Isaac Kolding, "*A Hazard of New Fortunes* and Political Speech," *American Literary Realism* 54, no. 2 (2022): 120–34.

32. Henry James, *The Portrait of a Lady* (1881; Boston: Houghton, Mifflin and Co., 1882), 12.

33. Ibid., 42.

34. Joseph H. Friend, "The Structure of *The Portrait of a Lady*," *Nineteenth-Century Fiction* 20, no. 1 (1965), 87; Carrie Tirado Bramen, "James, Pragmantism, and the Realist Ideal," in *Cambridge History of the American Novel*, 309–11.

35. James, *Portrait of a Lady*, 510.

36. James W. Gargano, "The Middle Years," in *A Companion to Henry James Studies*, 121–30; Friend, "Structure," 91–94; Dominie J. Bazznella, "The Conclusion to *The Portrait of a Lady* Re-examined," *American Literature* 41, no. 1 (1969): 55–63; Robert Shulman, "Realism," in *The Columbia History of the American Novel*, ed. Emory Elliott (New York: Columbia University Press, 1991), 166–68.

37. Henry James, *The Princess Casamassima* (London: Macmillan and Co., 1886), 257; Alex Beringer, "The Pleasures of Conspiracy in Henry James's *The Princess Casamassima*," *Studies in American Fiction* 39, no. 1 (2012): 23–42; Gargano, "Middle Years," 121–36.

38. James, *Princess Casamassima*, 365; Christopher Stuart, "'Bloom[ing] on a Dog's Allowance': Hyacinth Robinson and the Redemption of the Working Class in Henry James' *The Princess Casamassima*," *American Literary Realism* 36, no. 1 (2003): 22–39.

39. Louisa May Alcott, *Jo's Boys* (1886; New York: Grosset & Dunlap, 1949).

40. Burnett was another transatlantic author like James or Wharton, but whose crossings went the other way. She was born in England and came to America with her family when she was sixteen. See "Frances Hodgson Burnett," *American National Biography*.

41. Lisa Tetrault, *The Myth of Seneca Falls: Memory and the Women's Suffrage Movement, 1848–1898* (Chapel Hill: University of North Carolina Press, 2014), 37–80, 145–72; the essays in Nancy A. Hewitt, ed., *No Permanent Waves: Recasting Histories of U.S. Feminism* (New Brunswick: Rutgers University Press, 2020), raise questions about the concept of "waves"; see also the discussion in chapter 4.

42. Lew Wallace, *Ben-Hur, A Tale of the Christ* (1880; London: Sampson Low, Marston, Searle & Rivington, 1881), 449; James D. Hart, *The Popular Book: A History of America's Literary Taste* (New York: Oxford University Press, 1950), 164; Frank Luther Mott, *Golden Multitudes: The Story of Best Sellers in the United States* (New York: R. R. Bowler Company, 1947), 172.

43. Barbara Bardes and Suzanne Gossett, *Declarations of Independence: Women and Political Power in Nineteenth-Century American Fiction* (New Brunswick, NJ: Rutgers University Press, 1990), 132.

44. Harriet Beecher Stowe, *My Wife and I; or, Harry Henderson's History* (New York: J. B. Ford & Company, 1871), 110.

45. James, *American*, 38.

46. James, *Portrait of a Lady*, 43.

47. Henry James, *The Bostonians* (London: Macmillan, 1886), 22.

48. Ibid., 334.

49. Bardes and Gossett, *Declarations of Independence*, 174.

50. Henry James, *Daisy Miller* (1878; New York: Harper & Brothers, 1906), 79–80.

51. James, *Princess Casamassima*, 582.

52. Louisa May Alcott, *Little Men* (1871: Toronto: W. Briggs, 1996), 229–30.

53. Louisa May Alcott, *Work: A Story of Experience* (1873; New York: Schocken Books, 1977), 1, 426.

54. Alcott, *Jo's Boys*, 5–6, 33, 75.

55. George Washington Cable, *The Grandissimes: A Story of Creole Life* (New York: Charles Scribner's Sons, 1880), 336–37; Sean Pears, "A Speculative Reading of Black Feminist Resistance in George Washington Cable's *The Grandissimes*," *Arizona Quarterly* 76, no. 2 (2020): 115–40.

56. Sarah Orne Jewett, *A Country Doctor* (1884; Boston: Houghton, Mifflin and Co., 1887), 826.

57. John Habberton, *Helen's Babies, with some account of their ways*.... (1876; New York: Frederick A. Stokes, Co., 1921), 158.

58. Most critics agree with this assessment. See, for example, Trygve Thoreson and Trygve Thorson, "'Virtuous According to Their Lights': Women in Mark Twain's Early Work," *Mark Twain Journal* 21, no. 4 (1983): 52–56; Stahl, "American Myth," 215. However, Laura E. Skandera-Trombley, *Mark Twain in the Company of Women* (Philadelphia: University of Pennsylvania Press, 1994), 4, argues that Twain "evolved into a defender of reformist, liberal, feminist interests." Skandera-Trombley shows that many women were important in Twain's life, but is less convincing in her analysis of his novels. See also Ann M. Ryan, "The Voice of Her Laughter: Mark Twain's Tragic Feminism," *American Literary Realism* 41, no. 3 (2009): 192–213; Horst H. Kruse, "A Matter of Style: How Olivia Langdon Clemens and Charles Dudley Warner Tried to Team and to Tame the Genius of Mark Twain," *The New England Quarterly* 72, no. 2 (1999): 232–50.

59. Mark Twain and Charles Dudley Warner, *The Gilded Age: A Tale of Today* (1873; Hartford, CT: Hartford American Publishing Co., 1874); Twain to Dr. John Brown, February 28, 1874, *Mark Twain's Letters, Volume 6: 1874–1875*, ed. Michael B. Frank and Harriet Elinor Smith (Berkeley: University of California Press, 2002), 53; Andrew Lawson, "Twain, Class, and the Gilded Age," in *Cambridge History of the American Novel*, 368–71.

60. Howells, *Silas Lapham*, 42. For similar passages, see Howells, *Lady of the Aroostook*, 52; Howells, *Modern Instance*, 201; Howells, *Hazard of New Fortunes*, 98.

61. Martha S. Jones, *Vanguard: How Black Women Broke Barriers, Won the Vote, and Insisted on Equality for All* (New York: Basic Books, 2020), 73–117; Rosalyn Terborg-Penn, *African American Women in the Struggle for the Vote, 1850–1920* (Bloomington: Indiana University Press, 1998), 8–19.

62. Michael Kimmel, *Manhood in America: A Cultural History* (New York: The Free Press, 1996), 102.

63. E. Anthony Rotundo, *American Manhood: Transformations in Masculinity from the Revolution to the Modern Era* (New York: Basic Books, 1993), 199.

64. *Thoughtful*, for example, follows the same arc as *trustworthy*.

65. William Laffan, *New York Sun*, February 1879, quoted in Margaret C. Conrads,

Winslow Homer and the Critics: Forging a National Art in the 1870s (Princeton, NJ: Princeton University Press, 2001), 151; Lloyd Goodrich, *Winslow Homer* (New York: Whitney Museum of Art, 1973), 11–12; Bruce Robertson, *Reckoning with Winslow Homer: His Late Paintings and Their Influence* (Cleveland, OH: Cleveland Museum of Art in cooperation with Indiana University Press, 1990), 9–10; Jules D. Prown, "Winslow Homer in His Art," *Smithsonian Studies in American Art* 1, no. 1 (Spring 1987): 34–35; Randall C. Griffin, *Winslow Homer: An American Vision* (New York: Phaidon Press, 2006), 71–76, provides a close analysis of *Snap the Whip*.

66. George Sheldon, *New York Evening Post*, March 5, 1880, quoted in Conrads, *Winslow Homer*, 170–71.

67. Goodrich, *Winslow Homer*, 30–33.

68. Prown, "Winslow Homer," 33–41, emphasizes the sexual elements in *The Life Line*; Griffin, *Winslow Homer*, 8; Goodrich, *Winslow Homer*, 38–40; Robertson, *Winslow Homer*, 3, 13–14; Hunter Ingalls, "Elements in the Development of Winslow Homer," *Art Journal* 24, no. 1 (1964): 18–22.

69. Griffin, *Winslow Homer*, 123–201; Goodrich, *Winslow Homer*, 45;

70. John Wilmerding, "The Tensions of Biography and Art in Thomas Eakins," in *Thomas Eakins*, ed. Wilmerding (Washington, DC: Smithsonian Institution Press, 1993), 16; Robert Erwin, "Who Was Thomas Eakins?" *The Antioch Review* 66, no. 4 (2008): 655–64.

71. Henry Adams, *Eakins Revealed: The Secret Life of an American Artist* (New York: Oxford University Press, 2005); Sylvan Schendler, *Eakins* (Boston: Little, Brown and Company, 1967); David Lubin, "Projecting an Image: The Contested Cultural Identity of Thomas Eakins," *The Art Bulletin* 84, no. 3 (2002): 510–22.

72. Thomas Eakins to Benjamin Eakins, 1868, quoted in Gordon Hendricks, *The Life and Work of Thomas Eakins* (New York: Grossman Publishers, 1974), 47.

73. Even *The Gross Clinic* (in contrast to the later *Agnew Clinic*) is softened by a note of sentimentality. A woman, either the sister or mother of the patient, covers her face in horror as the operation proceeds. She signals to the viewer (like Tom and Huck's fright at the graveyard murder in *Tom Sawyer*) that a horrific act is taking place

74. Elizabeth Johns, *Thomas Eakins: The Heroism of Modern Life* (Princeton, NJ: Princeton University Press, 1983), 3.

75. "Catalog," *Thomas Eakins*, ed. Wilmerding, 109, quotes Eakins.

76. This table draws from the complete listing of Eakins's works. The online version, based largely on Lloyd Goodrich's catalogue with various updates, is available at https://en.wikipedia.org/wiki/List_of_works_by_Thomas_Eakins.

In constructing the table, I have followed these principles: (1) Only oil on canvas paintings are considered; (2) Sketches and studies are excluded; (3) Works that are known to have existed, but now are lost or destroyed, are excluded; (4) Finished and nearly finished paintings are counted; (5) Paintings that have a larger setting, even with a named individual, such as *John Biglin in a Single Scull*, are not considered portraits. Some modifications to these assumptions, along with some judgement calls, might lead to minor changes in the percentages—but would not challenge the larger pattern.

Chapter 6

1. Edith Wharton, *A Backward Glance*, intro. Louis Auchincloss (1933; New York: Charles Scribner's Sons, 1964), 293–95.

2. Herman C. Voeltz, "Coxey's Army in Oregon, 1894," *Oregon Historical Quarterly* 65, no. 3 (1964): 263–95; Lawrence Goodwyn, *The Populist Moment: A Short History of the Agrarian Revolt in America* (New York: Oxford University Press, 1978), 69–71; Robert H. Wiebe, *The Search for Order, 1877–1920* (New York: Hill and Wang, 1967), 84–91; David O. Whitten, "The Depression of 1893," http://eh.net/?s'depression+of+1893; H. W. Brands, *The Reckless Decade: America in the 1890s* (New York: St. Martin's Press, 1995), 90–214.

3. Jane Addams, *Twenty Years at Hull House* (1910; rpt. New York: Signet Classic, 1999), 64.

4. Wiebe, *Search for Order*, 82–83, 91–107.

5. Marc Egnal, *Divergent Paths: How Culture and Institutions Have Shaped North American Growth* (New York: Oxford University Press, 1996), 143–45; Gabriel Kolko, *The Triumph of Conservatism: A Reinterpretation of American History, 1900–1916* (New York: Free Press of Glencoe, 1963), 18–20; John Milton Cooper, Jr., *Pivotal Decades: The United States, 1900–1920* (New York: W. W. Norton & Company, 1990), 3–12, 82–83, 132–36, 210, 306–23; James Weinstein, *The Corporate Ideal in the Liberal State, 1900–1918* (Boston: Beacon Press, 1968).

6. Cooper, *Pivotal Decades*, 89–99

7. Roosevelt made this remark in a 1907 speech, "On the occasion of the laying of the cornerstone of the Pilgrim memorial monument," https://www.bradford-delong.com/2018/03/document-teddy-roosevelt-1907-the-malefactors-of-great-wealth.html.

8. *Historical Statistics of the United States: Millennial Edition Online*, ed. Susan B. Carter et al. (New York: Cambridge University Press, 2006), tables Aa1–Aa5, Aa39–Aa92, Aa699–715.

9. Booth Tarkington, *The Magnificent Ambersons* (New York: Doubleday & Page, 1918), 478; T. J. Jackson Lears, *No Place of Grace: Antimodernism and the Transformation of American Culture, 1880–1920* (Chicago: The University of Chicago Press, 1983), 32–36.

10. Marc Egnal, "Re-Visioning American Literary Naturalism," *Canadian Review of American Studies* 48, no. 2 (2018): 171–90, presents a fuller discussion of these arguments; see also Eric Carl Link, *The Vast and Terrible Drama: American Literary Naturalism in the Late Nineteenth Century* (Tuscaloosa: The University of Alabama Press, 2004), 3–10, 14–17. Chuck Robinson, "Scale Shifts from Polk Street to a Broken Earth; or, Literary Naturalism's Geontological Affordances," *CR: The New Centennial Review* 20, no. 3 (2020): 47–73, responds to my contentions.

11. Vernon Louis Parrington, *Main Currents in American Thought: An Interpretation of American Literature from the Beginnings to 1920. Volume Three: 1860–1920, The Beginnings of Critical Realism in America* (1930; New York: Harcourt, Brace & World, Inc., 1958), 323–29, quotations on 323, 324.

12. Donald Pizer, "Late Nineteenth-Century American Literary Naturalism: A

Re-Introduction," *American Literary Realism* 38, no. 3 (2006): 189–202; Charles Child Walcutt, *American Literary Naturalism, A Divided Stream*. (Minneapolis: University of Minnesota Press, 1956); Eric Carl Link, "Defining American Literary Naturalism," in *The Oxford Handbook of American Literary Naturalism*, ed. Keith Newlin (New York: Oxford University Press, 2011), 71–91; Gregory Phipps, "American Literary Naturalism and Its Descendants," *Studies in American Naturalism* 15, no. 1 (2020): vii–xiv.

13. Ann Douglas, *Terrible Honesty: Mongrel Manhattan in the 1920s* (New York: Farrar, Straus and Giroux, 1995), 28, observes that Einstein showed "there are no absolutes in time or space. The laws that concerned the 1920s generation were not those of man or God, at least not as their Victorian predecessors had understood man or God."

14. Winfried Fluck, "Misrecognition, Symptomatic Realism, Multicultural Realism, Cultural Capital Realism: Revisionist Narratives about the American Realist Tradition," in *Revisionist Approaches to American Realism and Naturalism*, ed. Jutta Ernst et al. (Heidelberg: Universitätsverlag Winter, 2018), 1–34, esp. 11–17, discusses demands to expand the canon of Realist (and Naturalist) works to include more multicultural novels.

15. Rick Armstrong, "'First Principles of Morals': Evolutionary Morality and American Naturalism," *Oxford Handbook*, 139–53; Donna Campbell, "The Rise of Naturalism," *The Cambridge History of the American Novel*, ed. Leonard Cassuto, Clare Virginia Eby, and Benjamin Reiss (New York: Cambridge University Press, 2011), 505–7.

16. Theodore Dreiser, *Jennie Gerhardt* (1911; New York: Boni and Liveright Publishers, 1926), 23; Carol A. Schwartz, "*Jennie Gerhardt*: Fairy Tale as Social Criticism," *American Literary Criticism, 1870–1910* 19, no. 2 (1987): 16–29.

17. Jack London, *Call of the Wild* in *The Call of the Wild, White Fang, and Other Stories*, ed. Andrew Sinclair (1903; New York: Penguin Books, 1981), 64.

18. Frank Norris, *McTeague: A Story of San Francisco* (1899; New York: Doubleday, Page & Company, 1900), 30.

19. Theodore Dreiser, *The Financier* (New York: A. L. Burt, 1912), 18.

20. Frank Norris, *The Octopus: A Story of California* (New York: Doubleday, Page & Company, 1901), 651; Daniel Darvay, "The Naturalist Sublime in Frank Norris's *The Octopus*," *Studies in the Novel* 47, no. 1 (2015): 43–59; Steven Frye, "Presley's Pretense: Irony and Epic Convention in Frank Norris' *The Octopus*," *American Literary Realism* 39, no. 3 (2007): 213–21.

21. Theodore Dreiser, *Sister Carrie* (1900; Cleveland: World Publishing Company, 1927), 89; Donald Pizer, "The Problem of American Literary Naturalism and Theodore Dreiser's *Sister Carrie*," *American Literary Realism* 32, no. 1 (1999): 1–11; Charles Harmon, "Cuteness and Capitalism in *Sister Carrie*," *American Literary Realism* 32, no. 2 (2000): 125–39.

22. Michael Davitt Bell, *The Problem of American Realism: Studies in the Cultural History of a Literary Idea* (Chicago: University of Chicago Press, 1993), 134, quotes Crane.

23. Dreiser, *Financier*, 13; Joe Fernandez, "Economic Reciprocity and Darwinian Evolution in Theodore Dreiser's *The Financier*," *The Journal of the Midwest Modern Language Association* 46/47, no. 1/2 (2013–14): 11–36; Alex Pitofsky, "Dreiser's *The Financier* and the Horatio Alger Myth," *Twentieth Century Literature* 44, no. 3 (1998): 276–90.

24. Edith Wharton, *The House of Mirth* (1905; New York: Rinehart and Winston, 1962), 350; among those noting elements of naturalism in the novel are Donald Pizer, "The Naturalism of Edith Wharton's *The House of Mirth*," *Twentieth Century Literature* 41, no. 2 (1995): 241–48; and Jacquelyn Scott, "The 'lift of a broken wing': Darwinian Descent and Selection in Edith Wharton's *The House of Mirth* and *Summer*," *Edith Wharton Review* 25, no. 2 (2009): 1–9.

25. Edith Wharton, *The Custom of the Country* (New York: Charles Scribner's Sons, 1913), 437.

26. Edith Wharton, *Ethan Frome* (1911; New York: Charles Scribner's Sons, 1970), 134.

27. Kate Chopin, *The Awakening* (1899; New York: Avon Books, 1972), 25.

28. Willa Cather, *O Pioneers!* ed. Susan J. Rosowski et al. (1913; Lincoln: University of Nebraska Press, 1992), 64.

29. Paul Laurence Dunbar, *The Sport of the Gods* (1902; New York: Dodd, Mead, 1981), 76–77; Charles R. Larson, "The Novels of Paul Laurence Dunbar," *Phylon* 29, no. 3 (1968): 257–71.

30. Winston Churchill, *The Crisis* (Toronto: Copp, Clark, 1901), 118.

31. Edgar Rice Burroughs, *Tarzan of the Apes* (1912; New York: The Library of America, 2012), 72.

32. Zane Grey, *Riders of the Purple Sage* (New York: Harper & Brothers, 1912), 70; Cathryn Halverson, "Violent Housekeepers: Rewriting Domesticity in *Riders of the Purple Sage*," *Rocky Mountain Review of Language and Literature* 56, no. 1 (2002): 37–53.

33. Gail Bederman, *Manliness & Civilization: A Cultural History of Gender and Race in the United States, 1890–1917* (Chicago: The University of Chicago Press, 1995), 23.

34. Jack Salzman, "The Critical Recognition of *Sister Carrie*, 1900–1907," *Journal of American Studies* 3, no. 1 (1969): 123–33.

35. Owen Wister, *The Viriginian* (New York: Macmillan Publishers, 1902), 97, 489.

36. Grey, *Riders of the Purple Sage*, 129, 141, 163; Halverson, "Violent Housekeepers," 41.

37. Burroughs, *Tarzan*, 242; Bederman, *Manliness & Civilization*, 217–32.

38. London, *Call of the Wild*, 105, 108, 123.

39. Henry James, *What Maisie Knew* (1897; New York, Penguin Books, 1985), 86; Chopin, *Awakening*, 16, 189.

40. Miriam Hansen, "Adventures of Goldilocks: Spectatorship, Consumerism and Public Life," *Camera Obscura* 22, no. 1 (1990): 52–53; William R. Leach, "Transformations in a Culture of Consumption: Women and Department Stores, 1890–1925," *Journal of American History* 71, no. 2 (1984): 320.

41. Robert Herrick, *Together* (1908; Cabin John, MD: Wildside Press LLC, 2007), 515; Lori Merish, "Engendering Naturalism: Narrative Form and Commodity Spectacle in U.S. Naturalist Fiction," *Novel: A Forum on Fiction* 29, no. 3 (1996): 322; Jennifer L. Fleissner, "Wharton, Marriage, and the New Woman," in Cassuto ed., *Cambridge History*, 454–56; Brynnar Swenson, "Resistance to the Gilded Age: Robert Herrick's Radical Middle Class," *The Journal of the Gilded Age and Progressive Era* 16, no. 2 (2017): 143–62.

42. Dreiser, *Sister Carrie*, 111; Rachel Bowlby, *Just Looking: Consumer Culture in Dreiser, Gissing and Zola* (New York: Methuen, 1985), 52–65; Walter Benn Michaels, *The*

Gold Standard and the Logic of Naturalism: American Literature at the Turn of the Century (Berkeley, CA: University of California Press, 1987), 31–58; Harriet Beecher Stowe, *Pink and White Tyranny* (Boston: Roberts Brothers, 1871), 110.

43. Dreiser, *Jennie Gerhardt*, 173–74.

44. Wharton, *House of Mirth*, 17–18; Wharton, *Custom of the Country*, 20; Merish, "Engendering Naturalism," 324.

45. Stephen Crane, *Maggie: A Girl of the Streets* in *Great Short Works of Stephen Crane* (1893; New York: Harper & Row, 1965); Kate Chopin, *Awakening*, 188.

46. Dreiser, *Sister Carrie*, 101, 103; Fleissner, "Wharton, Marriage, and the New Woman," 453.

47. Dresier, *Jennie Gerhardt*, 93, 98; Dreiser, *Financier*, 526–27; Pitofsky, "Dreiser's *The Financier*," 286, quotes the *New York Evening Mail*.

48. Wharton, *Backward Glance*, 207.

49. Wharton, *Custom of the Country*, 590; Ariel Balter, "What does **** Want? Desire and Consumerism in Edith Wharton's *The Custom of the Country*," *American Literary Realism, 1870–1910* 27, no. 3 (1995): 19.

50. Wharton, *Summer* (1917; New York: Charles Scribner's Sons, 1964), 154, 176–77; Martha Billips, "Misunderstanding, Motivation, and Marriage in Edith Wharton's *Summer*," *American Literary Realism* 51, no. 3 (2019): 189–99.

51. Willa Cather, *My Ántonia* (1918; Cambridge, MA: Houghton Mifflin Company, 1926), 401.

52. Charlotte Perkins Gilman, "The Yellow Wallpaper" (1892; New York: The Feminist Press, 1973), 10; Chopin, *Awakening*, 87.

53. Frances Harper, *Iola Leroy, or, Shadows Uplifted* (1892; Philadelphia: Garrigues Brothers, 1893), 205.

54. Jean Rohloff, "'A Quicker Signal': Women and Language in Sara Orne Jewett's *The Country of the Pointed Firs*," *South Atlantic Review* 55, no. 2 (1990): 41; Anita Duneer, "Sarah Orne Jewett and (Maritime) Literary Tradition: Coastal and Narrative Navigations in *The Country of the Pointed Firs*," *American Literary Realism* 39, no. 3 (2007): 222–40.

55. Cather, *My Ántonia*, 412.

56. Theodore L. Gross, *Thomas Nelson Page* (New York: Twayne Publishers, 1967), 24, 27, 43–44.

57. John M. Gonzalez, "The Warp of Whiteness: Domesticity and Empire in Helen Hunt Jackson's *Ramona*," *American Literary History* 16, no. 3 (2004): 446.

58. Among the works praising Jim's courage and intelligence are Tom Quirk, "The Flawed Greatness of *Huckleberry Finn*," *American Literary Realism* 45, no. 1 (2012): 47; Richard Hill, "Overreaching: Critical Agenda and the End of *Adventures of Huckleberry Finn*," *Texas Studies in Literature and Language* 33, no. 4 (1991): 501, and Jocelyn Chadwick-Joshua, *The Jim Dilemma: Reading Race in Huckleberry Finn* (Jackson: University Press of Mississippi, 1998). Essays viewing Twain's depiction of Jim as racist include John Wallace, "*Huckleberry Finn*: Literature or Racist Trash," in *The Critical Response to Mark Twain's* Huckleberry Finn, ed. Laurie Champion (New York: Greenwood, 1991): 147–55; Jane Smiley, "Say it ain't so, Huck," *Harper's Magazine* (January 1996), 64; and Toni

Morrison, *Playing in the Dark: Whiteness and the Literary Imagination* (1992; New York: Vintage Books, 1993), 54–57.

59. The one significant exception to this depiction of Jim is his resolve to shield Huck from knowledge of Pap's death.

60. James Grove, "Mark Twain and the Endangered Family," *American Literature* 57, no. 3 (1985): 380, calls her a "proud passionate force"; Myra Jehlen, "The Ties that Bind: Race and Sex in *Pudd'nhead Wilson*," *American Literary History* 2, no. 1 (1990): 43, notes her "shrewdness"; Lee Clark Mitchell, "'De Nigger in You': Race or Training in *Pudd'nhead Wilson*?" *Nineteenth-Century Literature* 42, no. 3 (1987): 307, notes the "unalterable traits" burdening Blacks in the novel.

61. Twain, *Pudd'nhead Wilson and Those Extraordinary Twins* (1894; New York: W. W. Norton & Company, 1980), 73.

62. George Washington Cable, *The Grandissimes: A Story of Creole Life* (New York: Charles Scribner's Sons, 1880), 219; Louis D. Rubin Jr., "The Division of the Heart: Cable's *The Grandissimes*," *Southern Literary Journal* 1 (1969): 27–47, reprinted in *Critical Essays on George W. Cable*, ed. Arlin Turner (Boston: G. K. Hall & Co., 1980), 195–208; Elmo Howell, "George Washington Cable's Creoles: Art and Reform in *The Grandissimes*," *Mississippi Quarterly* 20 (1972–73), 42–53, reprinted in *Critical Essays*, 221–28.

63. Michael J. Pfeifer, *Rough Justice: Lynching and American Society, 1874–1947* (Urbana: University of Illinois Press, 2004).

64. Thomas Dixon Jr., *The Clansman: An Historical Romance of the Ku Klux Klan* (New York: Doubleday, Page & Company, 1905), 267, 304.

65. Burroughs, *Tarzan*, 162; Bederman, *Manliness & Civilization*, 223.

66. Booth Tarkington, *Penrod* (New York: Doubleday, 1914), 147; Upton Sinclair, *The Jungle* (1906; Middlesex, UK: Penguin Books, 1965), 328.

67. Henry Louis Gates Jr., "Harlem on Our Minds," *Critical Enquiry* 24, no. 1 (1997): 1–12, argues that African American writing at the turn of the twentieth century marked the first of four Black "renaissances." The others came in the 1920s, from 1965 to the early 1970s, and after 1987.

68. Harper, *Iola Leroy*, 256; Carole Lynn Stewart, "Iola's War on Alcohol, Lynching, and the Rise of the Carceral State," *Canadian Review of American Studies* 49, no. 2 (2019): 185–204.

69. Charles Chesnutt, *The Marrow of Tradition* (1901; Boston: Bedford/St. Martin's, 2002), 227.

70. Harper, *Iola Leroy*, 279; James Weldon Johnson, *The Autobiography of an Ex-Colored Man* (Boston: Sherman, French, & Company, 1912), 97.

71. W. E. B. Du Bois, "The Talented Tenth," 1903, http://teachingamericanhistory.org/library/document/the-talented-tenth/.

72. Johnson, *Autobiography*, 152; Chesnutt, *Marrow of Tradition*, 82; Susan Danielson, "Charles Chesnutt's Dilemma: Professional Ethics, Social Justice, and Domestic Feminism in *The Marrow of Tradition*," *The Southern Literary Journal* 41, no. 1 (2008): 76.

73. Harper, *Iola Leroy*, 276; Dunbar, *Sport of the Gods*, 56; Larson, "Paul Laurence Dunbar," 265–69.

74. Barbara Haskell, *The American Century: Art & Culture, 1900–1950* (New York: W. W. Norton & Company, 1999), 11–47; Edith DeShazo, *Everett Shinn, 1876–1953* (New York: Clarkson N. Potter, 1974), 64–65.

75. Robert Hughes, *American Visions: The Epic History of Art in America* (New York: Alfred A. Knopf, 1997), 318–335, quotation on 325.

76. Barbara Rose, *American Art Since 1900*, rev. ed. (New York: Praeger Publishers, 1975), 9–27, quotation on 20; Haskell, *American Century*, 61–65, 79–91.

77. Hughes, *American Visions*, 338–94; Haskell, *American Century*, 93–100, 109–18.

78. Rose, *American Art*, 28–45, 65–68, quotation on 35.

79. JoAnne M. Mancini, "'One Term is as Fatuous as Another': Responses to the Armory Show Reconsidered," *American Quarterly* 51, no. 4 (1999): 833–70; Rose, *American Art*, 49–61; Hughes, *American Visions*, 353–62; Haskell, *American Century*, 106–7; New York Historical Society, "The Armory Show at 100," http://armory.nyhistory.org/category/artworks/. These accounts differ in the proportion of European art in the show, placing it at one-third (Mancini, Rose), one-half (New York Historical Society), or two-thirds (Hughes).

Part 3: The Modern Era

1. F. Scott Fitzgerald, *The Great Gatsby* (New York: Charles Scribner's Sons, 1925), 82; Harry Levin, "What Was Modernism?" in *Refractions: Essays in Comparative Literature* (New York: Oxford University Press, 1966), 291; *The Cambridge History of American Literature*, vol. 6, *Prose Writing, 1910–1950*, ed. Sacvan Bercovitch (New York: Cambridge University Press, 2002), xvii; Henry Steele Commager, *The American Mind: An Interpretation of American Thought and Character Since the 1880s* (New Haven, CT: Yale University Press, 1950), 406–08.

2. Ernest Hemingway, *A Farewell to Arms*, The Hemingway Library Edition (1929; New York: Scribner, 2012), 167.

3. F. Scott Fitzgerald, *This Side of Paradise* (New York: Charles Scribner's Sons, 1920), 58; Nancy F. Cott, *The Grounding of Modern Feminism* (New Haven, CT: Yale University Press, 1987), 148–52.

4. For other interpretations of modernism, see the essays by David Minter, Rafia Zafar, and Werner Sollars in *Cambridge History of American Literature*, vol. 6; Commager, *American Mind*, 406–43; Maxwell Geismar, *American Moderns: From Rebellion to Conformity* (New York: Hill and Wang, 1958); Levin, "What Was Modernism?"; Norris W. Yates, "What Makes the Modern American Novel Modern?" *Jahrbuch für Amerikastudien* 11 (1966): 59–68; Earl Rovit, "The Twenties," *The Sewanee Review* 122, no. 1 (2014): 115–23.

5. Warren I. Susman, "'Personality' and the Making of Twentieth-Century Culture," in Susman, *Culture as History: The Transformation of American Society in the Twentieth Century* (New York: Pantheon Books, 1984), 271–85; Chip Rhodes, "Twenties Fiction, Mass Culture, and the Modern Subject," *American Literature* 68, no. 2 (1996): 385–404.

6. Dale Carnegie, *How to Win Friends and Influence People* (1936; London: Pocket Books, 1981), 63.

7. Yates, "Modern American Novel," 68. Cultural historians of Britain and continental Europe regularly date "modernism" from the late nineteenth-century. See Peter Gay, *Modernism: The Lure of Heresy* (New York: W.W. Norton, 2007).

8. *Cambridge History of American Literature*, vol. 6, xix.

9. Margot Norris, "Modernist Eruptions," in *The Columbia History of the American Novel*, ed. Emory Elliott (New York: Columbia University Press, 1991), 311–30.

10. Carmen W. Holsberry, "Faulkner, Fitzgerald, and Pynchon: Modernism and Postmodernism in Secondary School," *The English Journal* 70, no. 2 (1981): 26; Geismar, *American Moderns*, 10, 27; Levin, "What Was Modernism," 283.

11. Holsberry, "Faulkner, Fitzgerald, and Pynchon," 26.

12. Irving Howe, "Mass Society and Post-Modern Fiction," 1959, in *The American Novel Since World War II*, ed. Marcus Klein (Greenwich, CT: Fawcett, 1969), 124–41.

13. Levin, "What Was Modernism," 277.

14. Marty Jezer, *The Dark Ages: Life in the United States, 1945–1960* (Boston: South End Press, 1982), 177–93.

Chapter 7

1. Sinclair Lewis, *Babbitt* (New York: Collier, 1922), 2, 15.

2. Thomas S. Hines Jr., "Echoes from 'Zenith:' Reactions of American Businessmen to *Babbitt*," *The Business History Review* 41, no. 2 (1967): 123–40, quotations on 128, 132, 133; Clare Virginia Eby, "*Babbitt* as Veblenian Critique of Manliness," *American Studies* 34, no. 2 (1993): 5–23.

3. U.S. Bureau of the Census, *Historical Statistics of the United States*, 2 vols. (Washington, DC: U.S. Government Printing Office, 1975), 301–2; William E. Leuchtenburg, *The Perils of Prosperity, 1914–1932* (Chicago: The University of Chicago Press, 1958), 178–80; Michael E. Parrish, *Anxious Decades: America in Prosperity and Depression, 1920–1941* (New York: W. W. Norton & Company, 1992), 30–45.

4. Leuchtenburg, *Perils of Prosperity*, 179–92; Parrish, *Anxious Decades*, 71–72; John H. Lorant, "Technological Change in American Manufacturing During the 1920s," *The Journal of Economic History* 27, no. 2 (1967): 243–46.

5. Leuchtenburg, *Perils of Prosperity*, 193–94; Parish, *Anxious Decades*, 81–92; George Soule, *Prosperity Decade: From War to Depression, 1917–1929* (New York: Holt, Rinehart and Winston, 1947), 175–86, 275–89; Roger W. Garrison, "Reflections on Reflections: A Consensus about the Great Depression?" *The Independent Review* 8, no. 1 (2003): 113–20, discusses economists' differing views about the causes of the downturn.

6. G. Mayer, *Union Membership Trends in the United States* (Washington, DC: Congressional Research Service, 2004), page CRS-23, accessed online; William L. Leuchtenburg, *Franklin D. Roosevelt and the New Deal, 1932–1940* (New York: Harper & Row, 1963), 24–25, 111–14, 239–41; for dissent on end of the downturn, Frank G. Steindl, "What Ended the Great Depression? It Was Not World War II," *The Independent Review* 12, no. 2 (2007): 179–97.

7. Leuchtenburg, *Perils of Prosperity*, 244–62; Leuchtenburg, *Roosevelt*, 120–25; Nich-

olas Crafts and Peter Fearon, "Lessons from the 1930s Great Depression," *Oxford Review of Economic Policy* 26, no. 3 (2010), 285–317, suggests slightly lower figures for unemployment (287).

8. *Historical Statistics*, 301; Giles Kemp and Edward Claflin, *Dale Carnegie: The Man Who Influenced Millions* (New York: St. Martin's Press, 1989), 141–51.

9. Stanley Coben, "A Study in Nativism: The American Red Scare of 1919–20," *Political Science Quarterly* 79, no. 1 (1964): 52–75.

10. F. Scott Fitzgerald, *This Side of Paradise* (New York: Charles Scribner's Sons, 1920), 220, 292, 304; Clinton S. Burhans Jr., "Structure and Theme in *This Side of Paradise*," *The Journal of English and Germanic Philology* 68, no. 4 (1969): 615.

11. Edna Ferber, *So Big* (Garden City, NY: Doubleday, 1924), 285–86, 335, 358.

12. F. Scott Fitzgerald, *The Great Gatsby* (1925; New York: Charles Scribner's Sons, 1953), 2, 73, 80.

13. Edith Wharton, *The Age of Innocence* (1920; New York: Washington Square Press, 1995), 17, 165, 276–77.

14. Ernest Hemingway, *The Sun Also Rises* (New York: Charles Scribner's Sons, 1926), 22, 25.

15. Ernest Hemingway, *A Farewell to Arms*, The Hemingway Library Edition (1929; New York: Scribner, 2012), 94.

16. Ibid., 216.

17. Theodore Dreiser, *An American Tragedy* (1925; New York: The Modern Library, 1956), 397.

18. Willa Cather, *Death Comes for the Archbishop* (1926; New York: Alfred A. Knopf, 1927), 26, 276–77; Merrill Maguire Skaggs, "*Death Comes for the Archbishop*: Cather's Mystery and Manners," *American Literature* 57, no. 3 (1985): 395–406; James M. Dinn, "A Novelist's Miracle: Structure and Myth in *Death Comes for the Archbishop*," *Western American Literature* 7, no. 1 (1972): 39–46.

19. Fitzgerald, *Great Gatsby*, 121.

20. John Woolley and Gerhard Peters, eds., "Franklin D. Roosevelt: XXXII President of the United States, 1933–1945," First Inaugural Address, March 4, 1933," The American Presidency Project, http://www.presidency.ucsb.edu/ws/index.php?pid'14473.

21. Pearl S. Buck, *The Good Earth* (1931; New York: The John Day Company, 1932), 90, 221; Richard Jean So, "Fictions of Natural Democracy: Pearl Buck, *The Good Earth*, and the Asian American Subject," *Representations* 112, no. 1 (2010): 96; Colleen Lye, *America's Asia: Racial Form and American Literature, 1893–1945* (Princeton, NJ: Princeton University Press, 2005), 213.

22. William Faulkner, *Light in August* (New York: Harrison Smith and Robert Haas, 1932), 320–21, 424; Karl E. Zink, "Faulkner's Garden: Woman and the Immemorial Earth," in *Faulkner and His Critics*, ed. John N. Duvall (Baltimore, MD: The Johns Hopkins University Press, 2010), 149–61, quotation on 160.

23. Erskine Caldwell, *Tobacco Road* (New York: Grosset and Dunlap Publishers, 1932), 89.

24. John Steinbeck, *Of Mice and Men* (1937; New York: Penguin Books, 1994), 38.

25. James T. Farrell, *Studs Lonigan* (1932–1935; New York: The Vanguard Press, 1935), 438.

26. Michael Gold, *Jews Without Money* (New York: Liveright, 1930), 309; Morris Dickstein, "Hallucinating the Past: *Jews Without Money* Revisited," *Grand Street* 9, no. 2 (1990): 159, 164.

27. Laura Hapke, *Daughters of the Great Depression: Women, Work, and Fiction in the American 1930s* (Athens: The University of Georgia Press, 1995), 145–80; John Marsh, "Women on the Breadlines," in *The Cambridge History of American Women's Literature*, ed. Dale M. Bauer (Cambridge, UK: Cambridge University Press, 2012), 477–500, surveys the proletarian novels involving women.

28. Grace Lumpkin, *To Make My Bread* (1932; Lanham, MD: Rowman & Littlefield, 2014), 328.

29. Introduction by Warren French to John Steinbeck, *In Dubious Battle* (1936; New York: Penguin Classics, 1992), xvii.

30. Steinbeck, *In Dubious Battle*, 198.

31. Jackson J. Benson and Anne Loftis, "John Steinbeck and Farm Labor Unionization: The Background of *In Dubious Battle*," *American Literature* 52, no. 2 (1980), quotes Steinbeck, 197.

32. John Steinbeck, *Grapes of Wrath* (1939; New York: The Viking Press, 1967), 436.

33. Jenn Williamson, "'His Home Is Not the Land': Caretaking, Domesticity, and Gender in *The Grapes of Wrath*," *Modern Language Studies* 40, no. 2 (2001): 41.

34. Hemingway, *Farewell to Arms*, 161.

35. Ernest Hemingway, *For Whom the Bell Tolls* (1940; New York: Scribner Classic, 2002), 315.

36. David Sanders, "Ernest Hemingway's Spanish Civil War Experience," *American Quarterly* 12, no. 2 (1960): 133–43, quotation on 141; for different readings of the novel, see Walter J. Slatoff, "The 'Great Sin' in *For Whom the Bell Tolls*," *The Journal of Narrative Technique* 7, no. 2 (1977): 142–48; Michael J. B. Allen, "The Unspanish War in *For Whom the Bell Tolls*," *Contemporary Literature* 13, no. 2 (1972): 204–12.

37. William Faulkner, *The Hamlet* (New York: Random House, 1940), 171–72.

38. Wharton, *Age of Innocence*, 121.

39. Fitzgerald, *Great Gatsby*, 99.

40. F. Scott Fitzgerald, *Tender Is the Night* (New York: Charles Scribner's Sons, 1934), 201, 293.

41. Gold, *Jews Without Money*, 230; Michael Kimmel, *Manhood in America: A Cultural History* (New York: The Free Press, 1996), 192–93, 199–202.

42. Farrell, *Studs Lonigan*, 743.

43. Williamson, "His Home Is Not the Land," 51; Michael Szalay, *New Deal Modernism: American Literature and the Invention of the Welfare State* (Durham, NC: Duke University Press, 2001), 162–84.

44. Claude McKay, *Home to Harlem* (1928; Boston: Northeastern University Press, 1987), 114.

45. Margaret Mitchell, *Gone with the Wind* (1936; New York: Scribner, 2011), 859.

46. Robert Penn Warren, "Hemingway," *The Kenyon Review* 9, no. 1 (1947): 2; W. J. Stuckey, "'The Killers' As Experience," *Journal of Narrative Theory* 5, no. 2 (1975): 128–35; Philip Durham, "Ernest Hemingway's Grace Under Pressure: The Western Code," *Pacific Historical Review* 45, no. 3 (1976): 425–32.

47. Hemingway, *Sun Also Rises*, 174.

48. Hemingway, *For Whom the Bell Tolls*, 174.

49. Fred H. Marcus, "*A Farewell to Arms:* The Impact of Irony and the Irrational," *The English Journal* 51, no. 8 (1962): 527; John I. Irwin, *Unless the Threat of Death is Behind Them: Hard-Boiled Fiction and Film Noir* (Baltimore, MD: Johns Hopkins University Press, 2006), 188–91.

50. Raymond Chandler, *The Big Sleep* (1939; New York: Vintage Books, 1992), 113–14.

51. James M. Cain, *The Postman Always Rings Twice* (1937; New York: Perennial Classics, 1986), 97.

52. Parrish, *Anxious Decades*, 136–45, 400–4; Alice Kessler-Harris, "Gender Ideology in Historical Reconstruction: A Case Study from the 1930s," *Gender and History* 1 (1989): 31–44.

53. Parrish, *Anxious Decades*, 147–52; Nicole C. Cox, "Selling Seduction: Women and Feminine Nature in 1920s Florida Advertising," *The Florida Historical Quarterly* 89, no. 2 (2010): 186–209.

54. Andria Taylor Hourwich and Glady L. Palmer, eds., *I Am a Woman Worker: A Scrapbook of Autobiographies* (New York: Affiliated Schools for Workers, 1936); Estelle B. Freedman, "The New Woman: Changing Views of Women in the 1920s," *The Journal of American History* 61, no. 2 (1974): 372–93; Nancy F. Cott, *The Grounding of Modern Feminism* (New Haven, CT: Yale University Press, 1987), 115–74.

55. Thomas D. Snyder, ed., *120 Years of American Education: A Statistical Portrait* (Washington, DC: National Center for Education Statistics, 1993), 83, https://nces.ed.gov/pubs93/93442.pdf

56. Fitzgerald, *Great Gatsby*, 69, 77.

57. Hemingway, *Sun Also Rises*, 183.

58. Barbara Foley, "Women and the Left in the 1930s," *American Literary History* 2, no. 1 (1990): 150–69.

59. Faulkner, *Light in August*, 245.

60. Cain, *Postman Always Rings Twice*, 21.

61. Hemingway, *For Whom the Bell Tolls*, 182.

62. Fitzgerald, *Tender is the Night*, 151–52.

63. Faulkner, *Light in August*, 244; Diane Roberts, "A Precarious Pedestal: The Confederate Woman in Faulkner's *Unvanquished*," *Journal of American Studies* 26, no. 2 (1992): 233–46.

64. Hemingway, *For Whom the Bell Tolls*, 32.

65. Nellie McKay, "'Happy[?]-Wife-and-Motherdom': The Portrayal of Ma Joad in John Steinbeck's *The Grapes of Wrath*," in *New Essays on The Grapes of Wrath*, ed. David Wyatt (New York: Cambridge University Press, 1990), 66.

66. Williamson, "His Home Is Not the Land," 40–53; Jackson J. Benson and Anne

Loftis, "John Steinbeck and Farm Labor Unionization: The Background of *In Dubious Battle*," *American Literature* 52, no. 2 (1980): 194–223; Hapke, *Daughters of the Great Depression*, 18–20, 35–38.

67. Hapke, *Daughters of the Great Depression*, 145–80.

68. Charles Rowan Beye, "*Gone with the Wind* and Good Riddance," *Southwest Review* 78, no. 3 (1993): 375.

69. Frederick Lewis Allen, *Only Yesterday: An Informal History of the Nineteen-Twenties* (1931; New York: Harper & Row, 1964), 49–62.

70. Fitzgerald, *Great Gatsby*, 45.

71. Hemingway, *Farewell to Arms*, 222.

72. Gold, *Jews Without Money*, 16.

73. Steinbeck, *Of Mice and Men*, 53.

74. Mitchell, *Gone with the Wind*, 23, 654.

75. Edmund L. Volpe, *A Reader's Guide to William Faulkner* (New York: Farrar, Straus and Giroux, 1964), 16.

76. George E. Kent, "The Black Woman in Faulkner's Works, with the Exclusion of Dilsey: Part II," *Phylon* 36, no. 1 (1975): 55–67, quotation on 67.

77. Lumpkin, *To Make My Bread*, 350.

78. Hemingway, *For Whom the Bell Tolls*, 123.

79. F. Scott Fitzgerald, *The Last Tycoon* (1941; New York: Penguin Books, 1965), 116.

80. Alain L. Locke, *The New Negro: An Interpretation* (New York: A. and C. Boni, 1925), 4, 6, 7; Daylanne, K. English, "Selecting the Harlem Renaissance," *Critical Enquiry* 25, no. 4 (1999): 807–21; Sidney H. Bremer, "Home in Harlem, New York: Lessons from the Harlem Renaissance Writers," *PMLA* 105, no. 1 (1990): 47–56.

81. Nella Larsen, *Quicksand* (1928; Overland Park, KS; Digireads.com., 2016), 75.

82. Zora Neale Hurston, *Their Eyes Were Watching God* (1937; New York: Perennial Classics, 1998), 133.

83. McKay, *Home to Harlem*, 267; Langston Hughes, *Not Without Laughter* (1930; Mineola, NY: Dover Publications, 2008), 212.

84. Larsen, *Quicksand*, 89.

85. Hurston, *Their Eyes*, 97.

86. Hughes, *Not Without Laughter*, 180.

87. McKay, *Home to Harlem*, 191.

88. Charles Scruggs, "'All Dressed Up But No Place to Go': The Black Writer and His Audience During the Harlem Renaissance," *American Literature* 48, no. 4 (1977): 553, quotes Toomer.

89. Alain Locke, "American Literary Tradition and the Negro," *The Modern Quarterly* 3, no. 2 (1926): 215–22, quotation on 221.

90. Jean Toomer, *Cane* (1923; New York; Liveright, 1975), 152; Benjamin Kahan and Makoka Kishi, "Sex under Necropolitics: Waldo Frank, Jean Toomer, and Black Enfleshment," *Journal of American Studies* 54, no. 5 (2020): 926–50.

91. Hughes, *Not Without Laughter*, 155.

92. McKay, *Home to Harlem*, 77.

93. Kevin Hillstrom, *The Harlem Renaissance* (Detroit: Omnigraphics, 2008), 83, quotes McKay; Henry Louis Gates Jr., "Harlem on Our Minds," *Critical Inquiry* 24, no. 1 (1997): 3–4.

94. Sheldon Brivic, "Conflict of Values: Richard Wright's *Native Son*," *NOVEL: A Forum on Fiction* 7, no. 3 (1974): 231–45; Masaya Takeuchi, "Bigger's Divided Self: Violence and Homosociality in *Native Son*," *Studies in American Naturalism* 4, no. 1 (2009): 56–74.

95. Robert Hughes, *American Visions: The Epic History of Art in America* (New York: Alfred A. Knopf, 1997), 379–80; Barbara Haskell, *The American Century: Art & Culture, 1900–1950* (New York: W. W. Norton, 1999), 145–47, 169–70.

96. Karen Lucic, *Charles Sheeler and the Cult of the Machine* (London: Reaktion Books, 1991), 80–98, quotation on 92.

97. Karen Lucic, "Charles Sheeler and Henry Ford: A Craft Heritage for the Machine Age," *Bulletin of the Detroit Institute of Arts* 65, no. 1 (1989): 36–47, quotation on 39; Hughes, *American Visions*, 382–86; Haskell, *American Century*, 153–56.

98. Wanda M. Corn, "The Birth of a National Icon: Grant Wood's *American Gothic*," in *Reading American Art*, ed. Marianne Doezema and Elizabeth Milroy (New Haven, CT: Yale University Press, 1998), 387–408, quotation on 404; Hughes, *American Visions*, 437–43; Haskell, *American Century*, 224–26.

99. Haskell, *American Century*, 221.

100. Barbara Rose, *American Art Since 1900* (New York: Prager Publishers, 1975), 98.

101. Hughes, *American Visions*, 446–53, quotation on 447; Haskell, *American Century*, 245, 256–61, 281; Rose, *American Art*, 105–7.

102. Ellen Wiley Todd, "The Question of Difference: Isabel Bishop's Deferential Office Girls," in *Reading American Art*, 409–39.

103. Hughes, *American Visions*, 454–57; Haskell, *American Century*, 231–34.

104. Linda Nochlin, "Edward Hopper and the Imagery of Alienation," *Art Journal* 41, no. 2 (1981): 136–41; Gail Levin, *Edward Hopper: The Art and the Artist* (New York: W. W. Norton & Company, 1980), 5–6, 39–40; Hughes, *American Visions*, 422–28.

105. Levin, *Edward Hopper*, 27.

106. Ibid., 27, 29.

107. Ibid., 6, 9.

Chapter 8

1. Andrew Wilson, *Beautiful Shadow: A Life of Patricia Highsmith* (New York: Bloomsbury, 2003), 186, 188; Patricia Highsmith, *The Talented Mr. Ripley* (1955; New York: Vintage Books, 1992); Russell Harrison, *Patricia Highsmith* (New York: Twayne Publishers, 1997), 20–29.

2. William H. Chafe, *The Unfinished Journey: America Since World War II*, 6th ed. (New York: Oxford University Press, 2007), 107–8; Marc Egnal, *Divergent Paths: How Culture and Institutions Have Shaped North American Growth* (New York: Oxford University Press, 1996), 168.

3. Egnal, *Divergent Paths*, 162; Marty Jezer, *The Dark Ages: Life in the United States, 1945–1960* (Boston: South End Press, 1982), 215; Jeffrey Madrick, *The End of Affluence: The Causes and Consequences of America's Economic Dilemma* (New York: Random House, 1995), 58–63; Michael Urquhart, "The Employment Shift to Services: Where Did It Come From?" *Monthly Labor Review* 107, no. 4 (1984): 15–22; Chafe, *Unfinished Journey*, 108–10.

4. Jezer, *Dark Ages*, 215; Chafe, *Unfinished Journey*, 8, 106.

5. Elaine Tyler May, *Homeward Bound: American Families in the Cold War Era* (New York: Basic Books, 1988), 3–14, 166–69; Chafe, *Unfinished Journey*, 105, 106, 112, 117–18.

6. May, *Homeward Bound*, 170–71; Michael Harrington, *The Other America: Poverty in the United States* (New York: Macmillan Co., 1962), 1, 182; Chafe, *Unfinished Journey*, 137–38.

7. Herman Wouk, *The Caine Mutiny* (Garden City, NY: Doubleday & Co., 1951), 446, 468.

8. James R. Browne, "Distortion in the Caine Mutiny," *College English* 17, no. 4 (1956): 216.

9. J. D. Salinger, *The Catcher in the Rye* (1951; Boston: Bantam Books, 1964), 85, 126, 213.

10. Jack Kerouac, *On the Road* (New York: The Viking Press, 1957), 208.

11. Ibid., 309; J. T. Barbarese, "Fifty Years of Jack Kerouac's On the Road," *The Sewanee Review* 112, no. 4 (2004): 592–93.

12. Sloan Wilson, *The Man in the Gray Flannel Suit* (New York: Simon and Schuster, 1955), 301.

13. Robert Penn Warren, *All the King's Men* (New York: Harcourt, Brace and Company, 1946).

14. Philip Roth, *Goodbye, Columbus* (Boston: Houghton Mifflin Co., 1959); Sean McCann, "Training and Vision: Roth, DeLillo, Banks, and the Postmodern Aesthetics of Vocation," *Twentieth-Century Literature* 53, no. 3 (2007): 298–301.

15. Salinger, *Catcher in the Rye*, 173.

16. Saul Bellow, *The Adventures of Augie March* (New York: The Viking Press, 1953), 457.

17. Roth, *Goodbye, Columbus*, 95.

18. Harper Lee, *To Kill a Mockingbird* (New York: J. B. Lippincott Co., 1960), 213.

19. Erich Fromm, *Man for Himself: An Inquiry into the Psychology of Ethics* (New York: Holt, Rinehart and Winston, 1947), 4.

20. Wilson, *Man in the Gray Flannel Suit*, 121, 180.

21. Saul Bellow, *Henderson the Rain King* (New York: The Viking Press, 1959), 3, 25.

22. John Updike, *Rabbit, Run* (1960; New York: Penguin Books, 1964), 219.

23. Frank Newport, "Five Key Findings on Religion in the U.S.," December 23, 2016, *Gallup News*, http://news.gallup.com/poll/200186/five-key-findings-religion.aspx; Chafe, *Unfinished Journey*, 115.

24. Lists taken from Alice Payne Hackett, *70 Years of Best Sellers, 1895–1965* (New York: R. R. Bowker Co., 1967), 121–214. Books were counted each time they appeared on these annual top ten lists.

25. Carl Bode, "Lloyd Douglas: Loud Voice in the Wilderness," *American Quarterly* 2, no. 4 (1950): 340–52, quotation on 349.

26. Lloyd C. Douglas, *The Robe* (Boston: Houghton Mifflin, 1942), 371–72.

27. John T. Frederick, "*The Robe* and *The Apostle*," *The English Journal* 33, no. 6 (1944): 281–88. Sholem Asch, another bestselling religious author, underwent (like Douglas) a dramatic shift in his outlook and writing around 1940.

28. Joanne Meyerowitz, ed., *Not June Cleaver: Women and Gender in Postwar America, 1945–1960* (Philadelphia, PA: Temple University Press, 1994); Cynthia Harrison, *On Account of Sex: The Politics of Women's Issues, 1945–1968* (Berkeley: University of California Press, 1988), 3–49, 89–92, 170–72; Claudia Goldin, *Understanding the Gender Gap: An Economic History of American Women* (New York: Oxford University Press, 1990), 62.

29. Wilson, *Man in the Gray Flannel Suit*, 7.

30. Yvonne Fonteneau, "Ralph Ellison's *Invisible Man*: A Critical Reevaluation," *World Literature Today* 64, no. 3 (1990): 408–12.

31. Lillian Smith, *Strange Fruit* (New York: Reynal & Hitchcock, 1944), 90.

32. John Steinbeck, *Cannery Row* (New York: The Viking Press, 1945), 98.

33. Warren, *All the King's Men*, 79.

34. Bellow, *Augie March*, 215, 232.

35. Douglas, *Robe*, 694.

36. Betty Smith, *A Tree Grows in Brooklyn* (Philadelphia: The Blakiston Co., 1943); Rebecca DeWolf, "The Equal Rights Amendment and the Rise of Emancipationism, 1932–1946," *Frontiers: A Journal of Women Studies* 38, no. 2 (2017): 47–80, discusses the strength of the women's movement during the early 1940s; Michael Szalay, *New Deal Modernism: American Literature and the Welfare State* (Durham, NC: Duke University Press, 2003), 184–94.

37. Constante González Groba, "The Intolerable Burden of Femininity in Carson McCullers' *The Member of the Wedding* and *The Ballad of the Sad Café*," *Atlantis* 16, no. 1/2 (1994): 133–48, quotation on 134.

38. Carson McCullers, *The Ballad of the Sad Café and Other Stories* (Boston: Houghton Mifflin Co., 1951), 5.

39. Groba, "Intolerable Burden of Femininity," 146.

40. Edna Ferber, *Giant* (New York: Doubleday & Co., 1952), 54.

41. James Gilbert, *Men in the Middle: Searching for Masculinity in the 1950s* (Chicago: The University of Chicago Press, 2005), surveys the "crisis" men faced in the 1950s and its historiography.

42. Ernest Hemingway, *The Old Man and the Sea* (1952; New York: C. Scribner's Sons, 1980), 85.

43. Several popular books (and much pulp fiction) stand outside the mainstream, exalting men who disdain conformist society. Tough-talking Mike Hammer, the hero of Mickey Spillane's *I, The Jury* (1947) exemplifies that outlook. In *The Fountainhead* (1943) and *Atlas Shrugged* (1957), the Russian-born libertarian novelist Ayn Rand exalts a creative elite—industrialists, scientists, and architects—whose powers, she argues, have been foolishly limited.

44. Leslie Fiedler, "Come Back to the Raft Ag'in, Huck Honey," *Partisan Review* 15, no. 6 (1948): 664–71.

45. John D'Emilio and Estelle B. Freedman, *Intimate Matters: A History of Sexuality in America*, 3rd ed. (Chicago: University of Chicago Press, 2012), 289; George Chauncey, *Gay New York: Gender, Urban Culture and the Making of the Gay Male World, 1890–1940* (New York: Basic, 1994), 226–86, 313, 327–355, suggests repression began in the 1930s.

46. F. Scott Fitzgerald, *The Great Gatsby* (1925; New York: Penguin Books, 1950), 32, 34.

47. John Dos Passos, *The 42nd Parallel* (New York: Harper & Brothers Publishers, 1930), 229–30.

48. Emilio and Freedman, *Intimate Matters*, 292–95; Robert J. Corber, *Homosexuality in Cold War America: Resistance and the Crisis of Masculinity* (Durham, NC: Duke University Press, 1997), 2–10; Arthur Redding, *Turncoats, Traitors, and Fellow Travelers: Culture and Politics of the Early Cold War* (Jackson: University Press of Mississippi, 2008), 79–97.

49. Salinger, *Catcher in the Rye*, 142.

50. Corber, *Homosexuality in Cold War America*, 49–53; Kerouac, *On the Road*, 73.

51. Updike, *Rabbit, Run*, 13.

52. Highsmith, *Talented Mr. Ripley*, 25–26.

53. Harry Thomas, "'Immaculate Manhood': *The City and the Pillar, Giovanni's Room*, and the Straight-Acting Gay Man," *Twentieth-Century Literature* 59, no. 4 (2013): 596–618.

54. Yasmin Y. DeGout, "Dividing the Mind: Contradictory Portraits of Homoerotic Love in *Giovanni's Room*," *African American Review* 26, no. 3 (1992): 425–35; Aliyyah I. Abur-Rahman, "'Simply a Menaced Boy': Analogizing Color, Undoing Dominance in James Baldwin's *Giovanni's Room*," *African American Review* 41, no. 3 (2007): 477–86.

55. Wouk, *Caine Mutiny*, 289.

56. Kerouac, *On the Road*, 180.

57. James Baldwin, *Nobody Knows My Name* (New York: The Dial Press, 1961), 231; Mark Richardson, "Peasant Dreams: Reading *On the Road*," *Texas Studies in Literature and Language* 43, no. 2 (2001): 218–42; Victoria A. Elmwood, "The White Nomad and the New Masculine Family in Jack Kerouac's *On the Road*," *Western American Literature* 42, no. 4 (2008): 335–61; Jason Vredenburg, "'Solitary Bartlebies': Kerouac's *On the Road* and the Ideology of the Superhighway," *Twentieth-Century Literature* 62, no. 2 (2016): 170–96.

58. Naa Baako Ako-Adjei, "Why It's Time Schools Stopped Teaching *To Kill a Mockingbird*," *Transition*, 122 (2017), 182–200, quotations on 186, 194, 198. Ako-Adjei also points out that the racist Atticus in Lee's *Go Tell a Watchman* is very much in keeping with his character in *Mockingbird*. *Watchman* was written before *Mockingbird* but not published until 2015. For similar arguments, see Joseph Crespino, *Atticus Finch: The Biography* (New York: Basic Books, 2018), esp. 89–99.

59. Ralph Ellison, *Invisible Man* (New York: Random House, 1952), 3; Redding, *Turncoats, Traitors, and Fellow Travelers*, 67–78.

60. Ellison, *Invisible Man*, 439, 435; Barbara Foley, "The Rhetoric of Anticommunism in *Invisible Man*," *College English* 69, no. 5 (1997): 530–47, quotation on 530; Christopher Z. Hobson, "*Invisible Man* and African American Radicalism in World War II," *African

American Review 39, no. 3 (2005): 355–76; Tony Tanner, *City of Words: American Fiction, 1950–1970* (New York: Harper & Row, 1971), 50–63.

61. James Baldwin, *Go Tell It On A Mountain* (1953; New York: The Dial Press, 1963), 20, 38.

62. John Henry Merryman, Albert E. Eisen, Stephen K. Urice, *Law, Ethics, and the Visual Arts*, 5th ed. (Alphen aan Den Rinj, Netherlands: Kluwer Law International, 2007), 644–55, Dondero quotation, 645; Jane de Hart Mathews, "Art and Politics in Cold War America," *American Historical Review* 81, no. 4 (1976): 766, 772–73.

63. Mathews, "Art and Politics," 777, 779, for Truman and Eisenhower quotes.

64. Robert Hughes, *American Visions: The Epic History of Art in America* (New York: Alfred A. Knopf, 1997), 507–9; Otto Kallir, ed., *Art and Life of Grandma Moses* (New York: A. S. Barnes and Co., 1969), 45.

65. Hughes, *American Visions*, 467, quotes Gorky.

66. Erika Doss, *Benton, Pollock, and the Politics of Modernism: From Regionalism to Abstract Expressionism* (Chicago: University of Chicago Press, 1991), 330, 331, quotes Pollock and Benton.

67. Ben Shahn, *The Shape of Content* (Cambridge, MA: Harvard University Press, 1966), 58. [These are the Charles Eliot Norton Lectures, 1956–1957], 40, 58.

68. Doss, *Politics of Modernism*, 341, 345, quotes Gottlieb and Motherwell. One possible exception to the apolitical nature of abstract expressionism is Motherwell's series of paintings "Spanish Elegies," which pays homage to the Spanish Republic of the 1930s. Still, unlike Picasso's highly graphic *Guernica*, Motherwell's paintings feature only abstract shapes whose political import would be hard to discern without their titles.

69. Eve Cockcroft, "Abstract Expressionism, Weapon of the Cold War," *Artforum* (June 1974), 40.

70. David and Cecile Shapiro, "Abstract Expressionism: The Politics of Apolitical Painting," *Prospects* 3 (1977): 175–214, quotation on 207.

71. Serge Guilbaut, *How New York Stole the Idea of Modern Art: Abstract Expressionism, Freedom, and the Cold War*, trans. Arthur Goldhammer (Chicago: University of Chicago Press, 1983), 3.

Part 4: The Postmodern Era

1. Paul Goodman, *Growing Up Absurd: Problems of Youth in the Organized Society* (New York: Random House, 1960), ix, xiv, xvi.

2. Andrew Hoberek and Sean McCann also root postmodernism in the changing structure of society. See Hoberek, "Introduction: After Postmodernism," *Twentieth-Century Literature* 53, no. 3 (2007): 233–47; Hoberek, "Postmodernism and Modernization," *Twentieth-Century Literature* 57, no. 3/4 (2011): 341–53;. Hoberek, *The Twilight of the Middle-Class: Post-World War II American Fiction and White-Collar Work* (Princeton: Princeton University Press, 2005); Sean McCann, "Training and Vision: Roth, DeLillo, Banks, Peck, and the Postmodern Aesthetics of Vocation," *Twentieth-Century Literature* 53, no. 3 (2007): 298–326.

3. For example, support for same-sex marriage rose from 36 percent in 2007 to 62 percent in 2018, David Greenberg et al., "Fifty Years After Stonewall," https://www.prri.org/research/fifty-years-after-stonewall-widespread-support-for-lgbt-issues-findings-from-american-values-atlas-2018/; "Religious Landscape Study," Pew Research Institute, 2014, https://www.pewforum.org/religious-landscape-study/belief-in-god/; Jerry Rubin, *Growing (Up) at Thirty-Seven* (New York: M. Evans and Co., 1976), 1–34, discusses one protester's response to the aftermath of the 1960s.

4. Robert L. McLaughlin, "Post-Postmodern Discontent: Contemporary Fiction and the Social World," *symplokē* 12, nos. 1–2 (2004): 53–68, quotations on 59, 64; John Barth, "The Literature of Exhaustion," *The Atlantic*, August 1967, 62–76.

5. Wendy Steiner, "Postmodern Fictions, 1960–1990," in *The Cambridge History of American Literature*, ed. Sacvan Bercovitch, vol. 7 (New York: Cambridge University Press, 1999), 425–538, quotations on 428, 431, 441. Presenting similar arguments are Ursula K. Heise, "Postmodern Novels," in *The Cambridge History of the American Novel*, ed. Leonard Cassuto (New York: Cambridge University Press, 2011), 964–85; Kimberley Chabot Davis, "'Postmodern Blackness': Toni Morrison's *Beloved* and the End of History," *Twentieth-Century Literature* 44, no. 2 (1998): 242–60; Paula Geyh et al., eds., *Postmodern American Fiction: A Norton Anthology* (New York: W. W. Norton & Co., 1997); Amy Hungerford, "On the Period Formerly Known as Contemporary," *American Literary History* 20, nos. 1/2(2008): 410–19.

6. Philip Roth, "Writing American Fiction," *Commentary* 31, no. 3 (March 1, 1961): 223–233, quotation on 231.

7. Rachel Adams, "The Ends of America, the Ends of Postmodernism," *Twentieth-Century Literature* 53, no. 3 (2007): 248–72, quotation on 249; Andrew Hoberek, "Introduction: After Postmodernism," *Twentieth-Century Literature* 53, no. 3 (2007): 240; Alan Kirby, *Digimodernism: How New Technologies Dismantle the Postmodern and Reconfigure Our Culture* (New York: Continuum, 2009).

8. Andrew Hoberek, "Epilogue: 2001, 2008, and After," in *Cambridge History of Postmodern Literature*, ed. Brian McHale and Len Platt (Cambridge, UK: Cambridge University Press, 2016), 497–513, quotation on 499.

9. Jeffrey T. Nealon, *Post-Postmodernism, or, The Cultural Logic of Just-In-Time Capitalism* (Stanford, CA: Stanford University Press, 2012), 8.

10. David Foster Wallace, "E Unibus Pluram: Television and U.S. Fiction," *Review of Contemporary Fiction* 13, no. 2 (1993): 151–94, quotations on 183, 193; Paul Giles, "Sentimental Posthumanism: David Foster Wallace," *Twentieth-Century Literature* 53, no. 3 (2007): 327–44; Adam Kelly, "Dialectic of Sincerity: Lionel Trilling and David Foster Wallace," *Post* 45, October 17, 2014.

11. Lee Konstantinou, "Periodizing the Present," *Contemporary Literature* 54, no. 2 (2013): 411–23, provides an insightful review of Nealon's book.

12. Brian McHale, "1966 Nervous Breakdown; or, When Did Postmodernism Begin?" *Modern Language Quarterly* 69, no. 3 (2008): 391–413; Hungerford, "On the Period," 413; Andreas Killen, *1973 Nervous Breakdown: Watergate, Warhol, and the Birth of Post-Sixties America* (New York: Bloomsbury, 2006).

13. Frederic Jameson, *Postmodernism, or The Cultural Logic of Late Capitalism* (Durham, NC: Duke University Press, 1991), 1.

14. David Cowart, *The Tribe of Pyn: Literary Generations in the Postmodern Period* (Ann Arbor: University of Michigan, 2015), 199, notes the "intergenerational continuities that augur postmodernism's longevity."

Chapter 9

1. Interview with Paul Levine, "The Writer as Independent Witness," 1978, in *E. L. Doctorow: Essays and Conversations*, ed. Richard Trenner (Princeton, NJ: Ontario Review Press, 1983), 69; Gillian Brassil, "The Real Lives of Early 20th-Century Celebrities, as Depicted in 'Ragtime,'" *New York Times*, September 7, 2022; Nicky Marsh, *Credit Culture: The Politics of Money in the American Novel of the 1970s* (New York: Cambridge University Press, 2020), 10–16.

2. Robert J. Donovan, *Eisenhower: The Inside Story* (New York: Harper & Brothers, 1956), 25.

3. Lee Konstantinou, *Cool Characters: Irony and American Fiction* (Cambridge, MA: Harvard University Press, 2016), 81; Vance Packard, *The Naked Society* (New York: David McKay Co., 1964), 1–90; http://archive.fortune.com/magazines/fortune/fortune500 _archive/full/1955/; Maryann Keller, *Rude Awakening: The Rise, Fall, and Struggle for Recovery of General Motors* (New York: William Morrow & Co., 1989), 19–54; Ira C. Magaziner and Robert Reich, *Minding America's Business: The Decline and Rise of the American Economy* (New York: Knopf, 1988), 155–68; David Halberstam, *The Reckoning* (New York, 1986), 23; Marc Egnal, *Divergent Paths: How Culture and Institutions Have Shaped North American Growth* (New York: Oxford University Press, 1996), 159–67.

4. John Kenneth Galbraith, *The New Industrial State* (Boston: Houghton Mifflin Co., 1967), 3, 5, 6, 76.

5. Egnal, *Divergent Paths*, 179–81; Annie McClanahan, "Introduction: The Spirit of Capital in an Age of Deindustrialization," *Post45*, January 10, 2019, http://post45 .research.yale.edu/2019/01/introduction-the-spirit-of-capital-in-an-age-of -deindustrialization/.

6. Benjamin P. Bowser, *The Black Middle Class: Social Mobility—and Vulnerability* (Boulder, CO: Lynne Rienner, 2006). See also chapter 10, below.

7. Roger Rosenblatt, "The Age of Irony Comes to an End," *Time*, September 24, 2001, 79.

8. Sanford Pinsker, "Reassessing *Catch-22*," *The Sewanee Review* 108, no. 4 (2000): 602–10, quotations on 608, 609.

9. Kurt Vonnegut, *Slaughterhouse-Five, or, The Children's Crusade* (New York: Delacorte Press, 1969), 23, 87, 171.

10. Don DeLillo, *End Zone* (Boston: Houghton Mifflin Co., 1972), 240.

11. Don DeLillo, *White Noise* (1985; New York: Penguin, 1986), 70.

12. Cormac McCarthy, *Blood Meridian; or, The Evening Redness in the West* (1985; New York, Random House, 1992), 250; Jordan Carson, "Drawing Fire from the Text: Narrative and Morality in *Blood Meridian*," *The Cormac McCarthy Journal* 12 (2014): 20–38.

13. Bret Easton Ellis, *Less Than Zero* (1985; New York: Vintage Contemporaries, 1998), 187, 188.

14. Sander Gilman, *Difference and Pathology: Stereotypes of Sexuality, Race, and Madness* (Ithaca, NY: Cornell University Press, 1985), 127, quoted in Joshua L. Charlson, "Ethnicity, Power and the Postmodern in Saul Bellow's *Mr. Sammler's Planet*," *The Centennial Review* 41, no. 3 (1997): 532.

15. Joan Didion, *Play It As It Lays* (1970; New York: Washington Square Press, 1978), 165–166.

16. Carl Hiaasen, *Double Whammy* (New York: G. P. Putnam's Sons, 1987), 155.

17. Walker Percy, *Love in the Ruins: The Adventures of a Bad Catholic at a Time Near the End of the World* (New York: Farrar, Straus & Giroux, 1971), 17, 167.

18. William Kennedy, *Ironweed* (New York: The Viking Press, 1983), 25.

19. Jay Ellis, "'What Happens to Country' in *Blood Meridian*," *Rocky Mountain Review of Languages and Literature* 60, no. 1 (2006): 85.

20. Thomas Pynchon, *The Crying of Lot 49* (Philadelphia: J. B. Lippincott Co., 1966), 124

21. Ibid., 178; there are also hints, and adamant denials, that one of Inverarity's companies, Beaconfield, used human bones in its filter cigarettes.

22. Quoted in Thomas Blues, "The Moral Structure of *Catch-22*," *Studies in the Novel* 3, no. 1 (1971): 64.

23. Joseph Heller, *Catch-22* (New York: Dell Publishing Co., 1961), 15, 88, 329.

24. Richard Yates, *Revolutionary Road* (Boston: Little, Brown and Company, 1961), 330.

25. E. L. Doctorow, *Ragtime* (1975; Toronto: Bantam Books, 1976), 153, 155, 158.

26. DeLillo, *White Noise*, 111, 115, 130, 205, 228, 279, 280, 299.

27. Rosalind Rosenberg, *Divided Lives: American Women in the Twentieth Century*, revised ed. (New York: Hill and Wang, 2008), 180–244; Diana Furchtgott-Roth, *Women's Figures: An Illustrated Guide to the Economic Progress of Women in America* (Washington, DC: AEI Press, 2012), 1–52, 139–176.

28. Heller, *Catch-22*, 221.

29. Vonnegut, *Slaughterhouse-Five*, 147.

30. Jordan J. Dominy, "Walker Percy's *Love in the Ruins* and the Modern Conservative Identity," *The Southern Literary Journal* 47, no. 2 (2015): 115.

31. Pynchon, *Crying of Lot 49*, 138.

32. Charles Portis, *True Grit* (New York: Simon & Schuster, 1968), 215.

33. Saul Bellow, *Mr. Sammler's Planet* (New York: The Viking Press, 1970), 16.

34. Doctorow, *Ragtime*, 126.

35. Toni Morrison, *Beloved* (New York: Alfred A. Knopf, 1987), 273.

36. Louisa Erdrich, *Love Medicine* (1984; New York: Harper Perennial, 1993), 218.

37. Laura L. Mielke, "'The Saga of the Third World Belle': Resurrecting the Ethnic Woman in Ishmael Reed's *Flight to Canada*," *MELUS* 32, no. 1 (2007): 3–27, quotation on 21.

38. Michael S. Kimmel, "The Contemporary 'Crisis' of Masculinity in Historical Perspective," in *The Making of Masculinities: The New Men's Studies*, ed. Harry Brod (Boston: Unwin Hyman, 1987), 121–53; Richard L. Ochberg, "The Male Career Code and the

Ideology of Role," in *Making of Masculinities*, 173–91; Jennifer Lemon, "'Masculinity in Crisis?'" *Agenda: Empowering Women for Gender Equalilty* 24 (1995): 61–71.

39. Pynchon, *Crying of Lot 49*, 15.

40. Sally Robinson, "'Unyoung, Unpoor, Unblack': John Updike and the Construction of Middle American Masculinity," *Modern Fiction Studies* 44, no. 2 (1998): 331–63.

41. Erich Segal, *Love Story* (New York: Harper & Row, 1970), 13, 15.

42. Pat Conroy, *The Prince of Tides* (1986; New York: The Dial Press, 2005), 471, 663.

43. Morrison, *Beloved*, 48.

44. Saul Bellow, *Herzog* (New York: The Viking Press, 1964), 225–26.

45. Bellow, *Mr. Sammler's Planet*, 32, 60.

46. Philip Roth, *Portnoy's Complaint* (New York: Random House, 1969), 13, 172.

47. Percy, *Love in the Ruins*, 15–16.

48. John Updike, *Rabbit Redux* (New York: Alfred A. Knopf, 1971), 208.

49. Doctorow, *Ragtime*, 212.

50. McCarthy, *Blood Meridian*, 235.

51. Conroy, *Prince of Tides*, 7, 9.

52. Kevin B. Smith, "The Politics of Punishment: Evaluating Political Explanations of Incarceration Rates," *The Journal of Politics* 66, no. 3 (2004): 925–938, quotation on 934; Dan Baum, "Legalize It All: How to Win the War on Drugs," *Harper's* 332, no. 1991 (April 2016), 22, 24–32; https://www.macrotrends.net/2508/unemployment-rate-by-race; Patrick A. Langan, *Race of Prisoners Admitted to State and Federal Institutions, 1926–1986* (US Department of Justice, NCJ-125618, May 1991); Ibram X. Kendi, *How to Be an Antiracist* (New York: One World, 2019), 183–85.

53. Herbert G. Gutman, *The Black Family in Slavery and Freedom, 1750–1925* (New York: Vintage Books, 1976), 461–67.

54. Alice Walker, *The Third Life of Grange Copeland* (1970; New York: Pocket Books, 1988), 80, 342.

55. Jacqueline Bobo, "Sifting Through the Controversy: Reading *The Color Purple*," *Callaloo* 39 (1989): 337; Kimberly Springer, "Third Wave Black Feminism?" *Signs* 27, no. 4 (2002): 1059, 1074–75.

56. James Berger, "Ghosts of Liberalism: Morrison's *Beloved* and the Moynihan Report," *PMLA* 111, no. 3 (1996): 408–20.

57. Toni Morrison, *The Bluest Eye* (1970; London: Picador, 1990), 35.

58. Walker, *Grange Copeland*, 111–12.

59. Ibid., 198.

60. Morrison, *Bluest Eye*, 164.

61. Ishmael Reed, *Flight to Canada* (New York: Avon Books, 1977), 162.

62. Morrison, *Beloved*, 255; Berger, "Ghosts of Liberalism," 416.

63. Diana B. Elliott, Kristy Krivickas, Matthew W. Brault, and Rose M. Kreider, *Historical Marriage Trends from 1890–2010: A Focus on Race Difference*, SEHSD Working Paper, no. 2012-12 (2012), 18, 19.

64. Didion, *Play It As it Lays*, 2, 4; Chip Rhodes, "The Hollywood Novel: Gender and Lacanian Tragedy in Joan Didion's *Play It As It Lays*," *Style* 34, no. 1 (2000): 134.

65. Walker, *Grange Copeland*, 181.

66. Barbara E. Cooper, "Milkman's Search for Family in Toni Morrison's *Song of Solomon*," *College Language Association* 33, no. 2 (1989): 145–156, quotation on 156.

67. Erdrich, *Love Medicine*, 65, 227.

68. Pepe Karmel, "The Negro Artist's Dilemma: Bearden, Picasso, and Pop Art," *Studies in the History of Art* 71, Symposium Papers 48 (2011): 249–68; Gerard Malanga, "A Conversation with Andy Warhol," *The Print Collector's Newsletter* 1, no. 6 (1971): 125–27; Erika Doss, *American Art of the 20th–21st Centuries* (New York: Oxford University Press, 2017), 151–67, 203–16; Robert Hughes, *American Visions: The Epic History of Art in America* (New York: Alfred A. Knopf, 1997), 518–20.

69. Arthur C. Danto, *The Philosophical Disenfranchisement of Art* (New York: Columbia University Press, 1986), x–xv, 81–115, 187–210, quotations on x, 81, 210; David Carrier, "The Era of Post-Historical Art," *Leonardo* 20, no. 3 (1987): 269–72.

70. Rosalind Krauss, "Overcoming the Limits of Matter: On Revising Minimalism," in *American Art of the 1960s*, ed. James Leggio and Susan Weiley (New York: Harry N. Abrams, 1991), 122–41, quotation on 125; Hughes, *American Visions*, 558–62; Doss, *American Art*, 175–81.

71. Malanga, "Conversation with Andy Warhol," 127, quotes Warhol; Hughes, *American Visions*, 539–41; Tilman Osterwold, *Pop Art* (Cologne, Germany: Taschen, 1991), 168–77; Elizabeth Athens, "Andy Warhol's Production Kitchen," *Gastronomica* 9, no. 2 (2009): 45–50.

72. Donald B. Kuspit, "Pop Art: A Reactionary Realism," *Art Journal* 36, no. 1 (1976): 31–38, quotation on 33.

73. Osterwold, *Pop Art*, 172–77, quotation on 174; Doss, *American Art*, 167.

74. Robert Slifkin, *Out of Time: Philip Guston and the Refiguration of Postwar American Art* (Berkeley: University of California Press, 2013), 22, 78–79, 97–98, 108–9, quotations on 22. For the conflict over his Klan paintings, see "Why Philip Guston Can Still Provoke Such Furor, and Passion," *New York Times*, October 2, 2020, https://www.nytimes.com/2020/10/02/arts/design/guston-painter-career.html; Susan Tallman, "Philip Guston's Discomfort Zone," *New York Review of Books* 68, no. 1 (2021): 12–15.

75. Kaluma ya Salaam, "Historical Overviews of The Black Arts Movement BAM," October Gallery, April 25, 2012, https://octobergallery.com/2012/04/25/historical-overviews-of-the-black-arts-movement/

76. Laurie A. Rodrigues, "'SAMO© as an Escape Clause': Jean-Michel Basquiat's Engagement with a Commodified American Africanism," *Journal of American Studies* 45, no. 2 (2011):227–43, quotation on 234.

77. Linda Nochlin, "Why Have There Been No Great Women Artists?" *Art News* 69 (1971): 22–39, 67–70, quotation on 25.

78. "The Dinner Party by Judy Chicago," https://www.brooklynmuseum.org/exhibitions/dinner_party.

79. Renee Sandell, "Female Aesthetics: The Women's Art Movement and Its Aesthetic Split," *The Journal of Aesthetic Education* 14, no. 4 (1980): 106–110, quotation on 107; Doss, *American Art*, 208; Hughes, *American Visions*, 548, 587–90.

Chapter 10

1. Heidi Juliavits, "Interview with Jennifer Egan," *Bomb* 112 (2010): 85, 86; Jaron Lanier, *You Are Not a Gadget: A Manifesto* (New York: Vintage Books, 2010, 2011), introduction to the paperback edition, x; Alexander Moran, *Understanding Jennifer Egan* (Columbia: University of South Carolina Press, 2021), 47–60. This exchange continued when Egan and Lanier shared the stage for a City Arts Lecture, April 18, 2022, https://podcasts.apple.com/ca/podcast/city-arts-lectures/id1436346407?i'1000561476977.

2. "2017 Economic Report of the President," https://obamawhitehouse.archives.gov/administration/eop/cea/economic-report-of-the-President/2017; "The Clinton-Gore Administration: A Record of Progress," https://clintonwhitehouse5.archives.gov/WH/Accomplishments/eightyears-03.html.

3. Michael Perelman, "Retrospectives: Schumpeter, David Wells, and Creative Destruction," *The Journal of Economic Perspectives* 9, no. 3 (1995): 189–97.

4. Economic Policy Institute, "The Productivity-Pay Gap," July 2019, https://www.epi.org/productivity-pay-gap/; Greg N. Gregoriou and Luc Renneboog, "Understanding Mergers and Acquisitions: Activity since 1990," in *International M&A Activity Since 1990: Recent Research and Quantitative Analysis* (Amsterdam: Elsevier Finance, 2007), 1–20; Investopedia, "Who Killed Sears? Fifty Years on the Road to Ruin," July 1, 2019, https://www.investopedia.com/news/downfall-of-sears/; John Weir Close, *A Giant Cow-Tipping by Savages: The Boom, Bust, and Boom Culture of M&A* (New York: Palgrave Macmillan, 2013).

5. Congressional Research Service, "Real Wage Trends, 1979 to 2018," July 23, 2019, https://crsreports.congress.gov, R45090; Economic Policy Institute, "CEO compensation has grown 940% since 1978," August 14, 2019, https://www.epi.org/publication/ceo-compensation-2018/; Stanford Center on Poverty & Inequality, "20 Facts About U.S. Inequality that Everyone Should Know," 2011, https://inequality.stanford.edu/publications/20-facts-about-us-inequality-everyone-should-know; US Census Bureau, "Income Inequality," https://www.census.gov/topics/income-poverty/income-inequality/about.html.

6. Corporate data from *Fortune Magazine*. In 2021, labor shortages would improve conditions for some of these workers; Gad Levanon, "Why Wages are Growing Rapidly—Both Now and in the Future," *Forbes*, July 26, 2021.

7. Loïc Wacquant, *Punishing the Poor: The Neoliberal Government of Social Insecurity* (Durham, NC: Duke University Press, 2009), 41–75; United States Census Bureau, "Income and Poverty in the United States: 2018," September 10, 2019, Report #P60–266.

8. OECD Data, "Income inequality," https://data.oecd.org/inequality/income-inequality.htm. The American Rescue Plan, signed into law, March 11, 2021, temporarily strengthened the safety net for the least wealthy Americans.

9. Jonathan Franzen, *The Corrections* (Toronto: HarperCollins, 2001), 155, 443–44; James Annesley, "Market Corrections: Jonathan Franzen and the 'Novel of Globalization,'" *Journal of Modern Literature* 29, no. 2 (2006): 111–28; Ty Hawkins, "'A Smile and a Shoeshine': From F. Scott Fitzgerald to Jonathan Franzen, By Way of Arthur Miller: The American Dream in *The Great Gatsby*, *Death of a Salesman*, and *The Corrections*," *The Arthur Miller Journal* 2, no. 1 (2007): 49–68.

10. Ann Pancake, *Strange as this Weather Has Been* (Berkeley, CA: Counterpoint, 2007), 165.

11. Richard Powers, *Gain* (New York: Farrar, Strauss Giroux, 1998), 261

12. Ralph Clare, *Fictions Inc.: The Corporation in Postmodern Fiction, Film, and Popular Culture* (New Brunswick, NJ: Rutgers University Press, 2014), 159.

13. Jennifer Egan, *A Visit from the Goon Squad* (2010; New York: Anchor Books, 2011), 22–23. Egan continues the story of Salazar and the changing music business in *The Candy House: A Novel* (New York: Scribner, 2022).

14. Gary Shteyngart, *Lake Success* (New York: Random House, 2018), 159.

15. Ben Fountain, *Billy Lynn's Long Halftime Walk* (New York: HarperCollins, 2012), 131.

16. Bret Easton Ellis, *American Psycho* (New York: Vintage Books, 1991).

17. Thomas Pynchon, *Inherent Vice* (New York: Penguin Books, 2009), 7.

18. Kenneth L. Kusmer, *Down & Out, on the Road: The Homeless in American History* (New York: Oxford University Press, 2002), 3–12, 57–72, 239–47.

19. Sharada Balachandran Orihuela, "'Between Ownership and the Highway': Property, Persons, and Freeways in Karen Tei Yamashita's *Tropic of Orange*," *Journal of American Studies* 55, no. 4 (2021): 755–79.

20. David Foster Wallace, *Infinite Jest* (New York: Little, Brown and Company, 1996), 621, 948.

21. Shteyngart, *Lake Success*, 263.

22. Junot Diaz, "Apocalypse: What Disasters Reveal," *Boston Review*, May/June 2011.

23. Pancake, *Weather*, 239–40.

24. Díaz, *Oscar Wao*, 23.

25. Karen Tei Yamashita, *Tropic of Orange* (Minneapolis: Coffee House Press, 1997), 49, italics in original; Wenjia Chen, "Impasse, Time, Infrastructure: Politics of Reinhabitation in Karen Tei Yamashita's Petroapocalyptic Fictions," *Studies in American Fiction* 48, no. 1 (2021): 105–26.

26. Elliott Holt, *You Are One of Them* (New York: The Penguin Press, 2013), 290, italics in original.

27. Wallace, *Infinite Jest*, 58, 218.

28. Crawford Gribben, "Rapture Fictions and the Changing Evangelical Condition," *Literature and Theology* 18, no. 1 (2004): 89, quotes Jerry Jenkins and Tim LaHaye, *Nicolae, Left Behind*, vol. 3 (Carol Stream, IL: Tyndale House Publishers, 1997); Sherryll Mleynek, "The Rhetoric of the 'Jewish Problem' in the *Left Behind* Novels," *Literature and Theology* 19, no. 4 (2005): 370.

29. E. Annie Proulx, *The Shipping News* (New York: Simon & Schuster, 1993), 276, 290.

30. Richard Ford, *Independence Day* (New York: Vintage Books, 1995), 3, 451; Kathy

Knapp, "Richard Ford's Frank Bascombe Trilogy and the Post-9/11 Suburban Novel," *American Literary History* 23, no. 3 (2011): 500–28, quotation on 513.

31. Elizabeth Strout, *Olive Kitteridge* (New York: Random House, 2008), 43.

32. Barbara Kingsolver, *Pigs in Heaven* (New York: HarperCollins, 1993), 272.

33. Kathleen Godfrey, "Barbara Kingsolver's Cherokee Nation: Problems of Representation in *Pigs in Heaven*," *Western American Literature* 36, no. 3 (2001): 258–77, quotation on 266.

34. Amor Towles's bestselling novel, *A Gentleman in Moscow* (New York: Viking, 2016), fits well in this category. Under house arrest in the Hotel Metropol, Count Alexander Rostov maintains his courtly, cheerful demeanor, while revolutions, wars, and purges swirl around him.

35. US Bureau of the Census, "Percentage and Number of Children Living with Two Parents Has Dropped Since 1968," April 12, 2021, https://www.census.gov/library/stories/2021/04/.

36. Kingsolver, *Pigs in Heaven*, 12.

37. George Saunders, *Lincoln in the Bardo* (New York: Random House, 2017), 61.

38. Cormac McCarthy, *The Road* (New York: Alfred A. Knopf, 2006), 64.

39. Jeanine Cummins, *American Dirt* (New York: Flatiron Books, 2020), 295; Ignacio M. Sánchez Prado, "Commodifying Mexico: On *American Dirt* and the Cultural Politics of a Manufactured Bestseller," *American Literary History* 33, no. 2 (2021): 371–93, explores the controversy surrounding the novel, as does Pamela Paul, "The Long Shadow of 'American Dirt,'" *New York Times*, January 26, 2023, https://www.nytimes.com/2023/01/26/opinion/american-dirt-book-publishing.html.

40. Dorothy Allison, *Bastard Out of Carolina* (New York: Dutton, 1992), 307.

41. Junot Díaz, *The Brief Wondrous Life of Oscar Wao* (New York: Riverhead Books, 2007), 58.

42. Arlie Russell Hochschild, *Strangers in Their Own Land: Anger and Mourning on the American Right* (New York: New Press, 2016); Pew Research Center, "Religious Landscape Study," 2014, https://www.pewforum.org/religious-landscape-study.

43. Mleynek, "Rhetoric of the 'Jewish Problem,'" 381; Peter Ralph and James Larue, "Christian Fiction Labels: Help or Hindrance?" *American Libraries* 36, no. 11 (2005): 50–51; Marnie Jones, "'Spiritual Warfare' and Intolerance in Popular Culture: The *Left Behind* Franchise, the Commodification of Belief, and the Consequences for Imagination," *Studies in Popular Culture* 32, no. 1 (2009): 1–19; Paul C. Gutjahr, "No Longer Left Behind: Amazon.com, Reader-Response, and the Changing Fortunes of the Christian Novel in America," *Book History* 5 (2002): 209–36.

44. Jesmyn Ward, *Sing, Unburied, Sing* (New York: Scribner, 2017), 236.

45. McCarthy, *Road*, 4, 65, 143, 145.

46. Richard Russo, *Empire Falls* (New York: Vintage Books, 2001), 330.

47. Edward P. Jones, *The Known World* (New York: HarperCollins, 2003), 140.

48. Wallace, *Infinite Jest*, 40.

49. Pancake, *Weather*, 74.

50. Fountain, *Billy Lynn*, 46; Pew Research Center, "In U.S., Decline of Christianity

Continues at Rapid Pace," https://www.pewforum.org/2019/10/17/in-u-s-decline-of-christianity-continues-at-rapid-pace/

51. Allison, *Bastard*, 152.

52. See the tables in Department of Homeland Security, "2017 Yearbook of Immigration Statistics: Office of Immigration Statistics," https://www.dhs.gov/sites/default/files/publications/yearbook_immigration_statistics_2017_0.pdf.; Dorothee Schneider, *Crossing Borders: Migration and Citizenship in the Twentieth-Century United States* (Cambridge, MA: Harvard University Press, 2011), 214–50; Otis L. Graham Jr., *Unguarded Gates: A History of America's Immigration Crisis* (Lanham, MD: Rowhan & Littlefield, 2004), 87–133.

53. A shady business venture with a supply chain that sells to the rich and depends on underpaid workers lies at the heart of Lee's recent work, *My Year Abroad* (2021).

54. US Department of Labor, "Women in the Labor Force," https://www.dol.gov/wb/stats/NEWSTATS/facts.htm#WomenLF; Sarah Green Carmichael, "Gender Equality Starts in the Laundry Room," August 26, 2019, *Bloomberg Opinion*, https://www.bloomberg.com/opinion/articles/2019-08-26/gender-equality-in-the-boardroom-starts-in-the-laundry-room.

55. Quoted in R. Claire Snyder, "What is Third-Wave Feminism? A New Directions Essay," *Signs* 34, no. 1 (2008): 178.

56. Susan J. Carroll and Richard L. Fox, "Introduction: Gender and Electoral Politics in the Twenty-First Century," in *Gender and Elections*, 1–14; "Women Members by Congress," *History, Art & Archives*, United States House of Representatives, https://history.house.gov/Exhibitions-and-Publications/WIC/Historical-Data/Women-Members-by-Congress/; Ashwini Tambe, "The Women's March on Washington: Words from an Organizer: An Interview with Mrinalini Chakraborty," *Feminist Studies*, 43.1 (2017): 223–229; Susan Chira, "Donald Trump's Gift to Feminism: The Resistance," *Daedalus*, 149.1 (2020): 72–83; Jo Reger, "Finding a Place in History: The Discursive Legacy of the Wave Metaphor and Contemporary Feminism," *Feminist Studies* 43, no. 1 (2017): 193–221.

57. Catalyst, "Pyramid: Women in S&P 500 Companies," September 1, 2019, https://www.catalyst.org/research/women-in-sp-500-companies/; *Business Insider*, "7 charts that show the glaring bap between men and women's salaries in the US," https://www.businessinsider.com/gender-wage-pay-gap-charts-2017-3; Pew Research Center, "The narrowing, but persistent, gender gap in pay," March 22, 2019, https://www.pewresearch.org/fact-tank/2019/03/22/gender-pay-gap-facts/

58. Philip Roth, *American Pastoral* (New York: Vintage Books, 1997), 160.

59. Allison, *Bastard*, 91.

60. Pancake, *Weather*, 133, italics in original.

61. Kingsolver, *Pigs in Heaven*, 3.

62. Cormac McCarthy, *All the Pretty Horses* (1992; New York: Vintage Books, 1993), 230.

63. Jones, *Known World*, 130.

64. Allison, *Bastard*, 179, 263; Rachel Walerstein, "Recomposing the Self: Joyful Shame in Dorothy Allison's *Bastard Out of Carolina*," *Mosaic: An Interdisciplinary Critical Journal* 49, no. 4 (2016): 169–83.

65. Eric Murphy Selinger, "Review: Rereading the Romance," *Contemporary Literature* 48, no. 2 (2007): 307–24, quotes Greer 310; Melissa F. Zeiger, "'Less than Perfect': Negotiating Breast Cancer in Popular Romance Novels," *Tulsa Studies in Women's Literature* 32/33, no. 2/1 (2013–14): 107–28; Lynn S. Neal, *Romancing God: Evangelical Women and Inspirational Fiction* (Chapel Hill: University of North Carolina Press, 2006); Glen Thomas, "Romance: The Perfect Creative Industry? A Case Study of Harlequin-Mills and Boon Australia," in *Empowerment versus Oppression: Twenty-First Century Views of Popular Romance Novels*, ed. Sally Goade (Newcastle, UK: Cambridge Scholars, 2007), 20–29, quotations on 26, 28.

66. Emma Hagquist, "Toward Gender Equality in Practice? Cross-National Patterns of Change in the Gendered Division of Housework Over Two Decades," *Journal of Comparative Family Studies* 49, no. 3 (2018), 355–77.

67. Michael Kimmel, *Manhood in America: A Cultural History*, 4th ed. (New York: Oxford University Press, 2018), 275; Richard Reeves, *Of Boys and Men: Why the Modern Male is Struggling, Why It Matters, and What to Do about it* (Washington, DC: Brookings Institution Press, 2022).

68. Allison, *Bastard*, 23; Vincent King, "Hopeful Grief: The Prospect of a Postmodernist Feminism in Allison's *Bastard Out of Carolina*," *The Southern Literary Journal* 33, no. 1 (2000): 122–40; Kathleen McDonald, "Talking Back: Resistance to Stereotypes in Dorothy Allison's *Bastard Out of Carolina*," *Women's Studies Quarterly* 26, no. 1/2 (1998): 15–25.

69. Pancake, *Weather*, 133, italics in original.

70. Terry McMillan, *Waiting to Exhale* (New York: Viking, 1992), 332, italics added.

71. Kingsolver, *Pigs in Heaven*, 3.

72. Ellis, *American Psycho*, 376–77, italics in original.

73. Don DeLillo, *Falling Man* (New York: Scribner, 2007), 197.

74. Russo, *Empire Falls*, 126.

75. D. G. Meyers, "Michael Chabon's Imaginary Jews," *The Sewanee Review* 116, no. 4 (2008): 572–88, quotation on 574.

76. Margaret Wrinkle, *Wash* (New York: Atlantic Monthly Press, 2013), 139, 204.

77. Allison, *Bastard*, 86.

78. Saunders, *Lincoln in the Bardo*, 312.

79. Karen Russell, *Swamplandia!* (New York: Alfred A. Knopf, 2011), 200.

80. James Patterson, National Humanities Medal, 2019, https://www.neh.gov/award/james-patterson; James Patterson, biography, http://www.jamespatterson.com/biography.

81. Benjamin P. Bowser, *The Black Middle Class: Social Mobility—and Vulnerability* (Boulder, CO: Lynne Rienner, 2006), traces the origins of this group back to Reconstruction.

82. Touré, *Who's Afraid of Post-Blackness? What It Means to Be Black Now* (New York: Free Press, 2011), 200–201; Nigel I. Malcolm, "Slaves to the Community: Blacks and the Rhetoric of 'Selling Out,'" *Journal of African American Studies* 19, no. 2 (2015): 120–34; Barack Obama, *The Promised Land* (New York: Crown, 2020), 11–14, 41, shares that optimism.

83. Thabiti Lewis, "Bigger Still Haunts the American Imagination and Black Reality: Art with Purpose," *CLA Journal* 58, no. 3/4 (2015): 191–211, quotation on 205; K. Merinda Simmons, "Introduction: The Dubious Stage of Post-Blackness—Performing Otherness,

Conserving Dominance," in *The Trouble with Post-Blackness*, ed. Houston A. Baker and K. Merinda Simmons (New York: Columbia University Press, 2015), 1–20.

84. Tayari Jones, *An American Marriage* (New York: HarperCollins, 2018), 218.

85. McMillan, *Waiting to Exhale*, 184, 195.

86. Shauna Morgan Kirlew, "A Problematic Agency: The Power of Capital and a Burgeoning Black Middle Class in Edward P. Jones's *The Known World*," *South Atlantic Review* 79, nos. 1–2 (2014): 68–87, quotation on 69.

87. Ward, *Sing, Unburied, Sing*, 188.

88. Colson Whitehead, *The Underground Railroad* (New York: Doubleday, 2016), 33–34, 152–53.

89. Arthur Danto, "I'll Be Your Mirror," *The Nation*, May 1, 2006, 40; Erika Doss, *American Art of the 20th-21st Centuries* (New York: Oxford University Press, 2017), 288; Royal Academy of Arts, *USA Today: New American Art from the Saatchi Gallery* (London: Royal Academy of Arts, 2006), 11, provides a similar assessment.

90. *USA Today*, 34–45, 60–69, 244–47, 378–93; Rose G. Salseda, "The New Wave of Identity Politics: Juan Capistran's *White Minority*," *American Art* 28, no. 1 (2014): 24–31. All artists discussed in this section have their own web sites.

91. Ten of the forty artists profiled in *USA Today* were born outside the United States.

92. Mark A. Watson, "Jimmie Durham's *Building a Nation*: Across Post-Indian, Post-American Modernities," *American Art* 28, no. 1 (2014): 16–24; "When I Remember I See Red: American Indian Art and Activism in California," *Journal of American History* 108, no. 3 (2021): 568–71; Jessica L. Horton, "Seeing the National Museum of the American Indian Anew as a Diplomatic Assemblage," *American Art* 36, no. 3 (2022): 5–9.

93. Touré, *Post-Blackness*, 8, quotes Wiley.

94. Jessica L. Horton and Cherise Smith, "The Particulars of Postidentity," *American Art* 28, no. 1 (2014): 2–8; Doss, *American Art*, 313–19; Valerie J. Mercer et al., "Diversity of Contemporary African American Art," *Bulletin of the Detroit Institute of Arts* 86, no. 1/4 (2012): 88–123; see the websites of the artists mentioned; Zadie Smith, "What Do We Want History to Do to Us?" *New York Review of Books* 67, no. 3 (2020): 10–14, considers Kara Walker's art.

95. Julia Halperin and Charlotte Burns, "Museums Claim They're Paying More Attention to Female Artists. That's an Illusion," September 19, 2019, https://news.artnet.com/womens-place-in-the-art-world; Jill Fields, "Frontiers in Feminist Art History," *Frontiers: A Journal of Women Studies* 33, no. 2 (2012): 1–21; Derek Conrad Murray, "Mickalene Thomas: Afro-Kitsch and the Queering of Blackness," *American Art* 28, no. 1 (2014): 9–15; Angela Flournoy, "Mother of Invention: How the Artist Mickalene Thomas Lovingly Reconceives the Female Form," *New York Times Magazine*, October 17, 2021, 40–53; of the forty artists featured in *USA Today*, only nine are women.

Conclusion

1. The nineteenth-century works can be downloaded as free ebooks from www.gutenberg.org.

2. See the discussion in the introduction, particularly notes 17, 22, and 23.

INDEX

Page numbers in **boldface** refer to paintings and Ngram graphs. Ngram search terms are listed in *italics*.

abstract expressionism, 85, 175–77
Adams, Henry, 105
Adams, John, 21
Adams, Rachel, 182–83
Addams, Jane, 110
adultery and extramarital relations, 120–22
African American writers and artists, 6; artists, 207, 209, 235–36; assimilation and rebellion dialogue, 67–69; counterpoint to dominant (White) themes, 5, 66–69, 125–26; during genteel era, 84; humor and hard times, 148–49, 155–56; in late modern era, 174–75; in modern era/Harlem Renaissance, 6, 133, 153–56, 239, 280n67; naturalist school, 112, 115; portrayal of Blacks by Blacks, 67, 125–26, 151, 197–98, 200, 201–4, 229, 230, 232–34. *See also* race and racism; slavery; *individual writers and artists*
agriculture, 62, 138, 143–44; rural society, 27, 62, 76–77, 138. *See also* small-town society

Ako-Adjei, Naa Baako, 174
Alcott, Amos Bronson, 76
Alcott, Louisa May, 226; on *Huckleberry Finn*, 93; *Jo's Boys*, 96–97, 100; *Little Men*, 97, 99; *Little Women*, 3, 29, 64, 74, 76, 183; *Work*, 100
Aldrich, Thomas Bailey: *The Story of a Bad Boy*, 76
Allison, Dorothy: *Bastard Out of Carolina*, 221, 223, 227, 228, 229, 231
Allston, Washington, 29, 31; *Elijah in the Desert*, **42**, 43; *Tragic Figure in Chains*, 43
American Bible Society, 51–52
American middle class. *See* middle class
Ammons, Elizabeth, 69
Anthony, Susan B., 54, 71
anxiety, 165, 166–68, 177
apocalypse, 190, 217; graph, **191**
Applegate, Debby, 10
Armory Show (1913), 129–30, 136
art. *See* painting
Ashcan School, 127–30
asshole, 181; graph, **181**

baby boom, 163, 166, 169
babysitter, 204; graph, **204**

Bachinger, Katrina, 85
Baldwin, James, 161–62; *Giovanni's Room*, 169, 173; *Go Tell It on the Mountain*, 174–75; on Kerouac's *On the Road*, 174
Balter, Ariel, 122
Baptists, 51
Bardes, Barbara, 55, 98–99
Barth, John, 180
Barthelme, Donald, 180
Basquiat, Jean-Michel, 182, 209–10
Baur, John, 78
Bearden, Romare, 182, 209; *The Art of Assemblage*, 207
Bederman, Gail, 117, 125
Beecher, Catharine, 98; *A Treatise on Domestic Economy*, 50
Bell, Daniel, 162
Bell, Robert, 25; *Miscellanies for Sentimentalists*, 25–26
Bellow, Saul: *The Adventures of Augie March*, 166, 170, 190–91, 198; *Henderson the Rain King*, 167, 190–91, 198; *Herzog*, 191, 196–97, 199, 200; *Mr. Sammler's Planet*, 191, 196–97, 199, 200
Bellows, George, 129; *Cliff Dwellers*, **127**
Benton, Lori: *Burning Sky*, 222, 228
Benton, Thomas Hart, 157–58, 176–77; *America Today* mural, 158; *The Arts of Life in America* mural, 158
Bercovitch, Sacvan, 3–4
Berger, James, 204
betray, 36; graph, **36**
Beye, Charles, 152
Bible, 52
Bierstadt, Albert, 27, 77, 79–80; *The Rocky Mountains*, **79**
Bishop, Isabel, 158
black middle class, 187–88; graph, **188**
Blumin, Stuart, 10
Bode, Carl, 168
Boston Chronicle, 24
Boutwell, George, 62
Boydston, Jeanne, 49, 53

Brackenridge, Hugh Henry: *Modern Chivalry*, 35, 40
Braden, Thomas W., 177
Branson, Matthew: *Other People's Money*, 234; *People Who Divide People*, 234
Brodhead, Richard, 74
Brooke, Henry: *The Fool of Quality*, 26
Brooks, Van Wyck, 82
brotherhood, 227; graph, **226**
Brown, Charles Brockden, 11, 31, 35, 40, 266n38; *Arthur Mervyn*, 35; *Edgar Huntly*, 34, 35, 41–42; *Jane Talbot*, 34, 40; *Ormond*, 34, 35–36, 37–38, 39, 40; *Wieland*, 35, 40
Brown, William Hill: *The Power of Sympathy*, 22, 27, 37, 38, 39, 183
Brown, William Wells, 66; *Clotel*, 67, 68
Browne, James R., 164
Buck, Pearl S.: *The Good Earth*, 143
Burnett, Frances Hodgson: *Little Lord Fauntleroy*, 84, 97
Burney, Frances: *Evelina*, 26
Burroughs, Edgar Rice: *Tarzan of the Apes*, 116, 118, 125
business: big business and bureaucracies, 62–65, 80, 88–89, 162–63, 186, 187, 192–95, 212–13; civilization/culture of, 4, 131, 133–35, 136, 137, 142, 146–49, 192–95, 209; culture of in painting, 156–60; disdain for, 48, 161, 164–66, 179, 192–95, 234; from local to national market, 88; small units of production, 47. *See also* economy

Cable, George Washington: *The Grandissimes*, 96, 100, 124, 238
Cain, James M.: *The Postman Always Rings Twice*, 148, 150
Caldwell, Erskine, 112; *Tobacco Road*, 143, 150
Calvert, Karin, 20, 21
Cambridge History of American Literature, 13, 135

Cambridge History of the Novel, 13
Capistran, Juan: *Sympathy for the Devil*, 234
capitalism: community as antidote, 145; contradictory values, 48, 94, 194–95; department stores, 89; finance capitalists, 212–13; poverty and, 213; race and, 233; regulation of, 111; unregulated, 116, 213–15; women and, 37. *See also* business
Carnegie, Dale, 134; *How to Win Friends and Influence People*, 139
Carpenter, Frederic, 85
Cather, Willa, 239; naturalism, 112–13; *Death Comes for the Archbishop*, 142, 238; *My Ántonia*, 116, 122, 123; *O Pioneers!*, 115, 123
Chabon, Michael: *The Amazing Adventures of Kavalier and Clay*, 226, 230; *Mysteries of Pittsburgh*, 230; *Wonder Boys*, 230
chambers of commerce, 133, 137
Chandler, Raymond: *The Big Sleep*, 148
character (compared to *personality*), 56, 134; graph, **135**
Charles, Michael Ray, 235–36
Chesnutt, Charles, 84; *The Marrow of Tradition*, 6, 125–26, 154, 202
Chicago, Judy: *The Dinner Party*, 210
Chicago Art Institute, 130
Chicanx art exhibitions, 234
Child, Lydia Maria: on the middle class, 12; Transcendentalism, 76; *Hobomok*, 58
childhood, 75, 205; graph, **75**
children and childhood: child labor laws, 111; childrearing, 20–21, 76; importance in fiction and society, 74–76, 97, 166; maternalism, 73; parent-child bond, 204–6; single mothers, 201–2, 204–5
Chopin, Kate, 84; naturalism, 112–13; *The Awakening*, 6, 115, 119, 120–21, 122
Christianity, 51–52, 70. *See also* religion
Church, Frederic Edwin, 27, 77, 78; *The Heart of the Andes*, 80; *Niagara*, **78**, 78–79
Churchill, Winston: *The Crisis*, 116

Ciscernos, Sandra: *The House on Mango Street*, 224
civil rights movements, 173, 174, 180, 201, 203, 209. *See also* race and racism
Civil War, 4, 63, 67; as end of sentimental era, 29
Clare, Ralph, 214
class, 13, 19, 39, 64; upper class, 18, 23. *See also* middle class; poverty
Clay, Henry, 33, 55
Clemens, Samuel. *See* Twain, Mark
Cockcroft, Eva, 177
COHA database. *See* Corpus of Historical American English
Cole, G. D. H., 10
Cole, Thomas, 27, 77–78, 238; *Niagara Falls*, **77**, 78; *The Oxbow*, 59, **59**
colonial America, 20–21, 23–25
Columbia History of American Literature, 13
Columbia History of the American Novel, 34–35, 135–36
Comment, Kristin, 38
communism, 144–45, 156, 164, 174, 175; socialism, 94–95, 96, 111, 177
conformity, 133, 163; graph, **132**
conformity and criticism of, 133–35, 137, 139, 156–60, 161–66, 173–77
Conroy, Pat: *The Lords of Discipline*, 201; *The Prince of Tides*, 192, 197, 199–200, 201
Cooper, James Fenimore, 27, 28, 41, 238, 266n38; *The Chainbearer*, 48, 53; *The Deerslayer*, 52, 53, 57, 58; *The Last of the Mohicans*, 53, 58; Leatherstocking series, 48, 55–56, 57; Littlepage trilogy, 48; *The Oak Openings*, 52; *The Pathfinder*, 52, 57; *The Pioneers*, 3, 47, 48, 52, 57, 58; *The Prairie*, 47–48; *The Redskins*, 48; *Satanstoe*, 48, 65; *The Sea Lions*, 52; *The Spy*, 65; *The Ways of the Hour*, 55; *The Wing-and-Wing*, 52
Corbin Banking Company, 62
corporate greed, 111, 192, 213; graph, **193**
corporate power, 89, 192, 213; graph, **193**

306 INDEX

Corpus of Historical American English (COHA), 8–9, 56, 58, 75, 205, 239
Crafts, Hannah (Hannah Bond), 66; *The Bondwoman's Narrative*, 67, 68
Crane, Stephen, 112; *Maggie*, 6, 84, 114, 119, 120
Cronon, William, 41
Cummins, Jeanine: *American Dirt*, 220, 228
Cummins, Maria: *The Lamplighter*, 6, 70, 76
Curry, John Steuart, 157

damn, 131; graph, **132**
Danielson, Susan, 126
Danto, Arthur, 207, 234
Darwinism, 113, 114, 117, 121
Davidson, Cathy, 49; *Revolution and the Word*, 29, 37
de Balincourt, Jules: *People Who Play and People Who Pay*, 234; *U.S. World Studies III*, 234
de Beauvoir, Simone: *The Second Sex*, 195
deceit, 36; graph, **36**
Defoe, Daniel: *Robinson Crusoe*, 23
Delany, Martin R., 6; *Blake*, 66–67, 68
DeLillo, Don, 180; *End Zone*, 189; *Falling Man*, 229; *White Noise*, 189–90, 195, 199, 214
D'Emilio, John, 172
democracy, 36–37, 49, 93, 174
Demuth, Charles, 135, 239; *My Egypt*, 156
detective fiction, 148
Diaz, Junot: "Apocalypse: What Disasters Reveal," 217; *The Brief, Wondrous Life of Oscar Wao*, 217, 221, 224, 227
Didion, Joan: *Play It as It Lays*, 191, 205
Dillingham, William, 85
diversity, 224; graph, **132**
Dixon, Thomas: *The Clansman*, 124–25
Doctorow, E. L., 185, 239; *Ragtime*, 5, 185, 194–95, 197, 201
domesticity, 48–51, 53, 55, 57, 61–62, 69, 74; adultery, 119, 120; challenged, 71–73. *See also* maternalism

Dominy, Jordan, 196
Dondero, George, 175
Dos Passos, John: *The 42nd Parallel*, 172; *U.S.A.* trilogy, 146, 151
Doss, Erika, 234
Douglas, Ann, 29
Douglas, Lloyd, 168; *The Big Fisherman*, 168; *The Robe*, 168, 170, 222
Douglass, Frederick, 66; *The Heroic Slave*, 67, 68
Dove, Arthur, 85, 129
Dreiser, Theodore, 6, 84, 112, 239; *An American Tragedy*, 141–42; *The Financier*, 114, 117, 120, 121; *Jennie Gerhardt*, 113, 116, 120, 121; *Sister Carrie*, 12, 114, 115, 117, 120, 121, 123
drunkenness (and *temperance*), 90–91
Duane, Anna Mae, 67
Du Bois, W. E. B., 156; "The Talented Tenth," 126
duCille, Ann, 67
Dunbar, Paul Laurence, 6, 84, 112; *The Sport of the Gods*, 115, 126, 154
Durham, Jimmie: *Building a Nation*, 234

Eakins, Thomas, 7, 85, 103, 105–7, 127, 238; table of portraiture of, 107; *The Courtship*, 106, **106**; *The Gross Clinic*, 105, 275n73; *Walt Whitman*, 107, **107**
economy: affluence and optimism, 132–33; consumerism, 119–20; depressions and, 110, 133, 138–39, 142–46, 153, 156, 163; epoch divisions and, 13–14; genteel era, 81, 83–84, 88–89, 109, 110–11; middle-class culture and evolution of, 1–2, 4, 7, 11–13, 238; modern era, 138–39, 142–43, 162–63; postmodern era, 186–88, 211–13; pre-1800s, 16–26; prosperity of, 161–63; reconfiguring of, 212–13; sentimental era, 31–34, 39, 41, 45–48, 61, 62–64, 77; transportation systems, 33, 46, 63–64, 88, 111. *See also* business; capitalism; middle class
education: of African Americans, 67; girls

and boys compared, 37; of women, 37, 150, 196
Egan, Jennifer, 211; *A Visit from the Goon Squad*, 211, 214, 232, 297n1, 298n13
Eisenhower, Dwight D., 175
Ellis, Bret Easton: *American Psycho*, 215–16, 226, 229, 230, 231; *Less Than Zero*, 190, 192, 205, 215–16
Ellison, Ralph, 161–62; *The Invisible Man*, 3, 169, 174, 235
Emerson, Ralph Waldo: on communing with nature, 41, 57; on the self-reliant male, 56; Transcendentalism, 49, 57, 76, 78; on transportation, 46
Erdrich, Louise: *Love Medicine*, 198, 206
Eustace, Nicole: *Passion Is the Gale*, 21
evangelical Christianity, 51–52, 70, 218, 222, 228
Evans, Augusta J., 72; *St. Elmo*, 73–74, 268n60
executive, 134; graph, **134**

Farrell, James T., 112; *Studs Lonigan* trilogy, 144, 146, 147, 152
father, 50–51; graph, **50**
Faulkner, William, 136; *Absalom, Absalom!*, 153; *The Hamlet*, 146; *Light in August*, 143, 150–51, 153
Feke, Robert: *Isaac Royall and Family*, 20, **20**
feminism, 225; graph, **225**
Ferber, Edna: *Giant*, 171; *So Big*, 140, 146, 151, 159
Fern, Fanny: *Ruth Hall*, 73
Fetterley, Judith, 53
Fiedler, Leslie, 172
Fielding, Henry: *Joseph Andrews*, 23, 26; *Shamela*, 23; *Tom Jones*, 23, 26
Finney, Charles Grandison, 51
Fitzgerald, F. Scott, 85, 136; *The Great Gatsby*, 131, 133, 140, 142, 146–47, 150, 152, 172, 239; *The Last Tycoon*, 144, 146, 153; *Tender Is the Night*, 149, 151; *This Side of Paradise*, 132, 139, 146, 159
Fleissner, Jennifer, 121

Foley, Barbara, 174
Ford, Richard: *Independence Day*, 190, 219–20, 229
Foster, Hannah: *The Coquette*, 22, 34, 37, 38–39
Fountain, Ben: *Billy Lynn's Long Halftime Walk*, 190, 215, 223, 232
Frankenthaler, Helen, 210
Franklin, Benjamin, 10–11, 18, 39; "Advice to a Young Tradesman," 18; *Autobiography*, 15; "Father Abraham's Speech," 17, 18–19; *Pennsylvania Gazette*, 18; *Plain Truth*, 19; *Poor Richard's Almanac*, 17
Franzen, Jonathan: *The Corrections*, 214, 228, 229, 230, 231
Freedman, Estelle B., 172
French, Warren, 145
Friedan, Betty: *The Feminine Mystique*, 195–96
Fromm, Erich: *Man for Himself*, 166–67
fuck, 181; graph, **181**
Fuller, Margaret: *Woman in the Nineteenth Century*, 54
Fulton, Robert, 33

Gaddis, William, 180
Galbraith, John Kenneth: *The New Industrial State*, 187
Gass, William, 180
gays and lesbians, 172–73, 228, 230
gender roles. *See* men and women
genteel era, 81–130; overview, 13–14, 81–86, 87–89, 109–10, 238; African Americans, 93, 112, 115, 122–26, 123–26; children, 97; cities, growth of, 111; class divisions, 97; dating of, 85–86; economic depression, 110; industrialization, 92–97, 111; literature, 89–102, 109, 112–26; men, 101–2, 117–18, 121–22; naturalism, 112–17; natural world, 105; painting, 85, 103–7, 126–30; religion, 83–84, 97; small-town society, 82–83, 89–92, 103–4, 122; women, 98–101, 104, 118–23. *See also* economy

308 INDEX

Gershwin, Ira, 51
Gifford, Sanford Robinson, 77, 80
Gilman, Charlotte Perkins: "The Yellow Wallpaper," 122
Gilman, Sander, 191
Gilmore, Michael, 35
Gilpin, William, 41
Glackens, William, 129
Godey's Lady's Book, 72
Godfrey, Kathleen, 220
Goethe, Johann Wolfgang von: *The Sorrows of Young Werther*, 23, 25, 26
Gold, Michael: *Jews Without Money*, 144, 147, 151, 152
Goldsmith, Oliver: *The Vicar of Wakefield*, 26
Gombrich, E. H., 41
Gonzalez, John, 123
Goodman, Paul: *Growing Up Absurd*, 179
good manners, 29, 81, 84–85. See also genteel era
Gorky, Arshile, 175, 176
Gossett, Suzanne, 55, 98–99
Gottlieb, Adolph, 177
grandparents, 204; graph, **204**
Graydon, Alexander, 24
Great Depression, 133, 138–39, 142–46, 153, 156, 157–58
Greer, Germaine, 228
Grey, Zane: *Riders of the Purple Sage*, 116, 117–18
Griffith, D. W.: *The Birth of a Nation*, 124
Grimké, Sarah: *Letters on the Equality of the Sexes*, 54
Grisham, John: *A Time to Kill*, 201
Groba, Constante, 170–71
Guilbaut, Serge, 177
Guston, Philip: Ku Klux Klan studies, 209, 296n74

Habberton, John: *Helen's Babies*, 84, 97, 100–101, 102
Hale, Sarah Josepha, 72
Halverson, Cathryn, 118
Hansen, Miriam, 119
Harlem Renaissance, 6, 133, 153–56, 239
Harper, Frances, 6; *Iola Leroy*, 122–23, 125, 126, 202
Harrington, Michael: *The Other America: Poverty in the United States*, 163
Harris, Joel Chandler, 123
Harris, Susan, 74
Hart, Emma, 10
Hartley, Marsden, 129
Hatch, Nathan, 51
Hatcher, Jessamyn, 49
Hawthorne, Nathaniel, 6, 28, 61, 85, 238; "The Birthmark," 56; *The Blithedale Romance*, 64, 73; "Ethan Brand," 56; *The House of the Seven Gables*, 61, 64; *The Marble Faun*, 64; "Rappaccini's Daughter," 56; *The Scarlet Letter*, 39, 48, 51, 54–55, 56, 64, 76, 20
Heade, Martin Johnson, 77, 80
Heller, Joseph: *Catch-22*, 183, 189, 193–94, 196
Hemingway, Ernest, 148, 239; *A Farewell to Arms*, 131, 141, 145, 152; *For Whom the Bell Tolls*, 3, 145–46, 148, 150–51, 153; *The Old Man and the Sea*, 171; *The Sun Also Rises*, 141, 148, 150
Henri, Robert, 127, 129, 130
Hentz, Caroline Lee: *The Planter's Northern Bride*, 70, 76; "The Sex of the Soul," 73
Herrick, Robert: *Together*, 119–20
Hiaasen, Carl: *Double Whammy*, 191, 201
hierarchy, 39, 131, 135, 163, 164, 185, 193
Highsmith, Patricia, 161; *The Blunderer*, 161; *The Talented Mr. Ripley*, 161, 173
Hildreth, Richard: *The Slave*, 66
Hill, Richard, 93
The History of Constantius and Pulchera (author unknown), 38
Hitchcock, Enos: *Memoirs of the Bloomsgrove Family*, 37, 40
Hoberek, Andrew, 182–83

Holmes, Mary Jane, 72; *Tempest and Sunshine*, 69–70, 73
Holsberry, Carmen, 136
Holt, Elliott: *You Are One of Them*, 218
homeless, 216; graph, **216**
Homer, Winslow, 7, 103–5, 127, 238; *The Life Line*, **104**, 105; *Prisoners from the Front*, 103; *Snap the Whip*, 103, **103**
Hopper, Edward, 135, 158–60, 239; *Room in New York*, 158–59, **159**
House Un-American Activities Committee, 164
Howe, Irving, 136
Howells, William Dean, 6, 84, 85, 87, 238; Wharton on, 84; *A Hazard of New Fortunes*, 93–95, 102; *The Lady of the Aroostook*, 82, 90–91; *A Modern Instance*, 93–94; *The Rise of Silas Lapham*, 29, 93–94, 101, 102
Hudson River School, 59, 77
Hughes, Langston, 133, 156; *Not Without Laughter*, 151, 154–56
Hurston, Zora Neale, 133; *Their Eyes Were Watching God*, 146, 154–55

I Am a Woman Worker (collection), 150
IBM, 163, 186, 194, 213
immigration and multiculturalism, 63, 89, 116, 234–35; literature by immigrants, 224–25
incorporation laws, 63
Indigenous writers and artists. *See* Native Americans
individualism, 52–53, 55–57
industrialization: advances in productivity, 162, 212–13; continuous flow production, 88–89; cotton mills, 33, 46–47; deindustrialization, 187–88, 202, 212; impact of, 63–64, 92–93; mass media, 94; regulation of, 111; small-town feeling and, 83–84, 91–97; transportation and, 46–47. *See also* economy
industry and frugality, 15, 17–19, 18, 102

inequality, growth of, 211–13
Internet, 212
irony, 190
Irving, John, 246n10; *A Prayer for Owen Meany*, 181
Irving, Washington (*Sketch Book*), 53–54, 168; "The Legend of Sleepy Hollow," 47, 105, 219; "Rip Van Winkle," 54; "The Wife," 49, 53–54

Jackson, Helen Hunt: *Ramona*, 96, 123
Jacksonians, 48
James, Henry, 6–7, 29, 76, 84, 85; Wharton on, 84; *The American*, 90, 91, 98, 99; *The Bostonians*, 98–99; *Daisy Miller*, 90; *The Portrait of a Lady*, 5, 95–96, 97, 98, 99; *The Princess Casamassima*, 95–96, 97, 99, 238; *What Maisie Knew*, 119
Jameson, Frederic: *Postmodernism*, 183
Jarves, James Jackson, 77
Jefferson, Thomas, 39, 46
Jen, Gish: *Typical American*, 224–25
Jenkins, Jerry, and Tim LaHaye: *Left Behind* series, 218, 222, 226
Jewett, Sarah Orne, 84, 226, 238; *A Country Doctor*, 100; *The Country of the Pointed Firs*, 123, 238; *Deephaven*, 82, 90
Johnson, James Weldon, 84; *The Autobiography of an Ex-Colored Man*, 125–26
Jones, Edward P., 6; *The Known World*, 181, 223, 227, 230, 233
Jones, Tayari: *An American Marriage*, 222, 232, 233

Kaplan, Amy, 49
Kaser, David, 26
Kelley, Mary, 50
Kennedy, John Pendleton, 48, 65; *Horse-Shoe Robinson*, 53
Kennedy, William: *Ironweed*, 181, 192
Kensett, John Frederick, 77, 80
Kent, George, 153
Kerouac, Jack: *On the Road*, 165, 173–74

Kimmel, Michael, 102, 228–29
Kingsolver, Barbara: *Pigs in Heaven*, 220, 227, 229
Kirlew, Shauna, 233
Kiwanis, 133, 137; graph, **133**
Knott, Sarah: *Sensibility and the American Revolution*, 21
Konstantinou, Lee, 186
Krasner, Lee, 175, 176, 210
Krauss, Rosalind, 207

LaHaye, Tim, and Jerry Jenkins: *Left Behind* series, 218, 222, 226
Landry, Jordan, 66
Lane, Fitz Hugh, 77, 80
Lang, Amy, 69
Lanier, Jaron: *You Are Not a Gadget*, 211, 297n1
Larsen, Nella: *Quicksand*, 154–55
Lawrence, Jacob: *The Migration Series*, 158
Leach, William, 119
Lee, Chang-Rae: *My Year Abroad*, 300n53; *Native Speaker*, 224; *On Such a Full Sea*, 224
Lee, Harper: *To Kill a Mockingbird*, 166, 174
Leland, Thomas: *Longsword, Earl of Salisbury*, 24
lesbians and gays, 172–73, 228, 230
lê thi diem thúy: *The Gangster We Are All Looking For*, 224
Leverenz, David, 55
Levin, Harry, 136
Lewis, Sinclair, 1, 133; *Babbitt*, 1, 137, 146; *Main Street*, 1
Lewis, Thabiti, 232
libraries, 24, 25, 26
Lichtenstein, Roy, 207
Ligon, Glenn, 235
literature. *See* novels
Locke, Alain: *The New Negro: An Interpretation*, 153–54, 155
London, Jack, 112; *The Call of the Wild*, 113–14, 118

Lovell, Margaretta, 20
loving mother, 69, 119; graph, **119**
Lowell, Francis Cabot, 33
Luks, George, 129
luminist paintings, 78
Lumpkin, Grace: *To Make My Bread*, 144, 151, 153

Machor, James, 53
Maddox, Lucy, 53
Mailer, Norman: *The Naked and the Dead*, 131, 173
Main, Jackson: *The Social Structure of Revolutionary America*, 10
Mainardi, Pat, 210
manager, 134; graph, **134**
Mann, Herman: *The Female Review*, 38
manners. *See* genteel era
manufacturing. *See* industrialization
Marcus, Fred, 148
Marin, Cheech: *Chicano Visions: American Painters on the Verge*, 234
Marin, John, 129
Married Woman's Property Act (New York, 1848), 55
Mason, Bobbie Ann: *In Country*, 206
mass market fiction, 6
maternalism, 47–48, 69–70, 73, 119, 206, 220; mother, 50–51, 69, 119. *See also* domesticity
Mauer, Alfred H., 85
May, Henry, 85–86
McCarthy, Cormac, 112, 239; *All the Pretty Horses*, 227, 229–30; *Blood Meridian*, 190, 192, 201; *The Road*, 218, 220, 223, 226
McCarthy, Mary: *The Groves of Academe*, 170
McCormick, Cyrus, 46
McCullers, Carson: *The Ballad of the Sad Café*, 170–71; *The Member of the Wedding*, 170–71
McKay, Claude, 133, 156; *Home to Harlem*, 147, 151, 154–56

McLaughlin, Robert, 180
McMillan, Terry: *Waiting to Exhale*, 216, 227, 229, 232–33
McMillian, Rodney: *Supreme Court*, 234
Mein, John, 24
Melville, Herman, 28, 61, 238; "Bartleby," 63, 64; "Benito Cereno," 64, 66; *The Confidence-Man*, 64; *Moby-Dick*, 6, 56–57, 64, 66, 237; *Omoo*, 64, 66; *Pierre*, 61, 64; *Redburn*, 66; *Typee*, 64, 66; *White Jacket*, 66
men: Black men by Black authors, 67, 201–2; corporate, 64–65, 162–63; cult of the primitive, 117–18; ideal of manhood and business, 146–49; masculinity changing, 198–200, 228–30; narrowing roles of, 172; the self-made man, 55–57, 61–62, 289n43; as trustworthy, 65, 101–2; virile manhood, 65. See also genteel era; men and women; modern era; postmodern era; sentimental era
men and women: adultery and extramarital relations, 120–22; childrearing and gender roles, 76; emotional restraint, 19–20; two spheres doctrine, 48–51, 69–70, 83–84, 85, 95–96. See also domesticity; genteel era; men; modern era; postmodern era; sentimental era; women
Merish, Lori, 120
Methodists, 51
methodology: epoch divisions, 13–14, 250n45; Ngram collocates, 8–9, 56, 58, 75, 205; Ngram database and words, 7–9, 58; quantification, 9, 239, 247n23; use of literature and painting, 1–4, 6–7, 237–39, 246n10
Meyers, D. G., 230
Meyers, Marvin, 48
middle class: Black middle class, 12, 66–67, 187–88, 222, 232–33; context of emergence of, 15–26; defining of, 9–13, 85; income, 12, 138, 139, 162–63, 188, 213–14; occupations of, 11–12, 63, 89, 134, 149, 162–63; self-identifying as, 12–13; suburbia, 136, 163, 167, 179, 186, 188; urbanization of, 82–83, 111, 127–29, 131–36, 156–60. See also economy; genteel era; men; men and women; modern era; postmodern era; race and racism; sentimental era; women
middle class, 12, 187; graph, **13**; *black middle class*, 188; graph, **188**
Mitchell, Isaac: *Alonzo and Melissa*, 34, 41
Mitchell, Margaret: *Gone with the Wind*, 146, 147, 151–52, 153
modern era, 131–77; overview, 13–14, 131–36, 137, 161–62, 238–39; African Americans, 133, 148–49, 152–56, 161–62, 173–75; anxiety of, 165, 166–68, 177; business culture, 131, 133–34, 136, 137, 139–42, 146, 156–60, 162–63, 164–67; children, 166; cities, 131, 136, 156–60; collectives and communities, 144–46; dating of, 135–36; literature, 131–33, 137, 139–56, 161, 163–75; men, 146–49, 171–73, 289n43; painting, 156–60, 175–77; religion, 168; soil and agriculture, 143–44, 157–58; women, 149–52, 169–71. See also economy
modernists, 129–30
Moretti, Franco, 7
Morrison, Toni, 6, 239; *Beloved*, 5, 181, 197–98, 200, 202–4, 227, 233, 237; *The Bluest Eye*, 202–3; *Paradise*, 227; *Song of Solomon*, 197, 202–3, 205–6
Moses, Anna Mary Robertson (Grandma Moses), 176
mother, 50–51; graph, **50**; *loving mother*, 69, 119; graph, **119**
Motherwell, Robert, 175, 177
multiculturalism, 224; graph, **132**
Murfree, Mary: *The Prophet of the Great Smoky Mountains*, 96
Murray, Elizabeth, 210
Museum of Modern Art: *The Art of Assemblage*, 209; *Harlem on My Mind*, 209

Napoleonic Wars, 32
National Academy of Design, New York, 126–27, 129, 130
National Civic Federation, 110–11
National Women's Rights Conventions, 71
Native Americans: depictions of in novels, 35, 42–43, 52, 58, 90, 123, 220, 222, 227, 228, 266n38; depictions of in paintings, 43, 78; repression absent from fiction, 90; White women and, 53; writers and artists, 177, 198, 234–35, 234–36. See also *individual writers and artists*
naturalism, 84, 112–17; Ashcan School artists, 127–30; redefining of, 113
nature and the natural world: communing with the divine, 41, 57–59, 61–62; "harmonious" landscape, 41; as hostile, 41–43; redemptive power of soil, 143–44, 157–58; wilderness, 41–42, 57
Nealon, Jeffrey, 182–83
New-York Gazetteer, 24
New-York Journal: "A Tradesman," 11
Ngrams, 7–9, 239. See also *individual Ngrams*
nigger, 68, 124–25, 152, 200; graph, **68**
Niles, Hezekiah, 33
Nochlin, Linda: "Why Have There Been No Great Women Artists?" 210
Norris, Frank, 6, 84, 112; *McTeague*, 114; *The Octopus*, 114, 115
Norris, Margot, 135–36
Novak, Barbara, 77–78
novels: epoch divisions, 13–14; first American, 22, 27; imports of European, 22–24; increased accessibility of, 46; master narrative of American literature, 34–36, 47; methodology, 2–6, 97, 237–39. See also genteel era; modern era; postmodern era; sentimental era; *individual authors*
nurturing, 204; graph, **204**

O'Keeffe, Georgia, 129, 210
outsiders, 90, 92, 95

Page, Thomas Nelson, 123
Paine, Thomas: *Common Sense*, 21–22, 25
painting (art): abstract expressionism, 85, 175–77; American Scene painters, 157–58; attention to detail, 62, 79–80; genteel era, 85, 103–7, 126–30; methodological use of, 1–4, 6–7; modern era, 135, 156–60, 175–77; multiculturalism, 234–35; portraiture, 20–22, 85, 106–7; postmodern era, 182, 206–10, 234–36; Precisionism, 156; sentimental era, 29, 41–43, 59, 76–80; social realism, 176–77; women, 236
Pancake, Ann: *Strange as This Weather Has Been*, 214, 217, 221, 223, 227, 229, 230
Parrington, Vernon, 112
patriarchy, 50, 70, 119, 122. See also men and women
patriotism, 79
Patterson, James: *Along Came a Spider*, 231–32
Peale, Charles Willson: *The Peale Family*, 21, **22**
Percy, Walker: *Love in the Ruins*, 192, 196, 201
Perry, T. S., 93
personality (compared to *character*), 134–35; graph, **135**
picturesque, 41–42
picturesque, 8, 58, 263n61
piety, 39, 49, 51–52, 57, 70, 168
Pinsker, Sanford, 189
Pollock, Jackson, 7, 135, 175–77; *One: Number 31, 1950*, **176**, 177
Porter, Cole: "Find Me a Primitive Man," 118
Porter, Eleanor: *Pollyanna*, 83, 84
Portis, Charles: *True Grit*, 192, 196
portraiture, 20–22, 85, 106–7. See also painting (art)

postmodern era, 179–236; overview, 13–14, 179–83, 185–86, 239; African Americans, 187–88, 197–98; apocalyptic visions, 217–18; business culture, 179, 192–95, 213–17, 234; children and family, 204–6, 220–21; dating of, 136, 182–83; destruction and rebuilding, 180–82, 186–88, 195, 206–7, 209, 234; harmonious communities, 218–20; immigration and multiculturalism, 224–25, 234–35; lawlessness, 190–92; literature, 179, 180–81, 183, 185, 188–206, 211, 214–34; men, 198–200, 228–30; moral ambivalence, 188–90, 195, 209, 233; movements of resistance, 180, 195–97, 198, 201, 209, 226–27; painting and alternatives, 182, 206–10, 234–36; religion, 221–23; suburbia, 136, 179, 186, 188; women, 195–98, 225–28, 236

Pound, Ezra, 136

poverty: depicted in novels, 92–93, 96; economic depressions, 110, 143–46, 163; homelessness, 215–16; naturalism, 115; people of color and, 188, 213; portrayed in art, 129, 176; rise of unions and, 89

Powers, Richard: *Gain*, 214, 227

Precariat, 13

Prehal, Tim, 65

Presbyterians, 51

Prohibition, 91

Proulx, E. Annie: *The Shipping News*, 219–20, 221, 228, 230, 232

Pynchon, Thomas, 136, 180; *The Crying of Lot 49*, 183, 192–93, 196, 199, 215; *Inherent Vice*, 215, 226

race and racism: overview, 6; Black middle class, 12, 66–67, 187–88, 213, 232–33; civil rights movements, 173, 174, 180, 201, 209, 231; conformity and, 173–75; emotions as defining, 19; evangelical Christians, 222; homeownership and, 163; Jews, 94, 152, 222; lynching, 124–25, 153, 166, 209, 233–34; in modern era novels, 152–56; portrayal of Blacks by Whites, 65–66, 104, 123–25, 152–53, 166, 173–74, 191, 200–202, 226, 227, 231–32; portrayal of Indigenous people, 35, 42–43, 52–53, 58, 78, 90, 123, 142, 198, 234–35, 266n38; poverty, 213; repression absent from fiction, 90, 232; rights and social justice movements, 7, 173–75, 185, 186; suburbia, 136. *See also* African American writers and artists; slavery

Rauschenberg, Robert, 207

Reed, Ishmael: *Flight to Canada*, 198, 203

Reinhardt, Ad, 177, 207

religion: apocalyptic novels and, 218; communing with nature, 41, 57–59; decline in influence, 39–40, 78; evangelical Christianity, 51–52, 70, 222, 228; in genteel era, 84, 97; late modern turn to, 168, 175; piety, 52, 83, 85, 97; in postmodern era, 221–23; temperance, 91

Revolutionary War, 17, 24; revolutionary movement, 21–22

Reynolds, David, 28, 29

Rhodes, Chip, 205

Richardson, Samuel: *Clarissa*, 22, 23, 24, 26, 38; *Pamela*, 23, 26, 38; *Sir Charles Grandison*, 26

Riesman, David, 162

Ringe, Donald, 59

Rivington, James, 24

robbery, 190; graph, **191**

Robeson, Paul, 156

Rockwell, Norman, 175–76

Rodrigues, Laurie, 210

romance novels, 228

romantic, 8, 58, 140, 263n61; graph, **58**

Romero, Lora, 50

Roosevelt, Franklin, 139, 143

Roosevelt, Theodore, 111

Rosenblatt, Roger, 189
Rotarians, 133; graph, **133**
Roth, Philip, 182; *American Pastoral*, 221, 226, 231; *Goodbye, Columbus*, 165–66; *Portnoy's Complaint*, 199, 200–201, 206; on the "thought of the novelist," 3
Rothenberg, Susan, 210
Rothko, Mark, 7, 135, 175, 176, 177
Rotundo, E. Anthony, 102
Rousseau, Jean-Jacques: *Confessions*, 24; *Emile*, 21, 26; *Emilius and Sophia*, 26; *Julie; or, The New Heloise*, 23, 24, 26
Rowson, Susanna: *Charlotte Temple*, 34, 37, 38, 39, 75; *Reuben and Rachel*, 34, 39
Rubin-Dorsky, Jeffrey, 34–35
rural society, 27, 62, 76–77, 138; agriculture, 62, 138, 143–44. *See also* small-town society; urban society
Rush, Benjamin, 18
Russell, Karen: *Swamplandia*, 227, 231
Russo, Richard: *Empire Falls*, 221, 223, 227–28, 230, 237
Rust, Marion, 38
Ryan, Mary, 10

Saar, Betye, 182, 239; *The Liberation of Aunt Jemima*, **208**, 209
salariat, 162–63
Salinger, J. D.: *The Catcher in the Rye*, 164–65, 166, 172–73, 179, 198
Samuels, Shirley, 27, 28
Sanders, David, 146
Sansay, Leonora: *Secret History*, 38, 39
Santayana, George, 81–82, 85
Saunders, George: *Lincoln in the Bardo*, 181, 183, 220, 222–23, 226, 230, 231
Schumpeter, Joseph, 212
Schwab, Charles, 134
Sedgwick, Catharine Maria, 48; *Hope Leslie*, 53, 75
seduce, 38–39; graph, **38**
Segal, Erich: *Love Story*, 196, 199, 201, 206

sentimental era, 27–80; overview, 13–14, 15, 27–29, 61–62, 238, 255n10; African Americans, 65–69; children and youth, 74–76; dating of, 29, 183; emergence and context, 16–26; literature, 34–42, 47–59, 64–76; men, 55–57, 64–65; natural world, 40–43, 57–58, 78–80; painting, 29, 41–43, 59, 76–80; religion, 39–40, 51–52, 70, 78; women, 36–39, 48–55, 69–74
sex and sexuality, 120–22, 132, 149–50, 155–56, 170–71; homosexuality, 172–73, 228, 230
Shahn, Ben, 158, 177
Sheeler, Charles, 135, 156–57, 239; *American Landscape*, 157, **157**
Shinn, Everett, 129
shit, 181; graph, **181**
Shteyngart, Gary: *Lake Success*, 195, 214–15, 216–17, 229, 231
Sicherman, Barbara, 74
Sidney, Margaret: *The Five Little Peppers and How They Grew*, 84, 97, 100–101, 102
Simms, William Gilmore, 48, 73; *Guy Rivers*, 48, 56, 57–58; *Woodcraft*, 64, 73; *The Yemassee*, 53, 56, 65
Simpson, Eleanor, 66
sin, 8, 51
Sinclair, Upton: *The Jungle*, 3, 111, 125
sisterhood, 227; graph, **226**
slavery, 17, 21, 33, 46, 63, 65–66, 68, 70, 92–93, 153, 202, 210, 227–28, 231, 233–34, 235–36. *See also* African American writers and artists; race and racism
Sloan, John, 129
small-town society: 1870s as, 83, 88, 89–92, 238; 1880s and, 83, 92–97; genteel values, 81–82, 122
Smith, Betty: *A Tree Grows in Brooklyn*, 133, 170
Smith, Henry Nash, 85
Smith, Lillian: *Strange Fruit*, 169

INDEX 315

Smith-Rosenberg, Carroll, 37
socialism, 94–95, 96, 111, 177; communism, 144–45, 156, 164, 174, 175
Southworth, E.D.E.N., 72–73; *The Discarded Daughter*, 72, 76; *The Hidden Hand*, 64, 66, 72–73, 76, 238, 268n50
Soyer, Moses, 158
Spanish Civil War and anti-fascism, 145–46
Spencer, Herbert, 113
Stanton, Elizabeth, 71
Stearns, Harold E., 82
Stegner, Wallace: *The Spectator Bird*, 199
Steinbeck, John, 112; *Cannery Row*, 169; *In Dubious Battle*, 145, 151; *The Grapes of Wrath*, 116, 138, 145, 147, 151; *Of Mice and Men*, 143–44, 152–53; *Sweet Thursday*, 169
Steiner, Wendy, 180–81
Stella, Frank, 85, 207
Stella, Joseph, 129
Sterne, Laurence: *A Sentimental Journey through France and Italy*, 23, 25, 26
Stieglitz, Alfred, 7, 129–30
Still, Clyfford, 177
Stowe, Catharine: *A Treatise on Domestic Economy*, 69
Stowe, Harriet Beecher, 27, 69, 72, 238; *My Wife and I*, 73, 98, 102; *Pink and White Tyranny*, 82, 90–92, 102, 120; *Uncle Tom's Cabin*, 64, 65–66, 69–70, 75–76, 124, 183, 204
strong women, 54–55, 100, 118–19, 149, 169, 195; graph, **54, 149**
Strout, Elizabeth: *Olive Kitteridge*, 219–20, 221, 228
sublime, 58
suburbia: modern era, 163, 167; postmodern era, 136, 179, 186, 188. See also urban society
suffrage, 71, 73, 100–101, 119, 149. See also women
swearing, 131, 181

Tarkington, Booth: *The Magnificent Ambersons*, 83, 111; *Penrod*, 83, 84, 125
Taylor, George Rogers: *The Transportation Revolution*, 46
temperance, 91; graph, **91**
Thomas, Glen, 228
Thomas, Hank Willis, 236
Thomas, Mickalene, 236
Thoreau, Henry David, 78; *Walden*, 62
Ticknor, William, 61
Tocqueville, Alexis de, 45, 46–47, 53
toddler, 204; graph, **204**
Tompkins, Jane, 28, 35, 49, 69
Toomer, Jean, 155; *Cane*, 154, 155
Touré: *Who's Afraid of Post-Blackness?*, 232
Towles, Amor: *A Gentleman in Moscow*, 221, 299n34
tramps, 110, 215–16; graph, **216**
Transcendentalism, 49, 57, 76, 78
transportation systems, 33, 46, 63–64, 88, 111. See also economy
Truman, Harry S., 175–76
trustworthy, 65, 102, 117; graph, **102**
truthfulness, 109
Tucker, Nathaniel Beverly, 65
Tuckerman, Henry: *Book of the Artists*, 80
Twain, Mark (Samuel Clemens), 84, 85; on viewing Church's *The Heart of the Andes*, 80; *Adventures of Huckleberry Finn*, 6, 84, 92–93, 97, 101, 123–24, 237; *The Adventures of Tom Sawyer*, 76, 82, 90–91, 97, 101, 238; *A Connecticut Yankee in King Arthur's Court*, 92, 93, 101; *The Gilded Age* (with C. D. Warner), 101; *The Prince and the Pauper*, 5, 92, 101; *The Tragedy of Pudd'nhead Wilson*, 101, 124
Tyler, Royall: *The Algerine Captive*, 34, 35, 40

unions and labor strife, 89, 94–95, 110–11, 138–39, 144–45, 151, 186, 187, 212–13
Updike, John: *Rabbit, Run*, 167–68, 173, 199; *Rabbit is Rich*, 199; *Rabbit Redux*, 199, 201

316 INDEX

urban society: crime, 190–91; genteel era, 111, 127–29; modern era, 131–36, 157–60; naturalism, 114, 116; population, 82, 83,
urban society (*continued*)
111; small-town influence on, 82–83; suburban growth and, 136. *See also* small-town society; suburbia

Vanderlyn, John, 29; *The Murder of Jane McCrea*, 43
Vidal, Gore: *The City and the Pillar*, 173
Vietnam war, 180
violence, 190; graph, **191**
virile, 102, 117; graph, **102**
visual art. *See* painting
Volpe, Edmond, 153
Vonnegut, Kurt: *Slaughterhouse-Five*, 189, 199

Walker, Alice, 6; *The Color Purple*, 197, 199, 202–3, 205, 227; *The Third Life of Grange Copeland*, 199, 202–3, 205
Walker, Kara: *Alabama Loyalists Greeting the Federal Gunboats*, **235**, 236
Walker, Kelley, 234
Wallace, David Foster, 182–83; *Infinite Jest*, 216, 218, 223, 226, 230, 231
Wallace, Lew: *Ben-Hur*, 4–5, 84, 97, 98, 222
Walpole, Horace: *The Castle of Otranto*, 23
Ward, Jesmyn, 6; *Sing, Unburied, Sing*, 223, 230, 233
War for Independence. *See* Revolutionary War
Warhol, Andy, 182, 207, 239; *American Supermarket*, 209; *Death and Disaster* series, 209; *The Factory*, 209
Warner, Charles Dudley: *The Gilded Age* (with Twain), 101
Warner, Susan: *The Wide, Wide World*, 6, 51, 52, 70, 76, 222
Warren, Robert Penn, 148; *All the King's Men*, 165, 169–70

Washington, George, 24
Watt, Ian, 23
Webb, Frank J., 6, 66–67; *The Garies and Their Friends*, 67, 68, 76, 154, 202, 237–38
Weber, Max: *The Liberty Tower from the Singer Building*, **128**, 129
Weekly Anglo-African, 67
weep, 9, 28; graph, **28**
Weinstein, Cindy, 28
Welter, Barbara: "The Cult of True Womanhood, 1820–1860," 49–50
Wexler, Laura, 28
Wharton, Edith, 83, 84, 112–13, 114–15, 119, 239; *The Age of Innocence*, 116, 140–41, 146, 159; *A Backward Glance*, 84–85, 109, 121–22; *The Custom of the Country*, 114–15, 119, 120, 122; *Ethan Frome*, 85, 109, 115; *The House of Mirth*, 6, 84, 85, 114–15, 120, 121–22; *Summer*, 109, 116, 122
Whitehead, Colson, 6; *The Underground Railroad*, 181, 183, 228, 233
Whitman, Walt: on the middle class, 12
Whyte, William, 162
Wiebe, Robert, 88
Wiggin, Kate: *Rebecca of Sunnybrook Farm*, 82–83, 84
Wigglesworth, Michael, 41
wilderness, 41–42, 57. *See also* nature and the natural world
Wiley, Kehinde, 235
Williams, Raymond, 4
Williamson, Jenn, 145
Wilmerding, John, 105
Wilson, Harriet E., 66–67; *Our Nig*, 67, 68
Wilson, Sloan: *The Man in the Gray Flannel Suit*, 165, 167, 169, 172, 194, 198
Winans, Robert, 26
Wister, Owen: *The Virginian*, 117
Witherspoon, John, 25
women: artists, 210, 235–36; as book consumers, 25; domesticity and patriarchy, 49–51, 53, 55, 69–70; education of, 37,

150, 196, 210; gains and losses by, 36–39, 48–49, 169, 225–28; as independent, 122–23; individualism, 52–53; naturalism, 112; portrayals of Black, 67, 151, 197–98, 226; rights movements, 29, 54–55, 70–74, 98–101, 119, 149–50, 195–97, 198, 209, 226–27; shopping and consumerism, 119–20; as strong, 54, 98–101, 118–19, 149–52, 169–71, 195, 227–28; suffrage, 71, 73–74, 81, 100–101, 119, 149; in workforce, 149, 169, 225–26; writers, 37, 49–50, 61, 64, 74, 150–51, 180–81, 195–96. *See also* genteel era; men; men and women; modern era; postmodern era; sentimental era; *individual writers*
women (strong women), 54–55, 100, 118–19, 149, 169, 195; graph, **54, 149**
women's liberation, 196, 225; graph, **225**
women's rights, 71; graph, **71**
women's suffrage, 71; graph, **71**
Wood, Grant: *American Gothic*, 157–58

Woodhull, Victoria, 98
Woolson, Constance Fenimore: *For the Major*, 96, 97
Wouk, Herman: *The Caine Mutiny*, 164, 173, 198
Wright, Harold Bell: *The Shepherd of the Hills*, 84
Wright, Richard, 156; *Native Son*, 144, 156
Wrinkle, Margaret: *Wash*, 231
Wyeth, Andrew, 175–76

Yamashita, Karen Tei: *The Tropic of Orange*, 181, 183, 216, 217, 224
Yarington, Earl, 73
Yates, Norris, 135
Yates, Richard: *Revolutionary Road*, 194, 196, 198–99
Yellin, Jean, 66

Zink, Karl, 143
Zola, Émile, 112